Organization Theory for Public Administration

ORGANIZATION THEORY FOR PUBLIC ADMINISTRATION

Michael M. Harmon
George Washington University

Richard T. Mayer
George Mason University

Scott, Foresman and Company
Glenview, Illinois   London, England

Library of Congress Cataloging-in-Publication Data

Harmon, Michael, 1941-
  Organization theory for public administration.

  Bibliography: p.
  Includes index.
  1. Organizational behavior.   2. Organizational change.   3. Public administration.
I. Mayer, Richard T.   II. Title.
JF1525.073H37   1986   350′.0001   85-23738

Library of Congress Catalog Card No. 85-23738

ISBN 0-673-39022-5

5678910-RRC-9089

Printed in the United States of America

Credits

   Pages 7-8: "'System' Betrayed 5-Year-Old Boy, Dead of a Beating" by Wayne Slater reprinted by permission of AP Newsfeatures.

   Page 29: "Congress and Cigarettes" by A. Lee Fritschler, SMOKING AND POLITICS:
Policymaking and the Federal Bureaucracy, 2nd edition, pp. 118-120. Copyright © 1975 by
Prentice-Hall, Inc. Reprinted by permission of Prentice-Hall, Inc., Englewood Cliffs, NJ.

   Page 31: "The Organization Map" reprinted by permission of the publisher, from "The
Human Side of Enterprise" by Douglas Murray McGregor, MANAGEMENT REVIEW,
November 1957, pp. 23, 26-27, 88-89. Copyright © 1957 American Management Association,
Inc. All rights reserved.

   Pages 32, 45: Excerpt from Joel Handler PROTECTING THE SOCIAL SERVICE CLI-
ENT reprinted by permission of Academic Press, Inc. and Joel Handler.

   Page 39: Excerpt from THE POWER BROKER: ROBERT MOSES AND THE FALL OF
NEW YORK by Robert Caro reprinted by permission of Alfred A. Knopf, Inc. and International Creative Management, Inc.

(continued on page 427)

Preface

Certainly, few would contest that a knowledge of organizations is essential to both the study and the practice of public administration. Nearly all academic programs in the field include courses on organization theory, and many of the principal contributors to the organizational literature are acknowledged as luminaries in public administration academic circles. In view of organization theory's importance for public administration theory and practice, it is ironic that relatively little of the most influential writing about organizations directly addresses the unique character of *public* organizations. Organization theory, most of it written by scholars in other disciplines, has penetrated the permeable boundaries of academic public administration virtually unaltered in substance and interpretation. Further, given public administration's historical commitment to improving administrative practice, it is also ironic that much of the organizational literature has so narrowly construed—and in some instances, ignored altogether—the practical value of theory and theorizing for administrators. Finally, while the diversity of theoretical perspectives on organizations has become markedly more pronounced in the last decade or two, the opportunities for thoughtful discourse afforded by that diversity are only infrequently recognized, much less acted upon. The result has been the emergence of several bastions of theoretical activity that are isolated from one another and, more important, from the practical experience of public administrators.

In brief, these are the concerns that prompted the writing of this book. Our intent, as the book's title suggests, has been to write an introductory text to present organization theory to public administrators. In doing this, we have attempted to highlight and take advantage of the diversity among theoretical perspectives, explicating their unique salience for practical action in public organizations. The range of theoretical perpectives that we consider is substantially broader than that usually included under the heading of "organization theory." This broad sweep emphasizes that theorizing about organizations should not be limited to a narrow, mainstream literature, but rather should include a wide array of writers who have something to tell us about why and with what consequences people engage in organizing activity. At the same time, the book is not in any way intended to be a complete compendium of writings on organization theory. Instead, it focuses on the seminal contributors to a variety of theoretical perspectives whose original insights have guided subsequent research and thinking. At the same time that we have sketched the valuable insights of each perspective, we have also suggested the significant limitations that each has for comprehending the whole of organizing activity.

We believe that the primary benefit of this book will be to help students and teachers explore in some detail the competing explanations of organizational action. In doing this, we hope the text encourages the development of a self-reflective attitude about theorizing on the part of both student and teacher. With such an attitude, any discussion of "which theory should be applied to this particular situation" becomes meaningfully grounded in an understanding of both the power and limitations of the various perspectives.

Acknowledgments

During the more than three years we have spent preparing the manuscript, we have benefited greatly from the efforts of colleagues, students, friends, and family. Their contributions to this endeavor ranged from substantive criticisms and suggestions for improving the book, to careful proofreading of the manuscript, to some much-needed moral support on those occasions when we doubted that the project would ever be completed. Thus, we offer our thanks to the following people who helped in these ways and others, while keeping their doubts to themselves: Robert Abbey, William C. Adams, Dennis Affholter, Patricia Aronsson, Bayard Catron, Pieter Degeling, Jerry Harvey, Ralph Hummel, Robert Hutchens, Lluana McCann, Cynthia McSwain, Wahib A. Soufi, Esther Williams Strongman, Frederick Thayer, Peter Vaill, Charles Washington, and Orion White.

Eight individuals spent an inordinate amount of time (and patience) reviewing our work in progress. Each provided us with assistance and clarity, and for that we thank them: Dean Michael Aiken, University of Pennsylvania; Professor Samuel B. Bacharach, Cornell University; Professor David Bresnick, Baruch College; Professor Nealia S. Bruning, Kent State University; Professor Judith J. Hendricks, California State College, Stanislaus; Dr. Jeanne Marie Kielman, New York University; Professor Lawrence B. Mohr, University of Michigan, Ann Arbor; and, especially, Professor Richard L. Schott, The University of Texas at Austin, whose review not only was thoughtful and helpful, but also stands as an example of the spirit of academic collegiality so often spoken of, yet seldom met. Special thanks go to David P. Lipsky, Consulting Editor, for providing editorial direction and encouragement.

We thank Astrid Merget, who, as Chair of the Public Administration Department at George Washington University, cheerfully contributed more department resources in support of this project than even she is aware of; we also thank the staff of GWU's computer center for their technical wizardry, general good humor, and endless supply of paper.

A special thanks is needed for Jane Mayer; without her support, love, and patience, at least half of this project would never have come this far.

Finally, we want to extend our appreciation to Alex Greene of Little, Brown, whose patience and encouragement saw us through to the end.

MMH
RTM

Contents

Organization Theory for Public Administration

1

THE PUBLIC ADMINISTRATION FRAMEWORK

The purpose of this book is to use organization theory to illuminate, from a variety of perspectives, the organizational contexts within which public administrators act. Our intention is ultimately practical. By "practical" we mean not only instrumental (*how* can we accomplish objectives?), but also moral (*should* a particular objective be regarded as worth pursuing and by what means?) and diagnostic (*why* is a particular state of affairs the way it is?). We do not offer prescriptions for administrative actions, but we attempt to show how theory may be of use in making sense of the past and present in order to suggest future possibilities for action.

Although we do not believe that *all* of what passes for organization theory has practical value for public administrators, neither do we believe that any one approach to theory embodies all or even most of what may have practical value. The meaning of "practical" is too complicated to permit such theoretical purity.

One immediate difficulty is how to deal with the diversity that falls under the rubric of "organization theory." Some have argued for synthesis: Competing "schools" of theory offer different views of the same object; therefore, one should gather together the similar strands (while making note of, but playing down, the differences) and draw them into a single theory of organizations. Another approach acknowledges the differences openly; here one uses different theories for different purposes: Systems theory is for assessing systemic issues, decision-set theory for decision-making issues, and human relations theory for interpersonal issues. In the first case, the intent is to create a grand theory that binds together our knowledge about organizations; in the second, it is to create a lineman's tool belt, with a theory for each purpose.

What we propose here is both more modest than synthesis and more useful than simply acknowledging the differences among theoretical approaches. Theory, like the organizations it addresses, is a human creation and must be understood as such. It therefore represents the theoretical interests that its creators have in describing the objects of their attention. "Interest" here is meant in neither a conspiratorial nor a political/economic sense, although one could assess any theoretical position in those terms. Rather, it simply underscores our guiding assumption about all theorizing:

> Thinking about organizational activity is always grounded in assumptions about human nature, in the purposes for examining such activity, and in the suppositions about the relationship between theory and practice.

Together, these form the interests that are at the base of creating and using theory in order to understand human activity in organizational settings. The utility of organization theory therefore lies in the perspectives it provides on organizational life, viewpoints that differ because of underlying assumptions about human action and its relationship to the social world.

A second aspect of organization theory with which we shall be concerned is its distinctive relevance to *public* organizations. This bears on the usefulness of various theoretical perspectives as frameworks not only for description and explanation, but also for normative evaluation. The actions of public administrators are *always* subject to public judgments, a fact seldom taken into account by the mainstream organizational literature. Through what we refer to as "normative vectors," the salience of organization theory to normative questions of public purpose and public value can and will be considered.

Parts II and III summarize and review a variety of perspectives on organization theory. Each chapter deals with several writers who either typify a particular approach or offer something unique to it. Although both the intellectual connections and the substantive boundaries between these approaches are sketched, there is no intention of being comprehensive. For example, systems theory looks at the organizational setting in a way that is very useful for understanding certain aspects that are highly relevant to public administration. We bring these out, not by reviewing all of the work in this area, but rather by capturing, through the work of a few characteristic writers, systems theory's assumptions about human nature, its purposes in examining organizational activity, and its suppositions about the relationship of theory and practice. Finally, these are then used as a lens, so to speak, for viewing the world of public administration. To do this, it is necessary to have a framework through which to view that world and apply the various theoretical perspectives. This framework is developed in Part I.

The framework is neither controversial nor novel in its explication of the work world of public administration. A different framework could be utilized for different purposes. This one reflects the interests of its authors in exposing the interplay between the personal and the organizational in day-to-day public administration. Our intention is to enable public administrators to bring the theoretical perspectives discussed here to bear on the problems they face, not in the sense of "solving" them, but rather in the sense of illuminating them for practical action.

A central concern of administration is decision making. For the public administrator, this concern is always enveloped within a particular kind of organizational context. This context can be broken up for analytical purposes; here, for example, we use the notion of *organizational arenas* within which administrators act and which bound their actions through the roles they must play in those arenas. Each public organization is a socially defined response to a special set of problems, namely, what we describe in some detail as *wicked problems*. Hence, the resulting decisions, large and small, that are organized in public ways, and that constitute public administration, are also socially mandated responses to these wicked problems. These mandates are played out in the organizational arenas, while underlying these mandates are the *normative vectors* of public administration.

Government, as objectification of the public will, operates through many agents. These agents, as public administrators, are both organizational and normative actors. As such, in carrying out public objectives, they are often motivated by altruism, public spiritedness, and other noble sentiments. However, the work they do, like that of most human beings, may also be based on selfish or venal motives; it may be done for petty reasons, for reasons of self-aggrandizement, for reasons of power, for reasons of control. In either case, their work is bounded both normatively and organizationally. The intent of the framework, the subject of Part I, is to illuminate the distinctively *public* context of the public administrator's world. Its primary use in this book is to provide a foil for examining the several theoretical perspectives discussed in Parts II and III. The book concludes, in Part IV, with a summary comparison of the diverse perspectives along six dimensions that implicitly permeate the organizational literature. This summary reflects an appreciation of the relation of theory to administrative practice within the context of the latter half of the twentieth century.

1

The Decisional Context of Public Administration

"Organization theory," as it is used throughout this book, refers to the body of knowledge and information that speaks to how and why people act as they do in organizational settings—that is, as members of organizations, as the recipients of goods and services provided by organizations, as initiators of actions that affect and are affected by organizations. Public administrators act, by definition, within an organizational context. In order to understand the relevance of organization theory to public administration, it is necessary first to lay out a framework that adequately bounds the field, the function of the three chapters in Part I. This chapter looks at the kind of decisions that constitute the bulk of public administration activity. The remaining two chapters outline the various *organizational arenas* within which public administrators make decisions and the *normative vectors* that help shape those decisions.

By "public administrators," we refer mainly but not exclusively to those, known in a more delicate age as civil servants, who have the responsibility for carrying out the work of the government. Within this group are all those who, in the course of their everyday work, administer the law of the land and carry out the civil dictates of society. This includes the Director of the Central Intelligence Agency, the Secretary of Human

Resources in Maryland, and the Director of Personnel in Lakewood, Ohio. But it also includes the social worker, the cop on the beat, the clerk in the water department, and the analyst in the county planning department. It includes all of these individuals *to the extent* that they are carrying out public responsibilities, administering the law, and bearing the public charge.

Simply put, public administration deals with decisions that

- Affect people's lives,
- Are made in the name of the public, and
- Use public resources.

Therefore, those who deal in public administration include more than the traditional group of civil servants. At every level of government, there now exist organizations—public agencies, commissions, public corporations, and official task forces—whose members carry out society's legal mandates and thereby work "in the public interest." These, too, may be regarded for our purposes as public administrators. The dividing line here is simple to define but difficult to draw: Public administration is the concern of all those who act on behalf of the public—on behalf of society in a legally mandated way—and whose actions have consequences for the members of society, singly or as a group.

All those who are engaged in public administration make decisions on the basis of public law, regulation, and tradition. In addition, however, their decisions reflect personal judgments based on individually held values and assessments that arise from unique configurations of factors in particular situations. Decisions, like the judgments on which they are based, emerge from an interplay of the general and the specific, the personal and the impersonal.

The complexity of this interplay is well illustrated by the story of Alan Madden, described in the accompanying box. Here, a five-year-old boy, who had once been removed by the state from his mother's care, was found beaten to death shortly after his return to her care. Although this story is special in its poignancy, it is not unique in that it captures the essence of the many dilemmas faced daily by public administrators: When to act or not act, how to maintain accountability, how to interpret personal responsibility, and how to determine the organizational limits of authority and responsibility.

The story emphasizes the kinds of problems (and therefore the kinds of decisions) that face public administrators. Touching cases such as Alan Madden's are written up in the newspaper, yet every day there are thousand of similar cases that pass unnoticed except by those directly involved. Their similarity lies not in the pathos or tragic consequences, but in the kinds of decisions being made: Decisions about people's lives, about the

'SYSTEM' BETRAYED 5-YEAR-OLD BOY, DEAD OF A BEATING

By Wayne Slater—Associated Press

QUINCY, Ill. Jan. 28—Alan Madden was pummeled for perhaps four hours before he died, at times with fists, at times with a wooden club wrapped with gauze and labeled "The Big Stick." He was 5 years old. Police found his frail body on the living room floor, his blond hair red with blood, his hands bruised from trying to deflect the blows.

He died Jan. 10. His mother and a boyfriend are charged with murder. But since his death, talk has centered not so much on those who may have killed him, but on those who did not.

- On the uncle, who now says he would have told anybody about the bruises he saw—but nobody asked.
- On the school principal, who went through all the proper channels when Alan came to kindergarten with blackened eyes.
- On the assistant state's attorney 100 miles away, confident that when investigators lay the blame they'll find "everybody did their job" by the rules in his county.
- And on the judge, who says he was shown no evidence of child abuse before he ordered Alan returned to his mother last August.

His mother, Pam Berg, 24, and his father, Gerald Madden, who disappeared years ago, had been questioned about possible child abuse in 1975, when Knox County authorities investigated bruises on the back and buttocks of Alan's sister Tina, 7.

"I remember little Tina waking up with nightmares screaming, 'Don't Mommy, don't!' I saw bruises that were suspicious on those kids . . . " said uncle Charles Kruger, who kept Alan and Tina for several months in 1976 while their mother served a prison sentence for forging a check.

After her release, Mrs. Madden headed for Colorado. Efforts to have Alan and Tina adopted were unsuccessful.

She returned several years ago with a new boyfriend and a new daughter, Nicole, and said she wanted her children back.

Hearings were held. The uncle wasn't asked about abuse. Past problems were blamed on the father or not discussed.

"She was very neat looking. She said she was going to school," said Circuit Court Judge William Richardson, whose hearing dealt only with the mother's interest in the children, where she would live and how she would pay for food and clothes.

Last August, Alan and Tina were returned to their mother, who was living with James Crain, 26. In October, Alan came to kindergarten with his face so bruised he couldn't be in the class picture. Principal Rick Baldwin alerted the local Department of Children and Family Services office.

Baldwin later called the department again. A neighbor, hearing screams, called police, but everything was kept confidential.

In December, just three weeks before Alan was killed, the Quincy office mailed a routine report to Richardson. It said the family was doing fine. *continued next page*

'SYSTEM' BETRAYED 5-YEAR-OLD *continued*

This week, following an internal investigation of the "almost incomprehensible" case, two DCFS employees were "suspended pending dismissal" and a second superior was demoted, according to Gregory Coler, state DCFS director. Six other social workers will be disciplined, he said.

Coler admitted his agency had ignored or failed to respond to warnings from a clergyman, school officials, a teacher and police.

Hundreds came to the funeral. Relatives didn't claim the body, which would have required they pay for the funeral, so the town donated a new set of clothes and a cemetery plot beneath evergreen trees.

Alan was buried with his teddy bear in a small blue coffin donated by strangers.

—from *THE WASHINGTON POST,* January 29, 1981.

conditions they work and live in, about the ways in which they will interact with one another.

These decisions, of course, are responses to perceived problems. Traditionally, we view public responses to problems as having two parts, with one being the "policy" and the other the "administration" of that policy. This traditional distinction between theory and practice in public administration serves well when "to administer" means simply to carry out a task. Increasingly, however, "to administer" means something much more complex, including sorting through interests, accounting for consequences, and justifying actions. Government activity deals almost exclusively with the mediation between one part of society and another. Although this mediation is not a new activity, our recognition of its pervasiveness *is* relatively new, as is our recognition of the role of the public administrator in that mediation.

In the case of affirmative action, for example, the rules and guidelines are set by the law and the courts (though not necessarily set clearly). Administrators, however, give substance to the policy of affirmative action by deciding how and when to intervene. Because of their intervention, affirmative action has altered not only the workplace in general, but also workers' perceptions of themselves. It has opened avenues and created opportunities that were once nonexistent; at the same time, it has—by making the very weakness of society explicit—raised both anxiety and hostility, while lowering cohesiveness and, potentially, short-run productivity of the workforce. Whether this bodes well or ill is not the main point here; the crucial point is that the administrator, as agent of the public will, alters the society from which that government springs. How this happens is primarily through the kind of problems that the society chooses for its government to address, namely, "wicked problems" like Alan Madden's.

Tame and Wicked Problems

Horst Rittel and Melvin Webber have noted that the kinds of problems that professionals in government were traditionally hired to deal with have in large part been solved—the roads are paved, the houses built, the sewers connected (albeit, not to everyone's satisfaction). These malleable problems, the ones that could be attacked with common sense and ingenuity, have in recent decades given way to a different class of problems. These are the problems with no solutions, only temporary and imperfect resolutions. They deal with the location of a freeway, the development of school curriculum, the confrontation with crime. Rittel and Webber characterize these as "wicked problems," in contrast to the "tame" ones of the engineer, the road builder, or the scientist:

> We are calling them "wicked" not because these properties are themselves ethically deplorable. We use the term "wicked" in a meaning akin to that of "malignant" (in contrast to "benign") or "vicious" (like a circle) or "tricky" (like a leprechaun) or "aggressive" (like a lion, in contrast to the docility of a lamb).[1]

Tame problems can be solved because they can be readily defined and separated from other problems and from their environment. This it not to trivialize them by suggesting they are easy to solve, but they do have an important feature: Whatever difficulties and complexities are encountered in their solution are mainly technical in nature. The landing of men on the moon and returning them safely to earth, for example, entailed the solving of a monumentally complex, time-consuming, challenging, costly—but nonetheless tame—problem.

By contrast, wicked problems have no definitive formulation and hence no agreed-upon criteria to tell when a solution has been found; the choice of a definition of a problem, in fact, typically determines its "solution." For example, take the categories that are used in defining a "problem" such as unemployment. The Bureau of Labor Statistics uses seven different definitions of the concept (and therefore the problem) of unemployment. These definitions differ depending on whether part-time workers are counted, or whether it is only heads of household, or dependents too, who are counted. Thus, in April 1977, the nation's unemployment was, variously, 1.9, 3.1, 4.4, 6.5, 7.0, 8.6, and 9.9 percent.

Such alternative definitions are so common that we sometimes forget their significance. This becomes clearer when one looks at the use of Western definitions applied to non-Western cultures. For example, Gun-

---

[1] Horst W. J. Rittel and Melvin Webber, "Dilemmas in a General Theory of Planning," *Policy Sciences* 4 (June 1973):160. The remainder of this section draws heavily on the tame/wicked-problem insight described in this article.

nar Myrdal, after reviewing various attempts to measure unemployment in South Asia, points out:

> But it would be fallacious to assume that the remedy for the shortcoming we have noted lies simply in the perfection of techniques and in the accumulation of cleansing experience. The fundamental difference lies in the analytical framework that has guided these inquiries. In general, these studies have been led to ask the kinds of questions Western economists would wish to investigate in their own countries. At the same time, however, it is often acknowledged that Western categories cannot be transferred intact to a South Asian environment.[2]

This comparison of Western to non-Western only highlights the difficulties of defining the problem. If the problem of unemployment is that it causes economic hardship for families, then one wants to employ all the breadwinners of those families. On the other hand, if the problem of unemployment is economic hardship *and* psychological well-being, then one wants to employ all who are able and wanting to work, including breadwinners and their dependents. It is not meaningful to argue that one of these solutions is correct, while the other is incorrect; it is possible, however, to argue that one is better (or worse) than the other at a particular time.

A social problem involves, in part, a discrepancy between how we see that things are and how we think that they should be. For a wicked problem, however, how we choose to describe this discrepancy at a particular time determines how the problem can be resolved at that time. One finds this interaction between seeing and choosing in the "poverty problem" in the United States. "Poverty," through legislative, judicial, and executive action, has been more or less consistently defined since the Nixon Administration as "the lack of money." (Alternative definitions could be in terms of social standing, education, or opportunity.) The "poverty level," defined solely in terms of income, became the only relevant measure. Efforts at solving the problem therefore focused on raising the income of the portion of the population that falls below that level. The "poverty problem" was thus turned into an "income distribution problem," one which is (technically and politically) more amenable to attack than if it were, say, a "cultural" problem.

Since wicked problems are subject to innumerable political definitions, there are no ultimate tests to measure the efficacy of their solutions. Once a bridge is built (a relatively tame problem, though deciding its location may not be), it is generally possible to determine if it has solved the problem it addressed, namely, to move certain kinds of traffic safely from one

---

[2]Gunnar Myrdal, *Asian Drama: An Inquiry into the Poverty of Nations* (New York: Pantheon, 1968), p. 2221.

place to another. For wicked problems, however, the solution itself potentially becomes a part of the problem: An employment training program produces skilled workers who each replace two less-skilled workers; a lower minimum wage for teenagers helps increase the proportion of teenagers employed, but at the expense of older workers requiring a higher minimum wage. Thus, every solution affects not only the target problem (one hopes), but also the problem of which the original one was a symptom—and the effects are not necessarily in the same direction.

Moreover, because of their uniqueness, wicked problems are not amenable to standardized routines for analysis and evaluation. Therefore, to the extent that it is possible to list solutions beforehand to a wicked problem, these solutions are unlikely to be mutually exclusive. We can lower unemployment by defining it in a different way, increasing the amount of work available, increasing the number of jobs, reducing the size of the workforce, or even changing the nature of work.

And, finally, in contending with wicked problems, public administrators as problem solvers have no right, in a political sense, to be wrong; they are responsible for the social consequences of their "solutions." The actions and inactions of public administrators affect the people whose lives are touched by the resulting consequences.

Organizations as Solutions to Wicked Problems

"Tame" and "wicked" represent the ends of a continuum, rather than distinct categories. As such, the notion of a wicked problem serves as a metaphorical reminder of our limitations in controlling the social world. In a sense, most of the problems that government deals with are, in at least some aspects, wicked. However, when government takes on a wicked problem, it finds it necessary to "tame" or bound the problem in some fashion. As critical players in these efforts, it is public administrators who apply instrumental analysis and rules to make wicked problems amenable to solution.

In separating means from ends, instrumental analysis enables us to judge whether a particular organizational action is correct and, by extension, whether those who took the action acted responsibly. Carrying the logic of instrumental analysis further, with sufficient knowledge of a problem and enough information and resources to solve it, structures of organizational authority are presumably available to assure the compliance of organizational members with organizational goals or standard operating procedures.

The metaphor of the wicked problem, however, challenges both our conventional descriptions of organizational problems, as well as our everyday beliefs about responsibility and authority. By implication, theories of organization that emphasize rational action as primarily or solely instrumental in character reveal the wickedness of administrative problems. By extension, they also reveal the limitations inherent in evaluating solutions either on solely instrumental grounds or by resort to formal organizational authority alone. If, for example, there is little agreement as to the appropriate division of moral, institutional, and legal responsibility for young Alan Madden's death, then who can say, even after the fact, how the solution to his *and* society's problem—the prevention of his death—might have been achieved? As with other wicked problems, Alan's death reveals that the problems and limitations of one agency are intertwined with those of other agencies and other actors.

Just as organizational actors will define problems in varying ways, theories of organization can define similar events, by virtue of the different questions they ask, in radically different ways.[3] Like wicked problems themselves, the corpus of the organizational literature possesses a distinctly Rashomon-like quality: Various theoretical approaches frame the same situations in different ways, ask differing questions about them, and thereby suggest differing solutions or preferred modes of action for contending with them.

The Administrator as Role-Taker

Although some problems are rather easily circumscribed in terms of the number of actors they affect, those problems that have particularly wicked aspects appear to span a wide range of organizational, political, and interpersonal domains. This presents an extremely confusing picture to both players and observers. In order to simplify this picture analytically, it is useful to employ several conceptual devices. One of these is the concept of *role*.

A role is the set of expectations that accompany a particular organizational relationship. There is a rather voluminous literature discussing various theoretical and empirical aspects of roles that is not necessary to review here. The point is merely to call attention to an idea that, in many ways, has become imbedded in everyday language. "To take a role" means, simply, to step into a relationship that already has many of its terms defined. These definitions are sometimes legal. For example, a public

---

[3]A good example of how different theoretical perspectives alter the interpretation of the same situation is Graham T. Allison, Jr., *Essence of Decision: Explaining the Cuban Missile Crisis* (Boston: Little, Brown, 1971), in which he analyzes the Cuban missile crisis from three different theoretical viewpoints.

administrator in the role of a manager has specified duties in relationship to subordinates as to hiring, firing, and supervising. There are also cultural expectations, often embodied in the law. The public administrator as manager, for instance, will generally be assumed to be the arbiter of disputes between subordinates. Some of the expectations concern power; the public administrator as manager is presumed to have more power—that is, is more likely to hold sway over internal and external forces and events— than do subordinates.

But roles are not pre-set; they are also defined by the individuals in them and those responding to them. The expectations we have toward a person enacting a role are modified by both the actions of that person and the actions of those with whom the role entails a relationship. As the range of concerns facing the public administrator increases—as he or she shifts from one role to another—significant changes are required in the skills, knowledge, and expertise needed. There is also a shift in the extent to which that performance, no matter how skillfully accomplished, can guarantee desirable solutions or outcomes.

Personal Action Versus Organizational Action

The actions—and inactions—of the officials involved in the Alan Madden incident portray some of the pathologies of public organizations in untypically stark and tragic terms. The case raises questions, however, that are generically similar to those wicked problems facing countless public administrators, and the answers are seldom, if ever, conclusive. Where, for example, is the proper dividing line between the responsibilities of government and those of private citizens? Confronted with scarce time, resources, and knowledge, how can public officials know, without benefit of hindsight, whether their actions are sufficiently responsive to the publics they serve?

In view of the relationships among the several agencies that are legally responsible for the welfare of any one citizen, is it possible to apportion blame reasonably among them when that citizen is inadequately cared for or mistreated? Does this apportionment of blame do very much to assure more responsive actions in the future? Finally, is the quality of government services a function more of the careful following of formal procedures or of the personal commitment of public officials to respond effectively to their clients' needs? The difficulties in obtaining definitive answers to these questions illustrate the problems encountered by public administrators in deciding not only how and when to act, but indeed *whether* to act.

If the actions of public officials seem hard to understand when taken individually, then consider the even greater difficulty in comprehending many such actions in relation to one another. Administrative decisions are difficult and complex precisely because they are made and acted upon in an organizational context, a web of relationships that often confounds not only observers, but even the actors themselves.

For example, despite the myriad rules and other mechanisms designed to check administrative error, both discretion and imperfect information are an inevitable part of administrative action. Although administrative discretion may sometimes lead to error, it is also the basis for the personal commitment that administrators need for conscientious performance of their tasks. Discretion, in other words, allows the administrator and client to shape the general rule of the specific circumstance. Without this commitment, as Max Weber recognized, the formalistic impersonality needed to insure efficiency in bureaucracy can also generate a pathology of its own in the form of indifference.[4] Thus, Alan Madden may well have died for reasons related less to the breakdown of a formal system of rules and procedures than because not enough people cared enough at the right time.

Even this assessment, however, may be misleading because of the distinction it implicitly draws between organizational and personal action, that is, between action taken according to rules and roles, and that motivated by personal commitment. Although the force of that distinction is manifestly evident in the premium that modern organizations place on efficiency (and therefore on impersonality), it is nevertheless artificial. Organizations are first and foremost human creations. Replete with impersonal rules, roles, and procedures, they seem to take on a life and a legitimacy of their own in the minds of those who work in them and are affected by them. Indeed, the history of modern organizations—and of organization theory—is the history of the process by which laymen and scholars alike have come to believe in the separation of the personal from the organizational. That this belief is implicit and even unconscious testifies to the power that we allow organizations to have over us. Despite the material benefits that we have reaped by virtue of this artificial separation, it has also led us to believe wrongly that there is a clear and meaningful difference between organizations and the people who inhabit them. To say, therefore, that Alan Madden died either from a breakdown of a system of rules and procedures or from human neglect and indifference are actually two ways of saying the same thing.

This separation of the personal from the organizational has been essential to the process by which modern organizations have evolved into an efficient means for the accomplishment of predefined ends. To the extent they are efficient, modern organizations conform to a key normative pre-

---

[4]See especially the concluding remarks in Max Weber, *The Protestant Ethic and the Spirit of Capitalism,* Talcott Parsons, trans. (London: G. Allen & Unwin, 1930), pp. 180–83.

cept, namely that of instrumental rationality. This contemporary action can be deemed rational only to the extent that it effectively accomplishes predefined goals. Action, then, is seen only as a means toward or an instrument for the attainment of ends; such action is thus valued positively only insofar as the amount of activity required to attain those ends is kept to a minimum. This is the common meaning of "efficiency," the *measure* of how well organizational action satisfies this criterion. An important way in which organizations try to foster efficiency is to sustain the belief that the unique and personal projects of individuals are separate and distinct from and subordinate to the efficient conduct of the organization's business. "Rational action" has come to be identified almost solely with what one does within an organizational setting and especially with what one does to further the goals and objectives of that organization.

The importance of all this is that instrumental rationality is at the heart of public administration and of virtually all organization theory. That people treat organizations as a means to an end or that people's actions are measured in an instrumental fashion is neither startling nor necessarily harmful to anyone. The difficulties arise when these are seen as the *only* ways by which to judge administrative action.

2

The Organizational Context of Public Administration

This chapter explores three related issues that figure prominently in the examination of the major theoretical perspectives on organizations in Parts II and III. The first concerns the ways in which the word "organization" has been variously defined in the theoretical literature. Our purpose here is not to reach any conclusions regarding a correct or preferred definition, but to show how various definitions, in juxtaposition, reveal the richness and also the contentiousness of the field of organization theory.

Second, we explore a long-standing controversy about how empirical differences between public and private organizations have historically influenced the role of organization theory in public administration. The main questions to be considered are whether these empirical differences (1) should make for significant variation in theorizing about public organizations, and (2) affect the salience of "generic" organization theory to public administration.

Finally, we describe the three "organizational arenas" that delimit the organizing context for public administration. Collectively, they provide a descriptive and analytic setting for examining the various perspectives on organization theory presented in Parts II and III. The arenas, combined with the "normative vectors" described in Chapter 3, constitute the framework for public administration. This is used throughout the remainder of the book to bring organization theory to bear on issues of specific concern to public administrators.

Defining "Organization"

Like the theories they represent, definitions direct our attention toward the objects—in this case, organizations—of our intuitive and common-sense experience. Some definitions are comforting because they clarify and provide substance to what we know implicity; others force us to recon-sider what we already think we know and therefore initially may be unwelcome intrusions into our seemingly well-ordered world. Offering any definition of "organization" as a preferred one to guide the reader through the discussions here would largely defeat a major purpose, namely, to induce an appreciation of the diversity and novelty that various theories (as well as theorizing in general) can bring to our understanding of organizations.

For example, in the accompanying box are eight definitions of "orga-nization" that are fairly representative of the organization literature. These definitions of organizations, of course, hardly reveal all that is inter-esting and significant either about the theories with which they are asso-ciated or about organizations themselves. Nevertheless, the various defi-nitions illustrate the diversity of opinion about what organizations are and how they may be productively viewed. Each definition emphasizes certain aspects to the exclusion of others. Thus, Katz and Kahn stress *patterns* and *flows of energy*, while Weber emphasizes the notion of *social domi-nation*. No definition here necessarily denies, however, the possible valid-ity of any other definition; that is, one could combine these eight defini-tions into a single large one and not have any conflicting elements. The definitions are, effectively, additive: each tells us a little more and some-thing different about human organization and organizing.

Like the tip of the proverbial iceberg, any definition of organization hides, but also provides clues to discovering, what lies beneath its surface. Mere differences between definitions are transformed into often-serious disagreements as one explores their varying implications for a deeper understanding of organization. On further examination, each definition reveals a distinctive and fairly coherent perspective from which to order our comprehension.

The idea of perspective provides a highly useful metaphor for differ-entiating among organizational theories. For the painter, "perspective" refers to the size, distance, and relation among objects in the field of view. Similarly, for the organization theorist, perspective suggests a particular kind of relation among, and emphasis on, aspects of organizing that are of practical and intellectual significance. Theoretical perspectives may be distinguished from one another along a variety of dimensions, of which six are especially prominent in the organizational literature:

- *The differing cognitive interests supported by theories.* A cognitive interest refers to the type of practical purpose that is potentially

EIGHT DEFINITIONS OF "ORGANIZATION"

MAX WEBER

A circle of people who are accustomed to obedience to the orders of *leaders* and who have a personal interest in the continuance of the domination by virtue of their own participation and the resulting benefits, have divided among themselves the exercise of those functions which will serve ready for their exercise. (This is what is meant by "organization.")

—Max Weber, *Economy and Society*, Vol. 2, Guenther Roth and Claus Wittich, eds. (Berkeley, Calif.: University of California Press, 1978), p. 952, emphasis in original.

DWIGHT WALDO

. . . organization may be defined as *the structure of authoritative and habitual personal interrelations in an administrative system.*

—Dwight Waldo, *The Study of Public Administration* (New York: Random House, 1955), p. 6, emphasis in original.

CHESTER BARNARD

A formal organization is a system of consciously coordinated activities or forces of two or more persons.

—Chester Barnard, *The Functions of the Executive* (Cambridge: Harvard University Press, 1938), p. 73.

PHILIP SELZNICK

. . . formal organization is the structural expression of rational action.

—Philip Selznick, "Foundations of the Theory of Organizations," *American Sociological Review* 13:1 (1948):25.

DANIEL KATZ AND ROBERT L. KAHN

Our theoretical model for the understanding of organizations is that of an energic input-output system in which the energic return from the output reactivates the system. Social organizations are flagrantly open systems in that the input of energies and the conversion of output into further energic input consists of transactions between the organization and its environment.

All social systems, including organizations, consist of the patterned activities of a number of individuals. Moreover, these patterned activities are complementary or interdependent with respect to some common output or outcome; they are repeated, relatively enduring, and bounded by space and time.

—Daniel Katz and Robert L. Kahn, *The Social Psychology of Organizations*, 2nd ed. (New York: John Wiley and Sons, 1978), p. 20.

continued next page

EIGHT DEFINITIONS *continued*

DAVID SILVERMAN

Organisations . . . are social institutions with certain special characteristics: they are consciously created at an ascertainable point in time; their founders have given them goals which are usually important chiefly as legitimating symbols; the relationship between their members and the source of legitimate authority is relatively clearly defined, although frequently the subject of discussion and planned change [by members who seek to coordinate or control].

—David Silverman, *The Theory of Organisations* (New York: Basic Books, 1971), p. 147.

KARL WEICK

. . . organizing [in contrast to organization] . . . is defined as a *consensually validated grammar for reducing equivocality by means of sensible interlocked behaviors.*

—Karl Weick, *The Social Psychology of Organizing*, 2nd ed. (Reading, Mass.: Addison-Wesley Publishing Co., 1979), p. 3, emphasis in original.

MICHAEL COHEN, JAMES MARCH, AND JOHAN OLSEN

An organization is a collection of choices looking for problems, issues and feelings looking for decision situations in which they might be aired, solutions looking for issues to which they might be the answer, and decision makers looking for work.

—Michael D. Cohen, James G. March, and Johan P. Olsen, "A Garbage Can Model of Organizational Choice," *Administrative Science Quarterly* 17:1(1972):2.

served by a theory. Theories may serve, for example, interests of social control by explicating cause-effect relations among variables that are regarded as important by the theorist; they may provide a means for interpreting problematic situations as they are understood by the actors involved in them; or theories may provide a carefully reasoned basis for normative criticism.

- *Dominant metaphors.* Metaphors are indispensable both to our everyday comprehension of the social world, as well as to theoretical understanding. Differences in theoretical perspectives are to a great extent reducible to differences in their dominant metaphors. A metaphor provides the theorist with an overall image of his or her subject matter that affects both methodologies for research and normative evaluation.

- *Primary units of analysis.* A primary unit of analysis provides the theorist with a starting point for investigation. A unit of analysis reflects a presumption regarding what is most real about, and therefore most basic to an understanding of, a subject of inquiry. Primary units differ from one another with respect to the *levels* of analysis to which they direct attention (e.g., the organization as a unified whole, the small group, the individual), as well as the presumed *motives* or *purposes* that they embody.

- *The relation of the individual to the organization.* Differences in theoretical stances regarding this dimension reveal differing and unique combinations of assumptions about human nature and the nature of the social order. A given combination of assumptions, in turn, influences the theorist's beliefs about whether organizations are fundamentally instruments of domination or benign associations of cooperative activity. These beliefs about the nature of organizations subsequently affect beliefs about the particular meaning of human fulfillment in organizational settings.

- *The meaning of rationality.* Many organization theorists define rational action instrumentally, that is, as action that attains pregiven ends. This meaning is widely disputed, however, as both an accurate and a normatively desirable characterization of human action. Arguments about the relevance of instrumental rationality for organization theory turn on the underlying question of whether thought mainly precedes and informs action or, alternatively, action (regarded as spontaneous or driven by unconscious energy) mainly precedes and gives rise to thought.

- *The primary values embodied in theoretical perspectives.* The primary values that are associated with any theoretical perspective are selected neither arbitrarily nor independently of other theoretical considerations. Rather, values are products of the particular manner in which theorists variously grapple with each of the five preceding dimensions. Values, for theorists, are embodied in their particular stances toward cognitive interests, dominant metaphors, primary units of analysis, the relation of the individual to the organization, and the meaning of rationality.

Each of these dimensions carries with it implications for the way in which a theoretical perspective will view particular problems, offer unique solutions, and generally approach the question of how humans organize themselves for collective activity over time. As we explore the various perspectives on organization theory, these dimensions should be kept in mind, for it is through them that the distinctive character of each perspective presents itself. Although the discussion in Parts II and III implicitly takes these dimensions into account, they alone cannot provide sufficient grounding to relate organization theory to public administration. This requires, at a minimum, appreciating the differences between public and private organizations.

Organization Theory and the Public/Private Distinction

Wallace Sayre's ironic aphorism that public and private management are fundamentally alike in all *unimportant* respects neatly summarizes a long-standing and highly contentious issue in public administration discourse about organizations. Assuming that Sayre is correct, then differences in modes of managing obviously imply differences in the kinds of organizations that are managed. By extension, if public and private organizations differ from one another in significant ways, then questions naturally arise about how theorizing might, both descriptively and normatively, take due account of those differences.

Historically, these questions have not been seriously addressed by mainstream organization theorists, whose ties have usually been to disciplines other than public administration. For scholars in these disciplines, chiefly sociology and business administration, the public/private distinction has traditionally been minimized, if not ignored altogether, resulting in what is conventionally termed "generic" organization theory.[1] In broad brush, generic theory has relied upon theoretical constructs and methodological approaches intended to help explain the structural aspects and modes of practice common to all organizations generally, irrespective of time, place and, most especially, social and political context.

Chapters 5 and 6 document the historical evolution of the generic view—from its early (and naive) emphasis on using the scientific method to reveal universal, prescriptive principles of organization and management to a far more sophisticated (and far less prescriptive) concern with scientific, value-free description and explanation.[2] But, despite the substantial changes generated by its increasing sophistication about the meaning and role of science, the generic view obscures what have come to be regarded by public administration scholars as the significant differences

---

[1]The term "generic theory" is used here to characterize any theory of organization or organizing that does not adhere to a distinction between public and private organizations as a theoretical starting point, rather than to describe any particular theoretical perspective.

[2]Especially important in this latter regard is Herbert Simon, whose works are examined in Chapter 6 and in Chapter 8's discussion of the debate between the "rationalists" in organization theory and the "later human relationists." For his thoughts relevant to the present discussion, see Herbert A. Simon, "The Proverbs of Public Administration," *Public Administration Review* 6:4(1946):53–67; and *Administrative Behavior*, 3rd rev. ed. (New York: The Free Press, 1976).

between public and private organizations. That these differences are masked by the generic view is attributable less to its proponents' stated belief that the "public" (or political) character of government organizations is unimportant than to their overriding concern for generalizations that transcend the public/private distinction. Partly this is owing to the generic theorists' acceptance of a radical distinction between facts and values. Values, seen as essentially emotional attachments devoid of any rational basis for explanation or justification, are considered as beyond the ken of science, which by definition is (or ought to be) value-free.

This commitment to a value-free science of organizations, in turn, precludes (or at least appears to) a consideration of the values that infuse public organizations. During its first half-century as a self-conscious field of study (roughly from the late 1880s to the mid-1940s), public administration's orthodoxy was firmly grounded in Woodrow Wilson's stern admonition that administration be kept separate from politics. The idea that administration and politics are logically and normatively separate activities served as a basic underpinning for the early public administration orthodoxy. This separation, or so it was thought, would enable the formulation of generalized scientific principles of administration that would not be contaminated by the vulgar intrusion of politics.

Beginning in the 1940s, Herbert Simon sought to demolish the early public administration orthodoxy by exposing its fundamental misunderstanding of science and, by extension, the pretentiousness of its claims to have discovered universal principles of organization and management. Nevertheless, by grounding his overall perspective on organization theory in the logical-positivist separation of fact from value, Simon in effect sustained one of that orthodoxy's principal beliefs: the logical distinction of administration from politics. His belief that organizations, whether public or private, could be studied scientifically rested on the assumption that issues of political value could and should be excluded from that enterprise, and, once excluded, scientific analysis would uncover organizational behavior that was constant across all organizational settings, public or private. Simon argued, it must be emphasized, against the particular "principles" of the early orthodoxy, not against the possibility of discovering such principles that would apply across all organizations.

As the influence of Simon's position spread, so too did an important countervailing current of thought. It emerged to challenge both Simon's positivism as well as the earlier public administration orthodoxy. As reflected in the works of Paul Appleby, Robert A. Dahl, and Dwight Waldo, this newer current of thinking established the public/private distinction as an idea of great importance in the study of public administration.

Paul Appleby's writings provide a striking, if perhaps unintended, counterpoint to Simon's argument for a generic science of organization.

In asserting that "Public administration is policymaking,"[3] Appleby sought to establish the inherently political character of public administration and, thereby, demonstrate its essential differences from private administration. Government is different from business, he argued, by reason of the breadth of the scope and impact of its decisions, the fact of its public accountability, and its fundamentally political rather than rational character.[4] Appleby's account of the nature of government organizations anticipated what are now commonplace observations about the distinctive character of public in contrast to private organizations, including an emphasis on service as opposed to profit, the sterner strictures of legal accountability, the greater difficulty of measuring effective goal attainment, the pluralistic and more publicly visible nature of decision making, and the fact of their responsiveness to public wants mainly through nonmarket forces.[5]

Appleby's project was not simply to document the distinctive character of government organizations in descriptive terms. In addition, he sought to *legitimate* the inherently political role of administration in a democratic society. Establishing that legitimacy, however, entailed much more than making a virtue of necessity by simply defending as appropriate a political role for administration that was, in any case, inevitable. Appleby believed that effective public executives, in addition to possessing qualities of political astuteness and professionalism, should also be guided by a clear commitment to democratic values and a sense of an overarching public interest.[6]

Although Appleby's recognition of the political nature of administration dampened the force of the generic school of organization theory in public administration, it did not constitute a direct rebuttal to the "scientific" assumptions on which the generic view was based.[7] At about the

[3]Paul B. Appleby, *Policy and Administration* (University, Ala.: University of Alabama Press, 1949), p. 170.

[4]Appleby, "Government Is Different," in Jay M. Shafritz and Albert C. Hyde, eds., *Classics of Public Administration* (Oak Park, Ill.: Moore Publishing Co., 1978), p. 105; reprinted from *Big Democracy* (New York: Alfred A. Knopf, 1945).

[5]See Robert B. Denhardt, *Theories of Public Organization* (Monterey, Calif.: Brooks/ Cole Publishing Company, 1984), pp. 40–68. Another useful discussion is Graham T. Allison, Jr., "Public and Private Management: Are They Fundamentally Alike in All Unimportant Respects?" in *Setting Public Management Research Agendas: Integrating the Sponsor, Producer and User*, in OPM Document 127–53–1 (Washington, DC: Office of Personnel Management, February 1980), pp. 27–38; this can be found reprinted in Richard J. Stillman II, *Public Administration: Concepts and Cases*, 3rd ed. (Boston: Houghton Mifflin, 1984), pp. 453–67.

[6]See Appleby, *Morality and Administration* (Baton Rouge, La.: University of Louisiana Press, 1952).

[7]Appleby was not principally a theorist, but rather an active participant in and a philosopher of public organization. Before becoming Dean of the Maxwell School of Citizenship and Public Affairs at Syracuse University, Appleby served as a high-level official with the United States Department of Agriculture during the administration of Franklin Roosevelt.

same time that Appleby wrote, however, two younger scholars, Robert A. Dahl and Dwight Waldo, took up more directly the theoretical challenge posed to public administration by the generic school. Dahl did so by disputing the then-prominent belief that a "science of administration" was either possible or desirable. Although he did not quarrel directly with the generic school's rejection of a meaningful public/private distinction, Dahl questioned the relevance to public administration of the "scientific" assumptions on which the generic view based its claims. He argued that difficult normative considerations could seldom be excluded from public administration problems. Problems of value and fact are almost inevitably co-mingled in the *practice* of administration. Since politics and administration converge almost to the point of being indistinguishable from one another, administration is inevitably concerned not just with the *implementation* of public ends, but with their *creation* as well. As Dahl puts it,

> [In] most societies, and particularly in democratic ones, ends are often in dispute; rarely are they clearly and unequivocally determined. Nor can ends and means ever be sharply distinguished, since ends determine means and often means ultimately determine ends.[8]

In addition, the possibilities of a generic science of administration are limited, he argued, both by the severe methodological difficulties in understanding the complex and variable nature of individual psychology in administrative settings, as well as by the cultural differences that necessarily impinge on administrative activity. Thus, Dahl concludes,

> No science of public administration is possible unless: (1) the place of normative values is made clear; (2) the nature of man in the area of public conduct is more predictable; and (3) there is a body of comparative studies from which it may be possible to discover principles and generalities that transcend national boundaries and peculiar historical experiences.[9]

Dahl's argument, however, holds chiefly as a rebuttal to the *early* generic organization theorists who claimed that science provided the means for discovering universal, prescriptive principles of organization and management. Later proponents of the generic approach, such as Simon, also rejected the earlier pretensions to universal principles, but did so by arguing that the assertion of such principles simply reflected a naive misunderstanding of science. Although science could not establish the normative legitimacy of particular values and modes of practice, the methods of science *could* enable a more sophisticated understanding of how

---

[8]Robert A. Dahl, "The Science of Public Administration: Three Problems," Shafritz and Hyde, p. 125; originally appearing in *Public Administration Review* 7:1(1947):1–11.
[9]Ibid., p. 133.

the realization of various values in organizational settings is influenced by differing psychological and cultural orientations and situational contexts. The later generic theorists seldom felt obliged to deny in explicit terms the obvious differences in normative, psychological, and cultural orientations, or even to deny salient differences between public and private organizations. Science, in short, could serve to appreciate difference as well as similarity.

Although nothing in the espoused logic of the scientific method necessarily precluded acknowledgment of the differences between public and private organizations, an appreciation of those differences nevertheless did not figure prominently in the emerging literature that reflected a generic viewpoint. To Dwight Waldo (writing in 1948), the failure of the generic literature to stress the distinctive character of public administration was not simply a matter of happenstance.[10] Rather, the scientific commitments of the generic theorists inevitably led them to focus almost exclusively on technical aspects of administrative efficiency, which were amenable to study through the scientific method. By being conceived in strictly technical terms, this generic view of administration excluded from consideration precisely what made public administration "public": a set of values derived from democratic political theory. In radically dividing fact and value, the positivists of the generic school, Waldo argued, not only conceptually *separated* matters of administrative technique from matters of political value, but implicitly sought to *replace* theories of political values with scientific theories relevant only to questions of administrative technique. To Waldo, however, the essence of *public* administration lay precisely in the democratic political theory that the generic theorists saw as irrelevant to both organization theory and public administration.[11]

Arguments such as those offered by Appleby, Dahl, and Waldo did not defeat the generic view, but they did diminish somewhat its development *within* the public administration academy. The generic theorists, however, found congenial climates elsewhere (mainly in sociology) in which they continued to prosper, making frequent inroads through the highly permeable boundaries of academic public administration. In the meantime, the emerging mainstream of the public administration literature readily embraced the *empirical* distinctions between public and private organizations emphasized by Appleby, Dahl, Waldo, and others.

Interest was largely absent, however, in developing the *normative foundations* of a theory of public organization derived from democratic theory as Waldo had urged. In recognizing that "public administration is

---

[10]For a fuller elaboration of his argument, see Dwight Waldo, *The Administrative State: A Study of the Political Theory of American Public Administration* (New York: The Ronald Press, 1948), pp. 159–91.

[11]For a discussion of the implications of Waldo's argument to the subject of "democratic administration," see Chapter 8.

different" (i.e., political), scholars in the field renewed their historical ties with the discipline of political science, but at a time when political scientists were largely renouncing normative political philosophy as the core of *their* discipline. By the early 1950s, the "behavioral revolution" was in full swing in all the American social sciences. That revolution embraced scientific and methodological commitments almost identical to those of the generic school of organization theory—against which Waldo had so eloquently argued. One consequence of this was the emergence of the so-called "bureaucratic politics" literature, which although acknowledging the distinctive character of government bureaucracies in an empirical sense, contributed only modestly to systematic theorizing about and philosophical analysis of public organizations.[12]

Although acknowledging that public organizations differ in important ways from their private counterparts, academic public administration did not produce, during the 1950s and 1960s, a body of literature and research on public organization theory commensurate with that produced by the generic theorists. Especially notable by their absence were serious efforts to ground theories of public organization within more encompassing theories of political values, democratic or otherwise. By the early 1970s, however, the public administration literature began to show substantial interest in responding to Waldo's challenge. Symbolized in part by the so-called "New Public Administration," which flourished briefly during and shortly after the United States involvement in Vietnam and the "War on Poverty," a body of literature began to appear that explicitly joined, often by way of critique, the organization theory literature with political theory.[13] Although short-lived as a unified voice of dissent from more traditional opinion, the New PA gave stimulus to subsequent efforts linking democratic and other political theory to both established and emerging perspectives in the generic organizational literature. These include the later human relations tradition inspired by the works of Abraham Maslow (see Chapter 8), interpretive and critical theories (discussed in Chapter 10), theories of emergence (Chapter 11), and to a lesser extent public choice theory (Chapter 9). The cumulative effect of this newer but highly varie-

---

[12]Although we will not explore the bureaucratic politics literature here, for a representative sampling see Graham T. Allison, Jr., *Essence of Decision: Explaining the Cuban Missile Crisis* (Boston: Little, Brown, 1971); Herbert Kaufman, "Administrative Decentralization and Political Power," *Public Administration Review* 29:1(1969):3–15; Norton E. Long, "Power and Administration," *Public Administration Review* 9:3(1949):257–64; Kenneth J. Meier, *Politics and the Bureaucracy* (North Scituate, Mass.: Duxbury Press, 1979); Francis E. Rourke, *Bureaucracy, Politics, and Public Policy* (Boston: Little, Brown, 1976); Rourke, ed., *Bureaucratic Power and National Politics* (Boston: Little, Brown, 1978); Harold Seidman, *Politics, Position and Power*, 2nd ed. (New York: Oxford University Press, 1975); and Aaron Wildavsky, *The Politics of the Budgetary Process*, 4th ed. (Boston: Little, Brown, 1984).

[13]See Frank Marini, ed., *Toward a New Public Administration: The Minnowbrook Perspective* (Scranton, Pa.: Chandler Publishing Co., 1971); and Dwight Waldo, ed., *Public Administration in a Time of Turbulence* (Scranton, Pa.: Chandler Publishing Co., 1971).

gated literature was to reestablish crucial linkages between public administration and at least some segments of the literature on organization theory. In doing so, the public/private distinction in organization theory attained renewed prominence.

Prior to these more recent developments, however, the more-established perspectives in the generic literature, especially organizational systems theories (Chapter 7) and the work of Simon and his colleagues (Chapter 6), occupied an anomalous position within the public administration academic community. Although this generic literature was read and often appreciated by public administration scholars, it was seldom analyzed in terms of its possibly valuable contributions to an understanding of the normative and political character of public organizations. This was especially regrettable inasmuch as, by the late 1950s, much of the generic organizational literature, although continuing to neglect the public/private distinction, had abandoned much of the positivistic and technocratic character of the earlier generic theory that had so offended writers such as Dahl and Waldo.

The discussion that begins in the next section grounds a descriptive and valuational framework of public administration within which the organization theory literature can be assessed. Then, starting with Chapter 5, we use this framework to examine the salience of a wide variety of theoretical perspectives on organizations to the study of public administration. That some of this literature still largely ignores what is distinctive about public organizations is taken as an invitation to explore its salience, rather than as a reason to reject it as irrelevant or merely incidental to public administration.

Three Arenas of Public Organization

Administrative action, by definition, takes place in an organizational context. For the public administrator, this is a context that is by and large strewn with wicked problems having political as well as instrumental, technical solutions. These solutions come about as a result of the actions of many organizational players. As one of these players, the public administrator moves in and out of roles in a variety of organizational settings. The numerous roles of the public administrator can be most easily visualized analytically as coalescing in three general arenas: inter-organizational, intra-organizational and organization-to-individual.

In the *inter-organizational* arena, the public administrator acts as representative of and agent for an organization as he or she meets, talks, argues, and deals with similar agents from other organizations. This arena is often clouded over because the language used to describe it is that of organization meeting with organization, rather than people dealing with people.

The second arena is the *intra-organizational*. Here the language is often that of the organization chart, of who reports to whom. The public administrator has a place in the organization and from that place works with others in the organization. The third arena is the *organization-to-individual*, in which the public administrator—again acting as agent—confronts, directs, cajoles, and interacts with individuals. These individuals are both inside (coworkers, subordinates, superiors) and outside (clients, citizens) of the organization.

The importance of being aware of this mixture is that various perspectives on organization theory deal only with particular bits and pieces of this picture. In order for theory to be most helpful, we need to be able to recognize the aspects of the picture to which each perspective speaks. The arenas, as an analytical tool, are imprecise; the lines between any two are always blurred. Their purpose is primarily to call attention to the different—and at times, opposing—roles that the public administrator is required to play.

Inter-Organizational Relations

The broadest of the administrative arenas is the *inter-organizational*. Here the administrator deals with representatives of other units of his agency outside his immediate control, as well as other agencies, legislative and judicial bodies, and interest and client groups. Many of these relationships are formally defined, either by statute or constitution, whereas others are defined by history and practice (e.g., the review of agency activities by legislative committee). Still others are defined informally (e.g., through personal friendship and acquaintance networks). In every case, these relationships are ultimately organization-to-organization, affecting, defining, and modulating the agency's perception of its mission and, therefore, the activities of its administrators.

The inter-organizational arena, more so than any other, requires a great diversity of both administrative roles and performance within those roles. It also requires an appreciation by actors and observers of the widest variety of social and political values in order to understand the effective performance of those roles.

Inter-organizational relations are in many ways the most significant for the public administrator in that they provide both the understructure and the legitimacy for the organization's work. Descriptions of this arena invariably speak of organizations as the relevant entities, rather than individuals, who often appear almost incidental. A good example of this comes from A. Lee Fritschler's description of the conflict between the

CONGRESS AND CIGARETTES

In view of most congressional oversight, the actions of Congress against the Federal Trade Commission's attempts to require health warnings for cigarette smokers were unusual both in their form and severity. Congress passed a bill in 1965 that reduced in very specific terms a small portion of the FTC's powers. Oversight legislation of a punitive nature is frequently introduced by an irate member, but it seldom is passed or even given serious committee consideration. Normally reprimands of agencies are informal, handled by committees through threatened action or by actual reduction of an agency's budget. Either of these occurrences may take place without the introduction of legislation or without public hearings.

Open controversy between Congress and an agency is almost always avoided, . . . But in the mid-1960's, the pressure on the Federal Trade Commission by the health interests and the Surgeon General's report encouraged the commission to take an action that was to invoke the full wrath of Congress. The threat of a warning being required on cigarette packages and in all advertising was more than Congress was prepared to accept. . . .

The resulting congressional reprimand of the Federal Trade Commission was unexpectedly severe in its intensity. It involved lengthy hearings in both houses of Congress and on the substance and wisdom of the FTC action. The legislation that emerged from those hearings specifically negated the commission's rule and temporarily took away its rulemaking powers relating to cigarette advertising. . . .

The pinpointing by Congress of a specific action and the commission's inability to muster support for what it had done left the Federal Trade Commission a bit shaken. . . . [T]he fact that Congress has the power to rise up in awesome dissent, at least occasionally, serves to remind administrators that the road to success is paved with quietly negotiated accommodation of agency policy to the views of key congressmen. In this way Congress exercises rather firm control over agency activities.

—From: A. Lee Fritschler, *Smoking and Politics*, 2nd ed. (Englewood Cliffs, N.J.: Prentice-Hall, 1975), pp. 118–20.

Congress and the Federal Trade Commission over the issue of health warnings about the danger of cigarette smoking (see the accompanying box).

Clearly, at the inter-organizational level, issues of organizational survival, responsiveness, and political legitimacy are most acute. As we shall see in Parts II and III, organizational theories vary both in the extent of their sensitivity to inter-organizational concerns and in the value stances this implies for the administrative roles used in coping with those concerns. In view of the legal/political nature of many inter-organizational issues, it is especially important, as will be evident throughout the book, to assess organizational theories in terms of their adequacy in comprehending and evaluating the distinctly *public* characteristics of public organizations.

Intra-Organizational Relations

A second clustering comprises administrative roles directed at *intra-organizational* relationships, that is, those creating the internal structure of and defining relations within organizations. The now-classical distinction between the formal and informal organization is especially salient to this clustering of administrative roles, with "formal" designating those relations that are authoritatively prescribed and publicly agreed to (and usually depicted on an organization chart), while "informal" refers to relations that emerge from convenience and tradition. Both formal and informal relations may also be thought of as the channels through which power and information flow throughout the organization. Although they are clearly affected by personal relationships, administrative roles required in the intra-organizational arena are mainly conceived as unit-to-unit or position-to-position, rather than person-to-person.

Intra-organizational issues typically differ in significant degree, if not in kind, from inter-organizational ones. Although it is certainly true that *within* an organization a particular unit's survival, its responsiveness to other units, and its perceived legitimacy may often be problematic, these issues are most often dealt with in implicit, sub rosa, even internecine fashion. At an explicit level, intra-organizational concerns typically center on the most basic, traditional issues found in the organizational literature: order and control, efficient attainment of goals, coordination, and the maintenance of effective communication. In response to such issues, the call has been for administrative roles conceived in mainly rational-instrumental terms, with intra-organizational problems conceptualized, if sometimes unwisely, as tame problems susceptible to technological rather than, say, political solutions.

Douglas McGregor captures the spirit of this traditional view of intra-organizational relationships when he speaks of the logic of traditional organizational structure (see the accompanying box). Although he is speaking about the business firm, the picture he draws is clearly applicable to the typical agency as well.

Although virtually all organization theories, especially generic theory, address intra-organizational concerns, the range of focus diverges widely. How best to define "organization," and even whether organizations exist in a real or concrete sense, are vigorously debated in the literature. Opinion also differs on the possibility and desirability of instrumentally rational action and, at least implicitly, on the relative tameness or wickedness

THE ORGANIZATIONAL MAP

One map of a portion of reality upon which managers have relied for many decades is the organization chart and its associated set of position descriptions. This map represents the organization as a structure of responsibilities and a structure of authority. The logic for viewing organizational reality this way is persuasive, and the tendency, therefore, has been to accept this map as a good representation of reality.

The familiar view is that, in a small company, the president . . . carries on all managerial functions. With growth of the firm, some division of labor becomes necessary. Consequently, the president hires other managers to whom he assigns responsibilities for certain parts of the total function. However, in doing so, he retains the overall responsibility for the organization, even though he no longer carries on all the managerial activities.

As the organization grows, each of these subdivisions of responsibility may be further divided, but with the same conception that each manager retains responsibility for everything that is assigned to him from above. He can delegate some of this authority, but he cannot delegate his responsibility. Each managerial position on the chart thus depicts what a man is responsible for, although not necessarily what he does.

. . .

Thus we have a map of the organization, constructed from a series of positions, which defines a structure of responsibility and a structure of positions. It tells who interacts with whom in terms of command or compliance. In addition, the necessary policies and procedures are formulated to define the interrelationships involved (i.e., the "controls" for making the structure operational). This map is essentially static, in that changes can be effected only by a formal reorganization of these relationships. Minor adjustments to individual positions, of course, can and do occur without reorganization.

—From: Douglas McGregor, *The Professional Manager*, Warren G. Bennis and Caroline McGregor, eds. (New York: McGraw-Hill, 1967), pp. 32–33.

of intra-organizational problems. While some theories accept the instrumentally rational emphasis as both natural and desirable, others offer thoroughgoing critiques on practical, political, and moral grounds.

Organization-to-Individual Relations

The third arena of administrative roles deals with *organization-to-individual* relations. Perhaps more accurately, the focus here is on administrators acting under the auspices of organizational authority with or in regard to individuals both within and outside the organization. These include, for example, manager-to-worker and agency-to-client relationships. At this level, administrative roles must contend with such issues as personal discretion in the application of rules, employee motivation, and styles of interpersonal relations.

One student of the effect of social service programs on their clients, Joel Handler, captures a view of the kind of issues involved in the organization-to-individual arena:

> In theory, the existence of discretion in the delivery of social services creates a bargaining relationship between the client and the social services officer. Discretion gives the officer authority to make choices which are based, on the one hand, on the rules, standards, and guidelines of the program and on his professional judgment and expertise, and on the other hand, on the requests, information, reasons, and arguments of the client. The client attempts to persuade the officer that benefits or services should be granted and promises to abide by the conditions of the grant. There are constraints on the bargaining relationship. Both the client and the officer, at least in theory, are bound by the procedural and substantive rules of the program, and, ... remedies are available with which to enforce these constraints.
>
> . . .
>
> ... Caseworkers and supervisors may treat clients kindly and wisely, or suspiciously and with hostility; they may view the law and the program liberally or restrictively, but in most cases the law does not tell them which path to choose. Administration depends on the proclivities of the administrators, not on the boundaries and principles of a legal framework.[14]

Unfortunately, much of the organizational literature is either silent about organization-to-individual concerns or tends to treat them in a perfunctory or derivative manner. The portion that does speak seriously to this arena has either of two general emphases. One concentrates on the moral/ethical considerations involved in the discretionary judgments that public administrators make. Here, individual needs and rights are balanced against, and in some cases integrated with, the values associated with the inter- and intra-organizational arenas. These issues, however, are only infrequently addressed by the generic organizational literature owing to its primary focus on business and private enterprises rather than government and public organizations.

The second emphasis is drawn from the psychological and social-psychological literature and addresses such problems as individual motivation and the effectiveness of small-group interaction. Here there is a conflict within the generic literature. Examining this conflict effectively brings out the tensions between the values implicit in the administrative roles in the

[14]Joel F. Handler, *Protecting the Social Service Client* (New York: Academic Press, 1980), pp. 23, 25.

organization-to-individual arena and those tacitly underlying the other, more encompassing arenas. Illustrative of this tension is a generalization by Chris Argyris:

> Formal organization strategy tends to reward communication, openness, experimentation on the rational level. It tends to penalize openness, levelling, and experimentation on the interpersonal and emotional levels. This, in turn, tends to decrease the participants' interpersonal competence within the organization.
>
> The emphasis upon rationality tends to create an organizational climate in which feelings are considered to be "bad," "immature," "irrational," and many times irrelevant....[15]

Although the three organizational arenas are, to be sure, somewhat artificial in their distinctions, they do seem to conform in large measure to the common-sense distinctions made by both organizational actors and those who write about organizations. Although it is certainly the case that administrators implicitly know that their roles in the three arenas interact with and complicate one another, they also often perceive one arena—and therefore one role set—as more compelling or legitimate than the others. This may be a function of personal proclivities, professional training and experience, the perceived nature of the situation or problem at hand, or of the level in the organizational hierarchy occupied by the particular administrator.

A similar tendency to stress the importance of one arena over the others pervades the literature of organization theory. Differences of opinion about the relative importance of the three arenas of organizational concern extend not only to the ways in which organizational problems are defined and the relative priority of values that are associated with the various arenas, but also to disagreements about which arena is "most real" or most fundamental to a "true" understanding of organizations.

The organizational arenas of public administration constitute half of the framework used here to assess organization theory. The other half, the "normative vectors," is described in the next chapter.

---

[15]Chris Argyris, "Explorations in Consulting-Client Relationships" in Warren G. Bennis et al., eds., *The Planning of Change*, 3rd ed. (New York: Holt, Rinehart and Winston, 1969), p. 436.

3

The Normative Context of Public Administration

"Public administration is detailed and systematic execution of public law. Every particular application of general law is an act of administration."[1] So declared Woodrow Wilson one hundred years ago in an at-the-time obscure essay that is now considered a classic formulation of the role of public administration. His essay, "The Study of Administration," provided the intellectual basis for a distinction that brought years of frustrating debate: the dichotomy of policy and administration.

This debate centers around a two-pronged question, namely, where is the line that divides policy from administration and, assuming that it can be found, how useful is it in its application? The importance of these questions stems primarily from our notions of responsibility and accountability. If, as a public administrator, I am merely the executor of the law, then the responsibility for the consequences of that execution lies with those who propound the law. As long as my actions can be grounded in that law, I am acting properly; such would appear to be a straightward measure of administrative propriety. The difficulty, of course, shows itself when one moves down to cases: Is the welfare worker, in deciding that a family is ineligible for assistance, merely executing the law or is he in some way also formulating policy? Does the federal auditor, in disallowing a state's

[1]Woodrow Wilson, "The Study of Administration," *Political Science Quarterly* 2:2(1887):197.

charges against a particular account, only "carry out the rules" or does she in some fashion, by virtue of applying the rules, also remake those rules in the process?

This debate is unlikely to be resolved, at least in the terms in which it is usually drawn, and it is one returned to in many different guises when examining the various perspectives of organization theory. Meanwhile, several points underlying this debate are useful to pursue. The most important is that the central component of administering is decision making: Decisions are the core around which all other acts of the public administrator revolve.

This emphasis on decisions, however, can sometimes make them appear too grandiose. Much of the public administration literature, for example, gives the impression that the only decisions that really qualify for that title are the *big* decisions. Given this state of affairs, it is not difficult to see that when the policy/administration discussion attempts to draw the line between "big" and "little" decisions, the discussion becomes muddied. Part of the difficulty is that Paul Appleby's definition of policy is still the best: A policy decision is any decision made at *your* level or higher. In other words, trying to distinguish in any but a superficial way between "policy decisions" and "administrative decisions," between "big" and "little" decisions, is not very helpful. Although the welfare worker's decision is clearly administrative, from the client's perspective it is just as clearly a policy decision. Different ways out of this thicket have been proposed, ranging from the notion that the administrator should be a good person and follow his instincts, to the caution that she must be a literalist in all applications of rules. Neither of these proposals, however, assists us in confronting the serious dilemmas inherent in the administrator's role as decision maker.

If the primary activity of the administrator is to decide, then what should be the normative grounds for making decisions? We have already explored the scope of the public administrator's decisions; the three organizational arenas show us the where, the with-whom, and the toward-whom of these decisions. To understand the grounds for these decisions, the why, we need to move from a geographical context into a normative one.

The Normative Base for Decision Making

Decision making means making choices: selecting from among real or imagined alternatives, picking one thing or another, one person or another, one action or another. Some aspects of decision making deal with authority (who is legitimately entitled to make a decision), while others speak to power (who has the wherewithal to enforce a decision). Yet other aspects are concerned with the quality of the decision (is it the best one in the circumstance). Choices, at least those made at a conscious level of awareness, entail judgment in reference to a standard. This is just a formal way of saying that people do not make conscious choices, except in terms of what they think they want to happen or where they want to go or what they want the result to be. Standards, however, are seldom useful substitutes for judgment. Even when explicit, they still need to be interpreted within a specific decisional context.

"Every particular application of general law is an act of administration." Translating Wilson's statement into the terms we are using here: "Every particular application of a standard (be it embodied in law, regulation, or cultural norm) is an act of judging." To explore the standards by which public administrators make judgments is to explore the values inherent in public administration.

Both in defining their roles generally and in making specific decisions, administrators inevitably make choices about values in two senses. The first is to infuse their role definitions and actions, at an implicit and even unconscious level, with assumptions and beliefs about what is prudent, practical, and desirable. At this level, roles and actions may not be self-consciously thought of as having moral/ethical content. The values that underlie them appear to be so obvious and compelling that they are simply taken for granted. But all action is by definition *motivated* and, with rare exceptions, this motivation directs action toward that which is thought to be *worth* doing; in other words, it is valued. This may appear to be simply a truism, but it needs to be underscored in view of a pervasive tendency, especially in bureaucratic organizations, for people to think mainly in rational/instrumental terms or to regard particular actions as determined by "situational imperatives."

The second influence of values on administrative roles and actions is at a self-aware level. Here administrators consciously weigh competing values, to some extent abstractly, but usually in terms of their apparent fit with or relevance to particular contexts. In the public administration literature, two terms have been historically influential in framing value (or normative) questions: the public interest and administrative responsibility. Much, and certainly the best, of this literature is intended to be of practical benefit by highlighting and making critical sense of the tensions between those values with whose concrete manifestations administrators must routinely contend. Yet little consensus is discernible about either what the public interest is or what it means to be a responsible administrator. (This attests as much to the complexities of administrative life as to the muddle-headedness of those who write about such subjects.) These complexities have become sufficiently daunting that public administration academics, out of prudence or frustration, have pretty much given up on the public interest as a concept having any analytic usefulness.[2]

It is probably unimportant, and perhaps even salutary, that no agreement has been reached about the precise meanings of the public interest and administrative responsibility. Absence of agreement, after all, may be evidence of a continuing healthy dialogue that ought never to be seen as directed toward reaching final consensus.

In any event, although the academic debates continue (or even subside for a time), public administrators are still faced with making choices and judgments that, by one account or another, both are responsible and satisfy the public interest. Like the member of every other profession, the public administrator's actions are circumscribed by law and custom. At the same time, particular circumstances work to delineate the goals and ideals toward which administrative action is directed. The norms or values that operate in the sphere of public administration can be grouped into three general areas, or normative vectors:

- Concerns about efficiency and effectiveness, which focus primarily on the workings of government itself and the way its goods and services are distributed and delivered;

- Concerns about rights and the adequacy of governmental process, which direct scrutiny toward government's (and those acting in its name) relationship with its citizens; and

- Concerns about representation and the exercise of discretion, which aims attention at the control that the citizenry has over the workings of its government and its agents.

In mathematics, a vector is any quantity, such as velocity, which has both direction and magnitude. This image of vector is useful here because these value clusters have, in essence, both direction and magnitude as well. These qualities are determined by the peculiar combination of politics, culture, and economic conditions in the society at a particular historical time. The utility of the image will become clearer as we examine each vector in turn. The values that each vector circumscribes, though shifting and altering in specific application, always operate in relationship to one another. Understanding these vectors and the tensions within and between them is key to making sense of public administrators' various roles in the organizational arenas within which they act. Although no action of a par-

---

[2]One of the last serious attempts to deal with the subject, Glendon Schubert's aptly-titled *The Public Interest*, reluctantly concludes at the end of two hundred fifty pages that there is no such thing; Glendon Schubert, *The Public Interest* (Glencoe, Ill.: The Free Press, 1960).

ticular administrator in any one instance is determined by these vectors, they do inform, define, and circumscribe administrators' actions, albeit only implicitly. Perhaps even more important, they inform the way in which those actions are understood—and condoned or reviled—by the citizenry at large.

Efficiency and Effectiveness

An important social value that underlies this vector is the historical manner in which the public dollar is considered as a public trust to be used with a caution that is never even suggested in other areas of life. This requires, for example, judging an act of a public official to be a criminal offense, an act that, when committed by a person who is *not* a public official, is condoned as a sensible (or at least necessary) business practice. Public administrators have in this respect always been judged by a standard significantly different from those used by society's members to judge themselves. The effect of this standard's application can be seen in the explicit requirements that are usually attached to expenditures of public funds. These requirements, though often resulting in "red tape," are based on a firm social and historical footing.

Government's historical concern about efficiency and effectiveness is grounded in the belief that a public dollar should be expended with as much care and deliberation as possible, that it should be used properly, and that the effects of its use should be explicit to the extent possible. Public administration's self-conscious concern with efficiency first surfaced in the late nineteenth and early twentieth centuries with, for example, the passage of the Pendleton Act at the national level and the emergence of the Good Government movements in state and local governments. While these events are relevant to the other two normative vectors, the watchword for public administration in these early years was "efficiency in government." This attitude toward government emphasized the ability to mobilize, organize, and direct resources. Government's efforts were aimed primarily at what planners call the infrastructure: the transportation, public health, and education systems, for example. Such activities became (and remain) principal elements in the budgets at every level. The ideological base of both the good government movements and the engineering mode of government, inspired by the Scientific Management movement, included a strong emphasis on running government scientifically and efficiently. As the management sciences developed, beginning in the early part of the century, they reinforced the idea of efficiency as the central instrumental value for the public administrator.

In his biography of Robert Moses, Robert Caro catches the spirit of this shift:

> In setting out to reform New York City's civil service, Bob Moses was setting out to break into the plunderhouse of politics.
>
> The wheels of the Tammany war machine might be greased with money, but the machine was pulled by men, the men who voted Democratic themselves, the men who rounded up newly arrived immigrants and brought them in to be registered Democratic, the men who during election campaigns rang doorbells and distributed literature to those immigrants and to their own friends and neighbors and on Election Day shepherded them to the polls to vote Democratic. And the most succulent of the carrots that lured these men forward, that kept their shoulders braced against the ropes that pulled the Tammany machine, was the carrot of jobs, jobs for themselves, jobs for their wives, jobs for their sons. The only source of jobs on the scale required was the city itself. So the jobs Tammany had to control in order to control the city were the city's jobs—positions as policemen, firemen, sanitation workers, court clerks, process servers, building inspectors, secretaries, clerks. There were, in 1914, 50,000 city employees and this meant 50,000 men and women who owed their pay checks—and whose families owed the food and shelter those pay checks bought—not to merit but to the ward boss. Patronage was the coinage of power in New York City. And reforms of the civil service such as Moses was to propose were therefore daggers thrust at the heart of Tammany Hall.
>
> . . .
>
> James and Moskowitz [newly appointed to the Municipal Civil Service Commission and charged by Mayor John Purroy Mitchel to "clean up the civil service"] asked Moses for a plan of action. Moses said that the first step had to be a reform of the city's efficiency rating system, the system of ratings given by supervisors to their subordinates to help determine whether to promote a civil service employee or give him a pay raise; under the present method, ratings didn't give the Civil Service Commission enough information for a sound judgment. Making an evaluation system precise was perhaps the most difficult job in civil service, Moses explained; each job had to be broken down into component parts, so that each part could be graded, and in totaling the grades each part had to be given a mathematical weight corresponding to its importance in the job as a whole.[3]

And devise such a system he did. Using ten assistants, Moses observed city employees at their jobs for days so that each position could be divided into the appropriate components and graded. The result, in 1915, was the "Detailed Report on the Rating of the Efficiency of Civil Service Employees, Excepting Members of the Uniformed Forces in the Police and Fire Services and in the Lower Ranks of the Street Cleaners." The report was a proposal "of a purity, a strength and a scope that was almost more reli-

---

[3]Robert A. Caro, *The Power Broker: Robert Moses and the Fall of New York* (New York: Knopf, 1974), pp. 71, 73.

gious than governmental." In it, all government service was broken into sixteen categories, each of which was in turn divided into specific jobs. Each of these was analyzed to show its "functions" and "responsibilities." These were each given a mathematical weight and totaled to yield a precise grade.

> ... No aspect of conduct on the job was too small to be graded. Even personality must be reduced to number. "Personality," Moses said, "includes those intangible elements the existence of which do not readily admit of proof, but nevertheless . . . each employee *must* be rated on personality." Men would have to make sacrifices for the sake of the system: Acknowledging that some present employees would not score high enough on his tests for the jobs they held, he had a simple solution—such employees would have to accept demotions and pay cuts. Unnecessary employees, he said, would have to be eliminated.[4]

A third reinforcing trend, though it did not appear that way at first, came out of the social change ideology nurtured as a response to the Great Depression. As both state and federal governments moved more and more into social legislation, efficiency became less and less satisfying as an organizing principle. This seemed to be happening for several reasons. A proposal such as Moses's was difficult enough to swallow politically (the version that was eventually installed in New York City was a considerably watered-down one), although it did seem to make some sense for at least some types of jobs. As government at all levels began providing more *services* (such as day care for both adults and children) and relatively fewer *things* (such as buildings), the whole idea of grading jobs and dividing them up into tasks made less and less sense. But an even more fundamental problem was that the heavy top-down organization and management style implied and reinforced by such systems began to be questioned. Not that the hierarchical structures suffered any radical change or that civil service assessment programs were discarded, but there was a softening of attitude in two directions. One was toward an acceptance of the idea that a worker's motivation and initiative are essential to the proper running of an organization. Any organization that stifled these elements in its workforce could hardly be called efficient, no matter how good the numbers, it was argued. Second, as government in general moved into a more proactive role, that is, one that instigated change (particularly social change) rather than simply maintaining the infrastructure, there was increasingly the question of "efficiency for what?"

Effectiveness thus became an added concern, focusing both on getting a job done and on whether that job had an effect appropriate to the goals and objectives of the agency. As a chief of management systems in the federal Office of Management and Budget has put it:

[4]Ibid., p. 75.

... Over the years, varying emphasis was placed on efficiency and effectiveness by the management program [in the federal government], with efficiency tending to receive more consistent attention. While stress on efficiency in government programs is quite natural due to continuing pressure to hold taxes down and simultaneously expand government services, there is a point of diminishing returns when unbalanced emphasis on efficiency is pursued too far. At this point, the quality of the outputs produced and the timeliness of the services rendered may be jeopardized in terms of an effective response to human needs by the government.[5]

ZBB, PBBS, MBO and other acronymic attempts at systematizing the production function of government were, at least in part, attempts to capture the elusive notion of effectiveness.

In times of fiscal plenty, the luxury could be afforded of asking "how well are our programs achieving what we set out to do?" With leaner times, efficiency returned to the forefront, renamed "productivity"—"the biggest bang for the buck." Here, for example, is a Secretary of Commerce writing in a 1972 symposium on "Productivity in Government":

Improving productivity in the public sector of the U.S. economy is fundamental to the success of the current federal effort to create through a variety of policy initiatives an environment that will spur a higher rate of productivity growth—over the long term—in the economy as a whole.

It is fundamental, first, because the public sector is such a large and rapidly growing part of the whole. But it is crucial, also, because no government program to encourage higher rates of productivity growth in the private sector will succeed if government itself sets a bad example (or, because of inadequate measurement or popular mythology, is widely thought of as a bad example).[6]

In the literature of organization theory, the "management values" of efficiency, effectiveness and, most recently, productivity find their closest referent in Max Weber's treatment of the idea of legal-rational (instrumental) authority. Weber's description of the organizational manifestation of this form of authority, bureaucracy, is now familiar to any beginning public administration student. Its major elements include: hierarchy of authority, organization bound by rules, specified spheres of competence for office holders, administrative acts recorded in writing, and the separation of administrative staff from ownership of the means of production.

The distinction of public from private organization was not particularly relevant to Weber's discussion of legal-rational authority, in large part owing to the pervasiveness of the bureaucratic form of organization

[5]Gordon T. Yamada, "Improving Management Effectivenesss in the Federal Government," *Public Administration Review* 32:6(1972):765.
[6]Peter G. Peterson, "Productivity in Government and the American Economy," *Public Administration Review* 32:6(1972):740.

across all sectors of industrial societies, even at the time Weber wrote. The bureaucratic model that he described was, and still is, common to church, governmental, military, and industrial organizations. These sectors might pursue widely differing ends, but the bureaucratic means of administrative control through the exercise of legal-rational authority provide a uniformly compelling instrument for their attainment.

The values of efficiency, effectiveness, and productivity necessarily assume, in Rittel and Webber's terminology, the existence of tame rather than wicked problems. The limitations of those values, quite obviously, are most evident when organizations, public ones especially, confront problems exhibiting characteristics of wickedness. Wicked problems require different, or at least additional, value orientations in order for one to cope sensibly with them. The bureaucratic norms of rationality and efficiency, however, encourage the tendency for organizational members to regard intra-organizational relationships as more stable, predictable, and controlling than is warranted by the nature of the problems they confront. When this happens, wicked problems are treated as though they are tame and the inevitable consequences ensue: The wicked problems remain or are replaced by new ones.

The normative vector of efficiency and effectiveness is clearly most relevant to the intra-organizational and, to a lesser extent, the organization-to-individual arenas. For the inter-organizational arena, efficiency typically gives way to other values. Given the often politically charged and turbulent nature of the environments of most public organizations, efficiency usually becomes a standard for administrative performance only *after* more global issues, such as organizational survival and adaption, are duly accounted for. The relevance of efficiency depends on a relatively stable context, free from external interference, with organizational goals fairly viable and fixed, and relationships within the organization routinized and predictable. This is not always the case, of course, even *within* the confines of organizations, but such stability is typically more evident within than without. When these concerns are no longer problematic, efficiency emerges as a more appropriate guiding value for public administrators.

Rights and the Adequacy of Process

Individual liberty and the concomitant set of rights that have evolved to protect it are so basic to the American culture that any comments about their importance may sound trite and platitudinous. Yet public administrators are principal actors in the drama that has played out this evolution. Administrators' roles, from the perspective of the individual whose rights are in need of protection, are anomalous at best. As agents of government, administrators are charged with making specific the generality of law by creating the procedures for applying it to individual cases. This essential element in the power relationship between administrators and clients is reinforced through the hierarchical structures generally used to organize administrative action. The resulting and necessary exercise of discretion creates dilemmas for administrators.

One aspect of these dilemmas is that administrators are expected to follow what they perceive to be the letter of the law (that is, after all, what they were hired for). The result, however, can be an even-handedness in the general and a trampling on individual rights in the specific. This possibility (and, too often, actuality) creates the basis for both legislative and judicial action in the form of administrative codes and administrative law decrees. Their effect is not only to guide and bound administrative action, but also to reinforce the recognition of individual rights as a socially legitimate touchstone for administrative action. This leads to the other horn of the dilemma.

Embedded in the idea of individual liberty is a sense of equity, namely, that each should be treated according to his or her circumstances. This becomes operational in a notion of fairness and is one of the foundations, for example, of means-testing in income maintenance programs, with a corollary being that one should get only what one deserves. The result has been an attempt in many cases to particularize governmental action by providing services to fit individual circumstances. This individualization, generally backed by insufficient resources to meet all acknowledged need, is then criticized for its lack of horizontal equity.

This "damned if you do, damned if you don't" situation is made even more complex for administrators who apply rules and procedures in light of professional values and local political norms. Welfare administration provides a clear example of all these difficulties.

The core of the welfare program is the cash grant. Once a family meets categorical requirements (e.g., that there is only one parent in the home), means-testing is how a locality decides, first, whether a family is eligible for a grant, and second, if eligible, the amount of the grant they are entitled to receive. State law in most cases sets out what constitutes a "needy family." Regulation then specifies the manner in which various elements of income and need are counted. The changes and shifts in these elements illustrate the play of the different normative aspects.

For example, to determine eligibility and the amount of payment, it is necessary for a state to set a "standard of need." This is determined by balancing the amount of money that a family needs to live on with the amount that a state is willing to provide. The resulting standard of need (or a set percentage of it) then becomes the measure of eligibility. For instance, if the standard of need is $410 a month for a family of four, then a family whose income is greater than $410 is ineligible to receive any cash assistance, and a family whose income is less than $410 is eligible to receive the difference between its income and the standard. (This is, in fact, an over-simplification, but it carries the main point.)

Until the mid-1960s and early 1970s, welfare administrators in some states, at the urging of local political sentiment, sought to bring individual equity (a grant comparable to one's need) into the process by recognizing that food, transportation, and housing costs vary substantially for otherwise similarly situated families. This meant that a single grant amount for all families was seen as basically unfair in that it did not recognize particular conditions. Several mechanisms were developed to handle this situation, all of which essentially involved providing special allowances to a family for the costs of these items. The first of these was, naturally, an additional grant amount for each additional family member. Thus, using the original number, the standard of need for a family of three might be $360 and $460 for a family of five. Since housing costs often vary substantially between, say, urban and rural areas, the $410 in the latter becomes $450 in the former. So too with fuel and transportation costs.

If nothing else, the sheer difficulty of trying to apply such a set of criteria in the name of individual equity became enormous. For example, in 1973, the Illinois Department of Public Aid began to use a new system for calculating the size of the cash grant; by that time,

> ... the size of the basic cash payment was dependent upon the number and ages of the children, where and with whom the family lived, and amount of income. Also, the family could receive special allowances for expenses not covered by the basic cash grant. Illinois had 90 special allowances (70 in the AFDC category) which could be applied in 135 different ways, depending on the particular family circumstances.[7]

In 1973, Illinois changed to what is called a "modified flat grant," consolidating fifty-one of the categories into a single amount. The effect was that, generally speaking, families of the same size were more likely to receive similar amounts (horizontal equity), although they were less likely to receive an amount that matched their particular need (individual equity). Another aspect of this shift, however, was a change in the relationship of the agency to the client's rights.

In order to obtain all the information required to make the calculations required for individualizing the grant, it was necessary for the welfare worker to probe deeply into the affairs of the client. This probing was further supported in many localities by a norm that insisted that only the "deserving" receive assistance and that the welfare agency was the legiti-

---

[7]Peter Bateman et al., *Administration of AFDC in Illinois: A Description of Three Local Offices* (Cambridge, Mass.: Abt Associates Inc., July 1980), p. 156.

mate authority for making such judgments. This, in turn, was reinforced by a professional ethic among social workers that viewed the client as dependent because of an inability of run his or her life properly (why else would they be on welfare?). Thus, in many places the potentially simple calculation of a grant amount became administratively complicated and overlaid with a variety of political, professional, and social intentions.

Then, beginning in the 1960s, more and more attention was focused on the relationship between public welfare administrators and their clients. Among other things,

> It was found that attempts often were made to impose standards of moral behavior on recipients. For example, in Louisiana, aid to needy families was cut off if the mother gave birth to an illegitimate child while on relief, unless she could prove that she no longer had "illicit" relationships. Some departments threatened neglect proceedings against applicants with illegitimate children, and there were various man-in-the-house rules, enforced by surprise midnight raids without warrants, which resulted either in loss of eligibility or in a reduction in payment. Other invasions of privacy involved inquiries made in the community among merchants, employers, and relatives of clients to check financial eligibility and need. Every state promulgated work tests as well. In New York, men were required to cut brush in deep snow, under threat of criminal prosecution, in order to receive their relief checks; in areas of the South and the Northwest, welfare checks were stopped when crops ripened, and whole families were required to go into the fields.[8]

That decade and the next saw extensive litigation aimed at clarifying the interplay between the exercise of administrative authority and individual rights. Much of this revolved around due process and equity; at the base was the public administrator's dilemma of acting both as an enforcing agent of authority and as a protector of individual rights.

This normative commitment to individual rights has its intellectual roots in the Federalist papers and constitutional democratic theory. These include the rights of individuals and groups in relation to one another and, more importantly, to the government itself. Thus, as the idea of due process evolved in constitutional and administrative law, rules of conduct, so to speak, were established to provide protection to the individual (and group), on the one hand, and redress for violations of those protections, on the other. The due process argument, as well as constitutional democratic theory, surfaced concerns for equity. What had early in this country's history been primarily a concern for equity between and across states became concern for equity between and across groups of individuals.

These issues—rights, due process, and equity—were found by many to be necessary but insufficient in insuring the maintenance and furtherance

[8]Joel F. Handler, *Protecting the Social Service Client* (New York: Academic Press, 1980), p. 4.

of democratic ideals. There was an increasing concern for the manner in which people are treated. As an extension of the due-process notion, this came to include such things as providing adequate notice and specifying maximum waiting times for the receipt of services. Thus, for welfare administration, the time from application to the arrival of the first check became an objective measure of the *quality* of the interaction between the agency and client. The issue expanded from whether or not one was entitled to a service and from the idea that one's rights should not be violated in the process of receiving that service to include the notion that the service should be timely and appropriate. This became the basis for the development of indicators of administrative performance, ones that could presumably be measurable through objective criteria.

The originally narrow meaning of due process was broadened in a second direction to include the adequacy of the process of interaction between administrator and client. This required an appraisal, or at least an appreciation, of quality from the standpoint of the recipient. Here the issue is not so much the legal entitlement of individuals to receive benefits and to be protected from government abuses; rather, it is the perceived quality of transactions between service provider and service recipient, with each transaction subject to its own unique and subjective evaluation, not amenable to legal (and therefore generalized) standards of assessment. The importance of the recipient's subjective perception of the quality of a transaction is underscored by the notion that services are not "produced," but rather, to borrow a term from Elinor Ostrom, they are co-produced.[9] This means that provider and recipient perform complementary roles by cooperating with one another in the joint production of services. The analysis of the organizational literature in later chapters is implicitly attuned to the extent to which particular theories either address or preclude any serious consideration of co-production—both in a descriptive sense as well as in terms of the normative assessment of its importance to administrative practice.

In addition to the protection of individual rights, the practice of public administration also moved in the direction of opening up the decision-making process through the inclusion not only of affected individuals and groups, but also of citizens in general. This phenomenon is discussed in the following section in terms of responsiveness; its relevance here is that public participation is often sought not merely as a check on government, but is also emphasized as both (1) a right of the citizens to knowledge about their government (as evidenced by passage of the Freedom of Information Act and other "sunshine" legislation at both national and state

---

[9]Elinor Ostrom, "The Design of Institutional Agreements and the Responsiveness of Police," in L. Rieselbach, ed., *People vs. Government* (Bloomington, Ind.: Indiana University Press, 1975).

levels), and (2) a necessary consideration for the development of a conscientious citizenry (i.e., one that is able to exercise its rights intelligently).

This emphasis, although contemporary in an administrative sense, is firmly rooted in the literature of democratic theory, going as far back as Aristotle. As the distinction between administration and politics has become more and more tenuous, it should not be surprising that traditional democratic values have therefore assumed a prominent role *within* administration, rather than apart from it.

Although the mainstream of generic organization theory has generally been insensitive to the normative importance of citizen participation, some newer literature, mainly from humanistic and organizational psychology, has focused on the normative importance of such notions as self-actualization and personal growth. Other sources, principally political science and particular branches of European social thought, have couched these psychological issues (at least by implication) in moral/political terms. While American political scientists emphasize the long tradition of democratic theory, the Europeans typically draw their inspiration from Karl Marx. Especially important in these contributions is their normative consideration of the political, and therefore the public, aspects of administration that is largely absent in the generic organizational literature.

Representation and the Control of Discretion

Representative government is, by definition, individuals (and groups) acting in the name of other individuals (and groups). Representativeness, then, is the criterion of how well such action is performed and by what authorities. Three aspects of this concern can be distinguished: accountability, reponsibility, and responsiveness.

The idea of accountability stipulates that external standards of correct action, be they legally or bureaucratically enacted, determine the correctness of and provide the motive for administrative action. Sometimes called "objective responsibility," accountability typically assumes that administrative action is most appropriately viewed as instrumentally rational, with ends presumed to have been defined prior to taking action. This complements—indeed is central to—the classical distinction between policy, in which ends are determined politically, and administration, in which action is construed as the "neutrally competent" attainment of those ends. Accountability is institutionalized when legal, political, and bureaucratic sanctions, such as rewards, promotions, termination of employment, and even civil and criminal penalties, are available to induce competent and conscientious administrative performance.

The belief that accountability could by itself insure representativeness became less and less tenable as the limitations of the rational/instrumental model of action became clearer. The inadequacy of that model was described in the public administration literature, beginning in the late 1930s, as the breakdown of the policy/administration dichotomy. By 1939, Leonard White said that

> There is no reason to believe that administration is incompetent to make an important contribution to policy. . . . Administration may be the best equipped branch of government to make a genuinely public policy free from overwhelming favoritism to one particular pressure group.[10]

In 1949, Paul Appleby, in *Policy and Administration,* described public administration as the "eighth political process."[11] In a similar vein, Luther Gulick declared, in 1964, that

> we have a new approach to the dichotomy between politics and administration. We no longer decline to recognize the policy content of "pure administration," nor are we minimizing the political significance of administrative decisions.[12]

This shift away from the sharp distinction between policy and administration reflected not only an academic unease with the categories, but a practical realization that in many cases it had become a distinction without clear difference, except in the extreme. This was especially evident, for instance, at the federal level where, during World War II, the application of emergency administrative regulations governing the economy became both politics and policy making in effect, if not in intent. This and similar developments led to an unease with the traditional, relatively simple sense of accountability. This tended to show itself in the numerous proposed (and accomplished) reorganizations of the executive offices at all levels, in the development of clarified rule-making processes, and in insertion of the legislative veto and other provisions in statute. These reflected countervailing concerns about the exercise of discretion, with some proposals widening it and others seeking to limit it.

Out of this grew a different approach to accountability, in which the earlier sense came to be supplemented, though in no way replaced, by variations on the idea of individual administrative responsibility. These variations intend a broadening of the meaning of accountability, while also increasing the available means to assure that public administration is indeed representative. One sense of administrative responsibility argues

[10]Leonard White, *The Study of Public Administration* (New York: Macmillan, 1939), pp. 12–13.

[11]Paul Appleby, *Policy and Administration* (University, Ala.: University of Alabama Press, 1949).

[12]Luther Gulick, "The Twenty-Fifth Anniversary of the American Society for Public Administration," *Public Administration Review* 25:1(1965):2.

that the individual must cleave to standards of professional and technical competence. As the work of the administrator has become more technically complex, this particular sense of administrative responsibility serves to separate a domain of activity that is to be immune from political meddling. Carl J. Friedrich, arguing for this viewpoint more than forty years ago, wrote in reaction to what he regarded as the naive belief in the capacity of political accountability to encompass adequately the major normative issues in the administration of democratic government. He argued that various institutional safeguards for accountability are necessary but insufficient to the task:

> . . . throughout the length and breadth of our technical civilization there is arising a type of responsibility on the part of the permanent administrator, the man who is called upon to seek and find the creative solutions for our crying technical needs, which cannot be effectively enforced except by fellow-technicians who are capable of judging his policy in terms of the scientific knowledge bearing upon it. "Nature's laws are always enforced," and a public policy which neglects them is bound to come to grief, no matter how eloquently it may be advocated by popular orators, eager partisans, or smart careerists.[13]

As scientists, both natural and social, entered government service and as government itself became more solutions-to-problems oriented, this stance became institutionalized. This is illustrated, for example, by the emergence of technical panels to act in an advisory capacity to administrative decision making. Another is the growing use of experts to provide "technical information and judgment" in the rule-making process. A third is the use of technical expertise, hired from research firms and think tanks, to develop policy alternatives. The general assumption underlying all of these is that the actors are governed by standards of professional and technical competence revealed by scientific and other presumably value-neutral means. When standards of accountability are absent or ambiguous in a particular situation, the view here, again voiced by Friedrich, is that civil servants—and, by extension, the experts they use in policy analysis—should also act in accordance with "prevailing public sentiment." Coupled with professional standards (he argues), this provides a sufficient framework—bounded, of course, by necessary institutional controls—within which individual public administrators can act in an administratively responsible fashion.

The other general sense of individual administrative responsibility maintains that administrators must act in accordance with their sense of moral obligation. This can be defined in general terms—the basic notions

---

[13]Carl J. Friedrich, "Public Policy and the Nature of Administrative Responsibility," in Friedrich and Edward S. Mason, eds., *Public Policy 1* (Cambridge: Harvard University, 1940), p. 14.

CODE OF ETHICS FOR THE AMERICAN SOCIETY FOR PUBLIC ADMINISTRATION PREPARED BY THE PROFESSIONAL STANDARDS AND ETHICS COMMITTEE

The American Society for Public Administration (ASPA) exists to advance the science, processes, and art of public administration. ASPA encourages professionalism and improved quality of service at all levels of government, education, and the not-for-profit private sector. ASPA contributes to the analysis, understanding and resolution of public issues by providing programs, services, policy studies, conferences, and publications.

ASPA members share with their neighbors all of the responsibilities and rights of citizenship in democratic society. However, the mission and goals of ASPA call every member to additional dedication and commitment. Certain principles and moral standards must guide the conduct of ASPA members not merely in preventing wrong, but in pursuing right through timely and energetic execution of responsibilities.

To this end, we, the members of the Society, recognizing the critical role of conscience in choosing among courses of action and taking into account the moral ambiguities of life, commit ourselves to:

1 demonstrate the highest standards of personal integrity, truthfulness, honesty and fortitude in all our public activities in order to inspire public confidence and trust in public institutions;

2 serve the public with respect, concern, courtesy, and responsiveness, recognizing that service to the public is beyond service to oneself;

3 strive for personal professional excellence and encourage the professional development of our associates and those seeking to enter the field of public administration;

4 approach our organization and operational duties with a positive attitude and constructively support open communication, creativity, dedication and compassion;

5 serve in such a way that we do not realize undue personal gain from the performance of our official duties;

6 avoid any interest or activity which is in conflict with the conduct of our official duties;

7 respect and protect the privileged information to which we have access in the course of official duties;

8 exercise whatever discretionary authority we have under law to promote the public interest;

9 accept as a personal duty the responsibility to keep up to date on emerging issues and to administer the public's business with professional competence, fairness, impartiality, efficiency and effectiveness.

continued next page

CODE OF ETHICS FOR THE ASPA *continued*

10 support, implement, and promote merit employment and programs of affirmative action to assure equal employment by our recruitment, selection, and advancement of qualified persons from all elements of society;

11 eliminate all forms of illegal discrimination, fraud, and mismanagement of public funds, and support colleagues if they are in difficulty because of responsible efforts to correct such discrimination, fraud, mismanagement or abuse;

12 respect, support, study, and when necessary, work to improve federal and state constitutions and other laws which define the relationships among public agencies, employees, clients and all citizens.

Revised March 19, 1984
Committee Approved April, 1984
Approved by National Council April 8, 1984

—From: *Public Administration Times*, 7:10 (May 15, 1984):4.

of fairness, justice, and equity, for instance—or in more specific terms, such as those used in a code of ethics or professional principles. A good example of the latter is the twelve principles adopted in 1984 by the American Society for Public Administration (see the accompanying box).

In either case, the obligation is to a fairly general set of standards intended to check what might otherwise be an unquestioning obedience to legal or bureaucratic edict. Unlike the reliance on professional or technical competence, which tends to be given a primary position, the obligation here is viewed as a guide for action when laws or formal procedures are too general or vague to provide answers to unique problems. This theme permeates much of the recent public administration literature, carrying with it the general sense that the public administrator is first and foremost a good citizen, one who understands and is committed to working for the social good. This can be seen, for example, in proposals for reform of civil service that emphasize the importance of a general liberal arts education for administrators. Compatible sentiments are also evident in some of the "New Public Administration" literature, such as when H. George Frederickson urges that "The search for social equity provides Public Administration with a real normative base."[14]

In both cases—professional and technical competence, and moral obligation—the standards of correctness are external to the individual and, as

[14]H. George Frederickson, "Toward a New Public Administration," in Frank Marini, ed., *Toward a New Public Administration: The Minnowbrook Perspective* (Scranton, Pa.: Chandler Publishing Co., 1971), p. 328.

such, can be viewed as perhaps necessary but definitely insufficient to provide the base for responsible administrative action. The difficulty here, theorists such as Orion White argue, is that there must also be a sense of *personal* responsibility for one's actions.[15] Without this, generalized external standards can be (and often are) used to mask otherwise morally reprehensible action. Such personal responsibility entails the public administrator's recognition of the existential nature of all action: Ultimately, it is always personal, even when cloaked in external standards of legitimacy. When they act, therefore, administrators cannot legitimately escape the moral brunt of their actions by claiming they were compelled by circumstance, authority, professional standard, or even moral principle. Personal responsibility as an important normative idea represents for the administrator the furthest departure from, and is therefore in the greatest tension with, the classical notion of accountability.

Today, few would argue that any one of these stances falling under the general rubric of representativeness deserves a status that excludes the others. Opinion about their proper priority and relationship to one another does differ, however, given the inevitable tensions between them. Each, taken singly, may generate its own pathologies for which the other values may serve as effective checks. More important, however, is the recognition that variations in their relative priority, although subject to the vagaries of personal taste as well as philosophical debate, depend mainly on the differing contexts that call for "representative" administrative action. Both moral obligation and personal responsibility, for example, obviously gain in relevancy as the wickedness of problems becomes more evident. Similarly, responsibility based on personal, existential commitment to others appears especially salient where services are co-produced; here generalized standards of correctness necessarily give way to more idiosyncratic and qualitative judgments subjectively made by all the involved and fitted to their situation.

A final notion that completes the overall meaning of representativeness is responsiveness. Although in some senses the two terms may be redundant, the emphasis here is necessarily from the perspective of those being served. How well, for example, are the public's needs and demands being satisfied by government, irrespective of how skillfully and conscientiously administrators may implement programs, apply professional expertise, and follow legally mandated rules and procedures? Responsiveness is especially problematic in the inter-organizational and organization-to-individual arenas discussed earlier. A prominent concern in Parts II and III is the extent to which various organization theories have been sensitive to the problem of organizational responsiveness. The literature is clearly mixed

---

[15]See especially Orion F. White, Jr., "The Concept of Administrative Praxis," *Journal of Comparative Administration* 5:1(1973):55–86.

on this issue, not only in the degree of interest in it, but also on the particular moral and political significance accorded to responsiveness.

Taken together, these three aspects—accountability, responsibility, and responsiveness—help us grasp the ways in which representation becomes operational in public administration activity. Further, they surface the flip side, the exercise of discretion, by speaking to the question of how it is used, monitored, and justified.

Completing the Public Administration Framework

Collectively, the three normative vectors discussed in this chapter and the three organizational arenas described in Chapter 2 make up the overall framework of public administration used in this book to assess the relevancy of organization theories. We have already noted both the tensions among the normative vectors as well as the seamlessness (in a sense, the artificiality of separation) of the organizational arenas. These aspects of the framework complicate, but may also be used to clarify, the variety of ways in which public administrators think about their roles, define problems, and make decisions in response to them. All of these are influenced both by the particular organizational arenas that most directly impinge on administrators' day-to-day decisions, as well as by their personal assessments of the tensions among competing values. The adage that "where you stand depends on where you sit," it seems, is only a partial truth about organizational life. It is only partial because the reverse also holds true, namely that priorities about values, even when implicit or unconscious, also influence where one *chooses* to stand, or look.

The public administration framework—the organizational arenas and the normative vectors—provides the backdrop against which to understand the diversity of and tensions between the principal approaches to theorizing about organizations. The various perspectives on organization theory considered in Parts II and III vary in terms of the values they implicitly regard as most legitimate and the particular organizational arenas to which they direct primary attention. None presents, nor should any of them necessarily be expected to present, a perfectly balanced approach to the two general aspects of the framework. Their limitations as theoretical perspectives, but also their strengths, are evident from the particular manner in which they explicate their priorities about values and preferred arenas of analysis. Finally, the various approaches to organization theory differ significantly in their views of what constitutes a theory in the first place and what it means for a theory to be practical. These latter subjects are addressed in Chapter 4.

II

INTRODUCING ORGANIZATION THEORY

The framework outlined in Part I focuses on a particular organizational actor, the public administrator. In Part II, we begin to bring organization theory to bear on this actor's context. To do this, it is necessary to sketch some of the ways in which people generally think about theory and theorizing; this is done in Chapter 4. Chapter 5 initiates the discussion of various theoretical perspectives by examining the work of three theorists: Max Weber, Frederick Winslow Taylor, and Chester Barnard.

This latter chapter introduces an odyssey that explores the evolution of American thinking about organizations and organizing. The account begins ironically, with a German sociologist, Max Weber, whose writing was virtually unknown in the United States until the late 1940s. He is, however, the most articulate describer of and theorist about bureaucracy. It is his descriptions that form the base of almost all criticism of bureaucracy in the last thirty years; all of the other writers examined in subsequent chapters have had to contend with the images that Weber traced (irrespective of whether they actually knew of his work). He is also at his most useful in helping us understand the place of bureaucracy in modern society; Weber's critique still sits as a standard for all who follow him.

In the same chapter, we examine two American writers on organizations, Frederick Taylor and Chester Barnard, as well as the early human relations writers. Their writings span not only time, but also a particular vision of how the everyday world of humans is controlled by their organizing activities. The organization, for these writers, is how work gets done.

The principal ideas of all three writers remain as cornerstones of organization thinking from which most of the more contemporary perspectives have originated. Together they also form a baseline of organization theory for public administration. Each perspective discussed in the chapters of Part III owes a debt to one or more of these theorists. These debts are not always straightforward intellectual ones, however; in several cases, a perspective developed in reaction against what a writer was seen as standing for. Thus, for example, a good deal of energy was used by the early human relations theorists in severely criticizing "Taylor and Taylorism." This attack focused less on what Taylor said than on the specter that he seemed to represent.

Two thoughts should be kept in mind when looking over the array of theoretical perspectives. First, the field of organization theory is littered with the bodies of straw men: "Taylorism" for the human relations theorists, "positivism" for the action theorists, "comprehensive rationality" for the market theorists, "bureaucracy" for the critical theorists. The resulting profusion of ghosts, mixed with what seems to be a constant urging to choose sides between the different perspectives, makes it difficult at times to get at our purpose here. This purpose is a simple one, namely, to understand the ways in which each perspective enables both practitioners and students to clarify particular aspects of the world of public administration.

Second, in the field of organization theory, the dividing line between "prescriptive" and "descriptive" is often so fine as to be illusory. This requires some discussion of what "using" theory can mean and what it does mean here, both of which are dealt with in Chapter 4.

4
Theories and Theorizing

For many people "theory" means jargon and complex words to describe what appear to be otherwise relatively simple happenings. For others, it means something separate and distinct from, perhaps even alien to, the real world of practical work. For still others, "theory" carries the idea of conjecture and explanation, as in "I have a theory about what went wrong." In this book, we will do our best to avoid (but in some respects to appreciate) the first of these ways of understanding theory, try to correct some of the second, and do our best to adhere to the third.

Unfortunately, at least from the viewpoint of practitioners, much of the organization theory literature is produced to further the purposes of the academic community rather than of those who practice in organizations. An occasional practical application spills over now and then, or someone with a more "applied" turn of mind ferrets out a useful nugget, yet even these phrases suggest the psychological distance between those who practice in and those who write about organizations. This theory/practice gap has itself become the basis of a minor cottage industry in the literature.

Yet theory, as an explanation of what has happened or might happen, is really not all that foreign to our ways of dealing with the world. We use and make theory all the time, in the sense of forming suppositions, attributing causality and interrelatedness, and building conceptual structures to link past events and actions together with our opinions of what should be done next. There is an important difference, however, between this theory building that we do in our everyday activities and the sense of

theory intended when one talks of "organization theory." The latter usually points to something more formal, more rigorous and, especially, more
consistent. "Theory" in this sense, and as it will be used here, is often a
troublesome concept. This is a problem compounded by both the skepticism and, alternatively, the awe with which practitioners (and even some
theorists) often regard theorizing.

In their daily lives, administrators cannot avoid the undeniable reality
of organizations; out of self interest and curiosity, they are understandably
eager to learn more about those structures. The knowledge they seek,
however, is from their perspective practical knowledge, knowledge that
they can use to grapple with, control, or at least tame organizational problems. This leads to their understandable doubt that most of what they read
as organization theory will be of any use. In other cases, ironically, administrators expect too much from theory. This is particularly the case as they
search for general principles of administration, clear-cut prescriptions for
action, compelling moral justification for a particular decision, or, simply,
the truth about organizations: They are usually disappointed. Theory, as
judged by practitioners, would seem to suffer from expectations that are
both too high and too low.

Theory and Practice

There is a gulf between the notions of "theory" and "practice." This separation, which appears in most aspects of Western culture, is one between
thinking about action in the world and acting in the world. This "gap,"
embedded as it is in our ways of dealing with our reality, can be traced
from the early Greeks through medieval scholasticism into modern times.
The engine of the Industrial Revolution gave a particular twist to what
had been the meanings of practice and theory. They became entwined
with the rising views of individualism and personal freedom, society and
social good, and nature and control of the material world. This shift in
views about theory and practice marked a change as well in the views of
the relation between man and his society. By the mid-twentieth century
this had resulted in a frustrating paradox: On the one hand, society is seen
as malleable and perfectible, with the techniques for this lying close at
hand ("if we can put a man on the moon, then we should be able to
...."); on the other hand, our solutions continually fall short of the mark,
leaving us acutely sensitive to the limitations of our techniques.

Theory, in its broadest senses, once referred to convictions about the
beautiful, the true, and the good. Theory was a product of divine revela-
tion and natural reason. And politics was its handmaiden, with the purpose of creating the beautiful, the true, and the good within society. Over

time, politics lost its purpose of creating the good society and became instead the method for maintaining social stability in order for *individuals* to pursue, in relative peace, their *private* notions of good. With this, theory became more of an idea and less of a conviction, more essentially intellectual and less essentially religious.

In the same way, practice moved from being judged by its relationship to theory (i.e., to the good); day-to-day practice became "practical," in the sense of concern for the workings of the material world and for the techniques to alter, manipulate, and control the natural (and then the social) world. In this way, both practice and theory became political instruments in the sense of being socially directed toward remaking the world.

One consequence has been that notions of morality (of the good, the true, the beautiful) have been forced into more personalized (and relativistic) conceptions and, more important, into more ineffable, abstract clouds of vague "principles" and "values." A further consequence of this has been the detachment of practice from the pursuit of value. As the latter has become more individualized, it has become more difficult to define (and defend) socially and publicly. Practice, in turn, has become programmatic—the means to reach an end defined elsewhere. It has become, in other words, technique that is oriented to the control of a presumably malleable social world. Theory then moves from being the guide *for* practice into becoming the explicator *of* practice.

Public administration—both the thinking and the doing, the theoretical and the practical—is about administrative technology; as such, it is about the day-to-day, practical "detailed and systematic execution of public law," to use Woodrow Wilson's phrase. A microcosm of the interplay between modern-day notions of theory and practice, it is the "political instrument" par excellence: Public administration confronts both the hopes inherent in thinking of the social world as malleable and the frustrations in finding the promised technological perfections beyond its grasp.

Theory as Science

Much of the blame for this might rightfully be placed at the feet of those theorists who assume too easily that knowledge, especially scientific knowledge, necessarily serves the cause of human betterment. Although they are perhaps not wholly indifferent to the practical implications of their theory and research, they make light of the fact that for knowledge to be useful, it must in some meaningful way relate back to the reality it purports to describe or explain. The difficulty lies in the standard definition of "theory" employed by most organization theorists and social scientists. As Pieter Degeling and H. K. Colebatch put it, theory is "a coherent group of general propositions used as principles of explanations for a group of phenomena."[1] By this account, theory should enable rigorous explanation of the past and the present, as well as fairly reliable predictions of the future. Those who subscribe to this view are usually keenly aware of the formidable methodological difficulties in testing theories empirically. They nonetheless believe that in principle, if not always in practice, theories may achieve the purposes for which they are designed.

Especially in recent years, however, this definition of theory has been hotly contested throughout the social sciences. Disagreement about the legitimacy of its basic assumptions currently pervades the organizational literature and divides contending factions. The major question is this: Can the actions of people be explained through the use of deterministic notions—such as cause/effect and stimulus/response—that are at the root of this view of theory? This is not an issue of method or technique; rather it is one of human nature, and must be argued on philosophical rather than empirical grounds. That the actions of people might be principally explainable in terms of their own unique plans, reflections, definitions of situations, and even their unconscious motives forces us to take seriously the possibility that general explanatory theories of the classical mode suffer from far more than simply methodological limitations. Theories that effectively screen out the unique and personal aspects of actions in the interest of generalization run the risk of producing sterile caricatures of the social world that are both intellectually uninteresting and of dubious practical value.

Since we are mainly concerned here with the practical value of theory, let us look briefly at the manner in which the classical approach to social science theory and research is ordinarily assumed to have practical application. In examining a social policy problem, for example, the researcher constructs a theory, replete with testable hypotheses, to explain regularities and differences among the research subjects' behavior as they are seen by the researcher to bear on the problem that is selected and defined by the researcher. If the hypotheses suggested by the theory are supported by the accumulated data, then strategies, programs, or policies may be inferred from the theory.

Sometimes this seems to work, at least to a degree. When it does not, which is often, the problem usually has less to do with methodological imperfections in the research than with the failure of the theory, particularly in its assumptions about the nature of the problem, to match the research subjects' often diverse problem definitions and preferred solutions. Social policies, viewed as generalized solutions to social problems,

---

[1] Pieter Degeling and H. K. Colebatch, "On Talking Dirty: Sacred and Profane in Public Administration," paper presented at the annual conference of the American Society for Public Administration, Honolulu, March 1982, p. 18.

inevitably require the implicit cooperation and participation of the recipient population (of which the research subjects are presumably representative) in order to make the policy work. At a tacit level, in other words, effective policies are always, in an important sense, co-produced by policy makers and client populations. The likelihood of the policy not working as predicted, then, increases with the degree of mismatch between the theory and problem definition that are used by researchers and policy makers, on the one hand, and the problem definitions and desired solutions of the intended beneficiaries of the policy, on the other.

The mismatch is likely to be greater as the heterogeneity of the recipient population increases. Policy makers and administrators who in effect want to be "told what to do" by empirically supported theoretical findings, therefore, will often end up with results quite different than those predicted by the theory. This helps to illustrate, perhaps, the reasons for the sentiments in the frequent complaint by policy makers and administrators that "It may be good theory, but it doesn't work in practice." As an analytical statement, this complaint falls somewhat short of the mark in another respect, however, since it appears to assume that the "goodness" of a theory, by definition, has nothing to do with its practical relevance. That theorists, for reasons of their own, often unwittingly collude in that belief should already be evident.

Thus far we have painted a fairly bleak picture regarding the usefulness of theory for administrative practice and are therefore obliged to show cause why readers of practical inclination should continue reading. A successful attempt requires a considerably expanded and relaxed view of what can properly be called theory.

Practical Theory

For convenience, we shall define a theory as any intellectual construct that enables someone to make sense of a situation or a problem. A *practical* theory, then, is one that either illuminates possibilities for action that would not otherwise be apparent *or* stimulates greater understanding of what the person has already been doing. A second feature of a practical theory is its *novelty,* that is, its power to evoke new and unexpected insights that are different from those revealed by common sense or illuminated by other ways of looking at the situation.[2] Since novelty inevita-

---

[2]It is with some trepidation that we use the word "novelty." There is an unfortunate tendency for some theorists to use novel labels for commonplace occurrences. This promotes the opaque cover of jargon that often clouds much theorizing. The sense intended here, as can be seen in the discussion, is more along the lines of helping one view a situation in a new light, not merely putting old wine in new bottles.

bly wears off, theories in this sense must be continually augmented by new ones. There is a hazard, for example, in learning a theory too well, with the result that it becomes a substitute for thinking, rather than an aid to it. So, while theories permit a mental "engagement" with a situation, novel theories simultaneously require detachment by the observer, whether theorist or administrator, from whatever is being observed. This detachment serves two functions. The first is to enable critical reflection not only about the situation or problem in question, but also about one's own way of thinking. This is referred to as "reflexivity." That is, if we want to think critically about something "out there," we must also be able to think critically about *how* we think about it. Using several theories, with the multiple images they evoke, serves as a reminder of the difference—a difference that counts—between what we see and how we see it.

Another function of novelty in theory involves an important moral consideration concerning the relationship of theory to practice. The novelty permitted by continually shifting theoretical images dampens the tendency of observers to presume that theirs is the "correct" way to perceive the world. Such presumptions to truth lead people to believe, if only unconsciously, that courses of action illuminated by their preferred image of the world carry with them a compelling moral legitimacy. When this happens, responsibility is shifted from a personal level, in which people are aware of the subjectivity and the relative truthfulness of their definitions of situations, to an impersonal level in which people mistakenly assume that their knowledge will unerringly lead to correct action. Responsibility, then, becomes lodged in the theory that reveals those actions, which is to say that the *theory* becomes authoritative in a manner similar to the authority of laws and rules.

The power of theories, whether formal academic theories or the implicit theories of practicing administrators, however, may have even greater force in determining the course of administrative action than laws and rules. The reason for this, suggested by Peter Berger and Thomas Luckmann, is that theory about the social world, while it is intended to describe and explain, also helps to produce and sustain the world.[3] The power of administrators and others in positions of authority, by implication, derives from their abilities to define authoritatively those meanings and images that others are obliged to accept as true and legitimate. Thus, the behavior of subordinates is not so much controlled directly through the issuance of orders (although this does often occur) as it is subtly circumscribed and guided by authoritative definitions of problems and situations.

Happily, this power has its limitations, as evidenced by the persistence

---

[3] See Peter L. Berger and Thomas Luckmann, *The Social Construction of Reality* (Garden City, N.Y.: Doubleday and Co., 1966).

of competing definitions of problems and situations within even the most seemingly rigid organizations. This fact, coupled with the pervasive fluidity and wickedness of organizational problems, makes difficult the task not only of controlling the actions of others, but of even being able to know with certainty what a particular problem is and whether it will remain sufficiently stable to allow planned action to solve it.

The image of organizational life implicitly portrayed by the preceding discussion gives credence to a way of thinking about the use of theory for assisting administrative practice suggested by Orion White.[4] He makes the cautious assumption that administrators can seldom control, either through skill or authority, the overall flow of organizational events. The fluidity and the wickedness of the problems these events represent defy attempts to deal with them solely through rationally instrumental action on a comprehensive scale. In view of these limitations, theory cannot and should not be expected to prescribe administrative action in any direct sense. Instead, theory can only be used to "frame" temporarily the flow of organizational events as they pass before us, to hold them in brief suspension as we try to make some sense of them. The choices that administrators make as a result are personally generated, rather than inferred directly from the theory; thus theory may inform and provide context, but not prescribe. In helping to frame situations temporarily, theory aids action by allowing us to get more information; action, in other words, is a way of learning in order to make possible further action. White also notes that the choice of theories to fulfill the purposes he describes are likely to be successful to the extent that they include other people in their development, since organizational action is, by definition, a collective endeavor.

Theorizing as Retrospective Sense-Making

The above discussion has emphasized the prospective use of theory for administrative practice. That is, theory may enable an understanding of the present into order to act toward the future. Kark Weick offers a complementary approach to theory that adds an additional time perspective: Theory, he says, provides a means for understanding our past actions.[5] Casting further doubt on the rational-instrumental view of action, Weick argues that, in the main, people's understanding of what they are doing (or have done) can only be discovered retrospectively. Although he does not attempt a full-blown theoretical description of the unconscious

---

[4]See Orion F. White, Jr., "The Concept of Administrative Praxis," *Journal of Comparative Administration* 5:1(1973):55–86.

[5]Karl Weick, *The Social Psychology of Organizing*, 2nd ed. (Reading, Mass.: Addison-Wesley, 1979).

motives that lead to action, Weick holds that the actions people take result largely from more or less spontaneous responses to accidental events that they are predisposed to regard as significant. Theory, or to use Weick's preferred term "theorizing," provides an important means by which people make sense retrospectively of what they have done, which then makes them prone to particular kinds of accidents and situations in the future. The principal sentence in his book, *The Social Psychology of Organizing*, while whimsical in its tone, summarizes quite well the thrust of his approach, to wit: "How can I know what I think until I see what I say?" Part of his intended meaning is that we learn what we are up to *as a result of* our actions. Even when we act on the basis of some preconceived goal or objective, theorizing often retrospectively reveals to us additional, and sometimes contradictory, evidence about what our intentions really were.

Weick's notion of what theorizing entails clearly embraces the breadth of our own definition of theory noted earlier. Organizational theorizing involves the use of imagination and novelty, and includes such activities as:

> ... speculating ... , striving for interest ... , utilizing incongruity as a perspective, anthropomorphising, examining alternatives to positivism, reframing, intuiting, and any other tricks that help counteract sluggish imaginations. In the course of directing these various bits and pieces of bias and action at organizations, certain ideas will emerge. The ideas are important, but so is the process by which they were achieved. Our joint interest [is] in the activity of theorizing as well as the product of theorizing, coupled with our belief that the products of theorizing age quickly and have a short half-life.[6]

Among the additional devices for useful theorizing are metaphors, which, although perhaps limited in their generality, often simplify our understanding of organizational contexts with enough accuracy and novelty both to help us know what we have already been doing and thinking, and to inform our future actions.

> Metaphors treat things that are different as if they are alike, and technically that's a mistake. Managers talk about the climate of their organization and themselves as quarterbacks and conductors. Those are metaphors and mistakes. But the mistakes are only partial, because people see more things than they can describe in words. A metaphor can often capture some of the distinctive, powerful, private realities that are tough to describe to someone else. That's why it's sad that managers usually make such poor choices in the metaphors they use.[7]

Like other features of the social world, organizations are intangible and therefore cannot be seen or experienced directly through the senses. Thus, in a broad sense, our knowledge of organizations is always indirect and

[6]Ibid., p. 26.
[7]Ibid., p. 49.

metaphorical. Metaphors, then, are "not just nice," but are indispensable. Since we use them anyway, both to understand organizations and to guide our actions, the trick is to become more conscious of the implicit metaphors we use, more attuned to the consequences of our using them, and consciously seek alternative ones when our everyday metaphors are found wanting. As we shall see in Part III, metaphors underlie not only people's common-sense understanding of organizations, but those of theorists, as well. Weber's machine metaphor to describe bureaucracy and the systems theorists' use of the biological organism as a basic metaphor of organization come most readily to mind. The following chapters stress how metaphors and other modes of theorizing not only help to frame our experience and descriptions of organizations, but also enable, and perhaps even determine, the value judgments we make about them.

Theorizing as a Means of Critical Evaluation

In view of the undisputed importance that having knowledge about large organizations is to the study of public administration, it is surprising how little of the generic organizational literature directly addresses the major normative concerns (other than efficiency) discussed in Chapter 3. Derived mainly from public administration's heritage in constitutional-democratic theory, these normative concerns provide the foundations on which value judgments are made about administrative action in government agencies. That much of the organizational literature is silent on matters of larger social and political import is probably attributable to its origins in sociology and management science, in which the objects of study more often than not are business enterprises. The relative lack of crossover between the normative public administration and the organizational literature does not mean that the latter is irrelevant to the former, nor does it mean that organization theory is totally devoid of normative content. Its value emphases, which are usually implicit, are simply different from (or at least much narrower than) those deriving from democratic theory and normative social theory generally. This is particularly true of the mainstream of modern American organization theory, whose espoused apolitical posture has tended to stress instead such values as organizational survival, health, and adaptation. But the political and social consequences of these values are nonetheless made manifest by the dominant roles that public and private organizations play in virtually all aspects of contemporary life.

The clash of "organizational imperatives" (to use William Scott and David Hart's phrase)[8] with generally accepted political values has recently

---

[8]See William C. Scott and David K. Hart, *Organizational America* (Boston: Houghton Mifflin, 1979).

begun to receive attention from a few scholars whose interests bridge both disciplines. More will be said in later chapters about the tensions between the value orientations of public administration and organization theory; it is important, however, to stress here the practical as well as theoretical importance of those tensions. Just as practitioners absorb the democratic ethos of public administration, they are also likely to be influenced by and internalize the often-countervailing values engendered by large organizations. A critical understanding of the latter, from a variety of organization theory perspectives, would perform at least two functions. First, theories of organization, especially when juxtaposed against the normative ethos of public administration, help to clarify why the values associated with that ethos are often so difficult to realize in practice. For example, norms of rationality, whether broadly organizational or derived from individual self-interest, play a major role in theoretically explaining the logic of organizational action that is at odds with such democratic values as responsiveness and representativeness. Although such action may be judged as venal or otherwise inappropriate from a strictly normative standpoint, organization theories variously explain how the pressures for bureaucratic survival often render such action as reasonable or even necessary in the minds of organizational actors.

Second, making explicit the value premises of organization theories helps to illuminate administrators' implicit normative understanding of their own organizational experience. In some cases, theory may reinforce, complement, and provide a sense of legitimacy to that understanding; in other instances it may force a critical reevaluation of it. Recognizing this assists administrators in being more aware of the range of normative possibilities for organizational action, thereby widening their available range of moral choices and critical perspectives.

As a concluding observation about the practical use of theory, we should note that, like all theory about the social world, organization theory that intends to describe and explain is itself inevitably normative. As such, it influences not only value stances that inform the solutions to organizational problems, but also affects the manner in which organizational problems are defined. Understanding how a particular theory aids in defining problems, or even whether it permits the description of a given state of affairs as a "problem," is an essential part of making theory practical.

5

A Baseline for Organization Theory and Public Administration

Max Weber, Frederick Winslow Taylor, the work in the early human relations movement, and Chester Barnard together form an intellectual baseline for appreciating organization theory as it continues to inform the thinking and practice of public administration. The concepts and orientations toward organizational life as presented by these theorists are the stepping stones for most of the theoretical work described in Part III. For this reason, it is useful to examine their work in some detail and to see its relationship to the public administration framework.

While some might argue the redundancy of "rational machine," it is a useful metaphor here because it calls attention to the images central to these theorists. One of these is technology, a dominant element of Western civilization, particularly as represented by the machine. Encased in a durable, physical form and directed toward a specified, articulated end or object, a machine is, at base, a logically constructed process. The words "technical" and "technique" tend to conjure up the image of machine, although both have gone far beyond the simple bounds of the simple "mechanism." The role that technique plays in society, and the role of organizational action in that playing out, has been examined in some detail, as will be seen in later chapters. For these theorists, however, the image of machine-as-embodied-technique is important, because it not only presents for them a close analog to the functionings of organizations, but also sketches a normative portrait as well.

Affixing "rational" to this image flags a particular stance of these theorists toward the world. The history of our understanding of "rational," indeed of "reason" itself, is long and complicated, stretching well back to the ancient Greeks. Without retracing this path, it is sufficient to say that the theorists here, standing with feet well planted in this tradition, view rationality as the human attribute *sine qua non*. Although this is a view that is severely tempered in the work of Max Weber, it is unabashedly grasped by the Americans, Taylor and Barnard. Further, for these latter two especially, "rationality," "science," and "technique" are terms they always associate with the purposes of organizations: The organization is *the* machine that is constructed to manipulate, alter, and control the environment, both internal and external. Max Weber's work is important in this regard, primarily because of the way in which his ideas, particularly his concept of bureaucracy, have been received and used. (As we will see in later chapters, Weber's work has been claimed as the foundation for several different, and sometimes conflicting, theoretical stances.)

The chapter begins with a review of some of Weber's concepts, particularly his concept of ideal-typical bureaucracy. Frederick Winslow Taylor's ideas regarding Scientific Management are discussed next, followed by a brief discussion of the work of the early human relations theorists, and particularly the Hawthorne Experiments. The fourth section is an examination of Chester Barnard's *The Functions of the Executive*. The chapter ends with an attempt to relate these ideas about organizations to the framework for public administration.

Max Weber

Max Weber (1864–1920) is both a good and a poor place to begin. Considered a great sociologist—Raymond Aron refers to him as *the* sociologist—his work displays dazzling insight into the workings of human society. Although many argue with the specifics of his expositions and his method, both are the background against which progress in sociology in general and organization theory in particular is often measured. At the same time, access to his work has been difficult. The first translations from the German did not appear in the United States until almost twenty years after his death in 1920, and the piecemeal translations coming forth over the years have made it hard to assess Weber in any complete way. This, coupled with the difficulty of translating from the German in the first place, makes his work inaccessible without serious study. The result has been curious: Every recent textbook on organization theory takes account of Weber's description of bureaucracy, yet few attempt to place this description into a context that allows for interpretation other than as one of "how a bureaucracy *should* be run." Finally, the other theorists in this chapter show little awareness of Weber's work (although Barnard, for one, read him in the original German). Hence, there is a wide gulf between Weber, on the one hand, and Taylor, Barnard, and the early human relations work, on the other; at the same time a curious echoing of certain themes can be found.

The best way to tease out these themes is to begin with a brief summary of Weber's ideal-typical construct of bureaucracy. In content, this is not dissimilar to such summaries found elsewhere. In an attempt to clarify this concept, the summary is followed by a discussion of Weber's development and use of the ideal type as an analytic tool. This, in turn, is placed in the larger context of his sociological efforts at understanding the rationalizing aspects of modern society.

Bureaucracy

Although "bureaucracy" is a familiar word, its essence is difficult to capture. This is especially true in a time when we feel surrounded by bureaucracies and when the adjective "bureaucratic" is anything but a term of approbation. Simply put, Weber considered it to be *the* form of organization and administration in which the power of the organization is by and large in the hands of officials with the requisite technical skills.[1] "Technical skills" is the important term here, because the characteristics of bureaucracy suggest that the organization of the bureaucracy is oriented toward, first, insulating those skills from dilution by influences from outside and corruption from within the organization and, then, grouping and specializing those skills for efficient use. For Weber, the modern bureaucratic agency (public) or bureaucratic enterprise (private) operates within a defined jurisdictional area.[2] In doing so, it has three principal elements:

- The regular activities of the agents of the organization are defined as "official duties";

- These duties are relatively stable and the authority for performing them is strictly bound by rules, as is the coercive authority available for carrying them out; and

- There are regular, established ways for assuring the continuous enactment of these duties by (and only by) those individuals who meet additional general rules or qualifications.

[1] See Reinhard Bendix, *Max Weber: An Intellectual Portrait* (Berkeley, Calif.: University of California Press, 1960), Chapter 13, esp. pp. 452–53.

[2] The following general description of "bureaucracy" is based on Max Weber, *Economy and Society,* Guenther Roth and Claus Wittich, eds. (Berkeley, Calif.: University of California Press, 1968), pp. 956–94; in this section, all page references in parentheses are to this source; emphasis is in the original unless otherwise noted.

The organization operates on the basis of principles of office hierarchy in which there are clear lines of super- and subordination: The higher office supervises the lower office, but there is also a division of responsibility such that the higher office does not take over the work of the lower one. At the same time, a clear line for appeal "offers the governed the possibility of appealing, in a precisely regulated manner, the decision of a lower office to the corresponding superior authority" (p. 957). The office is managed by a salaried staff using written documents (maintained over time as "the files"): "The body of officials working in an agency along with the respective apparatus of material implements and the files makes up a *bureau*" (p. 957). An important characteristic of this bureau is that it separates the workplace from the home and the official's public life from his or her private life. The management of such an office presumes both that the official has some sort of prior training and that official business is his primary (rather than secondary) activity. Finally the management of the office operates on the basis of

> general rules, which are more or less stable, more or less exhaustive, and which can be learned. Knowledge of these rules represents a special technical expertise which the officials possess. (p. 958)

This rule-based knowledge encompasses the technical skills that characterize the definition of bureaucracy presented above. Their significance lies in the fact that

> The reduction of modern office management to rules is deeply embedded in its very nature. The theory of modern public administration, for instance, assumes that the authority to order certain matters by decree—which has been legally granted to an agency—does not entitle the agency to regulate the matter by individual commands for each case, but only to regulate the matter abstractly. This stands in extreme contrast to the regulation of all relationships through individual privileges and bestowals of favor . . . (p. 958)

In other words, the official acts by an authority that is legally established. In consequence, one's fealty is to the office that one holds, not to an individual or a ruler; one, in fact, *holds* office, one does not own it. The exchange for this is a secure existence and a regular salary. The relationship, in sum, is a devotion to impersonal and functional purposes.

Weber saw the development of modern bureaucracy as one of the important rationalizing mechanisms of Western society. Several paragraphs from his treatise, *Economy and Society,* point this out clearly and are worth presenting at length:

> The decisive reason for the advance of bureaucratic organization has always been its purely *technical* superiority over any other form of organization. The fully developed bureaucratic apparatus compares with other organizations

exactly as the machine with the non-mechanical modes of production. Precision, speed, unambiguity, knowledge of the files, continuity, discretion, unity, strict subordination, reduction of friction and of material and personal costs— these are raised to the optimum point in the strictly bureaucratic administration, . . . As compared with all collegiate, honorific, and avocational forms of administration, trained bureaucracy is superior on all these points. As far as complicated tasks are concerned, paid bureaucratic work is not only more precise but, in the last analysis, it is often cheaper than even formally unremunerated honorific services. . . . (pp. 973–74)

. . .

Bureaucratization offers above all the optimum possibility for carrying through the principle of specializing administrative functions according to purely objective considerations. Individual performances are allocated [to] functionaries who have specialized training and who by constant practice increase their expertise. "Objective" discharge of business primarily means a discharge of business according to *calculable rules* and "without regard for persons."

"Without regard for persons," however, is also the watchword of the market and, in general, of all pursuits of naked economic interests. . . . However, the second element mentioned, calculable rules, is the most important one for modern bureaucracy. The peculiarity of modern culture, and specifically of its technical and economic basis, demands this very "calculability" of results. When fully developed, bureaucracy also stands, in a specific sense, under the principle of *sine ira ac studio.* Bureaucracy develops the more perfectly, the more it is "dehumanized," the more completely it succeeds in eliminating from official business love, hatred, and all purely personal, irrational, and emotional elements which escape calculation. This is appraised as its special virtue by capitalism. (p. 975)

Ideal Types

This description of bureaucracy is neither startling nor novel, especially now that we have lived so many years with the phenomenon. What, if any, significance is there in it? And what makes it an "ideal type"?

It is easiest to begin with the latter. An "ideal type" is, first, a mental construct. Every commentator on Weber repeats this, but it bears saying again: "Ideal" refers only to "idea," to the mind, and *has absolutely nothing to do with a normative judgment.* One can construct an ideal type of rape or pillage as well as sainthood. An ideal type is a particular kind of mental construct, one that helps to make the world rationally intelligible. The purpose of all sciences, Weber argues, be they "hard" or "soft," is to make rational sense of the world. The ideal type is one tool that the social scientist uses to do this, a tool that every social scientist in fact *already* uses. Weber's purpose, he argues, is only to make its use explicit.

One way to clarify the concept of ideal type is to focus on a research question. For example, Alexis de Tocqueville, after his journey in America in 1831–32, made a number of observations about the way in which Americans seemed to be constantly forming associations, not only for political purposes, but for "moral and intellectual" ones as well.[3] Assume for the moment that we would like to compare this aspect of American life in the 1830s with the present. Our purpose in doing this is, for instance, to understand the nature of the changes in the ways that Americans use associations. There are at least three ways to go about this.

One could start by comparing the number of associations then and now, allowing for population growth. To do this we need a definition of "association" so that we know which groupings of people to count. We can create such a definition in several ways: count any group that calls itself an association, develop criteria (e.g., regular members, regular meetings, etc.), and so forth. Having done this, what does the comparison of then and now tell us? Can we determine if there have been changes and, more particularly, the nature of those changes? Probably not with much clarity.

Or we could compare the associations in the 1830s with the surrounding institutions, and then do the same for the present. Again, we would need categories and definitions ("association," "institution," and so on). An immediate question is: How do we judge one time period against the other; are they comparable?

A third way is to construct an ideal type of "association." To do this, we would develop a list of characteristics of "typical" associations. This list, however, is neither miscellaneous nor arbitrary. The characteristics must be both typical and logically connected with one another. For example, one characteristic of an association is that it is a voluntary grouping of individuals who agree to organize their efforts toward a common purpose. Is this complete? No, because we cannot distinguish between an association and some other grouping of individuals such as a corporation. Perhaps a corporation is one form of an association. What about a study group—it has voluntary membership and is usually organized toward some purpose. If both of these, the corporation and the study group, are associations, do we need additional characteristics to help clarify these two types and others? "Association" usually carries, for example, connotations of both regularity and membership; we should probably add these to the constellation of characteristics we are developing, specifying as clearly and logically as possible their connections with each other.

And so we proceed. Soon we have an explicit construct of "association," which itself has important characteristics: Notice that no one grouping of people, even if they call themselves an "association," has all of the characteristics in our constellation. Rather, each will have more or less the form and substance explicitly described by the ideal type. Also

[3]See Alexis de Tocqueville, *Democracy in America*, Richard D. Heffner, ed. (New York: New American Library, 1956), esp. pp. 198–202.

notice that, as we construct this ideal type, we abstract from reality guided by two concerns. One is that we find *salient characteristics*, that is, those that stand out as we look across many examples *from our point of interest*. But the second concern tempers their inclusion, namely that there be some *logical connection* between a particular characteristic and the others. This helps us distinguish between the characteristics of the ideal type itself and the ways in which any specific social institution that we examine manifests itself in a particular time and place.

With the ideal type, one has constructed a tool that is objective, in the sense of standing apart from both the observer and the subject matter. It is a tool that can be used by other observers (at least potentially) to observe the same phenomena and come to similar conclusions. It is important to emphasize that the ideal type has, more or less, objective *validity*, which is not to be confused with objective *reality*. In other words, the ideal type does not "exist in the real world" in any sense.

This process of developing ideal types, Weber argues, is what historians and most other social scientists do all the time, though usually not explicitly. This lack of explicitness can create two problems. One is that the basis on which the ideal type was developed is then hidden from view (and often this means hidden from the social scientist as well as outsiders); this leads to Weber's notion of social action, which will be examined in a moment. The other danger is that the ideal type is taken for reality itself. This happens when the ideal type, rather than being treated (rightfully) as only a construct of the observer and therefore bound by the interests and historical time and place of that observer, is seen as a statement of the totality of the social reality.

One other thing about Weber's uses of "ideal type" should be clarified here. As Raymond Aron points out, Weber actually uses the notion in at least two ways. One is to point out the "ideal-type tendency" that is present in all of our concepts in the cultural sciences. As such, it is an expression of the simplifying rationality that we use to grapple with the reality that confronts us. Aron describes this tendency succinctly when he points out:

> ... The concepts most characteristic of the science of culture—whether one is discussing religion, power, prophetism, or bureaucracy—involve an element of stylization or rationalization. ... All sociology is a reconstruction that aspires to confer intelligibility on human existences which, like all human existences, are confused and obscure. Never is capitalism so clear as it is in the concepts of sociologists, and it would be a mistake to hold this against them.[4]

And one could extend this to all, sociologists or not, who study organizations.

[4]Raymond Aron, *Main Currents in Sociological Thought: Durkheim, Pareto and Weber*, vol. 2 (New York: Anchor Books, Doubleday & Co., 1970), p. 245.

The other use of ideal type is, of course, as a specific description that Weber develops, such as "bureaucracy" or "capitalism." In these cases, the ideal type is never the end, only a means; logical analysis only *begins* when one has constructed the ideal type. In the same fashion, construction is seldom "complete." Because it is a construct and a tool, it can and should be altered to be most useful. But how does one use the ideal type for analysis? This brings us to Weber's understanding of the nature of social action.

Social Action

Max Weber's training was in law, history, and economics; only toward the end of his life did he consider himself a sociologist. His resistance to this designation was based on his aversion to sociology's heavy reliance on holistic concepts that were all too often, he argued, divorced from the self-conscious actions of individual people. Categories and typologies are useful tools in analysis of events and institutions, but they are not substitutes for that analysis. It was, of course, also clear to him that generalizations are necessary to the work of the historian and social scientist; however, he argued for the necessity of grounding these generalizations in the meaningful actions of individuals. Hence, the opening passages of *Economy and Society,* his uncompleted didactic treatise, carefully builds this framework:

> "Sociology" is a word which is used in many different senses. In the sense adopted here, it means the science whose object is to interpret the meaning of social action and thereby give a causal explanation of the way in which the action proceeds and the effects it produces. By "action" in this definition is meant human behavior when and to the extent that the agent or agents see it as subjectively *meaningful:* the behavior may be either internal or external, and may consist in the agent's doing something, omitting to do something, or having something done to him. By "social" action is meant an action in which the meaning intended by the agent or agents involves a relation to *another* person's behavior and in which that relation determines the way in which the action proceeds.[5]

[5] W. G. Runciman, ed., *Max Weber: Selections in Translation* (Cambridge: Cambridge University Press, 1978) p. 7, emphasis in the original. This passage has a slightly different translation in the volumes of *Economy and Society* cited earlier (Roth and Wittich, eds, p. 4), which bears comparison:
> Sociology (in the sense in which this highly ambiguous word is used here) is a science concerning itself with the interpretative understanding of social action and thereby with a causal explanation of its course and consequences. We shall speak of "action" insofar as the acting individual attaches a subjective meaning to his behavior—be it overt or covert, omission or acquiescence. Action is "social" insofar as its subjective meaning takes account of the behavior of others and is thereby oriented in its course.

Action, in Weber's terms, is both individual and social; in order to comprehend events, it is necessary to determine the social orientation of individual action, that is, the orientation toward other individuals, be they particular and immediate or present only in the actor's expectations. When I inadvertently collide with someone on the street, that is not itself a social action. It becomes one when I apologize (or the other person strikes me). And our use of money is, for example, a social action because of the expectations we have of others' reactions (even though no one is referencing any particular individual).

Key to grasping "social action" is the concept of meaning. Simply put, a social act on my part is an action that has meaning for me. "Action in the sense of subjectively understandable orientation of behavior exists only as the behavior of one or more *individual* human beings" (p. 13). To understand the meaning of the act requires comprehending the motive of the actor, with motive being a "complex of subjective meaning which seems to the actor himself or to the observer an adequate ground for the conduct in question" (p. 11).

Weber distinguishes four orientations of social action, none of which is ever likely to be found existing in isolation:

- *traditional*—This is action which comes from habit; it is clearly on the edge of "meaningfully oriented action" and can have different degrees of self-consciousness. Much of what we do in everyday life is action of this character.

- *affectual*—Action here is determined by the actor's emotion, feeling, affect; thus, striking in anger can be seen as being on the borderline of meaningfully oriented action.

- *value-rational* (wertrational)—Here action is consciously determined by a belief in a particular value for its own sake. It is distinguished from the previous mode "by its clearly self-conscious formulation of the ultimate values governing the action and the consistently planned orientation of its detailed course to these values" (p. 25). It is similar to affectual action in that in both cases the object of the action is, so to speak, not outside of the action itself (one does it for its own sake, without regard for consequences).

- *instrumentally rational* (zweckrational)—With action in this sense, the means, ends, and consequences are all taken into account and weighed. To quote Weber,

A person acts rationally in the "means-end" sense when his action is guided by consideration of ends, means and secondary consequences; when, in acting, he rationally *assesses* means in relation to ends, ends in relation to secondary consequences, and, finally the various possible ends in relation to each other. In short, then, his action is *neither* affectively determined (and especially not emotionally determined) *nor* traditional.[6]

This schema is useful because of the several things it suggests. One is the way in which rationality is clearly seen in a broader role than is common in much of the writing of the latter twentieth century. Since no action appears purely in any one of these forms, there is, equally clearly, the presupposition of a tension between, for example, the two modes of rational action. This particular interplay underlies, for instance, Weber's argument in his work on the relationship of capitalism and Protestantism.[7] The schema also underscores the idea of reciprocity in social action. Reciprocity, of course, does not suggest that either the expectations or the reactions of all parties to the social interaction are at all likely to even be similar, nor is there any intended implication of necessary cooperation.

Finally, this schema suggests a way, as we step back from the individual interaction to look at groups (or classes or states or organizations), in which to confront continually Weber's admonition that all of our constructs must be based on the self-conscious actions of individuals. A social relation exists because, and only because, there is a *probability* "that particular men, in the context of a relationship organized in a particular way, will perform actions in a way which is specifiable in terms of the meaning which on average they intend."[8] The schema thus suggests a way of comprehending actions and unearthing their meaning. For example, a social relationship can be bounded by mutual agreement. In some fashion, both parties make promises about their behavior in the future. When I engage in such a promise, I then assume (perhaps to varying degrees) that the other party will base his action on the agreement. In doing so, I am acting rationally in both senses:

> ... partly in the "means-end" sense, in that the meaning of [my] actions [are] more or less based on "fidelity" to this expectation, and partly in the sense of trying to realize the absolute value of "duty"—to adhere to the agreement which [I] have entered into in the sense intended by [me].[9]

From this regularity of social action comes the notion of a lawful order, although regularity is never complete because there is always the element of chance. As Raymond Aron illustrates:

> It is customary in universities for students not to compete with professors for attention. There is a probability, therefore, that the students will listen silently

---

[6]Runciman, p. 29, emphasis in original.
[7]Max Weber, *The Protestant Ethic and the Spirit of Capitalism,* Talcott Parsons, trans. (New York: G. Allen & Unwin, 1938), esp. Chapter 5.
[8]Runciman, p. 31.
[9]Ibid., p. 31.

to what the professor has to say, but this probability does not amount to a certainty.[10]

When regularity of social action is accompanied by social pressure, social convention is created; when accompanied by the threat of physical force, law is created. Notice that both conventional and lawful order are now defined in terms of the motives for obeying them. Social interaction is for Weber always, at base, voluntary (even if habitual).

And yet, viewing social convention and law in terms of the motives of those who obey can be misleading, from Weber's perspective, unless one realizes the stability that is usually inherent in social relationships. A key to this stability seems to lie in the notion of legitimacy. I tend to follow a social norm and to obey a law because each of these has a certain validity or legitimacy for me; I will also go along with them for a complex of other motives in any particular case, but the more I view them as legitimately grounded, the higher the probability that my actions will be stable in reference to them. Thus,

> ... When a civil servant appears in his office daily at a fixed time, he does not only act on the basis of custom or self-interest which he could disregard if he wanted to; as a rule, his action is also determined by the validity of an order (viz., the civil service rules), which he fulfills partly because disobedience would be disadvantageous to him but also because its violation would be abhorrent to his sense of duty (of course, in varying degrees). (p. 31)

Keeping in mind the potential motives for obeying, it is possible to turn this conception around and talk about the ways in which a legitimate order is maintained; in other words, the ways in which there is a probability that commands will be obeyed over time. This domination or authority makes a claim to legitimacy; when this exists, it also clearly implies at least minimal voluntary compliance (even though the motive for this compliance may be mixed). Power—"the probability that one actor within a social relationship will be in a position to carry out his own will despite resistance, regardless of the basis on which this probability exists" (p. 53)—is clearly evident in social relationships, yet it is too diffuse a concept to be workable on its own. "Domination" brings more clarity insofar as it helps toward an understanding of the way in which power is both legitimated and structured over time and across social relationships.

Weber talks of different types of domination, but the one of most interest to us here is the idea of legal domination. Legal authority, seen as a consistent system of abstract rules, is the basis for administration, which itself is

---

[10]Aron, p. 276.

held to consist in the application of these rules to particular cases; the administrative process in the rational pursuit of the interests which are specified in the order governing the organization within the limits laid down by legal precepts and following principles which are capable of generalized formulation and are approved in the order governing the group, or at least not disapproved in it. (p. 217)

This suggests some basic characteristics of rational legal authority. For example, official business is both continuous and rule-bound. It is also systematically divided, through specialization, and implies the notion of hierarchical ordering. To maintain the continuity of the abstract rules requires that these rules, as well as decisions made on the basis of them, be written so as to be readily available. As should be evident, we have come full circle, back into ideal-typical bureaucracy.

The reason for following this path of abstraction has been to provide some fullness to the concept of bureaucracy. Weber, in his many works, argued that one of the persisting (and increasing) peculiarities of Western culture is its apparent drive toward an ever more narrow and confining rationalism. A significant aspect of this rationalization of society is the "bureaucratization" of organizations:

... bureaucratic rationalization can also be, and often has been, a revolutionary force of the first order in its relation to tradition. But its revolution is carried out by *technical* means, basically "from the outside" ... ; first it revolutionizes things and organizations, and then, in consequence, it changes people, in the sense that it alters the conditions to which they must adapt and in some cases increases their chances of adapting to the external world by rational determination of means and ends.[11]

And finally:

Bureaucratic administration means fundamentally domination through knowledge. This is the feature of it which makes it specifically rational. This consists on the one hand in technical knowledge which, by itself, is sufficient to ensure it a position of extraordinary power. But in addition to this, bureaucratic organizations, or the holders of power who make use of them, have the tendency to increase their power still further by the knowledge growing out of experience in the service. For they acquire through the conduct of office a special knowledge of facts and have available a store of documentary material peculiar to themselves. (p. 225)

The social institution of bureaucracy, which Weber analyzed by use of his pure type, is a part of the entire modern social fabric. It involves, essentially, the transfer of power from the leader to the expert. As a way of

[11] Runciman, p. 231, emphasis in original.

organizing, through its separation of public and private life, creation of documents, division of labor and so on, it is a most efficient means of performing assigned tasks. At the same time, and this is an ambivalence that should be clear in the above summary, Weber saw this very efficiency as a reduction in the capacity of organizations to respond to the conditions that confront them. This is an important ambivalence to keep in mind as we move on to examine Taylor and Barnard.

Growth of the Railroads and Bureaucracy

As a way to make Weber's argument more concrete, it is useful to examine a particular historical situation and assess the changes that occurred both organizationally and administratively. The development of the railroads in the United States between 1840 and 1890 provides a particularly clear illustration of the processes of rationalization and bureaucratization of which Weber speaks. This discussion is also useful insofar as it provides some historical background for understanding the emergence of "efficiency" as a primary value in general and of Scientific Management in particular. Rationalization and bureaucratization in the public sector followed hand-in-glove that of the corporation in the private sector. The innovations described below are examples of what came to be the standard by which many would attempt to measure the efficiency of public organizations.

The first railroads were built in the 1830s and early 1840s to supplement existing road and canal systems. Technological advances in the 1840s made possible a tremendous expansion over the next several decades. By 1850, there were 4,000 miles of canal, but 9,000 miles of track. By 1890, the rail system was essentially complete; it looked then as it would look up through World War II.

By 1855, the railroad carried traffic that was equivalent to that handled by all forms of transportation twenty years earlier. Also by that time, more canals were being abandoned than being built. At least one reason for this success is almost self-evident: the several-times reduction in the travel time between two points. (When Chicago was founded in 1803, it took a traveler about six weeks to reach New York: in 1837, when it was incorporated, this was reduced to less than three weeks and to three days by 1857.) This was the first time in history that one could regularly travel (or send freight, for that matter) faster than the horse, in almost any weather.

But this technology required substantial changes in the way in which a business venture needed to be organized in order to be successful. One change concerned sheer size. In the 1850s, most manufacturing was done in shops of ten or so people, at most, with government offices of similar size. Railroads started relatively small as well, both in miles of track and number of employees, but by 1855 sixteen railroads each had more than 1,600 miles of track. This meant large numbers of employees to both run and maintain the line. The largest of the textile mills at this time had about 250 workers; the railroads often had 1,000 and more. In the large textile mills, where by this time spinning, weaving, and sizing had been integrated under one roof, a supervisory system had developed. The organization and administration of the mills was made somewhat easier by the skills required by the various tasks; unskilled workers could be trained (and retrained for other positions) fairly quickly. And the required skills were, in large, those of manual dexterity. On the railroads, on the other hand, the range of skills was considerably broader, many requiring judgment that developed only over time, others considerable training, and still others very high risk or large responsibility. In other words, a high degree of specialization almost necessarily developed.

The specialization grew not only in the actual work on the railroad; it was similarly required in the administering of that work as well. Organizing the maintenance efforts of several dozen crews spread across several thousands of miles of track necessitated both thinking about administration in different ways and learning about the managerial and administrative problems peculiar to that work. The same could be said for scheduling dozens of trains, running tens of depots, or determining and collecting thousands of fares and freight charges.

As noted earlier, Weber talks about bureaucracy as the shifting of power from leaders to experts. A good place to see this within the development of the railroads is in the changes that occurred in the use and handling of finances and money. Three areas illustrate this:

- the ways in which railroads came to be financed,

- the ways in which money was handled within the system itself, and

- the way in which these two combined with the high fixed cost of operating a railroad.

Financing Railroad builders required enormous capital investment in comparison to any development that had been envisioned in the United States up to that time. For example, in 1825 the Erie Canal was financed at $7 million, the largest single expenditure ever; twenty-five years later, three railroads were *each* capitalized at $10 million and, by 1859, there were ten.

To be able to finance these ventures, corporations (as opposed to the then-prevalent single ownerships and partnerships) had to be used in order to float large numbers of bonds. One effect was to encourage a separation of the financing from the running of a railroad, with each becoming a specialized group of tasks. This contributed, in part, to the growing distinction between the owners and the managers of the railroads. Alfred Chandler describes this neatly:

> ... The capital required to build a railroad was far more than that required to purchase a plantation, a textile mill, or even a fleet of ships. Therefore, a single entrepreneur, family, or small group of associates was rarely able to own a railroad. Nor could many stockholders or their representatives manage it. The administrative tasks were too numerous, too varied, and too complex. They required special skills and training which could only be commanded by a full-time salaried manager.[12]

The manager, who usually did not have the financial resources to play in the financing game, came to view his job of managing as a full-time occupation. Because of the technical skills required, he tended to view it as a lifetime one as well.

Money in the System You could buy a ticket in Santa Fe to take the train to Boston; this meant changing from one line to another. It also meant the fare had to be prorated between the two lines, with the proper amount ending up in each ledger. It also meant that the fare had to end up in the coffers of the railroad, not the pocket of the ticket agent. Or you could send a batch of dresses from New York west to Kansas City; the appropriate tariff had to be collected, including drayage charges, and those fees had to be portioned out to the right companies along the way, including the freight handlers on the other end who put the dresses in the warehouse. Added to this complexity was the setting of the "right" fare or tariff in the first place, changing it as needed, and (perhaps most important) communicating that change to everyone who needed to know. Setting rates clearly, quickly, and consistently was especially important because rates were the primary mode of competition between lines.

All this required specialization of several sorts. One was the development and maintenance of a system for the physical handling of money by hundreds of different individuals; a "rational" way to do this was to use written records: a tariff bill, with one copy to the sender, others to agents along the way as needed, with a final one in the hands of the receiver. Then the receipts were collected from the ticket agent's files and totaled to see that they matched the money in hand. Meanwhile (and further up in the hierarchy), the rates themselves were being determined—higher rates for those items that needed special handling (small packages of merchandise), lower ones for those that traveled in bulk (coal or wheat), and still lower ones for those where the shipper used his own cars. And then the rates changed by the distance, partly depending on how many times

[12]Alfred Chandler, *The Visible Hand* (Cambridge, Mass.: Belknap Press, 1977), p. 87.

the freight had to be shifted from one train to another. There were also rebates and kickbacks to hold on to customers, because this was the edge of competition on the trunk lines. At the same time, yet again further up in the hierarchy, representatives from the various competing railroads met to negotiate alliances to maintain stable agreements on rates (extremely rational behavior, from the railroads' point of view, even if socially frowned upon).

High Fixed Costs   Not only was it expensive to build a railroad, which required floating huge quantities of bonds, it was almost as expensive to maintain one. This required rolling those bonds over on a regular basis, which in turn put strong emphasis on making note payments in a very timely fashion. This situation was further complicated by the fact that the bonds were held by people who had more interest in getting a return on their investment than in making sure the railroad was run properly. (This itself was "rational" since they were usually bankers in Boston and New York, who themselves were working within their own emerging bureaucracies, following their own sets of rules, and so forth.)

The problem was one of high fixed costs. A train depot cost so much to staff and maintain, whether it served five or fifty trains on a particular day. A locomotive required an engineer and a fireman whether it pulled ten or forty cars. And so on it went through the entire system. In addition, much of the work on the railroad was, particularly in the earlier days, potentially dangerous and often immediately risky; it also required skill and training. Not surprisingly, the brotherhoods were formed, often to fight for safer trains and better maintenance; they also fought for higher wages. Labor, as the economists say, became inelastic, adding further rigidity to high fixed costs.

At the same time, rates were *the* source of income and *the* basis of competition. Cut the rates too much and the payments on the bonds could not be made. Cut them on the trunk lines but raise them on the spur lines (where there was no competition) and the farmers and small businessmen were liable to vent their fury through their local legislatures. There was no single solution to this problem; rate fixing, for example, brought stability to replace the cutthroat competition, but also brought charges of collusion and interference with trade (and therefore often brought government regulation). One thing became apparent: the margin between costs and income was crucial. If one could not increase income (except slightly) nor lower costs directly, then the forced choice, as a manager, was to run things more efficiently—get more out of the fixed resources. This spurred technological changes, such as faster engines that used less fuel and could haul more freight faster, more reliable switching mechanisms, more durable steel for tracks, and so on. But more important, from the perspective here, it also provoked a concern with unit costs and then with the question of the ways in which the tasks reflected in those unit costs were performed. One of the best means to develop useful unit costs and then to be able to disaggregate them into tasks was through uniformity and standardization, both of work and equipment. Thus, as Chandler points out,

> The 1880s and early 1890s witnessed the culmination of technological as well as organizational innovation and standardization. In those years the United States acquired a standard gauge and a standard time, moved toward standard basic equipment . . . and adopted uniform accounting procedures. On the night of May 31–June 1, 1886, the remaining railroads using broad-gauge tracks . . . shifted simultaneously to the standard 4'8½" gauge. On Sunday, November 18, 1883, the railroad men (and most of their fellow countrymen) set their watches to the new uniform standard time. The passage of the Railroad Safety Appliance Act of 1893 made it illegal for trains to operate without standardized automatic couplers and air brakes. In 1887 the Interstate Commerce Act provided for uniform railroad accounting procedures that had been developing for a quarter of a century. All four of these events resulted from two decades of constant consultation and cooperation between railroad managers.[13]

The ideal-typical understanding of bureaucracy helps to make sense of what was happening during that time. It is useful to recapitulate Weber's notion of the use of ideal type. For this, his own words are best:

> The ideal-type is a mental image, it is not historical reality or above all "authentic" reality, still less does it serve as a schema by which one might order reality by way of example. Its only significance is that of a limiting concept *(Grenzebegriff)* that is purely ideal, by which one measures *(messen)* reality in order to clarify the empirical content of certain important elements and with which one compares this reality. These concepts are images *(Gebilde)* in which we construct relations by utilizing the category of objective possibility which our imagination, formed and oriented by reality, deems adequate.[14]

The "forces" at play with the development of the railroads were the same ones underpinning Frederick Winslow Taylor's renowned emphasis on "the one best way."

Frederick Winslow Taylor

The "constant cooperation and consultation between railroad managers" to which Chandler refers took place, in large part, in the societies and associations that had sprung up around groupings of professional interests

---

[13]Ibid., p. 130.
[14]Weber, "Essais sur le theorie de le science," quoted in Aron, p. 311.

within the railroad industry. The training of many of these managers was, befittingly, technical; many, if not most, had at least some engineering background. As other industries grew larger and more complex, managers there saw developments parallel to those with the railroads: an emphasis on technical and engineering skills, the formation of societies and associations whose primary purpose was to share knowledge and work on common problems, and a growing appreciation for the relationship of income to high fixed costs.

One such association was the American Society of Mechanical Engineers. Founded in 1880, it was the first professional group that actively and consistently advocated systematic and scientific approaches to management. For example, "The Engineer as Economist," a paper presented in 1886 by Henry R. Towne, argued that the engineer must be concerned with more than "mere mechanical efficiency," such as costs and revenues. Instead, engineers must begin to think, like economists, in terms of how *all* resources should be utilized. Although this paper did not have a great influence on later papers that were presented to the society, it did have a profound effect on one member who was later to become the society's president, Frederick Winslow Taylor.

Taylor epitomizes the way in which those who ran large organizations (or at least large parts of them) came to think about the world. Often heralded as the "father of Scientific Management," he represents here a larger appreciation of the interaction of technology, work, and organizing. There are numerous debates about the "real influence" of Taylor and Taylorism. However, in an important sense, these are largely irrelevant to our present concern, because Taylor, no matter what his specific historical influence, characterizes a dominant way of thinking about and acting in organizations that is still common today. The son of a well-to-do Philadelphia family, Taylor (1856–1915) came from Quaker-Puritan stock and training that prepared him well for his life's work: It gave him "an intense spirit of inquiry for the truth, an urge to observe and verify facts, and a Puritan zeal to eradicate the evils of waste and slothfulness," as one biographer has put it.[15]

Educated at Phillips Exeter Academy, he passed the Harvard entrance exams with honors, but abandoned what was to have been a career in law because of ill health and poor eyesight. Instead of attending college, he began a four-year apprenticeship at the Enterprise Hydraulic Works of Philadelphia. He moved, in 1879, to Midvale Steel in the same city. Here he spent twelve years experimenting and testing both his notions of shop management and his ideas on metal working and cutting (he received at least eleven patents on improved machines and metals during this time).

[15]Daniel A. Wren, *The Evolution of Management Thought* (New York: Ronald Press, 1972), p. 112. The remainder of this biographical account is based on Wren, pp. 111–40.

At Midvale, Taylor would rise from common laborer to clerk, to machinist, to gang boss of the machinists, to foreman of the machine shop, to master mechanic in charge of repairs and maintenance throughout the plant, and to chief engineer—all in six years; a meteoric rise for this intense young man.[16]

He also enrolled in a home study course from Stevens Institute of Technology, graduating with a degree in mechanical engineering in 1883.

He left Midvale in 1890, going first to a wood pulp conversion firm as general manager, then setting up his own practice as a consultant, from 1893 to 1901. One of his first assignments, as he describes it, was "systematizing the largest bicycle ball factory in this country," the Simond's Rolling Machine Company, which manufactured steel ball bearings. At Simond's, one important operation was the inspection of the bearings after final polishing. Taylor conducted a number of experiments around this operation, changing procedures and personnel, all of which appeared to be successful. When he began, about 120 women each worked ten and one-half hours a day, five and one-half days a week. When he finished:

> the final outcome of all the changes was that *thirty-five girls did the work formerly done by one hundred and twenty.* And that the *accuracy of the work at the higher speed was two-thirds greater than at the former slow speed.*[17]

In addition, their workday had been cut to eight and one-half hours, with four ten-minute "recreation periods," while their wages were increased by 80 to 100 percent. On management's side, there was a "material reduction in the cost of inspection," as well as "substantial improvement in the quality of the product."[18] As Taylor himself summarizes this experience:

> These good results were brought about by many changes which substituted favorable for unfavorable working conditions. It should be appreciated, however, that the one element which did more than all of the others was the careful selection of girls with quick perception to replace those whose perceptions were slow ... [i.e.,] the scientific selection of the workers.[19]

From Simond's, Taylor moved on to Bethlehem Steel, largely at the instigation and urging of Joseph Wharton, who both owned a quarter of the company's stock and had founded the first business school. It was a tenet of Wharton's that scientific methods must be brought to bear on the problems of industry. At Bethlehem, Taylor conducted his now-famous

[16]Ibid., p. 114.
[17]Frederick Winslow Taylor, "The Principles of Scientific Management," *Scientific Management* (New York: Harper & Brothers, 1947), p. 95, emphasis in the original.
[18]Ibid., p. 96.
[19]Ibid., p. 97.

experiments in carrying pig iron and shoveling ore. As he would explain to a Congressional subcommittee some years later:

> There is a good deal of refractory stuff to shovel around a steel works; take ore, or ordinary bituminous coal, for instance. It takes a good deal of effort to force the shovel down into either of these materials from the top of the pile, as you have to when you are unloading a car. There is one right way of forcing the shovel down into materials of this sort, and many wrong ways. Now, the way to shovel refractory stuff is to press the forearm hard against the upper part of the right leg . . .[20]

By 1901, with earnings from his numerous patents, Taylor was ready to turn to spreading the word about his methods. The next fourteen years saw the publication of "Shop Management" and "The Principles of Scientific Management," his presidency of the American Society of Mechanical Engineers, lectures at Harvard and around the country, and consultations for the Army and the Navy. The "Taylor method" was receiving considerable publicity. For instance, Louis Brandeis helped coin the phrase "Scientific Management" when he used numerous witnesses sympathetic to Taylor's principles in arguing before the Interstate Commerce Commission on the inefficient management of the railroads. These hearings brought both fame and notoriety for Taylor.

On the negative side, organized labor (particularly the railroad brotherhoods) began to protest and then to work actively against the introduction of the new methods. One result, following testing of the methods, then protests and eventually a strike at the Army arsenal at Waterford, Massachusetts, was a Congressional investigation. Taylor spent twelve hours before this special committee, where the exchanges were often sharp and acrimonious. Copley, Taylor's most sympathetic biographer, speaks of the "terrorism in the air" as the unions set upon Taylor, and muckraker Ira Tarbell had these words to describe the scene:

> One of the most sportsmanlike exhibits the country ever saw was Mr. Taylor's willingness to subject himself to the heckling and the badgering of labor leaders, congressmen, and investigators of all degrees of misunderstanding, suspicion and ill will. To a man of his temperament and highly trained intellect, who had given a quarter of a century of the hardest kind of toil to develop useful truths, the kind of questioning to which he was sometimes subjected must have been maddening.[21]

---

[20]Taylor, "Taylor's Testimony before the Special House Committee," *Scientific Management* (New York: Harper & Brothers, 1947), p. 60.

[21]Ira Tarbell, *New Ideals in Business*, p. 315, cited in Frank Barkley Copley, *Frederick W. Taylor, Father of Scientific Management*, vol. 2 (New York: American Society of Mechanical Engineers, 1923), p. 347.

Even with all the abuse he received, this was in many ways his shining hour. He was able to make some of his clearest descriptions of the elements of Scientific Management; one passage in particular is worth quoting at length:

> Scientific management is not any efficiency device, not a device of any kind for securing efficiency; nor is it any bunch or group of efficiency devices. It is not a new system of figuring costs; it is not a new scheme of paying men; it is not a piecework system; it is not a bonus system; it is not a premium system; it is no scheme for paying men; it is not holding a stop watch on a man and writing things down about him; it is not time study; it is not motion study nor the analysis of the movements of men; it is not the printing and ruling and unloading of a ton or two of blanks on a set of men and saying, "Here's your system; go use it." It is not divided foremanship or functional foremanship; it is not any of the devices which the average man calls to mind when scientific management is spoken of. The average man thinks of one or more of these things when he hears the words "scientific management" mentioned, but scientific management is not any of these devices. I am not sneering at cost-keeping systems, at time study, at functional foremanship, nor at any new and improved scheme of paying men, nor at any efficiency devices, if they are really devices that make for efficiency. I believe in them; but what I am emphasizing is that these devices in whole or in part are not scientific management; they are useful adjuncts to scientific management, so are they useful adjuncts of other systems of management.
>
> Now, in essence, scientific management involves a complete mental revolution on the part of the working man engaged in any particular establishment or industry—a complete mental revolution on the part of these men as to their duties toward their work, toward their fellow men, and toward their employers. And it involves the equally complete mental revolution on the part of those on the management's side—the foreman, the superintendent, the owner of the business, the board of directors—a complete mental revolution on their parts as to their duties toward their fellow workers in the management, toward their workmen, and toward all of their daily problems. And without this complete mental revolution on both sides scientific management does not exist.[22]

The recommendation of the committee was that no legislation was needed. But, in spite of this stance, pro-labor factions began introducing a legislative rider to all military appropriation bills that forbade spending appropriated funds on the "Taylor system." (See the accompanying box.) Riders such as this one, which had been supported heavily by Senator Henry Cabot Lodge as a way to end "the days of slavery," continued to be placed on Army, Navy, and Post Office appropriations until 1949. "Taylorism," as Wren points out, "and the attempt to bring efficiency to government agencies was clearly crippled."

[22]Taylor, "Testimony," pp. 26–27.
[23]Wren, p. 140.

A LEGISLATIVE RIDER FORBIDDING SPENDING FOR "THE TAYLOR SYSTEM"

PROVIDED, That no part of the appropriations in this bill shall be available for the salary or pay of any officer, manager, supervisor, foreman, or other person having charge of the work of any employee of the United States government while making or causing to be made, with a stop-watch or other time-measuring device, a time study of any job of any employee while engaged upon such work; nor shall any part of the appropriations made in this bill be available to pay any premium or bonus or cash reward to any employee in addition to his regular wages, except for suggestions resulting in improvements or economy in the operations of any Government plant; and no claim for service performed by any person violating this proviso shall be allowed.

—From Frank Barkley Copley, *Frederick W. Taylor, Father of Scientific Management*, vol. 2 (New York: American Society of Mechanical Engineers, 1923), p. 350.

Following the hearings, Taylor was a celebrity. In part this was because he represented the effort to increase what President Theodore Roosevelt called at the time "the national efficiency." Hence, in the introduction to his "Principles of Scientific Management," Taylor sets the following objectives for his paper:

First. To point out, through a series of simple illustrations, the great loss which the whole country is suffering through inefficiency in almost all of our daily acts.

Second. To try to convince the reader that the remedy for this inefficiency lies in systematic management, rather than in searching for some unusual or extraordinary man.

Third. To prove that the best management is a true science, resting upon clearly defined laws, rules, and principles, as a foundation. And further to show that the fundamental principles of scientific management are applicable to all kinds of human activities, from our simplest individual acts to the work of our great corporations, which call for the most elaborate cooperation ...[24]

What had been an argument for method in "Shop Management" became an argument for philosophy in "Principles." Although he had offered the manuscript of the latter paper to the American Society of Mechanical

---

[24]Taylor, "Principles," p. 7. As Wren points out (p. 141, fn.): "This third point is a statement of the universality of scientific management but it does not necessarily hint at the same level of universality of management that will be seen later in the work of Henri Fayol." See Chapter 6 for a discussion of the work of Fayol and other writers such as Luther Gulick and Lyndall Urwick, all of whom attempted to construct universal principles of organization.

Engineers, he formally withdrew it after waiting a year for a response. Instead, he arranged to have it published, beginning in March 1911, in three issues of *The American Magazine*. There, he laid out the "duties of management," if management is to be truly scientific:

> *First*. They develop a science for each element of a man's work, which replaces the old rule-of-thumb method.
>
> *Second*. They scientifically select and then train, teach, and develop the workman, whereas in the past he chose his own work and trained himself as best he could.
>
> *Third*. They heartily cooperate with the men so as to insure all of the work being done in accordance with the principles of the science which has been developed.
>
> *Fourth*. There is an almost equal division of the work and responsibility between management and the workmen. The management takes over all work for which they are better suited than the workmen, while in the past almost all of the work and the greater part of the responsibility were thrown upon the men.[25]

These four "duties of management" embody not only the main thrust of Taylor's work, but also a theory about organizations that has continued to hold sway for many decades.

Taylor's Theory of Organizations

Taylor spent his entire life focused on making the work of the world more efficient. He did this in his professional life at Midvale, at Simond's, at Bethlehem Steel, at the Waterford Arsenal. He also did this in his private life, by devising the best way of taking a cross-country walk with the least fatigue, by inventing a two-handled golf putter (which was barred from the course), and by experimenting with different types of grass to develop the best putting green. But Taylor was hardly alone in his earnest desire to promote efficiency. At least a half-dozen other names must be counted as significant in the early days of this movement to rationalize the way in which business (particularly manufacturing) was conducted: Carl Barth, Henry L. Gantt, Frank and Lillian Gilbreth, Harrington Emerson, Morris L. Cooke. "These were the individuals," as Wren puts it, "who were in the vanguard in spreading the gospel of efficiency."[26]

And the gospel of efficiency was a popular tune in the years before the First World War. Efficiency clubs sprang up around the country, while efficiency experts became the butt of jokes and the bane of management's existence. As one commentator describes the situation:

[25]Taylor, "Principles," pp. 36–37.
[26]Wren, p. 127.

... social forces were generating and sanctioning an efficiency craze during the Taylor era. A proliferation of popular and technical literature appeared on efficiency in the home, in education, in conservation of natural resources, in the church, and in industry. The noted psychologist H. H. Goddard thought that the efficiency of group endeavors was not a function so much of intelligence but of the proper assignment of men to a grade of work which met their mental capacity. This psychological notion of the "first-class man" reflected the grip of Taylor's ideas on the academic community. American educational institutions, seeking reform and a broader base for their efforts, seized upon Taylorism and discovered the efficiency expert. Conservationists, spurred by Presidents T. R. Roosevelt and William Howard Taft, also found comfort in the gospel of efficiency. Feminists saw a saving grace in efficiency which would release the woman from the drudgery of housework and free her to assume her equal role in society. The Reverend Billy Sunday recommended functional foremanship for the church so that each department could obtain expert advice and lasting results.[27]

Time, motion and fatigue studies, economic incentive schemes, stop watches, Gantt charts, therbligs[28]—these were the various tools and techniques of Scientific Management. Guiding their use was a narrow, fairly specific theory of organization that has three interconnected elements:

- Particular assumptions about human nature,

- Presumed characteristics of the relationship between people and organizations, and

- A specific definition of "knowledge" and its role within the organization.

Human Nature and Motivation

Many Americans like myself who were born in the late nineteenth century and brought up in the early twentieth, look upon the years prior to 1914 as a golden age of the Republic. In part this feeling was due to our youth; in part to the fact that the great middle class could command goods and services that are now beyond their reach. But there was also a euphoria in the air, peace among the nations, and a feeling that justice and prosperity for all was attainable through good will and progressive legislation.[29]

In this way, historian Samuel Eliot Morison begins his account of the

[27]Ibid., p. 265.

[28]Frank Gilbreth "developed a list of 17 basic notions, each called a 'therblig' (Gilbreth spelled backwards with the 'th' transposed) such as 'search,' 'select,' 'transport loaded,' 'position,' 'hold,' etc. These fundamental notions could not be subdivided and gave Gilbreth a more precise way of analyzing the exact elements of any worker movement." Ibid., pp. 163–64.

[29]Samuel Eliot Morison, *The Oxford History of the American People*, vol. 3 (New York: Mentor Books, 1972), p. 167.

first Wilson administration. These sentiments also capture the underlying optimism that pervades Scientific Management; hence, Taylor opens his "Principles" with:

> The principal object of management should be to secure the maximum prosperity for the employer, coupled with the maximum prosperity for the employee.
> The words "maximum prosperity" are used, in their broad sense, to mean not only large dividends for the company or owner, but the development of every branch of business to its highest state of excellence, so that prosperity may be permanent.[30]

But this is a particular brand of optimism. It is not the type that merely thinks things will somehow turn out all right; rather, it is the kind of optimism that comes from knowing you can *make* them come out all right. The fertile ground from which Scientific Management sprang was essentially one of prosperity and expansion. With the gross national product doubling with every generation since the Civil War, this was a time in which it looked as though the only limits to progress were man's ingenuity and his stubbornness, his "goodwill and progressive legislation." Because of the nature of man and of the world, the key to progress was knowledge: Since both man and the world are malleable, they can be shaped and turned, with the right amount of pressure and heat, until— like a good piece of metalwork—they fit the job at hand.

But the natural condition is not in itself good. For example, Taylor's ideas about efficiency are based on the notion that if both management and labor are to prosper, then there need to be both high wages and low labor costs. The only way to obtain this is by enabling work to be done more productively. (This echoes the rationalization of work on the railroad described earlier.) One way is, of course, to use more machinery (or more productive machinery); Taylor himself was the holder of several patents on metal-working machines that did just that. The other way is to make people more productive; the problem Taylor saw was that "the greatest obstacle to the attainment of this standard is the slow pace which [workmen] adopt, or the loafing or 'soldiering,' marking time, as it is called."[31] He saw two kinds of soldiering, "natural" and "systematic":

> The natural laziness of man is serious, but by far the greatest evil from which both workmen and employers are suffering is the *systematic soldiering* which is almost universal under all the ordinary schemes of management and

[30]Taylor, "Principles," p. 9.
[31]Taylor, "Shop Management," *Scientific Management* (New York: Harper & Brothers, 1947), p. 30.

which results from a careful study on the part of the workmen of what they think will promote their best interests.[32]

There are several things of interest about this passage: People are assumed to be rational; workers engage in systematic soldiering because of what they see as their best interests. The way in which the world is organized is the cause of this soldiering; by changing one's scheme of management, this negative condition can be eliminated. And underlying both of these is the idea that this negative condition comes about in large part because those involved, labor and management, fail to see their real long-term interest. If they did, Taylor argues, they would see that their interests lie in high wages *and* low labor costs. The role of Scientific Management in this is a liberating one: By rationalizing the work process, it enables both labor and management to be their most productive. (This is the same way in which Weber talks of bureaucracy in relation to tradition.)

This rationalizing effort works in two ways. First, it determines the proper way of completing a task. To do this, it destroys "rule-of-thumb methods," rebuilding them "scientifically." Second, it is brought to bear on the selection of the people to do the work. From this comes Taylor's emphasis on finding "first-class men." Once both of these are done, there are two further steps: (1) alter the work environment to make it conducive to the best (most efficient) completion of tasks, and (2) provide appropriate and sufficient incentives for the work to get done.

Finally, the most important assumption about human nature in Taylor's thought is the emphasis and reliance on the individual. This is reflected in his constant search for the "first-class man," in his regular denigration of work gangs, and his analysis of systematic soldiering as being socially reinforced by the group. All of this is summed up well by David Silverman. For Taylor, he argues, "Man is an economic animal who responds directly to financial incentives within the limits of his physiological capabilities and the technical and work organization which is provided him."[33] At the same time, in all of Taylor's works, along with the glorification of the individual, there is a distinct distrust of *individualism* in the face of knowledge; hence, the need to teach the workman, rather than allow him to develop his own way of work. Nor does this emphasis on the individual lessen Taylor's strong emphasis on cooperation, but it is a cooperation in the pursuit of knowledge and efficiency, not mere camaraderie.

The Individual and the Organization For Taylor, the organizational relationships that are most conducive to productive work are those that

---

[32]Ibid., p. 32, emphasis in original.
[33]David Silverman, *The Theory of Organisations* (New York: Basic Books, 1970), p. 176.

are functionally aligned, with responsibilities clearly specified. One can see this clearly in his four objectives of Scientific Management, the last one of which bears repeating here:

> There is an almost equal division of the work and responsibility between management and the workmen. The management takes over all work for which they are better suited than the workmen, while in the past almost all of the work and the greater part of the responsibility were thrown upon the men.

"Better fitted"—this well defines the cutting edge for Taylor. The difficulty that he sees is simply that men are unable to grasp their own limitations. They tend to fall into bad habits (which are especially reinforced by peer pressure), and they have difficulty in seeing their own true interests. Therefore, it is clear that those who are "better fitted" (by being scientifically trained) should help guide and rationalize the behavior of those less-suited to understanding the real nature of work. In this fashion, each will find his proper niche: the place in the organization in which he can perform as a first-class man.

Taylor advocates exactly what Weber saw as the key shift with the coming of bureaucracy: the shift of power from both the owner and the worker to the expert. This shows very clearly in Taylor's emphasis on creating planning departments to administer the work in the factory:

> The shop, and indeed the whole works, should be managed, not by the manager, superintendent, or foreman, but by the planning department. The daily routine of running the entire works should be carried on by the various functional elements of this department, so that, in theory at least, the works could run smoothly even if the manager, superintendent and the assistants outside the planning room were all to be away for a month at a time.[34]

This functionalism of Taylor's was extreme; however, the basic concepts were accepted in business and used widely (and still are today).

In the Taylor system, a final element of the relationship of the individual to the organization is the emphasis on cooperation. The unions felt threatened by Scientific Management (as seen in the Congressional hearing and the legislative proviso described earlier). But so did employers. As Charles Perrow points out, Scientific Management

> "questioned [employers'] good judgment and superior ability which had been the subject of public celebration for many years." It reduced their discretion, placing it in the hands of technicians; it implied that management's failure to utilize the skills of the workers was the reason for workers' inefficiencies and restiveness.[35]

---

[34]Taylor, "Shop Management," p. 110.
[35]Charles Perrow, *Complex Organizations,* 2nd ed. (Glenview, Ill.: Scott, Foresman, 1979), p. 65, quoting Reinhard Bendix, *Work and Authority in Industry* (New York: John Wiley & Sons, 1956), p. 280.

However, the message of cooperation, iterated almost endlessly in the Scientific Management literature, seemed finally to have had an effect. The old ideologies, such as Social Darwinism, were no longer useful. The "survival of the fittest" came to be replaced with "ordering of the workplace." As organizations grew in size and unions became a permanent fixture, the adversarial ideologies were less and less helpful.[36]

The two keys to cooperation in the Taylor framework—and these were to be stressed in later management thought and organization theory—are manipulation and interposition, both on the basis of knowledge. The environment, the worker, even management, are all fair game for manipulation and control in order to enable work to be done more efficiently. Manipulation on the basis of scientific knowledge is the currency of this cooperation. And its banker is the expert who discovers and uses it by interposing himself first between the worker and his work, then between the worker and his immediate peers, and finally between the worker and the organization. One result of this is a sad irony: In all of his writings, Taylor consistently speaks of making life better for the individual worker, yet the system he developed and advocated had the effect of enhancing an already burgeoning impersonality in the workplace. This impersonality was made not only acceptable but even desirable because of being cloaked with scientific repute.

Knowledge and Scientific Management   There are several ways in which the concept of "knowledge" is thought of and used in Scientific Management. For example, knowledge is seen as liberating, in the sense of the Enlightenment, for it frees one from ignorance and sloth. This is the basis for Taylor's railings against soldiering, a practice based in ignorance.

Knowledge is also objective. Although one may need an expert to understand this knowledge in much the same way as one needed a shaman to discover truth, there is an important difference between the two. Knowledge in the former has an extremely public character (which includes, in part, its testability by others) that is lacking in the latter. This is reflected in the following description by Taylor during his Congressional testimony:

> No set of men under scientific management claims that the evolution (of knowledge) has gone on enough years . . ., but they do claim that the 30 years of scientific investigation and study of the instruments that are in use in any trade, whatever it may be, have enabled those engaged in this study to collect at least good instruments and good methods, and we ask our workman before he starts kicking: "Try the methods and implements which we give you: we

---

[36]Perrow, p. 65; as he points out (quoting Bendix, p. 294), by 1928 a management journal would urge, without embarrassment, "Trust workers as human beings. Show your interest in their success and welfare."

know at least what we believe to be a good method for you to follow; and then after you have tried our way if you think of an implement or method better than ours, for God's sake come and tell us about it and then *we will make an experiment to prove whether your method or ours is the best,* and you, as a workman, will be allowed to participate in that experiment.[37]

It is, in fact, this combination of "public-ness" ("standing in the open") and objective-ness ("as an object separate from ourselves") that is the driving force for Taylor. It is the foundation, for example, of his sharp distinction between planning for work to be done and performing that work. (This is now so obvious that it is difficult to realize that eighty years ago this was a foreign, provocative distinction.) Intimately connected with the idea of planning for work to be done is the notion of functionalism in the directing of its performance. Taylor's was a much more extreme and detailed functionalism than most, but it does epitomize what came to be a common way of specializing to deal with the performance of work.

This specialization is well illustrated in what Taylor called the "Exception Principle":

Under [this principle] the manager should receive only condensed, summarized, and *invariably* comparative reports, covering, however, all of the elements entering into the management, and even these summaries should all be carefully gone over by an assistant before they reach the manager, and have all exceptions to the past averages or to the standards pointed out, both the especially good and especially bad exceptions, thus giving him in a few minutes a full view of the progress which is being made, or the reverse, and leaving him free to consider the broader lines of policy and to study the character and fitness of the important men under him.[38]

The essence of this principle is that one should only deal at one's expected level of abstraction. Knowledge, at its various states of generalization, is what one uses to control and manipulate both the material and the social world. Further, as Wren points out, authority for Taylor is based on knowledge and not on position. This "enabled a check on who was and who was not meeting his delegated responsibility."[39]

Combining this specialization with as clear a separation as possible between what he called "brain work and manual labor" results in an emphasis on method as the essence of knowledge. It is here in Scientific Management that one begins to see a presumed identity between knowledge, rationality, and instrumentality. This is, for instance, an identity that Taylor assumes when he says,

[37]Taylor, "Testimony," p. 199, emphasis added.
[38]Taylor, "Shop Management," pp. 126–27, emphasis in original.
[39]Wren, p. 127.

Both sides [workmen and bosses] must recognize as essential the substitution of exact scientific investigation and knowledge for the old individual judgment or opinion, either of the workman or the boss, *in all matters relating to the work done in the establishment.*[40]

And, finally, what Scientific Management captures is a spirit that was pervasive and would only begin to flag after the Second World War: a certainty that there are principles and laws that order our knowledge of the world.

Critics regularly charged Scientific Management with dehumanizing the workplace. Its emphasis, they argued, was only on time measurement and task analysis, and not on the human factors within the organizations they studied. Although there is some truth in this (particularly in the case of many of the self-styled efficiency experts who descended on businesses to sell their techniques), it is also true that Taylor had a deep and abiding concern about working conditions. A regular part of his many lectures, for instance, was a chastisement of managers who, blinded to their long-term advantage because of their desire for short-term gain, treated workmen cavalierly by refusing to invest in their development.

This sense of appropriate working conditions ("a man must have the proper tools") was spurred on by the early research being done in industrial psychology. In what came to be called "the human relations school," this vein of research (including the later Hawthorne studies at Westinghouse) was important to our second American writer, Chester Barnard, as well. Taylor's emphasis on cooperation finds full-blown theoretical justification with Barnard. However, before examining his work, it is useful to explore briefly the early work in human relations.

Hawthorne: The Beginnings of the Human Relations Movement

A number of those engaged in Scientific Management were also interested in industrial psychology. Thus, Frederick Taylor avidly followed the work of Elton Mayo, the pioneer in that field, while Lillian Gilbreth, in 1914, published *The Psychology of Management: The Function of the Mind in Determining, Teaching and Installing Methods of Least Waste,*[41] along with her numerous works on Scientific Management. The two areas were clearly complementary and tended to proceed apace.

By the mid-1920s, the "cult of efficiency" had died down, but the con-

---

[40]Taylor, "Testimony," p. 31, emphasis added.

[41]Lillian Gilbreth, *The Psychology of Management: The Function of the Mind in Determining, Teaching and Installing Methods of Least Waste* (New York: Sturgis & Walton, 1914; reissued in 1921 by Macmillan).

cern with making workers more productive had not. Much of the early effort in industrial psychology focused on issues such as worker fatigue. It was just such a study, sponsored by the National Academy of Science, that began the twelve-year odyssey known as the Hawthorne Experiments. These famous studies affected a number of different areas. One effect was on writers such as Chester Barnard, who intently watched the progress of the research, seeing it as a confirmation of his theoretical perspective on organizational behavior. A second effect was on those researchers and writers who concerned themselves primarily with the ways in which organizations define, limit, and therefore impede individual human growth. (The work of these writers, including Douglas McGregor and Chris Argyris, are examined in Chapter 8.) A third effect came from the systems model developed by F. J. Roethlisberger and William Dickson in interpreting the findings from the studies. (Systems theories are examined in Chapter 7.) Because of this influence on organization theory, it is useful to look briefly at the Hawthorne Experiments.

It is worth taking the time to read a good account of the experiments, for it is then possible to get a sense of the excitement of discovery that they engendered.[42] Much of what the studies speak to has since become commonplace, just as "Hawthorne effect" has become a part of the social science neophyte's language. The Hawthorne research has, over the past fifty years, been subjected to intense criticism.[43] Although this has usually been directed more at the ideology underpinning the explanations derived from the research, the methodology itself has also been attacked as insufficient.[44] It is useful to examine the theoretical model on which most of the research was based because, criticized as it has been, it is still a schema that has held considerable sway in the thinking about organizations.

When the experiments began at the Western Electric Company's Hawthorne Works outside of Chicago in the 1920s, the management of AT&T was interested in discovering the relationships between working conditions (initially, illumination) and productivity (as reflected in the incidence of monotony and fatigue). As Roethlisberger and Dickson point out:

[42]For one such account, see Wren, pp. 235–90. The "official" account of the experiments is F. J. Roethlisberger and William J. Dickson, *Management and the Worker* (Cambridge: Harvard University Press, 1939). Because so many accounts of the experiments are available, the details are not recounted here.

[43]See Loren Baretz, *The Servants of Power* (Westport, Conn.: Greenwood Press, 1974); Gibson Burrell and Gareth Morgan, *Sociological Paradigms and Organisational Analysis* (London: Heinemann, 1979), pp. 130–43; Alex Carey, "The Hawthorne Studies: A Radical Criticism," *American Sociological Review* 32:2(1967):403–16; Charles Hampden-Turner, *Radical Man* (Garden City, N.Y.: Doubleday Books, 1971); and Perrow, pp. 90–98.

[44]See Michael Argyle, "The Relay Assembly Test Room in Retrospect," *Occupational Psychology* 27(1953):98–103; H. A. Landsberger, *Hawthorne Revisited* (Ithaca, N.Y.: Cornell University Press, 1958); A. J. Sykes, "Economic Interest and the Hawthorne Studies: A Comment," *Human Relations* 18(1965):253–63.

It was anticipated that exact knowledge would be obtained about this relation by establishing an experimental situation in which the effect of variables like temperature, humidity, and hours of sleep could be measured separately from the effect of an experimentally imposed condition of work.[45]

The spirit of Frederick Taylor and Scientific Management is definite and clear in this statement of purpose, a spirit never lost, even as the purpose of experiments shifted from examining those variables to linking supervisory behavior with productivity, and later to connecting informal organization with group efficiency. Through all, the idea was to discover cause-and-effect relationships, first between physical conditions and efficiency, then later between intangibles (such as worker attitudes) and efficiency.

An initial series of manipulations of the workers' environment and conditions yielded little in the way of clear knowledge about these causal relationships. There was a large increase in output that appeared unrelated to these manipulations; for example, productivity continued to increase despite raising *or* lowering the amount of illumination. After considerable puzzlement, Elton Mayo, leader of the "Harvard Group" that was called in, noted:

> The most significant change that the Western Electric Company introduced into its "test room" bore only a casual relation to the experimental changes. What the Company actually did for the group was to reconstruct entirely its whole industrial situation.[46]

With this recognition, the focus of the research became employee morale. The causal link had been found: Higher morale (more satisfied workers) yielded higher productivity. The researchers saw that the difficulty with earlier models of the relationships between individuals and work (such as embodied in Taylor's Scientific Management) was that they failed to take adequate account of what the researchers came to call "the informal organization" and "the logic of sentiments":

> Sometimes attempts to make employees more efficient unwittingly deprives them of those very things which give meaning and significance to their work. Their established routines of work, their cultural traditions of craftsmanship, their personal interrelations—all these are at the mercy of "logical" innovations. (p. 577)

In order to understand employee satisfaction, what was required was a

---

[45]Roethlisberger and Dickson, p. 3; in this section, all page references in parentheses are to this earlier cited source; emphasis is in the original unless otherwise noted.

[46]Elton Mayo, *The Human Problems of an Industrial Civilization* (New York: Macmillan, 1973), p. 73; cited in Wren, p. 278.

new theoretical model in which the industrial organization is viewed as a social system: "By 'system' is meant something which must be considered as a whole because each part bears a relation of interdependence to every other part" (p. 557). This is a notion that came to the Harvard Group from Vilfredo Pareto (through L. J. Henderson, who is cited at this point in the official account).[47] Its real significance is that the group adopted almost totally Pareto's ideas regarding the necessity of maintaining equilibrium. These created, in the Hawthorne model, a dichotomous view of the world such that any single thing (or feeling or action) is judged as contributing either to the maintenance of equilibrium or to the initiation (or continuance) of disequilibrium. This and the other dichotomies that resulted from this view tend to give a positive or negative cast to whatever they describe. For example, here are some of the pairs that are used throughout *Management and the Worker*:

equilibrium	disequilibrium
fact	sentiment
logic of efficiency	logic of sentiment
satisfaction	dissatisfaction
visible authority	invisible authority
personal authority	impersonal authority
formal organization	informal organization
manifest content	latent content
actual output	reported output

The ordering of these terms is not intended to suggest that all items in the left column foster equilibrium, nor that those in the right encourage disequilibrium. There is, however, a tendency to read these connotations in the terms, because of the way in which they are used in the Roethlisberger and Dickson book. This is softened somewhat by a sense, reflected in the previous quotation, that the issue is more one of balance than of choice between two extremes. This is not developed, however, to any clear extent.

One can see the difficulty in the conclusions that were drawn about how to interpret employee complaints. In order to investigate "employee morale," numerous interviews were conducted. The researchers found that, in their judgments, some things that were being complained of did not "objectively warrant" complaint. Instead, the complaints being made were often about something else; that is, they appeared (to the researchers) to be about personal feelings and situations, rather than about objective situations:

[47]See L. J. Henderson, *Pareto's General Sociology* (Cambridge, Mass.: Harvard University Press, 1935); and Vilfredo Pareto, *The Mind and Society,* Andrew Bongiorno and Arthur Livingstone, trans., 4 vols. (New York: Harcourt Brace Jovanovich, 1935).

Although [these complaints] gave a picture of how the employees felt about such matters [as plant conditions], they did not provide any immediate illumination as to why the employees felt as they did. (p. 266)

It is instructive to present the researchers' findings on this point (p. 326):

In order to fit their findings into a coherent whole, the investigators had to evolve a new way of thinking about the worker and those things about which he complained. Their conclusion emerged in terms of a conceptual scheme for the interpretation of employee complaints, which can be stated as follows:

- the source of most employee complaints cannot be confined to some one single cause, and the dissatisfaction of the worker, in most cases, is the general effect of a complex situation;

- the analysis of complex situations requires an understanding of the nature of the equilibrium or disequilibrium and the nature of the interferences;

- the interferences which occur in industry can come from changes in the physical environment, from changes in the social environment at work, or from changes outside the immediate working environment, and the "unbalances" which issue from such interferences may be organic (changes in the bloodstream), or mental (obsessive preoccupations which make it difficult to attend to work), or both;

- therefore, to cloak industrial problems under such general categories as "fatigue," "monotony," and "supervision" is sometimes to fail to discriminate among the different kinds of interferences involved, as well as among the different kinds of disequilibrium;

- and if the different interferences and different types of disequilibrium are not the same ill in every instance, they are not susceptible to the same kind of remedy.

From this one can easily draw both the feeling of sharp dichotomies and a suggestion toward balance between two extremes; it is also clear that the emphasis is on separation into categories. This is reinforced by the conceptual scheme depicted in Figure 5.1, reproduced from *Management and the Worker*. Here the worker is (passively) acted on by conceptually discrete "forces" such as "social demands." Further, these "forces" are by and large defined by researchers, using *their* interpretations of the answers to questions they asked. The thrust of these interpretations is clear: The dissatisfied individual (the source of the complaint) is to be manipulated by alterations in his or her position or status; this is achieved by manipulation, to the extent possible, of the social organization, etc. In addition, this schema enables one to defuse a complaint by attributing a stated dissatisfaction to a status or position held:

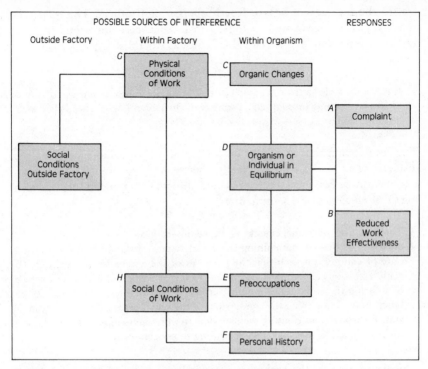

Figure 5.1　*Scheme for Interpreting Complaints and Reduced Work Effectiveness*
Source: F. J. Roethlisberger and William J. Dickson, *Management and the Worker* (Cambridge: Harvard University Press, 1939), p. 275.

For example, the meaning of many employee complaints about plant conditions could be understood only when they were interpreted in the light of the employee's position in the social organization of the company. More than any other aspect of the work situation, physical plant conditions differentiated supervisory and office groups from shop groups. Plant conditions, in other words, served to define an individual's position in the social organization of the company. Inasmuch as the lower status of the shop employee was indicated by the kind of plant conditions he enjoyed, he may have been somewhat more conscious of them. This interpretation would account for the fact that shop employees commented a great deal about plant conditions whereas the supervisors who were interviewed mentioned them relatively little. (p. 376)

Essentially, people are seen as socially motivated and controlled. Any increase in morale (and therefore in productivity) is, thus, necessarily related to change in the human and social conditions, not the physical environment or the material condition.

This development of the work organization as a social system was central to the message of Mayo, Roethlisberger, and others. The issue was that man is not motivated by logic and fact (at least not primarily), but rather by sentiment and social value. Thus, as Roethlisberger and Dickson put it:

> It is not possible to treat . . . material goods, physical events, wages, and hours of work as things in themselves, subject to their own laws. Instead they must be integrated as carriers of social value. (p. 374)

The equilibrium that one searches for is not only a balance between the discrete parts of the system but also between the technical and human organizations, between the formal and informal organizations, between logics of efficiency and sentiments:

> The function of management, as stated in its most general terms, can be described as that of maintaining the social system of the industrial plant in a state of equilibrium such that the purposes of the enterprise are realized. To achieve this objective, management has two major functions: (1) the function of securing the common economic purpose of the total enterprise; and (2) the function of maintaining the equilibrium of the social organization so that individuals through contributing their services to this common purpose obtain personal satisfaction that makes them willing to cooperate. (p. 569)

This distinction, as the authors acknowledge, is similar to that developed by Chester Barnard.

The results of the Hawthorne studies demanded a new combination of managerial skills: diagnostic (to understand human behavior) and interpersonal (to communicate, counsel, motivate, and lead), as well as (but more important than) technical skills. "Technical skills alone were not enough to cope with the man discovered at the Hawthorne Works."[48] It required a Chester Barnard to put together a theoretical description sufficient to house this new man.

Chester Barnard

> People are tractable, docile, gullible, uncritical—and wanting to be led. But far more than this is deeply true of them. They want to feel united, tied, bound to something, some cause, bigger than they, commanding them yet worthy of them, summoning them to significance in living.[49]

Such is the summary that Reinhard Bendix provides of Elton Mayo's and

---

[48]Wren, p. 290.
[49]Perrow, p. 65, quoting Bendix, p. 296.

Chester Barnard's view of human nature. And people, Barnard would argue, are "summoned to significance in living" by participating in organizational life. This is the substance of *The Functions of the Executive*,[50] the first American attempt at an academic, intellectual structure for understanding organizations.

Born in 1886 in Malden, Massachusetts, Barnard offers the picture of poor boy made good. He completed Harvard (on a scholarship) in just three years. Almost completed, that is, because he never actually received the degree, having neglected to take a laboratory science, despite otherwise completing his coursework with honors. His first job, in 1909, was with the Statistical Department of the American Telephone and Telegraph system; he became president of New Jersey Bell in 1927.

Barnard was infatuated with organizations. He spent much of his life studying them; he also spent much of his life working actively in them. As Wren describes it,

> . . . he helped David Lilienthal establish the policies of the Atomic Energy Commission, he served the New Jersey Reformatory, the United Service Organization (president for three years), the Rockefeller Foundation (president for four years), and was president of the Bach Society of New Jersey. Barnard was a self-made scholar who applied the theories of Vilfredo Pareto (whom he read in the original French edition), Kurt Lewin, Max Weber (whom he read in the original German edition), and the philosophy of Alfred North Whitehead in the first in-depth analysis of organizations as cooperative systems. By the time of his death in 1961, this Harvard "drop-out" had earned a place in history as a management scholar.[51]

"The Functions of the Executive"

In November and December 1937, Barnard gave a series of eight lectures at the Lowell Institute in Boston. He expanded these lectures the following year, publishing them (under the imprimatur of Harvard University) as *The Functions of the Executive*. Having read considerably, he found that the work describing organizations showed little appreciation for the processes of coordination and decision making, which he himself found central to understanding organizational life. And, as he points out in his preface:

> More important, there was lacking [in that literature] much recognition of formal organization as a most important characteristic of social life, and as being

[50]Chester Barnard, *The Functions of the Executive* (Cambridge: Harvard University Press, 1968, first published in 1938); in this section, all page references in parentheses are to this source; emphasis is in the original unless otherwise noted.
[51]Wren, pp. 310–311.

the principal structural aspect of society itself. Mores, folkways, political structures, institutions, attitudes, motives, propensities, instincts, were discussed *in extensio* but the bridge between the generalizations of social study on the one hand and the action of masses to which they related on the other were not included, I thought. (p. xxix)

Barnard intended for the theoretical framework described in *Functions* to become this bridge. The book concerns itself almost exclusively with the process by which the individual relates to (and is affected by) the organization. The core of this process is cooperation; hence, an organization is "a system of consciously coordinated personal activities or forces" (p. 72). This leads Barnard to a picture of organizational life that is at odds with then-common notions. Instead of an emphasis on structure, such as was the case with Taylor, for instance, an organization in Barnard's view is a "construct," "a field of personal 'forces,' just as an electromagnetic field is a field of electronic or magnetic forces" (p. 75). As such, the organization stretches beyond the traditional boundaries to include not only the employees of the firm, but the customers and suppliers as well. "Member of the organization" is a phrase he uses guardedly; the issue for him is not inclusion (i.e., membership) but contribution. Organizations require people; without them, an organization does not exist. To maintain an organization requires cooperation between people, a cooperation that "means self-abnegation, the surrender of control of personal conduct, the depersonalization of personal action" (p. 84).

For Weber and Taylor, each in his own way, the "glue" that holds organizations together is authority, especially hierarchical authority. Barnard, on the other hand, sees cooperation as the "cohesion of effort":

> Activities cannot be coordinated unless there is first the disposition to make a personal act a contribution to an impersonal system of acts, one in which the individual gives up personal control of what he does. (p. 84)

Thus, authority lies only in the "giving up of personal control": "If a directive communication is accepted by one to whom it is addressed, its authority for him is confirmed or established" (p. 163). And further:

> In the last analysis the authority fails because the individuals in sufficient numbers regard the burden involved in accepting necessary orders as changing the balance of advantage against their interest, and they withdraw or withhold the indispensable contributions. (p. 165)

In order to explore Barnard's theory of organizational life, it is useful to look at three areas: the organization as a system, formal and informal organizations, and the role of the executive.

The Organization as a System

The opinion that governs in this book is that when, for example, the efforts of five men become coordinated in a system, that is, an organization, there is created something new in the world that is more or less than or different in quantity and quality from anything present in the sum of the efforts of the five men. (p. 79)

Chester Barnard was intrigued with the experiments at the Hawthorne Works that were then rediscovering human motivation. At the same time, he found this work incomplete insofar as it offered no true theory of organization. And the then-dominant theories about organizations, notably those of Frederick Taylor and Henri Fayol,[52] Barnard found to be incomplete as well. Although Taylor and Fayol were at first seen as competing or contrasting with one another, the work of these two "fountainheads of management thought," as they have been called, was in fact highly complementary, insofar as both emphasized hierarchical order, planning, and reliance on "management principles."

The missing elements in these theoretical characterizations, according to Barnard, arose because their authors neglected to recognize that organizations are cooperative systems that coordinate the effort of individuals toward a purpose:

An organization comes into being when (1) there are persons able to communicate with each other (2) who are willing to contribute action (3) to accomplish a common purpose. (p. 82)

Purpose bounds and directs cooperative activity, but it "does not incite cooperative activity unless it is accepted by those whose efforts will constitute the organization" (p. 86). There is an important distinction for Barnard between organizational purpose and individual motive. It is, he says, as though each person in the organization has a dual personality, one organizational and the other individual:

Individual motive is necessarily an internal, personal, subjective thing; common purpose is necessarily an external, impersonal, objective thing even though the individual interpretation of it is subjective. (p. 89)

---

[52]The work of the French manager-engineer Henri Fayol did not become fully accessible in the United States until after a 1949 English translation of his work was published as Henri Fayol, *General and Industrial Management,* Constance Storrs, trans. (London: Sir Isaac Pitman and Sons, 1949). However, an influential paper, "The Administrative Theory of the State," was translated and published in 1937 in Luther Gulick and Lyndall Urwick, eds. *Papers on the Science of Administration* (New York: Institute of Public Administration, 1937), pp. 99–114. See Chapter 6.

An organization, then, is a collection of actions focused toward a purpose. For an organization to sustain itself, an equilibrium must be maintained: If the organization does not accomplish its purpose, it disintegrates; if it accomplishes its purpose, it goes out of business. This necessitates a constant reassessing and balancing that results in "dynamic equilibrium."[53] By using this term, Barnard emphasizes the interaction between the organization and its environment.

The organization comprises, for Barnard, all those whose cooperative actions are involved in an ongoing exchange. "Exchange" is fundamental: "An organization is a system of cooperative human activities the functions of which are (1) the creation, (2) the transformation, and (3) the exchange of utilities" (p. 240). The organization can then be analyzed as an interweaving of economies (pp. 240–242):

- The material economy—the "physical things and forces" that are *both* assigned as utility and controlled by the organization.

- The social economy—the set of relationships between the organization and other organizations and individuals not cooperatively connected to it.

- The individual economy—the interplay of the "power of the individual to do work" and the "ascribed utilities" of his "material and social satisfactions."

- The organization economy—the collection of "the utilities assigned by *it* to (1) the physical material it controls; (2) the social relations it controls; and (3) the personal activities it coordinates."

Each of the first three can be measured; each can be assessed in at least crude monetary terms. But the "organization economy," Barnard argues, can only be assessed "in terms of success or failure," because it either maintains an equilibrium or it does not. This equilibrium "requires that [the organization] shall command and exchange sufficient of the utilities of various kinds so that it is able in turn to command and exchange the personal services of which it is constituted" (p. 244). The other three economies exist only to support the organizational economy, because the latter enables the organization to maintain its dynamic equilibrium:

> The only measure of this economy is the survival of the organization. If it grows it is clearly efficient, if it is contracting it is doubtfully efficient, and it may in the end prove to have been during the period of contraction inefficient. (p. 252)

[53]This term is actually a later characterization by Barnard. See "Concepts of Organization" in Chester Barnard, *Organization and Management* (Cambridge: Harvard University Press, 1948), p. 133.

And finally: "Exchange is the distributive factor; coordination is the creative factor" (p. 254).

The organization thus begins as a cooperative enterprise, coordinated toward a purpose. It becomes a coordinated enterprise with the purpose not only of survival but of growth. For this to occur and to continue requires what Barnard calls "the executive process":

> What is required is the sense of things as a whole, the persistent subordination of parts to the total, the discrimination from the broadest standpoint of the strategic factors from among all types of factors. (p. 256)

Before examing this executive function, it is necessary to stand back for a moment and examine the concept of "organization" that Barnard has developed. One significant aspect of this concept as he uses it is that it constitutes the "formal" as distinguished from the "informal" organization.

The Formal and Informal Organization

The distinction between formal and informal organization is now commonplace, but when Chester Barnard was writing *The Functions of the Executive* it was a new idea, a new analytic tool. And it was a distinction that was receiving empirical backing and intellectual credence from the Hawthorne experiments. There, in the Bank Wiring Room for instance, the group acted through informal agreements and decisions, rather than through the formal structure, to maintain the rate and quantity of work.

The distinction was a relatively clear one for Barnard: Formal organization comprises the *consciously coordinated* activities of people; informal organization comprises the unconscious group feelings, passions, and activities of those same individuals. The latter is " . . . indefinite and rather structureless, and has no definite subdivision. It may be regarded as a shapeless mass of quite varied densities" (p. 115). Formal organization, on the other hand, with its primary characteristic of being consciously coordinated, is marked by purposefulness. It is cooperation toward an end.

The informal precedes the formal yet it is of short duration without the latter: "It is an observable fact that men are universally active, and that they seek objects of activity" (p. 117). With "objects of activity" come formal organization. By no means, however, does informal organization disappear. In order for the formalized structures and relationships to be maintained, the informal is essential. Barnard sees three ways in which it supports formal organization. The paramount one is the maintenance and facilitation of communication. This is, specifically,

The communication of intangible facts, opinions, suggestions, suspicions, that cannot pass through formal channels without raising issues calling for discussion, without dissipating dignity and objective authority. (p. 225)

Barnard makes a distinction between communication in the informal organization, on the one hand, and communication techniques in the formal organization, on the other. The former involves the more generalized, undifferentiated ways that people use to structure their interactions with one another:

The possibility of accomplishing a common purpose and the existence of persons whose desires might constitute motives for contributing toward such a common purpose are the opposite poles of the system of cooperative effort. The process by which these potentialities become dynamic is that of communication. (p. 89)

In the informal organization, communication is diffuse, because it is often "The ability to understand without words, not merely the situation or conditions, but the *intentions*" (p. 90). Other than citing this central role, Barnard spends little time on communication as such. His real interest is in the *techniques* of communication. These are the responsibility of the executive within the formal organization and speak directly to the ways in which communication is manipulated, controlled, and directed towards the purposes of that organization.

A second function of the informal within the formal is the "maintenance of cohesiveness . . . through regulating the willingness to serve and the stability of objective authority" (p. 122). For Barnard, there is an essential "fiction of superior authority." The belief that authority comes from above, from the "general to the particular," is a fiction that

merely establishes a presumption among individuals in favor of acceptability of orders from superiors, enabling them to avoid making issues of such orders without incurring a sense of personal subserviency or loss of personal or individual status with their fellows. (p. 170)

Barnard sees three categories of orders that one receives. There are those that will not be followed because they are clearly unacceptable. There are those that are just barely acceptable or unacceptable. Finally, there are those orders that are unquestionably acceptable because they lie in the "zone of indifference":

The person affected will accept orders lying within this zone and is relatively indifferent as to what the order is so far as the question of authority is concerned. (p. 169)

Finally, the "fiction of authority" is maintained by the communication within the informal organization insofar as the latter encourages cohesiveness and stability. This enables authority to operate within the formal organization in such a manner as to allow a person to take actions that might otherwise be avoided:

> Most persons are disposed to grant authority because they dislike the personal responsibility which they otherwise accept. . . . The practical difficulties lie in the reluctance [of individuals] to take responsibility for their own actions in the organization. (pp. 170–71)

The third function of the informal organization within the formal is "the maintenance of the feeling of personal integrity, of self respect, of independent choice" (p. 122). These are feelings to which the formal organization must remain oblivious if it is to maintain what Barnard sees as its necessary impersonality. Through the informal organization, the individual's attitudes are reinforced and shaped. Perhaps most important, because actions within the informal organization are not dominated by the necessary impersonality that is characteristic of formal organization, "interactions are [only] apparently characterized by choice." This is a necessary buttress against "certain effects of formal organizations which tend to disintegrate the personality" (p. 122).

Personal choice, while nurtured by the informal organization, can at the same time be at the base of "false and abortive effort":

> Often, as I see it, action is based on an assumption that individuals have a power of choice which is not, I think, present. Hence, the failure of individuals to conform is erroneously ascribed to deliberate opposition when they *cannot* conform. (p. 15)

This brings forward the role of the executive process in the formal organization. The executive affects the choices made by the individuals through "Altering the conditions of behavior, including a conditioning of the individual by training, by the inculcation of attitudes, by the construction of incentives" (p. 15).

The Role of the Executive

An organization is a set of consciously coordinated activities directed toward a purpose. For the organization to be maintained over time requires that certain functions be performed, which Barnard terms the "executive functions":

- The maintenance of organizational communication,

- The securing of essential services from individuals, and

- The formulation of purpose and objectives.

These functions are performed by executives, though they do not necessarily constitute all the work that executives do. As Barnard puts it, "Executive work is not that *of* the organization, but is the specialized work of *maintaining* the organization in operation" (p. 215).

The distinction is important in Barnard's conception of organizational life. The executive functions are in the same relationship to the organization as

> ... those of the nervous system, including the brain, [are] in relation to the rest of the body. It exists to maintain the bodily system by directing those actions which are necessary more effectively to adjust to the environment, but it can hardly be said to manage the body, a large part of whose functions are independent of it and upon which it in turn depends. (p. 217)

The executive functions, in order to adjust the organization to the environment, are directed at making organizational (rather than personal or individual) decisions. These have several characteristics. First, they are impersonal and, as such, may be delegated. In fact, "it may be said that often responsibility for an organization decision is not a personal responsibility until assigned" (p. 185). Second, these decisions, being of an essentially logical character, are used to adapt means to ends. They involve "logical processes, not as rationalizations after decision but as processes of decision" (p. 186).

The first executive function is the molding and shaping of communication within the organization through the use of controlling and directing techniques. Communication is the currency of the organization for Barnard, which requires attention to two regularly alternating "strategic factors" or phases: the scheme of the organization and its personnel. The first deals with the location and "the geographic, temporal, social, and functional specializations of unit and group organization" (pp. 218–19), all of which act as significant limiters on communication. The other speaks to the recruiting of appropriate individuals and "the development of inducements, incentives, persuasion and objective authority" (p. 219) that will make for effective services.

The second executive function is to secure essential services from individuals once they have agreed to "contribute" to the organization. Best summarized as "the maintenance of morale, the maintenance of the scheme of inducements, the maintenance of schemes of deterrents, supervision and control, inspection, education and training" (p. 231), this brings into play what Barnard terms "the economy of incentives," the base of which is persuasion.

Persuasion, in Barnard's terms, ranges from the "rationalizing of opportunity" (i.e., creating the idea that something is in one's best interests) to "inculcating motives." Force, propaganda, and education and training are essential tools in this process. They are necessary because the individual "Regardless of his history or his obligations ... must be induced to cooperate or there can be no cooperation" (p. 139). If the executive fails here, the organization itself will fail. The control of incentives is one-sided and in the hands of the executive. Because of the difficulty of putting together, for each individual, the exact proportion of objective incentives (e.g., material and nonmaterial inducements, opportunities for participation, etc.),

> the only alternative then available is to change the state of mind, or attitudes, or motives, so that the available objective incentives can become effective. (p. 141)

This, in turn, relates to the third general executive function, that of formulating purposes and objectives:

> ... an objective purpose that can serve as the basis for a cooperative system is one that is *believed* by the contributor ... to be the determined purpose of the organization. The inculcation of belief in the real existence of a common purpose is an essential executive function. (p. 87)

At the same time, the specification of purpose and objectives is not unitary. Rather, Barnard argues, the specification moves from the general executive to the department head to the division head and so on "until finally purpose is merely jobs, specific groups, definite men, definite times, accomplished results" (p. 232). Yet the movement is never smooth. Purpose and objective are always checked, altered, refined and modified as " ... back and forth, up and down, the communications pass, reporting obstacles, difficulties, impossibilities, accomplishments, redefining, modifying purpose level after level" (p. 232). Thus, like the "fiction of authority,"

> Responsibility for abstract, generalizing, prospective, long-run decision is delegated *up* the line, [and] responsibility for definition, action, remains always at the base where the authority for effort resides. (pp. 232–33)

These three functions of the executive encompass only the *technical* aspects of the leadership implicit in executive work. For Barnard, there is another side to leadership, one which is the aspect of individual superiority in determination, persistence, endurance, courage; that which determines the *quality* of action; which often is most inferred from what is *not* done, from abstention; which commands respect, reverence. It is the aspect of leadership we commonly imply in the word "responsibility," the quality which gives dependability and determination to human conduct, and foresight and ideality to purpose. (p. 280)

This is the "moral factor" in organization, that which justifies the existence of the organization and the propriety of the actions taken in its name. Not only do executive positions, by their very nature, both "imply a complex morality and require a high capacity of responsibility," they also require "the faculty for *creating* morals for others" (pp. 272, 277).

This "creative morality," as Barnard calls it, is the "essence of leadership" and the "highest test of executive responsibility." Without it, those in the organization will be unable to coalesce around the proper things to be done in the name of the organization. By means of this leadership function, the organization itself becomes a moral force, the ultimate measure of what is right. The essence of Barnard's theoretical statement about the morality of organizational life is best captured in one of the few examples from real organizational life that he provides in his book:

> I recall a telephone operator on duty at a lonely place from which she could see in the distance the house in which her mother lay bedridden. Her life was spent in taking care of her mother and in maintaining that home for her. To do so, she chose employment in that particular position, against other inclinations. Yet she stayed at her switchboard while she watched the house burn down. No code, public or organizational, that has any general validity under such circumstances governed her conduct, and she certainly violated some such codes, as well as some of her own. Nevertheless, she showed extraordinary "moral courage," we would say, in conforming to a code of her organization—the *moral* necessity of uninterrupted service. This was high responsibility as respects that code.[54] (p. 269)

The organization cannot remain in existence without "enduring cooperation," which is "the catalyst by which the living system of human efforts" can continue the constant, necessary interchange of energies and satisfactions. "Cooperation, not leadership, is the creative process; but leadership is the indispensable fulminator of its forces" (p. 259).

The Framework for Public Administration

The perspectives presented by Weber, Taylor, and Barnard have formed the principal basis for theoretical writing and practical thinking about

---

[54]Barnard points out in a footnote: "The mother was rescued."

organizations over the last fifty years. The values implicit and the concepts explicit in these descriptions create a backdrop for the ways in which organizations have been viewed in everyday life. The perspectives do not offer a unitary vision; however, they do cohere around some themes.[55] The results are rich in insight, but limited in their range of subject. The picture they develop focuses almost exclusively on two arenas of the public administration framework, the intra-organizational and the organization-to-individual.

The theoretical perspectives described in this chapter tend to emphasize structural relationships that are stabilized by authority in an impersonal framework of incentives. Herein lies their richness: Weber highlights the efficiency of the rationalizing aspects of modern organizations. Taylor takes this one step further by emphasizing the necessary role of objective knowledge in defining the means for achieving organizational objectives. Barnard combines these, seeing the potential of the modern organization as a moral force for societal purposes.

The limitations of this picture, however, are also evident. Barnard's references to the interactions of organization and its environment notwithstanding, the perspectives discussed above treat organizations as self-sufficient entities. As such, they illuminate little of the inter-organizational arena of public administration.

A second limitation is that each writer assumes that hierarchy is *the* efficient (and necessary) organizing mode. Their views on hierarchy are based on two sets of related assumptions:

- Power, knowledge, and moral legitimacy are lodged at the top of the hierarchical pyramid.

- Questions of fact and value, knowledge and sentiment, rational and nonrational action are all dichotomized. To do so is a choice, particularly for Taylor and Barnard, that has consequences for the ways in which the world (for them) is organized.

The consequences of this view of hierarchy are to limit organizational analysis in a variety of ways. In terms of the three organizational arenas discussed in Part I, the *inter-organizational* is largely excluded from analysis, since inter-organizational relations are seldom hierarchical. Rather, they frequently involve relations in which each organization has a more-or-less independent source of power. The result is that inter-organizational relations tend to be mediated by processes of exchange and bargaining rather than by the imposition of hierarchical authority. With

---

[55]Weber's work as a whole clearly goes beyond what is discussed below. However, it can be reasonably argued, his bureaucratic ideal type (particularly to the extent it has been taken by others as a normative model) is illuminating in many of the same ways that the works of Taylor and Barnard are. For this reason, the discussion of Weber here is limited to that ideal type.

respect to the *intra-organizational* arena, the notion of hierarchy is often incapable of explaining complex interactions among several organizational levels or subgroups. Here, too, these relationships are often mediated by market-like processes of bargaining and mutual adjustment, rather than solely through hierarchical control. Finally, for the *organization-to-individual* arena, the *a priori* legitimacy of hierarchy, coupled with its impersonality, subordinates the interests and motives of individuals, both those within and those outside the organization, to the rational imperatives of the organization.

The third limitation is that the organization-to-individual arena is unidirectional. All three writers emphasize that authority and power flow from the organization to the individual and, within the organization, from the top downward. Especially for Taylor and Barnard, this is reflected in the various dichotomies between fact and value, knowledge and sentiment, and rational and nonrational action. For example, the individual *qua* individual in the organization is seen as motivated mainly by sentiment and emotion. This plays out in Taylor's "soldiering" and Barnard's "informal organization."[56] In both cases, the individual is assumed to be normatively and objectively submerged in the organization, indistinguishable from his neighbor.

The consequences of these limitations become clear when one looks at these perspectives in terms of the normative vectors of public administration.

Efficiency and Effectiveness

Efficiency is clearly the preeminent normative force in this baseline view. *The* object of organizing is the efficient use of resources toward some purpose: Efficiency is the explicit *raison d'etre* of the organization for Weber, Taylor, and Barnard. The motive force of rationalizing that creates bureaucracy is, for Weber, the efficient use of resources in pursuit of effective legal domination. With Taylor, efficiency is the measure of "the one best way." It is a simple algorithm transforming energy expended into products created. For Barnard, efficiency takes on a broader meaning: "The efficiency of cooperation . . . depends upon what it secures and produces on the one hand, and how it distributes its resources and how it changes motives on the other."[57]

Barnard also creates what has come to be a commonplace distinction between efficiency and effectiveness. The first speaks exclusively to the exchange of resources, while the second speaks to the attainment of specified ends. The way in which both are obtained is through the logic of instrumental rationality. For all three writers, this logic sweeps aside that

---

[56]This view of the world was reinforced strongly by the Hawthorne work.
[57]Barnard, *Functions* p. 59.

which is not directly seen as capable of being manipulated for a purpose. For this reason, given their narrow (and hierarchical) construction of this logic, Taylor and Barnard especially are forced to the position of insisting on an opposition of fact and sentiment. This can be seen very clearly in Taylor, with his insistence both on measurement as the basis of knowledge and on the role of knowledge as the arbiter of proper action. This leads to the conclusion that those who are "better fitted" (by being scientifically trained) should help guide and rationalize the behavior of those less suited to understanding the real nature of the work at hand.

The purpose of organizing is to rationalize the behavior of actors toward some end. Basic to this is specialization in term of both the types of work performed and the methods by which that work is done. This can be seen in Taylor's ideas on the need for planning departments (types of work) and his scientific studies of work (methods). This is also what Barnard does through his specification of the "executive functions," which delineate the boundaries of executive work and responsibility. Both of these require the creation of boundaries (maintained, Weber would argue, by impersonal rules) between different work responsibilities. Such boundaries are independent of the particular people who are involved in and affected by the organization.

Finally, the emphasis on efficiency leads ultimately to the belief that organizationally established, impersonal authority is normatively superior to personal authority. In addition, knowledge produced (or at least sanctioned) by the organization is the only objective knowledge. This objective knowledge is used, in a means-to-ends fashion, to support the purposes and objectives of the organization. Impersonality in applying this knowledge must be maintained if the organization is to remain in "dynamic equilibrium," to use Barnard's term.[58] The application of objective knowledge leaves public administration with two unresolved questions: How are organizational purposes and objectives to be defined, and who is to determine the legitimate meaning and boundaries of impersonal knowledge and action?

Rights and the Adequacy of Process

To talk of rights is to speak of rules, at least in the organizational settings described in the baseline perspective. Any Enlightenment conception

---

[58]This is somewhat but not wholly an oversimplification. To investigate it further requires recognition and exploration of the dominant empiricism/positivism that was becoming imbedded in American society at the time that Weber, Taylor, and Barnard were writing. In a similar fashion, the emphasis on efficiency should not be surprising, given the historical context (as was pointed out in the discussions of Weber and Taylor, in particular, above). The issue here is that (a) these writings contributed to the notion, still held now in many quarters, that efficiency *should* be the dominant (if not the only) value by which to judge organizational action, and (b) these writings, by focusing so extensively on efficiency, are limited in their utility in regard to seeing other relevant aspects of organizational life.

of natural rights is set aside, replaced by one of organizationally defined, rule-encompassed rights. It is not so much that the former is denied, rather that it is not seen as relevant. As a consequence, "rights" are treated solely as procedural matters.[59] In mirror-like fashion, responsibility is by and large narrowly construed as accountability. This is clear in both Weber's discussion of bureaucracy and Taylor's notion of functional foremanship. In the case of Barnard, it is somewhat more complex.

For Barnard, responsibility means being governed by moral codes. In the case of the executive, as one moves higher in the organization, situations grow more complex, thereby increasing the likelihood of conflict between organizational decisions and individual codes. Resolving disputes requires of the executive a "complex morality" in which "organization codes" are added to his personal, individual code. Barnard is quite explicit on this point: "The *organization* codes to which he should conform are . . .," proceeding to list nine codes that are organization based, including "the code that is suggested in the phrase 'the good of the organization as a whole.'"[60] All is well so long as each code, organization and personal, is congruent with every other.[61] When there is a conflict, adroitness is required on the part of the executive, because:

> . . . these conflicts can only be resolved by one of two methods: either to analyze further the pertinent environment with a view to a more accurate determination of the strategic factor of the situation, which may lead to the discovery of that "correct" action which violates no codes; or to adopt a new detailed purpose consistent with general objectives, that is, the more general purposes.[62]

This leaves Barnard with a crude "survival of the fittest" in which those who continue as executives are only those who are able to negotiate between conflicting codes by redefining either the organization's purposes or its environment. There is no question for Barnard that the struggle to resolve the conflict must ultimately benefit the organization, rather than the individuals in it. When organizational purpose and individual motive clash, there is only one survivor.

This robust picture ties back into accountability through the way in which Barnard ultimately grounds organizational responsibility. The individual who finally carries out the organizationally directed action is the

---

[59]Again, it is important to see this in its context. The shift of the discussion about rights to encompass primarily procedural issues was taking place across numerous areas of social life at the time these theorists were writing. The significance of the work described here lies in the way in which it supports this larger trend and thereby limits the possibility of seeking alternatives.

[60]Barnard, *Functions*, p. 273, emphasis in the original.

[61]Barnard does not deal with the possibility that the organization codes can be incongruent with one another, a situation that public administrators face with regularity.

[62]Ibid., p. 276.

one to be held as primarily responsible. Just as authority comes from the bottom up rather than the top down, responsibility lies with those who carry out decisions, not solely with those who make them. This results in a map of accountability that links the executive function of making a decision with the nonexecutive function of carrying out the desired action. Unfortunately, although this clarifies the two end points of the chain, what is left ambiguous are the decision points in between: What is my responsibility as a somewhere-down-in-the-organization supervisor? How far does my culpability extend for the acts of my crew?[63]

The normative concern with the adequacy of process revolves around questions of how individuals are treated when they are affected by actions taken in the name of an organization. One part of this concern is about the treatment of an organization's members, while another part is about the treatment of its clients. The first aspect was discussed above; the emphasis on impersonality, on organizational purpose over individual motive, on rule-bound behavior all entail a clear separation between organization and individual personality. They also support Weber's characterization of "legal domination."

The second aspect, the manner in which the organization treats its clients, must be extrapolated, since the interests of Weber, Taylor, and Barnard are generally restricted to activities within the organization. This is not difficult to do, because the same instrumental logic would hold, making the organizational perception of purpose (and, therefore, the perception of the presenting problem) dominant over any individually formulated statement. This is further complicated by the knowledge/sentiment dichotomy, particularly in both Taylor's and Barnard's work: Organizations define knowledge; individuals embody sentiment. Because of this, one sees Taylor's presumption that individuals misperceive their own interests (and, hence, engage in systematic soldiering) and Barnard's insistence that the only available alternative to adapting organizational purpose to individual motive is to change the individual's perception of that motive.[64]

Representation and the Control of Discretion

Although Weber, Taylor, and Barnard are silent on the normative vector of representation and the control of discretion, there are clear implications for how discretion is (and should be) controlled. In Weber's discussion of the characteristics of bureaucracy, for example, he finds a

---

[63]Barnard does not add any clarity when he tells us that "often responsibility for an organization decision is not a personal responsibility until assigned." Ibid., p. 185.

[64]All of which was again strongly supported by the initial interpretations of the Hawthorne work.

distinct separation between a higher and lower office: The former, even while supervising the latter, cannot take over its activities. Specialization of work, combined with the rule-binding aspects of hierarchy, insists on a clear separation between the two and provides a limit on discretion.

Taylor, on the other hand, emphasizes relieving the worker of all discretion in the name of efficient procedure. He objects to the way the man chooses to shovel the ore because it is not efficient: "There is one right way of forcing the shovel down into materials of this sort, and many wrong ways."[65] He argues against the "rule-of-thumb" (i.e., discretionary) methods used by workers; the duty of management is to train and teach the worker the "one best way." There must, therefore, be careful control of every aspect of organizational work.[66]

The situation with Barnard is murky because he does not approach this question directly. However, it is clear this balance is tilted in the same direction as the others, given the priority of organization purpose and the locus of decision making that is embodied in Barnard's "executive." For Barnard, discretion is implicit in the process by which organizational objectives are altered as they are communicated up and down the organizational chain. As long as one stays within this chain, the exercise of discretion is presumably acceptable. This is reminiscent of Weber's discussion of the avenues of appeal available for decisions made in other offices. In both cases, discretion is limited by formal rules. Within the situations governed by those rules, "proper judgment" is allowed (and even expected).

[65]Taylor, "Testimony," p. 60.

[66]In fairness to Taylor, he directed his efforts toward producing objects in the most efficient way, not services (the primary "product" of public administration). Unfortunately, as was seen earlier, under the banner of scientific management all aspects of life were deemed suitable for being made more efficient.

III

PUBLIC ADMINISTRATION PERSPECTIVES ON ORGANIZATION THEORY

Part I laid out a general framework for examining the world that confronts the public administrator. Part II explored the use of theory and the basic groundwork upon which is built today's theorizing about organizations. The main intent of Part III is to see how various theoretical perspectives illuminate different aspects of the public administration framework. The six perspectives discussed here are:

- *Neo-classical theories:* Organizations as Decision Sets

- *Systems theories:* Organizations as Purposive Entities

- *Later human relations theories:* Integrating Individuals and Organizations

- *Market theories:* Organizing as Revealed Self-Interest

- *Interpretive and critical theories:* Organizing as Social Action

- *Theories of emergence:* Organizing as Discovered Rationality

Each perspective addresses only certain aspects of the public administrator's world, while ignoring, deemphasizing or even skewing other parts of it. The approximately forty thinkers and writers about organizations that are discussed in Part III, however, have several things in common.

First, as noted earlier, an important function of theory is its use of metaphor, and each writer here uses theory in this way, although some cleave more literally to their chosen image than do others. It is possible to group the writers here loosely under the rubric of several dominant metaphors so as to emphasize the distinctive themes that each perspective brings to the study of human organizing activities. The purpose of each chapter is to explore and characterize these themes, rather than to attempt a comprehensive survey of the literature of organization theory.

The chapters in Part III present six substantively different approaches to viewing organizations and organizing: Neo-classical theories, systems theories, human relations theories, market theories, interpretive and critical theories, and theories of emergence. In depicting broad perspectives on organizations, these terms are not intended to outline highly unified "schools of thought," although in some instances there has been a tendency for the theorists themselves to do this. Rather, these labels are merely devices to help readers keep track of the various strands of thought that, collectively, can be called organization theory. Each chapter describes the contributions of several writers whose works illuminate aspects of a particular perspective. But the perspectives, and the chapters, should be regarded as nothing more than convenient organizing devices, each encompassing an often-diverse, as well as rich and insightful, array of ideas. The hope is that the reader will come away with an understanding, not only of the unity and diversity *within* each of the perspectives, but also of how they relate to and often disagree with one another.

In addition to having common metaphors, the unifying aspects within each of the six chapters are their particular "meta-assumptions," that is, the overarching beliefs that form the basis for other assumptions. One central issue with which all six chapters are deeply concerned, but about which they differ mightily, is the meaning of "rationality" and its importance in grounding an understanding of human action. With some notable exceptions discussed in Chapters 8, 10, and 11, rationality tends to be equated with instrumental rationality, whose meaning was stressed so heavily by Weber, Taylor, and Barnard in the last chapter. Although there is significant disagreement as to whether this emphasis is an unalloyed good, every writer here would agree that the instrumental logic of means and ends has been the *raison d'etre* of large-scale organizing in modern Western culture.

Another meta-assumption that, at least, by implication, occupies the attention of writers in Part III is the belief that human destiny is malleable through human action. This marks their writings with a certain cast, that of wanting to tell how organizations and the people in them *should* or *might be* as well as how they *are*. This mixture of the normative and the descriptive exists in all of the literature discussed here, often causing a good deal of confusion amongst both proponents and critics as to what is "real" and what is "desired."

Linked closely to this belief in the capacity to change the human condition through human action is an additional meta-assumption: a fundamental belief in causality. The idea that A is related to B in such a way as to make B and only B happen is central to Western scientific thinking. When as scientists we ask "why?" we implicitly mean "how does this come to happen?" For the social scientists discussed in the following chapters, the pertinent question is "how do organizations come to be as they are?" The answers provided by the six perspectives present a spectrum that parallels the range of Western thought today. It also parallels a changing sense of the role and meaning of causality in the thinking about organizations.

6

Neo-Classical Theory: Organizations as Decision Sets

Certain images emerge from the previous chapter examining the baseline for theorizing about organizations. The clearest is the metaphor of the organization as a simple system: a machine, with levers and gears to be manipulated for smooth running. Another image is that of the leader, the executive in Barnard's terms, as the center of authority and power, as well as the giver of meaning and purpose in the organization. Here, the essence of the organization is the classical hierarchical relationship. A third image is that of the organization as the embodiment of purpose; it is the mechanism by which humans join together to accomplish that which cannot be done individually. This brings together the notions of both system and hierarchy, focusing attention on how the organization is structured to accomplish a purpose.

These three themes—system, hierarchy, and structure—are the touchstones for the writers about organizations discussed here in Part III. All of them expand, modify, and, in some cases, reject the meanings of these terms as defined by the baseline theories, but in all cases these terms define the boundaries of the discussion. Underlying the three themes is a belief about human rationality that has been central to all Western theorizing about organizations. This belief illuminates that aspect of rationality that decides, chooses, weighs, analyzes, and discriminates. Again, although many of the writers discussed in Part III are uncomfortable with the thrust and scope of instrumental rationality, all respond to it, if only to broaden or narrow its meaning. There is, however, one perspective in organization theory that is extremely satisfied with the primary emphasis on the human as analyzer and decider. Often referred to as "Neo-Classical organization theory," this perspective sees the organization as a decision set, that is, as a series of choices and resulting decisions rationally linked together and bounded by the purposes of the organization. This chapter explores the perspective of these decision-set theories.

Introduction

The Neo-Classical perspective, labeled here as "decision-set theories," regards instrumental rationality as the essence of that part of human organizing known as administration. This theoretical posture encompasses those writers who see the making of decisions as the primary explanatory factor in understanding behavior in organizations. For them, the decision (as well as some of the conditions under which it is made) is the primary unit of analysis, the central characteristic upon which their theoretical perspective is built. Organizations are seen, analytically, as the playing out of choice-making through a set of decisions that both determine and are determined by the organization's structure, hierarchical relations, and system-like qualities.

There are four characteristics of the decision-set perspective that bear noting:

1 Decision making is the focal point of administration. Administrative action, therefore, consists (for purposes of analysis) primarily of the activities encompassing the making of decisions, such as analysis of data, weighing of priorities, and communication of decisions.

2 The core mode of operation within administration is instrumental rationality. Hence, the emphasis is on finding the appropriate means to an already given end.

3 The primary measure of organizational and administrative capacity and activity is efficiency.

4 There is an emphasis within this perspective on organizational roles, rather than on individuals per se, as they relate to the decision-making process.

The preeminent work of this perspective is Herbert Simon's *Administrative Behavior*, originally published in 1947. This book had an effect on organizational thinking that, as we shall see in later chapters, went far beyond its neo-classical boundaries, primarily because, even while arguing strenuously for the supremacy of instrumental rationality, it clearly illustrated the limits of that rationality in organizational settings. This insight into the limitations of instrumental rationality became central to the development of several of the perspectives discussed here. For the decision-set perspective, however, *Administrative Behavior* emphasizes several interconnected ideas that form the basis of its particular outlook. These ideas are further refined in what is sometimes called the work of the Carnegie Mellon school; this school includes the work of James G. March and R. M. Cyert, as well as Simon.

Generally speaking, this perspective attempts to consolidate what is *scientifically* known about organizations and organizational behavior. Such a compilation is the primary purpose, for example, of James March's *Handbook of Organizations,* which includes a series of essays that reflect the current research in the field.[1] This is also the purpose of March and Simon's *Organizations,* which discusses propositions about organizational behavior using some 206 variables in order to "review in a systematic way some of the important things that have been said about organizations by those who have studied them and written about them."[2] In general, the intent is to develop what Robert Merton called "middle-range theory." Although he was speaking specifically of sociology when he wrote in the 1950s about the need to "separate the history from the systematic substance" of theory, Merton's emphasis on the development of theories to guide empirical investigation fell on appreciative ears in all the social sciences. He saw the theories of the middle-range as those

> that lie between the minor but necessary working hypotheses that evolve in abundance during day-to-day research and the all-inclusive systematic efforts to develop a unified theory that will explain all the observed uniformities of social behavior, social organization and social change.[3]

Postwar social science involved a strong turn toward behavioralism,[4] an orientation that assumes that truth, as least in the scientific sense, lies in the objective study of the observable behavior of organisms, rather than in speculation about the motives of individuals or presumptions about their individual or collective purposes. This orientation fostered a firm belief in both the measurability of human behavior and the possibility for

[1]James G. March, ed., *Handbook of Organizations* (Chicago: Rand McNally, 1965).
[2]March and Herbert A. Simon, *Organizations* (New York: John Wiley & Sons, 1958), pp. 4–5.
[3]Robert K. Merton, *On Theoretical Sociology,* (New York: Free Press, 1967), p. 39; this and the following citation come from an essay that was first published in 1957.
[4]The terms "behaviorism" and "behavioralism" are often confused. Here, the former refers to that particular school of psychology usually associated with B. F. Skinner that advocates such notions as "operant conditioning" as a causal explanation. The latter term, "behavioralism," is used to indicate a much more general approach, one that starts with the assumption that human behavior as observed by a third party can be causally explicated in terms of those observations alone.

developing causal explanation to describe it. Modeled on the scientific approach of classical physics in particular, social science was seen to afford the potential for predicting human behavior. Behavioralism, in encouraging all of this, is not a school of thought, as such; rather, it is an intellectual orientation to a methodology that defines observable and generalizable human behavior as the only legitimate subject for study in the social sciences. In view of its particular, rigorous methodological commitments, behavioralism is uncomfortable with much of the earlier theorizing, seeing it as too vague and grandiose to enable the systematic observation and measurement of human behavior that it deems necessary.

Robert Merton's discussion of middle-range theory attempted to bridge the gap between the earlier "grand theorizing" and behavioralism's insistence that theory construction be empirically based.[5] By dutifully constructing and testing middle-range theory, social science could (he argued) build a body of theoretical knowledge that would, in time, enable the accurate explanation and predication of human behavior.

> The middle-range orientation [to theorizing] involves the specification of ignorance. Rather than pretend to knowledge where it is in fact absent, it expressly recognizes what must still be learned in order to lay the foundation for still more knowledge. It does not assume itself to be equal to the task of providing theoretical solutions to all the urgent practical problems of the day, but addresses itself to those problems that might now be clarified in the light of available knowledge.[6]

The grounding of theory in empirical research and the reluctance to broaden theorizing beyond the immediate problem at hand became highly developed criteria for "good theory," particularly in the decision-set perspective. Along the same line, the "model of economic man," with its particular assumptions about human nature and human organizing, was used, with important modifications, as an analytical base for this perspective. This is seen at its sharpest in March and Cyert's *A Behavioral Theory of the Firm,* where the writers attempt to provide what they see as a more realistic concept of decision-making processes in the firm.[7] For them, economic theory's abstraction of "the entrepreneur" is limited insofar as it does not reflect the empirical reality that most decisions within the firms are actually organizational—and multi-individual—decisions. Cyert and

---

[5]In fact, the tendency of behavioralists was to avoid *any* theory building. However, Merton and others attempted to link theory construction with empirical data-gathering, seeing this as the only way to avoid what C. Wright Mills called "abstract empiricism," a tendency toward mere fact collection and data manipulation (because "it was there," so to speak), with little regard for its usefulness in the development of theory. See C. Wright Mills, *The Sociological Imagination* (New York: Oxford University Press, 1959).

[6]Merton, pp. 68–69.

[7]R. M. Cyert and March, *A Behavioral Theory of the Firm* (Englewood Cliffs, N.J.: Prentice-Hall, 1963).

March construct a link between organizational variables and specific types of decision making, such as price setting, in order to build a broader framework for describing the firm's general decision-making processes.

Herbert Simon's *Administrative Behavior* best illustrates the decision-set perspective, because it lays out all of the key elements of how this theoretical posture sees organizations and their roles in the public sector. Neoclassical theory, with its decision-set perspective, developed largely in reaction to pre-World War II writings in the organizational and public administration literature that emphasized the development of a science of administration through the articulation of general principles for administration. This latter work was briefly alluded to in the previous chapter on the baseline theories, but it is necessary to examine it in some detail here so that the specifics of the decision-set quarrel are clear. The earlier "science of administration" ideas are best developed and arrayed in the 1937 volume edited by Luther Gulick and Lyndall Urwick, *Papers on the Science of Administration*. A discussion of these papers is followed by a presentation of the major ideas in *Administrative Behavior*. The chapter ends with an assessment of the relationship between this perspective and the public administration framework developed earlier in the opening chapters.

The "Papers on the Science of Administration"

> It is the hope of the editors that the availability of these papers will advance the analysis of administration, assist in the development of a standard nomenclature, encourage others to criticize the hypotheses with regard to administration herein set forth and to advance their own concepts fearlessly, and to point the way to areas greatly in need of exploration. If those who are concerned scientifically with the phenomena of getting things done through co-operative human endeavor will proceed along these lines, we may expect in time to construct a valid and accepted theory of administration[8]

So reads the admonition in the Foreword to the 1937 classic *Papers on the Science of Administration*. This collection of eleven papers reflects the predominant mode of thinking about organizations in Europe and the United States prior to World War II, with the essays falling into two general groups. In the first half of the volume, the papers of Gulick, Urwick, James D. Mooney, and Henri Fayol all concentrate on the structural aspects of organizations, whereas those in the second half, written by L.

---

[8]Luther Gulick and Lyndall Urwick, eds., *Papers on the Science of Administration* (New York: Institute of Public Administration, 1937), Foreword; in this section, all page references in parentheses are to this source; emphasis is in the original unless otherwise noted.

J. Henderson, T. N. Whitehead and Elton Mayo, Mary Parker Follett, and V. A. Graicunas, emphasize those social and environmental elements that affect organizations. This is a division that would generally hold in theorizing about organizations up through the present.

The effect of the writings stressing the social context grew primarily out of the work of the early human relations theorists, particularly those associated with the Hawthorne Experiments discussed in the previous chapter. The extensions of their work are explored in Chapter 8, "Later Human Relations Theory."[9]

For purposes of the decision-making perspective, it is those writers stressing the structural aspects of organizations who had the most influence and who also later became the foil for Herbert Simon's critiques, particularly in *Administrative Behavior*. These are of primary concern here.

POSDCORB as an Organizing Philosophy

By far the most influential of the papers has been "Notes on the Theory of Organization" by Luther Gulick. Here he presents his now-famous acronym POSDCORB, used to describe the primary activities of the executive (see the accompanying box). POSDCORB summarizes a view of administration that would influence the teaching and thinking about public administration for the next fifty years. There are three primary consequences of this outlook on administration, consequences that have profoundly affected the way in which organizations in the public sector have developed.

First, this view encapsulates, albeit implicitly, the Wilsonian dichotomy between politics and administration. There is an emphasis on the *means* of administration, with little discussion of its purpose (except in the technical sense of "objectives"). The "purpose" of government, for Gulick and the others, is found in the constitutionally established forms of political leadership: "A democracy is characterized by the fact that there is built into the structure of government a systematic method of introducing changes in program and method as the result of the broad movements of public opinion" (p. 44). Because of this, administration requires specialists and experts to accomplish its objectives; however,

> The true place of the expert is ... "on tap, not on top." The essential validity of democracy rests upon this philosophy, for democracy is a way of government in which the common man is the final judge of what is good for him. (p. 11)

---

[9]One exception to this is Mary Parker Follett, who was somewhat of an anomaly for her time; see Chapter 11, "Theories of Emergence."

POSDCORB

"What is the work of the chief executive? What does he do?"
The answer is POSDCORB.

POSDCORB is, of course, a made-up word designed to call attention to the various functional elements of the work of a chief executive because "administration" and "management" have lost all specific content. POSDCORB is made up of the initials and stands for the following activities:

- *Planning,* that is working out in broad outline the things that need to be done and the methods for doing them to accomplish the purpose set for the enterprise;

- *Organizing,* that is the establishment of the formal structure of authority through which work subdivisions are arranged, defined and co-ordinated for the defined objective;

- *Staffing,* that is the whole body of bringing in and training the staff and maintaining favorable conditions of work;

- *Directing,* that is the continuous task of making decisions and embodying them in specific and general orders and instructions and serving as the leader of the enterprise;

- *Co-ordinating,* that is the all important duty of interrelating the various parts of the work;

- *Reporting,* that is keeping those to whom the executive is responsible informed as to what is going on, which thus includes keeping himself and his subordinates informed through records, research and inspection;

- *Budgeting,* with all that goes with budgeting in the form of fiscal planning, accounting and control.

—From Luther Gulick, "Notes on the Theory of Organization," in Gulick and Lyndall Urwick, eds., *Papers on the Science of Administration* (New York: Institute of Public Administration, 1937), p. 13.

Democracy for these writers is the anchor to which public administration is lashed. As Mark Lilla has pointed out, they thought about government in terms of a democratic ethos, which included an implicit trust between the public (in the person of legislatures and courts) and the public administrator:

No matter how much debate there was over the nature of administrative responsibility in a democracy, there was no question but that democracy in the U.S. was itself legitimate; the only question was how the moral public officials could best serve that democracy when government agencies and programs became large and complex, and administrators found themselves with discretion.[10]

This profound belief in democracy articulates the politics side of the politics/administration dichotomy in a way that would by and large be lost to later writers. Here there is a clarity of purpose, of value, that would become obscured as behavioralism became dominant. When its insistence on the clear separation of value from fact was combined with behavioralism's natural tendency to emphasize facts rather than values, the result was a theoretical, methodological, and substantive disregard for the values and purposes embodied in human action.

The second consequence of POSDCORB was to highlight the need for the division of work as the primary tool for accomplishing organizational objectives. Thus, Urwick, in his essay "Organization as a Technical Problem," argues

> ... [T]here are principles which can be arrived at inductively from the study of human experience of organization, which should govern arrangements for human association of any kind. These principles can be studied as a technical question, irrespective of the purpose of the enterprise, the personnel composing it, or any constitutional, political or social theory underlying its creation. They are concerned with the method of subdividing and allocating to individuals all the various activities, duties and responsibilities essential to the purpose contemplated, the correlation of these activities and the continuous control of the work of individuals as to secure the most economical and the most effective realization of the purpose. (p. 49)

This emphasis on the division of work as a primary focus led in two parallel directions. The first was toward an emphasis on developing principles, such as those described above by Urwick, to guide both the division of work and the resulting and necessary coordination of effort. Such principles were grounded in the notion that work can best be divided functionally, in terms of the objectives to be accomplished. This made for, in other words, a kind of intellectualized Scientific Management. Whereas Frederick Taylor said that "There is one right way of forcing the shovel down into materials of this sort . . .," James D. Mooney, for instance, talks of functions as being

> distinctions between *kinds of duties*. We know that authority is the determining principle of organization, but it is impossible to think of the variations of different jobs in terms of authority alone. Functionalism enters from the very first, from the first the central line of authority begins to throw off functions, and in the end it always breaks up into functional distinctions. Authority, rep-

[10]Mark T. Lilla, "Ethos, 'Ethics,' and Public Service," *The Public Interest* 63:2(1981):6.

resented in leadership, and operating through delegation of duties, has only one aim and purpose within the organization, namely the co-ordination of functions. (p. 94)

Such functional distinctions make sense when political objectives are clear and when the tasks at hand represent relatively tame problems. The work of government of which these writers speak (when they talk in specifics at all) is that of road building, hospital service, sewer construction, and the like. Because "modern" issues such as equity of service delivery were assumed to be dealt with by the body politic, the administrator was left with the task of coordinating means. It is not surprising, therefore, for administration to be seen as neutral and generalizable, "irrespective of the purpose of the enterprise," in Urwick's words. And this is only one step from assuming that there must be general principles that would guide its operation, principles on which to base administrative action.

The second direction in which the division of work as an operating principle led was toward a reliance on bureaucratic hierarchy, with the chief executive as the center of administrative interest. For example, POSDCORB, as a definition of the boundaries of the work (or duties, in Mooney's terms) of the executive, is also a statement of hierarchical division. The traditional distinction between line and staff takes on a clear meaning *only* within a bureaucratic structure, because as work is divided functionally and therefore laterally, it is further divided vertically. As Gulick points out,

> When the work of government is subjected to the dichotomy of "line" and "staff," there are included in staff all of those persons who devote their time exclusively to the knowing, thinking and planning functions, and in the line all of the remainder who are, thus, chiefly concerned with the doing functions. . . . Obviously those in the line are also thinking and planning, and making suggestions to superior officers. They cannot operate otherwise. But this does not make them staff officers. Those also in the staff are *doing* something; they do not merely sit and twiddle their thumbs. But they do not organize others, they do not direct or appoint personnel, they do not issue commands, they do not take responsibility for the job. Everything they suggest is referred up, not down, and is carried out, if at all, on the responsibility and under the direction of a line officer. (p. 31)

The division of work in this context leads almost naturally to two conclusions. The first is that as work is segmented, so is accountability, the lines of the former matching the lines of the latter. The second conclusion is essentially contradictory, at least on the surface, to the first: Because there is a single source of authority, namely the executive, there is but one source of accountability. This paradox is handled in both practice and theory by assigning responsibility and accountability to the office, bureau, or agency. Because of this, the link with Max Weber's description of ideal-typical bureaucracy is clear. It is the office, bureau, or agency, not the person occupying it, that becomes vested with authority. Thus, accountability is broken into discrete elements in terms of individuals performing work; at the same time, it is seen as unitary in terms of the office, bureau, or agency deemed responsible for the activity. There is no real difficulty so long as the activities are relatively discrete and the purposes for which they are performed relatively clear to all parties.

The third consequence of POSDCORB as an operating philosophy is the centrality of efficiency as the premier value by which to judge governmental activity. One must be cautious, however, with "efficiency" as it is used by these writers, because they are not using the term in the precise economic (and behavioral) sense that would later become the norm.[11] Gulick, in "Science, Values and Public Administration," the concluding essay in the book, sums up their view quite clearly:

> In the science of administration, whether public or private, the basic "good" is efficiency. The fundamental objective of the science of administration is the accomplishment of the work in hand with the least expenditure of man-power and materials. Efficiency is thus axiom number one in the value scale of administration. This brings it into apparent conflict with certain elements of the value scale of politics. . . . But both public administration and politics are branches of political science, so that we are in the end compelled to mitigate the pure concept of efficiency in the light of the value scale of politics and the social order. There are, for example, highly inefficient arrangements like citizen boards and small local governments which *may* be necessary in a democracy as educational devices. . . . But in any case the student of administration will not only explore relationships from the standpoint of efficiency within the framework afforded, *but will consider the effect of that framework upon efficiency itself.* (p. 193; second emphasis added)

In summary, POSDCORB outlines an operational philosophy for public administration that has three consequences:

1 There is an assumption of and stress on the Wilsonian dichotomy between politics and administration, with a particular emphasis on the democratic ethos as the political context.

2 The division of work, both functionally and hierarchically, is the primary mode for organizing public administration activities.

3 Efficiency, in terms of the best utilization of resources appropriate to the larger political context, is the paramount value for public administration.

[11]Cf., Herbert Simon's use of the term "efficiency," as described in the following section.

The operational philosophy behind these consequences is one in which administration seeks to operate on the basis of principles of action. These principles, which the writers here again and again suggest should be based in empirical experience, came to be lightning rods for the criticisms of later writers. The question that was seldom asked, however, as behavioralism began to dominate the ways of determining what was and was not "scientific," was the simple one of intent: What did these writers in fact mean when they spoke of "principles"? The answer is important, because it points out how the rules of the game, so to speak, have changed for the analysis of administrative action.

The Principles of Administration

In "Notes on the Theory of Organization," Luther Gulick outlines what he calls the "principle of homogeneity." According to this principle, one can functionally characterize every worker by the *major purpose* he serves, by the *process* he uses, by the *person* or *things* he deals with, or the geographical *place* where he works:

> Where two men are doing exactly the same work in the same way for the same people at the same place, then the specifications of their jobs will be the same under [each of these.] All such workers may be easily combined in a single aggregate and supervised together. Their work is homogeneous. But when any of the four items differ, then there must be a selection among the items to determine which shall be given precedence in determining what is and what is not homogeneous and therefore combinable. (p. 15)

He goes on to describe organizing by one or the other of these functions as "applying the principle of departmentalization."

Lyndall Urwick, in "Organization as a Technical Problem," summarizes a number of organizational principles, the most significant (he argues) being that of coordination. In this regard he approvingly cites two passages from the influential work by James Mooney and Alan Reilly, *Onward Industry:*

> [Coordination] expresses the principles of organization *in toto,* nothing less. This does not mean that there are no subordinated principles; it simply means that all the others are contained in this one of co-ordination. The others are simply principles through which co-ordination operates, and thus becomes effective.
>
> The supreme co-ordinating authority must rest somewhere and in some form in every organization. . . . It is equally essential to the very idea and concept of organization that there must be a process, formal in character, through

which this co-ordinating authority operates from the top throughout the entire structure of the organized body.[12]

Two "subordinated principles" that Urwick outlines are those of specialization and span of control. The former is essentially the division of work treated so thoroughly by Frederick Taylor, while the latter speaks to what "Students of administration have long recognized [namely] that, in practice, no human brain should attempt to supervise directly more than five, or at most, six other individuals whose work is interrelated" (p. 52).

Henri Fayol, the French industrialist and founder of the Centre for Administrative Studies in Paris, describes fourteen principles of administration:

1. Division of labor
2. Authority
3. Discipline
4. Unity of command
5. Unity of management
6. Subordination of individual interests to the common good
7. Remuneration
8. Centralization
9. The hierarchy
10. Order
11. Equity
12. Stability of staff
13. Initiative
14. Esprit de Corps

What was the intent in developing all these principles? Herbert Simon would come to argue that, like proverbs, any two contradictory principles can be found to fit a given situation. As will be seen in the next section, Simon maintains that these principles are unclear and ambiguous, containing poorly defined terms. As scientific principles, he asserts, they are not at all useful.

In a strict, contemporary sense, this criticism appears to have merit, since the contributors to the Gulick and Urwick volume do regularly use the term "scientific" to describe their approach to administration.[13] There is, however, an aspect of their approach that requires more clarification now than when these essays were originally written. This is the orientation of the principles toward administrative action, rather than research. Henri Fayol, for instance, makes clear that his intent is the former rather than the latter. Urwick, in "The Function of Administration," summarizes

---

[12]James D. Mooney and Alan C. Reilly, *Onward Industry* (New York: Harper & Brothers, 1931), p. 19; quoted in Gulick and Urwick, pp. 49 and 51.

[13]Popular discussion of science, particularly in the pre-war years, tended to focus on science-as-technology, rather than science-as-research. This is reflected in the "science of administration" discussions, such as appear in the Gulick and Urwick volume. Here science is used as a synonym for benign technology, the purpose of which was to bring a better, ordered life. There was little discussion of, much less the later preoccupation with, the "scientific method" as such. It is this seemingly innocent view of science as technology that underlies the postwar rejection of "science as administration."

Fayol's work, particularly his principles, and quotes him at length on this point:

> Of the principles of administration [Fayol] writes: "There is no limit to the number of principles of administration. Every administrative rule or device, which strengthens the human part of an organization or facilitates its working, takes its place among the principles, for so long as experience proves it to be worthy of this important position." He then summarizes fourteen such principles [listed above] and adds: "I shall leave the review of principles at this point, not because the list is exhausted—it has no precise limit—but because it seems to me particularly useful at the moment to endow the theory of administration with about a dozen well-established principles, on which public discussion can conveniently be focussed." . . . [Fayol] wishes to insist on elasticity in the application of administrative principles: "The same principle is hardly ever applied twice in exactly the same way." This is a fundamental concept in administration. (p. 121)

Of course, if the principles are intended as research guides, then (as we shall see) the notion of a principle "hardly ever being applied twice in exactly the same way" is a contradiction in terms. However, despite the colorings of "science" that these writers use, they clearly intend a different sense of the scientific endeavor than would be later taken up; they also clearly intended their principles to be general guides for administrative action, rather than unambiguous recipes, to aid individual administrators in understanding their organizational contexts.

Herbert Simon and "Administrative Behavior"

Although the Second World War symbolized a number of different things, to many it demonstrated the power, necessity, and even the inevitability of technological development. To this way of thinking, the heart of this technology was the normative and methodological essence of the scientific method. After the war, science as the way to a better life became a banner lifted high in the social science community. Many social scientists increasingly saw their charge as one of creating, through science, a social technology that would enable the accurate prediction and control of human behavior. For the study of administration, this translated into a desire to create an administrative technology that would make organizations efficient. This conception of social science was, in part, an intellectual extension of Scientific Management; at the same time, however, it was a reaction against earlier theorizing as being logically unstructured, inadequately scientific, and poorly grounded in empirical evidence.

The overall redirection of postwar social science, especially in the United States, embraced the methodological commitment to behavioralism. To the behavioralists, science meant generating and manipulating data about observable social behavior in order to test hypotheses constructed on a theoretically sound basis. As we saw earlier, in the field of sociology, Robert Merton argued for empirically grounded "theories of the middle range." Similarly, in political science, David Truman concluded, in a 1955 lecture at the Brookings Institution, that

> The developments in the behavioral sciences over the past quarter-century have been more striking in the realm of technique than in that of validated and expanded theory. In both there has been a growing influence on the work and thought of political scientists. Though both types of impact are important, I should argue that the concern for empirically based theory, for the discovery and statement of behavioral uniformities, is the more fundamental . . . I would fully accept the proposition that the advance of our discipline lies in the acceptance of generalization as its primary objective and of empirically testable theory as its principal method . . . [14]

And in 1946, Herbert Simon published a paper in the *Public Administration Review* entitled "The Proverbs of Administration."[15] Incorporated into his book *Administrative Behavior* two years later, that paper generally argued that

> It is a fatal defect of the current principles of administration that, like proverbs, they occur in pairs. For almost every principle one can find an equally plausible and acceptable contradictory principle. Although the two principles of the pair will lead to exactly opposite organizational recommendations, there is nothing in the theory to indicate which is the proper one to apply.[16]

"There is nothing in the theory to indicate which [principle] is the proper one to apply"—this statement sums up a significant shift in the meaning and purpose of administrative theory from that characterized by the Gulick and Urwick papers. It also captures a defining element of the decision-set perspective as outlined by *Administrative Behavior*. To clar-

---

[14]David Truman, *Research Frontiers in Politics and Government* (Washington, DC: The Brookings Institution, 1955); reprinted in Heinz Eulau, ed., *Behavioralism in Political Science* (New York: Atherton Press, 1969), pp. 64, 65.

[15]Herbert A. Simon, "The Proverbs of Administration," *Public Administration Review* 6:4(1946)53–67.

[16]Herbert A. Simon, *Administrative Behavior: A Study of Decision-Making Processes in Administrative Organization*, 3rd rev. ed. (New York: The Free Press, 1976), p. 20; first published in 1947; in this section, all page references in parentheses are to this source; emphasis is in the original unless otherwise noted.

ify this shift in meaning and appreciate its implications for thinking about organizations, it is useful to first look closely at Simon's argument against "the proverbs" and then examine the three themes developed in his book that define the decision-set perspective:

- The decision is the central act of organization;

- Instrumental reason is central to administrative decision making and organizational understanding; and

- Satisficing—a significant limit on rationality and its effect on organizational behavior—is the primary condition in decision making.

The "Proverbs" of Administration

Simon cogently sums up the thesis of *Administrative Behavior* on the opening page:

> Although any practical activity involves "deciding" and "doing," it has not commonly been recognized that a theory of administration should be concerned with the processes of decision as well as the processes of action. (p. 1)

More attention should be paid, Simon argues, "to the determining of what is to be done rather than to the actual doing" (p. 1).

This is also at the core of his criticism of the earlier literature, exemplified in Gulick and Urwick's *Papers on the Science of Administration*. The four principles that Simon examines in particular are described in the accompanying box.

These principles are like proverbs, he argues, because they provide no guidance about when they should be applied. The reason for this lack of guidance comes primarily from a lack of adequate definition and specification of terms in the principles. The difficulty is that the principles provide a set of choices in a situation, but are unclear about what should be the basis for choosing. For example, in examining the principle of organization by purpose, process, clientele, and place, which is supposed to increase administrative efficiency, Simon points out that

> . . . it is clear that this principle is internally inconsistent for purpose, process, clientele, and place are competing bases of organization, and at any given point of division the advantages of three must be sacrificed to secure the advantages of the fourth. (p. 28)

Not only is there competition amongst these bases of organization, there is also ambiguity in the terms themselves. Thus, even though "pur-

---

SOME ACCEPTED ADMINISTRATIVE PRINCIPLES

Among the more common "principles" that occur in the literature of administration are these:

1 Administrative efficiency is increased by a specialization of the task among the group.

2 Administrative efficiency is increased by arranging the members of the group in a determinate hierarchy of authority.

3 Administrative efficiency is increased by limiting the span of control at any point in the hierarchy to a small number.

4 Administrative efficiency is increased by grouping the workers, for purposes of control, according to (a) purpose, (b) process, (c) clientele, or (d) place. (This is really an elaboration of the first principle, but deserves separate discussion.)

—From Herbert A. Simon, *Administrative Behavior: A Study of Decision-Making Processes in Administrative Organization*, 3rd rev. ed. (New York: The Free Press, 1976), pp. 20–21.

---

pose" is the objective of an activity and "process" is the means for reaching that objective, purposes form a hierarchy of subpurposes, which themselves appear no different from processes. For example,

> A typist moves her fingers in order to type; types in order to reproduce a letter; reproduces a letter in order that an inquiry may be answered. Writing a letter is then the purpose for which the typing is performed; while writing a letter is also the process whereby the purpose of replying to an inquiry is achieved. It follows that the same activity may be described as purpose or process. (p. 30)

Similarly, in commenting on a recommendation by the British Machinery of Government Committee that urged unequivocally for purpose rather than clientele as the base for reorganization, Simon points out:

> The faults in this analysis by the committee are clearly obvious. First, there is no attempt to determine how *a* service is to be recognized. Second, there is a bald assumption, absolutely without proof, that a child health unit, for example, in a department of child welfare could not offer services of "as high a standard" as the same unit if it were located in a department of health. Just how the shifting of the unit from one department to another would improve or damage the quality of its work is not explained. Third, no basis is set forth for adjudicating the competing claims of purpose and process.... [T]he recommendations [of the committee] represented a choice, without any apparent logical or empirical grounds, between contradictory principles of administration. (p. 34)

"Without any apparent logical or empirical grounds ..."—it is here, in order to correct this deficiency, that Simon begins his resuscitation of administrative theory:

> ... much administrative analysis proceeds by selecting a single criterion, and applying it to an administrative situation to reach a recommendation; while the fact that equally valid, but contradictory, criteria exist which could be applied with equal reason, but with a different result, is conveniently ignored. A valid approach to the study of administration requires that *all* the relevant diagnostic criteria be identified; that each administrative situation be analyzed in terms of the entire set of criteria; and that research be instituted to determine how weights can be assigned to the several criteria when they are, as they usually will be, mutually incompatible. (p. 36)

As one might guess from his criticism of the earlier principles, Simon eschews the use of terms such as "authority," "centralization," and "span of control" because of their lack of operational definition. Rather than looking at these generalized organizational situations, he focuses instead on the individual organization member, specifically the decision-making individual in the organization. Because administrative theory, for Simon, "is concerned with how an organization should be constructed and operated in order to accomplish its work efficiently," it has a "rational character" that involves choosing the one alternative from among several that "leads to the greatest accomplishment of administrative objectives," when the expenditure is the same. From among those choices that would lead to accomplishing the same objective, the one selected should require the least expenditure (p. 39).

> ... [T]his "principle of efficiency" is characteristic of any activity that attempts rationally to maximize the attainment of certain ends with the use of scarce resources ... The "administrative man" takes his place alongside the classical "economic man." (p. 39)

The key to both the administrative- and economic-man models is their "rational character." The premise implicit in accepting this "rational man"as the model for administrative behavior is that the choice of an alternative is assumed to *necessarily* determine the subsequent action to be taken. Once the initial decision is made, the resulting actions are of only tangential concern to the theorist. This is sometimes known as "linear causality," because it posits a straight-line causal connection between A (the premise) and B (the conclusion). When confronted with a problem, the administrator turns it into a choice statement in order to make a decision. The choice is between a set of rationally constructed alternatives; once a choice is made (i.e., an alternative is decided upon), there is little theoretical concern here for the resulting implementation of that choice, except insofar as it presents other clusters of technical problems requiring further decisions. Once this is understood, Simon's criticisms of the "proverbs of administration" become clearer. Each principle, he argues, is actually a choice statement. Take, for instance, the principle of organization that was discussed above:

> Administrative efficiency is increased by grouping the workers, for purposes of control according to (a) purpose, (b) process, (c) clientele, or (d) place. (p. 21)

Note the construction of the principle as it is formulated by Simon. It is of the form "If A, then B" (if workers are grouped by place, then administrative efficiency is increased.) In other words, the principle has been reset as a choice statement. When one does this, then it follows, as Simon argues above, that the principle is internally inconsistent because there are competing premises (i.e., purpose, process, and clientele, as well as place).[17]

The notion of choice between alternatives is central to Simon's emphasis on the decision as the key to understanding organizational behavior. In turn, the principle of instrumental rationality (as in the means/ends logic of classical economics or the utility-maximizing logic of the rational man) underpins his entire theory of organizations. Although Simon generally adopts the principle of instrumental rationality, he does not accept all of the assumptions usually associated with it. For purposes of theorizing, for instance, an important assumption in economics is that rational man acts on the basis of "complete and perfect" information. Simon, however, sees both the *available* information and human psychological factors as significant constraints on the ability to make correct decisions. And this means that there are significant limits on an individual's ability to perform both administratively and organizationally. These limitations are the basis for his concept of "satisficing." These three areas—decisions as the basis for administrative theory, instrumental rationality, and satisficing—are described below.

The Decision as the Basis for Administrative Theory

> A general theory of administration must include principles of organization that will insure correct decision-making, just as it must include principles that will insure effective action. (p. 1)

As was clear in the above discussion of the Gulick and Urwick papers, earlier writings about organizing had centered almost exclusively on the

---

[17]To restate the principles in this way would seem to be to caricature them in a way that misses a salient feature, namely, their intent to offer guidance for action rather than to provide a basis for "scientific" investigation.

elucidation of principles as guides to effective administrative action. Span of control, division of work, and specialization are essentially statements about how work should generally be organized. As guides to action, these principles focused the study of administration on the resulting organizational configurations that resulted from applying them to specific situations.

Herbert Simon, however, shifts the focus of administrative study from action to analysis by starting from the implicit assumption that choice, which is based on analysis, determines subsequent action. "Choice" here is synonymous with making a decision, which itself is "a conclusion drawn from a set of premises—value premises and factual premises" (p. 123). Using this assumption as a starting point casts the resulting analysis in two characteristic ways. The first is that by emphasizing the point of decision (i.e., choice), there is a tendency to mask the subsequent ramifications of that decision as potentially integral elements themselves in the decision-making process. What tends to become clouded over is the dynamic aspect of administration in which some decision-making situations are in fact parts of reiterative sequences. By focusing on the decision, such situational aspects become lost, one effect of which is to treat organizational "problems" atemporally, that is, without due regard for the past or the future. Secondly, the focus on choice or decision means that the unit of analysis is necessarily limited to the *individual* who is "making" the decision, rather than the group, say, or the organization. Simon readily concedes that

> It should be perfectly apparent that almost no decision made in an organization is the task of a single individual. Even though the final responsibility for taking a particular action rests with some definite person, we shall always find, in studying the manner in which this decision was reached, that its various components can be traced through the formal and informal channels of communication [a la Chester Barnard] to many individuals who have participated in forming its premises. When all of these components have been identified, it may appear that the contribution of the individual who made the formal decision was a minor one, indeed. (p. 221)

This does not, however, gainsay the analytical difficulty: With the individual decision maker as the unit of analysis, the analytic task is limited to tracing, dividing, and summing the actions of one individual at a time. This theoretical perspective does not help the analyst to step outside of the framework centered on the individual in order to assess the combined effects of the decision process. This is further complicated by the way in which communication is defined here in terms of the transmittal of information, rather than the interaction of human beings. (Other possibilities, as we will see later, include seeing communication as a socially creative process.) Simon discusses communication within the organization, but that discussion begs the question, insofar as he considers that: "Communication may be formally defined as any process whereby decisional premises are transmitted from one member of an organization to another" (p. 154). Looking at communication in this fashion makes it a relatively simple matter to track the flow of "decisional premises." However, it also makes it difficult to estimate (or even consider as worthwhile) either the cumulative or the discretionary effects of those premises.

A decision in Simon's terms, as pointed out earlier, is "a conclusion drawn from a set of premises—value premises and factual premises." This distinction between fact and value premises is essential to the maintenance of Simon's approach to administrative theory, an approach grounded philosophically in logical positivism. The gist of this position is summarized neatly by Simon early in his book:

> The argument runs, briefly, as follows. To determine whether a proposition is correct, it must be compared directly with experience—with the facts—or it must lead by logical reasoning to other propositions that can be compared with experience. But factual propositions cannot be derived from ethical ones by any process of reasoning, nor can ethical propositions be compared directly with the facts—since they assert "oughts" rather than facts. Hence, there is no way in which the correctness of ethical propositions can be empirically or rationally tested. (p. 46)

One implication of this "fact/value dichotomy" is that the investigator should focus on the "facts" of a situation, on those elements that have an "empirical" basis. In doing this, the investigator sets aside the "value" elements, perhaps to be analyzed at another time or perhaps, as often happens, not to be dealt with at all. The latter is more likely because value elements are difficult, from this perspective, to analyze.

> The important point for the present discussion is that any statement that contains an ethical element, intermediate or final, cannot be described as correct or incorrect, and that the decision-making process must start with some ethical premise that is taken as "given." This ethical premise describes the objective of the organization in question. (p. 50)

Scientific reasoning and investigation, following Simon's line, applies only to questions of fact: What are the behavioral characteristics of the situation? How are these characteristics interrelated? How are they causally connected? The purpose of scientific research is to validate the factual propositions that result from such questions. Value judgments, on the other hand, cannot be investigated in this fashion: "The process of validating a factual proposition is quite distinct from the process of validating a value judgment. The former is validated by its agreement with the facts, the latter by human fiat" (p. 56).

The separation of facts from values results in dividing knowledge from the practical purposes for which it is used. Knowledge, from Simon's perspective, is neutral in any moral or ethical sense; it is the values of the *user* that imbue the application of knowledge with any meaning of "good" or "bad." Technology, being applied knowledge, is also neutral. How, why, and when people choose to use technologies available to them are important questions, but questions that are beyond the domain and scope of science. Herbert Simon, Donald Smithburg, and Victor Thompson, in their still widely used text, *Public Administration,* make this point and some of its implications quite clear, as can be seen in the accompanying box.

Administration is a technology that applies factual propositions about organizational settings; the science of administration tests and validates such propositions. When the latter is applied to the former, the result, for the administrator, is a set of decisions on which to base organizational action. Thus, an organizational decision is, once again, "a conclusion drawn from a set of premises—value premises and factual premises." The decision comes about because the administrator is faced with a choice. The administrator's responsibility, this perspective argues, is to assess that choice in a way that enables the specification of factually clear alternatives, to weigh those alternatives, and to make a decision.

There are two important aspects of this process that bear scrutiny. One is the question of how problems get defined in order to present themselves as choices to administrators. Understanding this requires a look at the role that instrumental rationality plays in the decision-set perspective, the subject of the next subsection. The other aspect is the way in which, according to Simon and his colleagues, the decision in fact comes to be made; this is the subject of the following subsection.

Instrumental Rationality as the Basis for Decision Making

Discussions of "rationality" are usually confusing, not the least for the varying shades of nuance and emphasis that each writer is intent on supplying. Nonetheless, it is possible to detect a shift over the last eighty years in the use of the term "rationality," parallel with the term "science," that has essentially narrowed its meaning. This shift has been especially accentuated by and is largely dependent on the influence of postwar behavioralism outlined earlier. For instance, as we saw in the last chapter, Max Weber in the first quarter of this century focused extensively on human rationality. He identified four orientations of social action: the traditional, the affectual, the value-rational and the instrumentally rational. The last is the one of interest here, the "means-end" sense of rationality, which characterizes social action in which the actor weighs the means, ends, and

ADMINISTRATION AS MANIPULATION

The position has been taken in these pages that knowledege of administration, like all knowledge, is amoral. It becomes "good" or "bad" only in terms of the value assumptions added to it by the person who uses it—in terms of his attitudes towards goals and methods. Knowledge gives man power—but power to do either good or evil. . . .

Knowledge of administration is amoral in an even deeper sense, for it is knowledge of how to manipulate other human beings—how to get them to do the things you want done. The study of administration discloses techniques for influencing human behavior. To carry out a program of action, the administrator is constantly trying to predict what the consequences will be of a particular course of action and to act in ways that will produce the behaviors he desires and inhibit those he does not want. Only this distinguishes a realistic plan from a vague wish.

One of the fundamental values in Western civilization has been the dignity of the individual human being. It is not easy to express the whole meaning of this value, but certainly it means, among other things, that human beings are not to be manipulated as marionettes attached to strings.

. . . [T]he dignity of the individual can be respected only in an administrative situation in which all participants will gain, in one way or another, from the accomplishment of the organization goal. In such a situation, administration can be "cooperative" in the broadest sense. It can be a constant process of behavioral interaction, with the plan being influenced by the reactions of the clientele and of all participants in the organization as often as by the conscious manipulative design of a "boss."

Nevertheless, we must not make the reassuring—but fallacious—assumption that this kind of cooperation will always be the most effective means of reaching the organization goal, unless this goal is defined broadly enough to include the values of all participants. This belief in some preordained harmony between administration that respects the individual and administration that is efficient in the usual sense mars the otherwise perceptive writings of Elton Mayo and others of the "Hawthorne Group."

—From Herbert A. Simon, Donald W. Smithburg, and Victor A. Thompson, *Public Administration* (New York: Alfred A. Knopf, 1950), pp. 22–23.

consequences of acting. It is useful to look once again at Weber's description of instrumentally rational action, because it throws into relief a particular characteristic of the decision-set perspective's own orientation forty years later:

A person acts rationally in the "means-end" sense when his action is guided by consideration of ends, means and secondary consequences; when, in acting, he rationally *assesses* means in relation to ends, ends in relation to secondary consequences, and, *finally the various possible ends in relation to each other*[18]

Compare this with Herbert Simon, writing in *Administrative Behavior:*

> ... Roughly speaking, rationality is concerned with the selection of preferred behavior alternatives in terms of some system of values whereby the consequences of behavior can be evaluated. [Simon then goes on to ask several complicating questions regarding this definition, concluding that] ... Perhaps the only way to avoid, or clarify, these complexities is to use the term "rational" in conjunction with appropriate adverbs. Then a decision may be called "objectively" rational if *in fact* it is the given situation. It is "subjectively" rational if it maximizes attainment relative to the actual knowledge of the subject. It is "deliberately" rational to the degree that the adjustment of means to ends has been deliberately brought about (by the individual or organization). A decision is "organizationally" rational if it is oriented to the organization's goals; it is "personally" rational if it is oriented to the individual's goals. (pp. 75, 76–77)

The difference between these two is striking. For Weber, being instrumentally rational means to weigh and assess *all* of the aspects of acting, comparing not only the alternatives that one faces, but also the purposes of those alternatives. For Simon, on the other hand, to be rational (no matter what adverb is in front) means to assess *only* those alternatives available within some pregiven system of values. The Weberian sense of rational was not limited to Weber, just as Simon's is hardly limited to Simon. In each case, the formulation represents a larger, historically time-dependent view. Implicit in the Weberian view is that the individual is rational and responsible, *despite* the surrounding organizational and social environment. By contrast, implicit in Simon's view is the belief that the individual is rational and responsible only *within* a particular organizational environment. It is the organizational environment, rather than autonomous individuals, that articulates the values that encompass the purposes of rational behavior. Moreover, values, regardless of where they come from, are essentially arbitrary, or, as Simon says, are only validated by "human fiat." Thus, no element of rationality (again, with any of its various adverbs) enables the individual to judge the widsom of those values or the purposes inferred from them.

Simon's conception of rationality is intimately connected with his description of an organization as a system in equilibrium, an idea borrowed directly from Chester Barnard:

---

[18]W. G. Runciman, ed., *Max Weber: Selections in Translation* (Cambridge: Cambridge University Press, 1978), p. 29, second emphasis added.

The organization has been described in this chapter [of Simon's book] as a system in equilibrium, which receives contributions in the form of money or effort, and offers inducements in return for these contributions. These inducements include the organization goal itself, conservation and growth of the organization, and incentives unrelated to these two.

The organization equilibrium is maintained by the control group, whose personal values may be of various kinds, but who assume the responsibility of maintaining the life of the organization in order that they may attain these values. (p. 122)

To Simon, the need for the organization to maintain equilibrium also requires that organizational purposes and goals predominate in guiding organizational action. Hence, to act rationally (with any adverb) means to act within the framework of the organization's pre-established goals and purposes. This has a direct bearing on the way in which problems come to be defined.

Given that decision making involves making choices about how to confront a "problem," it is surprising how little is said in this perspective about *where* problems come from and *how* they are formulated. The "problems" facing the administrator seem to be of two kinds. One could be called "extra-organizational," which is to say the kind of issue that develops as a "public problem." In their text, *Public Administration*, Simon, Smithburg, and Thompson treat this as an issue of the development of government organizations:

There is nothing automatic in the way that the community meets new problems as they arise. Before governmental activity is undertaken, a problem must exist not merely in fact, but in people's minds as well. . . . Meanwhile, tentative suggestions will begin to be made for possible solutions. Some of these may include programs of governmental service or regulation. Organized groups will begin to interest themselves in the issue. As the demands for some remedy grow louder, advocacy will begin to center around a few solutions, particularly about those that appear to have some likelihood of political acceptability. Sooner or later, specific proposals will be made in the form of legislative bills or requests for governmental appropriations.[19]

The intended solutions to public problems provide the organization with its goals and purposes. But other than simply acknowledging such problems, this perspective does little to clarify the relation of their complex and often general meaning to the specific and concrete choices that administrators face. To Simon, goals and purposes are taken as given;

[19]Simon, Donald W. Smithburg, and Victor A. Thompson, *Public Administration* (New York: Alfred A. Knopf, 1950), pp. 31–32.

thus, rationality has little bearing on the formulation of goals and purposes, nor on the values from which they derive (except of course in an
instrumental sense to those who participate in their development).

The second sort of "problem" is really a subset of the first. Public problems, once their ambiguity has been reduced or eliminated by politics or
higher authority (itself a heroic assumption), then become clusters of technical problems that Simon and others in this perspective implicitly assume
are self-evident to the administrator. They are the kinds of problems
toward which the entire text of *Administrative Behavior* is directed. That
administrative problems are self-evident is a crucial simplifying assumption of this perspective, an assumption on which so much else hangs.

In his theory of organizations, Simon's assumption about the predefined nature of problems plays out in his understanding of the meaning
and role of authority in the organization. "Authority," for Simon, is "the
power to make decisions which guide the actions of another." The importance of authority in the organization, however, lies not just in its power,
but also in the expectations that develop as a consequence of making decisions hierarchically: "The superior frames and transmits decisions with
the expectation that they will be accepted by the subordinate. The subordinate expects such decisions, and his conduct is determined by them"
(p. 125). This should strike a familiar note; Simon uses Barnard's term,
"zone of indifference," to describe the way in which most decisions are
accepted by subordinates. He goes on, however, to turn this concept
around:

> The most striking characteristic of the "subordinate" role is that it establishes
> an area of acceptance in behavior within which the subordinate is willing to
> accept the decisions made for him by his superior. His choice is then deter-
> mined, always within the area of acceptance, by his superior, and the relation
> of superior-subordinate holds only within this area.... The magnitude of the
> area is influenced by a large number of circumstances.... [and] Restraint of
> the superior is as important as obedience of the subordinate in maintaining the
> relationship. (pp. 133, 134)

Simon sums up the implication of this for decision making as follows:

> An analysis of organized behavior of all sorts will demonstrate that such behav-
> ior results when each of the coordinated individuals sets himself a criterion that
> makes his own behavior dependent upon the behavior of others.... [That is,]
> *he sets himself a general rule which permits the communicated decision of
> another to guide his own choices* (i.e., to serve as a premise of those choices)
> *without deliberation on his own part on the expediency of those premises.* (p.
> 125)

Although Simon generally embraces a "rational man" model in which the
individual is seen as a maximizer of utility (or efficiency), the force of that

model, he argues, is constrained, at least in part, by the limitations of social interdependence that characterize complex organizations, as well as by individual psychological limitations. It is the set of these limitations, discussed in the next subsection, that combine to form his notion of "satisficing."

Satisficing: Limits to Decision Making

As pointed out earlier in the chapter, Simon starts by declaring: "The 'administrative man' takes his place along side the classical 'economic man.'" To this point, we have explored several ways in which both function as representatives of the "rational man" model: described above the focus on choices and decision making; the given-ness of organizational premises, which is not dissimilar to the *ceteris paribus* of the economist; and the assumption of system equilibrium. An important contribution of Simon and the decision-set perspective, however, has been to emphasize the limits on administrative rationality that exist within organizational contexts.

First, it is useful to describe just what is meant by the "rational man," as it is often used in economics and statistical decision theory; the accompanying box contains a summary description by March and Simon. Essentially, he[20] "makes 'optimal' choices in a highly specified environment."[21] Rational man has two important characteristics for the purposes here. One is that, in his analysis of a problem, he takes in all the complexities of the situation, all of the possible alternatives, and all of their possible consequences. The other is that he maximizes, choosing the best alternative of all that are possible.

"Administrative man," on the other hand, approaches his choices with a seemingly slight, but important, difference. The defining characteristics of economic and administrative theory are the same, namely, "to maximize the attainment of certain ends with the use of scarce resources":

A fundamental principle of administration, which follows almost immediately from the rational character of "good" administration, is that among several alternatives involving the same expenditure that one should always be selected which leads to the greatest accomplishment of administrative objectives; and among several alternatives that lead to the same accomplishment the one should be selected which involves the least expenditure. (p. 39)

The difference between the two lies in the limited ability of administrative man both to perform generally in an optimal fashion and to make correct (which is to say, economically rational) decisions (p. 39). These limits derive not only from the organizational setting within which administrative decisions are made, but also from the psychological limitations of

THE RATIONAL MAN

1 When we first encounter him in the decision-making situation, he already has laid out before him the whole set of alternatives from which he will choose his action. This set of alternatives is simply "given"; the theory does not tell how it is obtained.

2 To each alternative is attached a set of consequences . . . Here the existing theories fall into three categories: (a) *Certainty:* theories that assume the decision maker has complete and accurate knowledge of the consequences that will follow on each alternative. (b) *Risk:* theories that assume accurate knowledge of a probability distribution of the consequences of each alternative. (c) *Uncertainty:* theories that assume that the consequences of each alternative belong to some subset of all possible consequences, but that the decision maker cannot assign definite probabilities to the occurrence of particular consequences.

3 At the outset, the decision maker has a "utility function" or a "preference ordering" that ranks all sets of consequences from the most preferred to the least preferred.

4 The decision maker selects the alternative leading to the preferred set of consequences. In the case of *certainty*, the choice is unambiguous. In the case of *risk*, rationality is usually defined as the choice of that alternative for which the expected utility is greatest. . . . In the case of *uncertainty*, the definition of rationality becomes problematic. One proposal that has had wide currency is the rule of "minimax risk": consider the worst set of consequences that may follow from each alternative, then select the alternative whose "worst set of consequences" is preferred to the worst sets attached to other alternatives.

—From James G. March and Herbert A. Simon, *Organizations* (New York: John Wiley & Sons, 1958), p. 139, emphasis in original.

human cognition. Rationality, in administrative settings, is actually "bounded rationality." It is bounded in three ways (p. 81):

1 Rationality requires a complete knowledge and anticipation of the consequences that will follow on each choice. In fact, knowledge of consequences is always fragmentary.

[20]Interestingly, no other semantic forms (e.g., he/she) are ever used in describing economic man. Presumably this is to keep the reader from giving economic man any individuality, a very important point from classical economic theory's point of view. "Rational man" and "economic man" are and must always remain abstractions; this is an important buttress for the analyst when his (or her) analyses are questioned.

[21]March and Simon, p. 137.

2 Since these consequences lie in the future, imagination must supply the lack of experienced feeling in attaching value to them. But values can only be imperfectly anticipated.

3 Rationality requires a choice among all possible alternative behaviors. In actual behavior, only a very few of all these possible alternatives come to mind.

Put another way, the rationality of the administrator is limited by his unconscious habits and skills, by his values and conceptions of purpose, and by the extent of his information and knowledge (p. 241).

The result of this bounding of rationality is that, rather than searching for optimal alternatives from all that are possible, the administrator instead "satisfices" by searching for an alternative that is *satisfactory* in terms of both conditions that prevail and the organization's purposes as he understands them:

> In actual organizational practice, no one attempts to find an optimal solution for the whole problem. Instead, various particular decisions, or groups of decisions, within the whole complex are made by specialized members or units of the organization. In making these particular decisions, the specialized units do not solve the whole problem but find a "satisfactory" solution for one or more subproblems, where some of the effects of the solution on the other parts of the system are incorporated in the definition of "satisfactory." (p. 272)

Finally, administrative man simplifies the world; he does not try to deal with all of its complexity:

> Administrative man recognizes that the world he perceives is a drastically simplified model of the buzzing, blooming confusion that constitutes the real world. He is content with this gross simplification because he believes that the real world is mostly empty—that most of the facts of the real world have no great relevance to any particular situation he is facing and that most significant chains of causes and consequences are short and simple. . . . Hence, he is content to leave out of account those aspects of reality—and that means *most* aspects—that appear irrelevant at a given time. He makes his choices using a simple picture of the situation that takes into account just a few of the factors that he regards as most relevant and crucial. (p. xxx)

Neo-Classical Theory and the Public Administration Framework

On several occasions, Herbert Simon states that organizations control behavior by virtue of controlling the *premises* on which organizational decisions are made. By extension, it might also be observed that theorists, by controlling the premises of academic discussion, also control its substance and conclusions. Certainly, few theorists are more certain of their premises or more rigorous in explicating the logical consequences of their application than Simon and his colleagues. *"Love me, love my logic,"*[22] as Simon once responded to a critic whose ideas reflected a more catholic (and to Simon, therefore, a less disciplined) intellectual bent.

Ironically, however, Simon's tremendous influence is probably attributable less to the logical and methodological rigor with which he *applies* his premises than to the intuitive appeal of the premises themselves to managers and observers of organizations who read his works.[23] Simon would probably not be wholly satisfied by this explanation of his influence. But it is also undoubtedly true that several of his premises capture quite accurately the beliefs and assumptions that guide practicing managers in their everyday activities. For example, managers, as problem solvers, do see their actions, by and large, as intendedly rational in the sense of being instrumentally calculated to solve apparently self-evident problems that present themselves. The seemingly self-evident nature of these organizational problems, moreover, reinforces Simon's belief that the criterion of efficiency is most central to assessing the efficacy of administrative action. Finally, Simon's observation that limitations of time, information, and resources force managers to settle for satisficing solutions injects a note of realism that tempers otherwise heroic expectations about managers as rational problem solvers. Thus, as Charles Perrow has observed,

> Herbert Simon and James March have provided, somewhat unwittingly, the muscle and flesh for the Weberian [bureaucratic] skeleton, giving it more substance, complexity, and believability without reducing organizational theory to propositions about individual behavior.[24]

But the position that Simon and those of the decision-set perspective have so carefully articulated, although often powerful in the logical extension of its initial premises, is at the same time limiting both in its range and in the manner in which it conceptualizes problems of organizational action. These limitations are particularly evident when we consider their

---

[22]Simon, " 'Development of Theory of Democratic Administration': Replies and Comments," *American Political Science Review* 46:2(1952):494, emphasis in the original.

[23]Indeed, Dwight Waldo, the critic referred to in the previous paragraph, has noted (to Simon's outrage) that "Herbert Simon has patently made outstanding contributions to administrative study. These contributions have been made, however, when he has worked free of the methodology he has asserted." Waldo, "Development of Theory of Democratic Administration," *American Political Science Review* 46:1(1952):97.

[24]Charles Perrow, *Complex Organizations: A Critical Essay,* 2nd ed. (Glenview, Ill.: Scott, Foresman, 1979), p. 140.

contributions in light of the three organizational arenas and the three normative vectors of the public administration framework spelled out in Part I.

The Organizational Arenas of Public Administration

As we shall see in the next chapter, the Neo-Classical perspective has been severely criticized for ignoring the relationship of organizations to the environments by which they are bound.[25] This criticism, although sometimes overdrawn, points out that the Neo-Classical perspective, by focusing mainly on issues of internal organizational functioning, illuminates what we have called the intra-organizational arena, while largely ignoring the inter-organizational arena. Simon's position, for example, provides a powerful explanation of the dynamics by which organizations maintain (or fail to maintain) internal equilibrium, but neglects an analysis of the contingent nature of that equilibrium on the environments from which organizations draw their sustenance. Although the systems theorists discussed in Chapter 7 emphasize this point with monotonous regularity, they also acknowledge that Simon has provided many of the central insights that form the basis of the systems approach.

Simon is often credited with bringing psychology to bear on organizational analysis. At first glance, this would appear to make his perspective highly relevant to the organization-to-individual arena, wherein the effects of organizational structures, rules, and processes on the complexities of individual behavior are explored. Yet Simon's contribution here, though insightful on its own terms, is extremely restricted and curiously negative in its tone. To Simon, "psychology" seems to be nothing more than a synonym for a regrettable human failing, namely, the inability to act rationally. Psychology, or at least his conception of it, simply helps to explain cognitive impediments to organizational efficiency. Although his noting the limits of rationality importantly serves to dampen the naive optimism spawned by classical theory's faith in "scientific principles" of management, a richer conception of psychology that Simon offers would tell us far more about both the creative as well as pathological aspects of human behavior in organizations. By conceptually linking psychology to the premise of intendedly rational action, Simon's psychology omits most of what is interesting about individual behavior and leaves us with an excessively narrow conception of the normative importance of psychology to the study of organizations.

---

[25]In fairness to Simon, we should note that the overall thrust of his earlier work does not necessarily preclude an analysis of organizational/environment relationships and that much of his later writing does address this subject directly. See, for example, Simon, *The Sciences of the Artificial*, 2nd ed. (Cambridge, Mass.: MIT Press, 1981).

The Normative Vectors of Public Administration

Herbert Simon is sometimes regarded as the intellectual successor to Chester Barnard. Clearly many parallels can be identified between *Administrative Behavior* and *The Functions of the Executive,* including their essentially bilateral view of organizational authority and the link between Simon's notion of "zones of acceptance" and Barnard's "zones of indifference." This is not surprising in view of Simon's warm acknowledgement of Barnard's influence in the preface to *Administrative Behavior* (to which Barnard penned the foreword).

There are crucial differences between Barnard and Simon, however, that point to some crucial limitations in the perspectives of both Simon and the Neo-Classical school for normative analysis in public administration. Where, in Barnard, one finds a profound concern with moral leadership, Simon's interests are principally empirical and are derived from his philosophical commitment to logical positivism—in particular its radical conceptual distinction between fact and value. Barnard's and Simon's widely divergent sentiments, for example, are apparent in the "models of man" that each espouses. Their differing beliefs about human nature, as Perrow notes, in turn explain how Barnard and Simon regard the moral nature (or lack thereof) of the organization. As Perrow puts it:

> In Barnard's model, man by himself is nonrational, but he achieves rationality through organizations. Simon's man is intendedly rational, but participation in the organization does not produce a more rational or superior man, nor does it produce an organizationally induced increment of rationality in the individual. . . . [Organization] members are made to "adapt their decisions to the organization's objectives" and they are provided with the information needed to make correct organizational decisions. The organization gains, not the individual. . . . Simon, in his model of organizational decision making, is concerned with the organization as a tool, or with individuals as tools of the organization. Barnard could not admit to this possibility, because organizations in his view are cooperative systems where the organizational and the individual objective must coincide. For Simon this is not the case; the individual satisfies his needs (for income, for example) through the organization, but his personal ends are not necessarily the ends of the organization.[26]

Simon's instrumental, rather than moral, view of organizations, coupled with his assumption of an intendedly rational (and morally atomistic) individual, colors his conception of administrative problems. From his stance as a logical positivist, Simon sees issues of value and issues of fact as neatly separable, in which the former can only be decided arbitrarily—or, in Simon's words, "validated by human fiat." In terms of the distinc-

---

[26]Perrow, p. 142.

tion noted in Part I between tame and wicked problems, administrative problems by Simon's definition must necessarily be seen as the former. This does not mean that they are simple; indeed, they may be extremely complex. But, at the same time, he sees administrative problems as principally technical and therefore amenable to logical or empirical analysis. Perhaps more importantly, insofar as their tameness is concerned, such problems, in Simon's view, must be taken as given. Their morally problematic character can be assumed as having been eradicated by prior moral discourse or political processes, both of which are largely arbitrary and apparently of scant interest.

The assumed technical character of administrative problems, which derives from Simon's acceptance of the fact/value dichotomy, meshes nicely with Woodrow Wilson's analogous distinction between administration and politics.[27] More precisely, the former dichotomy provides the logical (and epistemological) basis for the latter dichotomy. As ordinarily defined, politics refers to the authoritative allocation of values, whereas administration, to Simon, involves decisions rationally calculated from factual premises.

To the extent that this perspective deals with values, it is to assert that the instrumental value of efficiency is of paramount importance to organization and public administration theory. Because of this, Simon rejects as naive and contrary to empirical evidence the belief that efficiency is attained through the application of classical organizational principles, many of which seemingly contradict one another. He also astutely points out the organizational impediments to efficiency and, thereby, the conditions under which the traditional bureaucratic form of organization can or cannot satisfy that criterion.

Simon's success in explicating the conditions for efficient administration, however, is precisely what prevents him from regarding any normative issues other than efficiency as important. To be sure, Simon himself would not regard this as a serious limitation. For example, problems of individual rights and the adequacy of organizational processes, he would no doubt argue, are political ones, beyond the ken of rational analysis. To the extent such problems do have administrative implications, they are

---

[27]Although the label "Neo-Classical" that is appended to his writings most often refers to Simon's *organization* theory, it is an equally appropriate adjective for Simon as a *public administration* theorist. Vincent Ostrom has noted that Simon presented a radical challenge to the classical (Wilsonian) paradigm of public administration by using the efficiency criterion "to reject the presumption that perfection in hierarchical ordering is synonymous with efficiency." Vincent Ostrom, *The Intellectual Crisis in American Public Administration,* rev. ed. (University, Ala.: University of Alabama Press, 1974), pp. 45–46. Although Ostrom's statement of Simon's position is correct, it is arguable whether it constitutes a "radical challenge" to Wilson's classical formulation, since Simon sustains, via the fact/value dichotomy, the logical essence of Wilson's dichotomy between politics and administration. For further discussion of Ostrom's views of Simon's work, see Chapter 9.

dealt with by administrative technology and are therefore really questions of efficiency. Problems of rights and organizational process, by definition, are not administrative problems per se, unless they can be tamed by administrative technology. Similarly, although acknowledging the issue of administrative discretion, Simon treats it simply as evidence of the *limits* of rational, and therefore efficient, administration. Discretion is required, for example, to deal with "nonroutine" tasks that cannot be programmed through the preferred mode of normal bureaucratic channels. As Perrow notes, under such conditions, Simon believes that "there must be more emphasis on experience, 'feel,' or professionalization.... There is more craft, or art, or esoteric skills (in the case of professionals) involved."[28] While undoubtedly true, Simon's premises are of meager assistance in providing sage advice to professionals in making wise and judicious discretionary judgments.

Conclusion

Herbert Simon, as well as those who have followed in his intellectual footsteps, have in one sense been true to important traditions in classical public administration thought. This is apparent chiefly in their commitment to the value of efficiency and more broadly to the important role of science in guiding administrative theory and practice. In yet another and equally significant respect, however, they have parted company with the democratic ethos that informed, and continues to inform, the philosophical basis of public administration. This is not intended as a criticism of Simon and his contemporaries, whose disciplinary loyalties lie mainly in other fields of academic and professional endeavor. It does, however, suggest a warning to those in public administration who may, and often have, taken Neo-Classical organization theory as a sufficient theoretical foundation for their field. To do so, in effect, relegates democratic theory, and indeed political theory generally, to at best marginal status in public administration. The consequence is to restrict severely any normative awareness of the critical social role that public organizations play in the larger society.

As we shall see in the chapters that follow, Herbert Simon is a central figure with whom all perspectives in organization theory must contend. For some, especially those reviewed in the chapters that follow immediately, he provides vital insights and is criticized only for failing to extend his ideas far enough. From other perspectives, in particular many of the

---

[28]Perrow, p. 162.

theorists discussed in Chapters 10 and 11, Simon is regarded as not only fundamentally misguided, but as the purveyor of a pernicious social philosophy. Regardless of these disagreements, the decision-set perspective still forms the core of administrative practice, as well as the essential logic of administrative technology, as it has for half a century.

7

Systems Theory: Organizations as Purposive Entities

As we saw in the last chapter, looking at the organization as a decision set highlights the rational aspects of organizational decision making. That perspective aids in sensitizing both observers and participants to the means by which instrumental rationality both structures and determines the choices made by administrators. At the same time, the limitations of the view of the Neo-Classical school impede our understanding of other important aspects of organizations.

For example, the strong normative emphasis on efficiency tends to obscure the importance of other norms, such as representation and the control of discretion, that are also relevant to public administration settings. Similarly, the narrow focus on efficient means to attain previously specified ends may also serve to deflect attention from issues involving the protection of individual rights and the satisfaction of people's unique and therefore differing needs. Because the decision-set posture generally ignores the process of goal *setting* (taking it as a given), it offers little illumination of the place of public organizations within the larger social/governmental context.

At the time Herbert Simon published *Administrative Behavior*, a related but nonetheless distinctive perspective in organization theory began its emergence to a position of dominance in the field. Rooted in structural/functional sociology, "systems theory" has become such an integral part of our outlook on organizations that it is often difficult to separate its main ideas from much of the organizational thinking that has followed.

Introduction

Like most significant developments in social theory, organization theories that achieve widespread prominence not only are linked to earlier currents in intellectual thought, but also reflect the temper of their times. This is most certainly true of systems theory, which has sustained its position as the dominant school of thought in organization theory for a quarter of a century. In the United States, the aftermath of World War II fertilized both a vision of unlimited economic growth and abundance, and a conservative social and political climate. The latter appeared to stem in part from the complacency engendered by the former and was reinforced by the mood of postwar isolationism and the reality of the Cold War with the Soviet Union. The resulting economic and institutional growth in the United States was of unprecedented scale and complexity. The rapid social change of the late 1940s and 1950s thus produced was not the product of a progressive social ideology, but rather came about through swift adjustment to the imperatives of technological advancement engendered by that economic growth.

Social and technological change, coupled with the political conservatism of the postwar era, invited explanation and legitimation by social theorists. With social and technological change also came uncertainty and interdependence. This forced organization theorists to expand the earlier inward-looking belief in rationality as the handmaiden of efficiency, for the narrower definition no longer helped them account for organizational survival in a turbulent environment. Thus, they sought to explain not only the combination of change and conservatism, but also this alteration in the spirit of rationalism.

As we have seen, the foundation for a more sophisticated understanding of organizational rationality had already been laid. Chester Barnard and the early human relations theorists had begun to develop the notion of the organization as a social system that requires enlightened management in order to deal with such issues as equilibrium and stabilization. These were concerns that the narrower vision of rationality, such as Frederick Taylor's, had great difficulty encompassing. Finally, Herbert Simon, with the publication of *Administrative Behavior* in 1947, debunked much of the naive rationalism developed as "principles of administration" by describing the cognitive and psychological limits to rationality within organizations. Thus, his notion of "satisficing" became useful to the systems theorists as an explanation of the strategies used by organizations in surviving the perils of hostile, unpredictable environments. Simon, like Barnard who preceded him, was a pivotal figure in the transition from the rational machine image of organizations to that of the purposive entity, embodied most clearly in systems theory.

It is possible to abstract several general insights that this perspective offers. There are five characteristics of systems theory that form the basis of the discussion that follows:

1 Each part of an organization can only be understood in terms of its relation to the other parts of the organization.

2 The parts of the organization, including their interrelatedness, are important insofar as they contribute to the overall functioning of the organization.

3 Organizations, conceived as wholes, may be thought of metaphorically as biological organisms, replete with needs or goals that are superordinate to and conceptually separate from the conscious needs, purposes, and goals of individual parts or members.

4 These needs and goals of organizations may be conceived either statically (e.g., survival or maintenance of order) or dynamically (e.g., in terms of purposive evolution or change).

5 Organizational activity of any significance is understandable in terms of its relation to the external environment, which provides the resources and conditions on which the organization depends for its survival or the realization of its purposes.

The remainder of this chapter begins by briefly tracing the intellectual development of modern organizational systems theory from its origins in structural/functional sociology and general systems theory. This is followed by a summary of how these ideas were adapted by several organizational systems theorists to explain the structure and behavior of complex organizations. The next section examines some critiques of this perspective, as well as some attempts to rescue it by reorienting its description of organizational reality. The final section discusses how the systems perspective illuminates the framework of public administration.

The Intellectual Origins of Systems Theory

Although organizational systems theory owes considerable debt to Barnard and Simon, in a more comprehensive sense its origins lie in structural/functional sociology and general systems theory. Although these latter two grew out of very different traditions and diverged greatly in their respective research agendas, they have a similarity of assumptions and metaphors that makes them virtually indistinguishable from one another in many respects.

Structural/functionalism was well established as the leading school of thought in sociology by the mid-1950s. It received its initial articulation in social anthropology, principally through the writings of Bronislaw Malinowski and A. Radcliffe-Brown in the 1930s. Their functionalism was one that emphasized the interrelatedness of different aspects of a culture. Thus, Radcliffe-Brown argued that

> To turn from organic life to social life, if we examine such a community as an African or Australian tribe we can recognize the existence of a social structure. Individual human beings . . . connected by a definite set of social relations into an integrated whole. . . . The continuity of structure is maintained by the process of social life, which consists of the activities and interactions of the individual human beings and of organized groups into which they are united.[1]

The Sociology of Talcott Parsons

Talcott Parsons adapted this functionalist perspective to the study of sociology,[2] eventually integrating it with the sociological perspective of Max Weber, whose writings were just beginning to gain visibility in the United States.[3] Structural/functionalists such as Parsons ask one basic question: How is it that societies manage to keep functioning and survive? Although their answers deal to some extent with change, their major preoccupation is with explaining the nature of societal order in light of the constant turnover of individuals who populate the history of any social system. The individuals change, but one replaces another over time by stepping into already developed functional roles within the society.

For structural/functionalists, the starting point, or primary unit of analysis, is the social system conceived as a whole. The ongoing functions of systems, they argue, can only be seen in relationship to the whole. Their perspective, then, seeks to explain

> the relationship of the parts to the whole in order to show how what appear to be isolated, if not inexplicable, social phenomena may fulfill some wider purpose related to the stability of society.[4]

---

[1]A. Radcliffe-Brown, *Structure and Function in Primitive Society* (London: Cohen and West, 1952), p. 180.

[2]See Talcott Parsons, *The Social System* (New York: Free Press, 1951), especially Chapters 2 and 3.

[3]This was in large part due to the efforts of Parsons himself, who studied in Germany and later translated some of Weber's works into English. It is testimony to the richness (and perhaps the ambiguity) of Weber's work that he served as a major source of inspiration not only to Parsons, but also to some of the latter's principal detractors, such as C. Wright Mills and Alfred Schutz.

[4]David Silverman, *The Theory of Organisations* (New York: Basic Books, 1970), p. 45.

In other words, the structural/functional theorist, by virtue of this holistic approach, is primarily concerned with how systemic subunits (including both organized groups and individuals) contribute to the survival and stability of the system as a whole. To support the system's survival, particular subunits need not be consciously aware of the functions they perform within the system. Indeed, these functions are usually superordinate to (and sometimes in conflict with) the goals that individuals and groups may self-consciously pursue. "Function" is thus an overarching notion that applies to the system as a whole. One of the first explicit statements of this idea was made by the anthropologist Bronislaw Malinowski, who argued that functionalism:

> ... aims at the explanation of anthropological facts at all levels of development by their function, by the part which they play within the integral system of culture, by the manner in which they are related to each other within the system, and by the manner in which this system is related to the physical surroundings. ... The functional view of culture insists therefore upon the principle that in every type of civilization, every custom, material object, idea and belief fulfills some vital function, has some task to accomplish, represents an indispensable part within a working whole.[5]

Few of the later functionalists go as far as Malinowski in insisting that *every* part of the system necessarily fulfills a vital systemic need or purpose. Most, however, do rely on such themes as the imperative for system survival, the interdependency among system parts, and the contingent nature of the environment.

A clear example of this is Parsons's description of the four "functional imperatives" that any social system is driven toward and must satisfy if it is to continue to survive. The first, *adaptation,* consists of those actions of a system that, taken together, form linkages and relationships with the external environment on which it is dependent. In this way, the system secures, as any social system must, necessary resources from the environment and distributes them among the system subunits. *Goal attainment* is a management function involving the mobilization and use of resources. It encompasses those activities within the system that lead to and direct the accomplishment of ends. *Integration* is the coordination of the parts of the system such that control is established, deviancy is thwarted, and internal stability is maintained. Finally, *latent pattern-maintenance* deals

---

[5]Bronislaw Malinowski, "Anthropology," *The Encyclopedia Britannica,* Supplementary I, pp. 132–33, cited in Ernest Nagel, "Problems of Concept and Theory Formation in the Social Sciences," in Maurice Natanson, ed., *Philosophy of the Social Sciences* (New York: Random House, 1963), p. 193.

with "the problem of how to ensure continuity of action in the system according to some order or norm."[6]

As Parsons views it, the effective performance of these four functions is necessary for the survival of any living system, from a small natural organism to a large social collectivity. The norms make up the value system that serves to motivate and bound the actions of system subunits (groups and individuals). Adaptation and goal attainment relate to the efficiency of the system, while integration and latency affect its stability. Given the universality of these functional imperatives, the task of sociological analysis is, for Parsons, to identify and explain those structures and parts of social systems that perform and enhance, as well as limit, these functions.

Two implications of the functional imperatives bear examination. First, survival in this view is made possible by the efficiency and stability with which the system performs. This suggests that any undue change may well threaten the survival of the system. Change, particularly as heralded by conflict, is an indicator of discontinuity (between system and environment) or disequilibrium (within the system). This occurs when there is an imbalance between the stabilizing functions (integration and latency) on one hand and the efficiency-promoting functions (goal attainment and adaptation) on the other. From this comes the view that even though change may be internally generated, the conditions that give rise to it are evidence of a system pathology needful of remedy.

A second implication to note is that the organic metaphor implicit in the functional imperatives (and explicit in Parsons's work) tends to put a premium on survival in such a way that change, when it does occur, is viewed as an adaptive adjustment to externally imposed conditions made in the interest of restoring equilibrium. The main difficulty is that this is a circular, after-the-fact determination: If the system survives, the adjustment restored equilibrium; if not, then it failed. There is no way, however, to make a reasonable estimate of the probability of success. This tends to reinforce the opinions of those in power, rather than to offer any means of mediating between differing power positions. Nor do such *post hoc* explanations allow for seeing an act as a self-generated one, valuable for its own sake.

Ludwig von Bertalanffy and General Systems Theory

Concurrent with the rise of structural/functionalism, a transdisciplinary movement called general systems theory emerged from the work of

---

[6]Margaret M. Paloma, *Contemporary Sociological Theory* (New York: Macmillan, 1979), p. 114.

biologist Ludwig von Bertalanffy. His project has been to develop a generalized scientific language and methodology to be used in the "formulation of principles that are valid for 'systems' in general, whatever the nature of their component elements and the relations or 'forces' between them."[7] The need for the development of such principles, von Bertalanffy argues, derives from the complexity and interdisciplinary nature of practical problems. Identifying principles of scientific explanation common to all kinds of systems would make it possible to use the knowledge from highly understood systems to explore the less-understood ones.

Von Bertalanffy stresses that general systems theory is the science of "wholeness," in contrast to traditional (natural) science, which "tried to explain observable phenomena by reducing them to an interplay of elementary units investigatable independently of each other."[8] Systems, however, are truly understandable only in terms of the interplay among their constituent systemic elements and their relationship with their larger environment. Although a major part of the research agenda of general systems theory is to discover "general laws," these are not presumed to be deterministic, but rather are statistical or probabilistic in nature.

Guiding this search for laws are several concepts that form the basis of the systems perspective. For example, the initial context for most discussion in systems theory is the now-commonplace distinction between *open* and *closed* systems. The closed system metaphor depicts a self-contained entity in which the functioning of the component parts and their interrelationships are the primary objects of inquiry. Any simple machine operating as a self-contained mechanism, such as a lawn mower or an automobile, is a prototypical closed system. Similarly, bureaucracy is often seen as an organizational equivalent of a closed system. Its relationship to its environment is regulated and stabilized in such a way that one can, analytically, ignore that environment when describing, dissecting, and manipulating the system. This is what Max Weber does, for instance, when describing the characteristics of ideal–typical bureaucracy. In the same way, Frederick Taylor's discussion of the functions of the planning department essentially assumes that the firm's environment is stable, calculable, and likely to have little impact, in the sense of changing the work of the department.

As a metaphor, the closed system suggests that its natural tendency is toward *equilibrium* or balance amongst its systemic components. Its stability comes in large part from the regularized importing of energy from the environment. When this stability becomes unbalanced such that insufficient energy is imported, the system is said to undergo the process of

[7]Ludwig von Bertalanffy, *General Systems Theory* (New York: George Braziller, 1968), p. 37.
[8]Ibid., pp. 36–37.

entropy, "a law of nature in which all forms of organization move toward disorganization and death."[9] The closed system view is based on the assumption that support from the environment is forthcoming and predictable rather than problematic, so that attention may be focused on the internal efficiency with which system resources are used in the maintenance of equilibrium.

Few, if any, theorists have ever been advocates of the closed system approach. Rather, it is often an appellation used by systems theorists as a straw man and attributed to those theoretical approaches that have shown insufficient attention (from this point of view) to systemic relationships with the external environment. Thus, Barnard and Simon are sometimes labeled closed system (or equilibrium) theorists because of their preoccupation with the internal dynamics of organization.

The open system has been the dominant image in systems theory from the outset. Much of its literature embraces, if only loosely at times, the metaphor of the organization as a biological organism, thus emphasizing system survival rather than internal efficiency. This directs attention to the relationships between the system and its contingent environment. With this emphasis, the internal equilibrium concept is replaced by *homeostasis* (sometimes called "homeostatic equilibrium"). This is meant to depict a dynamic balance of forces and a constant exchange of energy with the environment that counteracts the entropic, disintegrating processes endemic to closed systems. *Negative entropy* (or "negentropy") entails, at a minimum, those processes enabling systems to maintain homeostatic equilibrium; other senses of the term convey a more positive meaning wherein systems are seen as naturally productive of growth, expansionistic, purposive, goal directed, and even creative. However, opinion differs as to whether or to what extent negative entropy should be regarded as a force internally generated within a system, as opposed to a necessary outcome produced when a system receives more energy from its environment than it needs for mere survival.[10] With the principle of negative entropy, systems are seen as *purposive.*

The purposiveness of a system is one of the most elusive concepts to clarify. To add to the difficulty, there is a distinction between "purposive" and "purposeful" that is honored more often in the breach. "Purposive" means acting or appearing to act toward an end or goal. "Purposeful" carries with it the additional sense of a conscious intention by the actors

[9]Daniel Katz and Robert L. Kahn, *The Social Psychology of Organizations,* 2nd ed. (New York: John Wiley and Sons, 1978), p. 25.

[10]Whatever the nuances of the various meanings of negative entropy, critics have chided systems theorists for choosing a clumsy, incongruous term to describe the essentially creative and growthful nature of human systems. "Negative entropy," as Charles Hampden-Turner points out, is a little like "referring to life as undeath." Charles Hampden-Turner, *Radical Man* (Garden City, N.Y.: Anchor Books, 1971), p. 13.

in a system in the selection of the end or goal toward which they orient their actions. Systems theorists appear divided (if not confused) on this matter. Sometimes, they include conscious intent as a defining feature of purposiveness; more often, however, the apparent purposiveness of social systems is an interpretation *by the theorist,* based on his or her own perceptual frame of reference, which is independent of the intentions and goals of the system members being studied.

Used in this latter sense, purpose refers to those conditions or states that individuals and, collectively, systems actively work to bring about or, in some cases, avoid. "Goal-oriented action" and purpose underlie Parsons's functional imperatives; they also underlie such open systems concepts as negative entropy. They do this by being, ultimately, the measure by which one determines whether, for example, the system is deteriorating. Thus, a presumed purpose of every system (though by no means in any conscious sense) is stability and continued existence.[11]

In the open systems perspective, with the notion of purposiveness the additional principle of *equifinality* follows. The idea is that an end state can be reached by a variety of paths and from widely different initial conditions. Essentially this is a notion of causality, but one that differs radically from that embodied in, for instance, the work of Frederick Taylor. For Taylor, as we saw earlier, the concept of causality was very narrow. It was embodied in a statement such as "Under given conditions, when A happens, then B follows." With this direct, linear idea of causality, prediction was seen as both possible and realizable; all one needed was to determine the first half of the statement and the second half would follow. Equifinality, on the other hand, severely undermines such a concept. To the extent that it is present in a system, it means there is no real possibility of determining B from A in any linear fashion. From the systems perspective, "the one best way" does not exist.[12]

Inputs, throughputs, and *outputs* are relational terms that depict, respectively, the energy and resources imported into the system from its environment, the transformation or processing of the energy and resources within the system, and the export of the transformed inputs back into the environment. (See Figure 7.1.) The emphasis of this kind of analysis is on the process rather than on who benefits. In other words, so long as a system's outputs satisfy the demands of its environment, and so

---

[11]The idea that a system has a purpose, when put so baldly, smacks of the worst sort of reification. For this reason, most writers from Parsons on (including von Bertalanffy) have assiduously avoided any such direct statement that would seem to imply that a "system chooses a purpose." Nonetheless, as will be seen below, this has been a distinction that has been a fine line to walk.

[12]At the same time, however, instrumental rationality is still central to systems theory for the judging of whether an activity is appropriate in the attainment of a goal, and, once having judged that, in selecting the means to accomplish the activity.

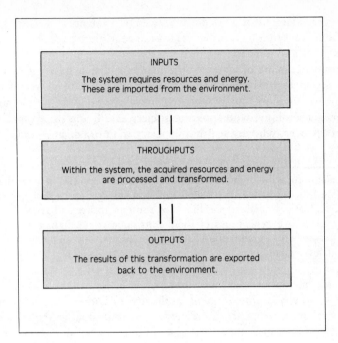

Figure 7.1 *The System and Its Environment*

long as it is able to import as much or more energy and resources than it expends or exports, then it is irrelevant to the analysis who the beneficiaries (or casualties) of the input-throughput-output process are.

In order to understand the effectiveness with which work is accomplished in the system (that is, in the throughput part of the process), two concepts are basic. *Feedback* "signals to the [system's] structure about the environment and about its own functioning in relation to the environment."[13] Thus, negative feedback permits the system to correct for inadvertent deviations from its desired course. *Differentiation* is the process by which a system develops specialized structures and processes for dealing with the complex, multifaceted tasks of sensing what is going on in the environment and transforming energy and resources into usable outputs. Differentiation is what Taylor engaged in as he analyzed jobs and broke them down into evermore discrete tasks. It is also what Weber meant when he talked of the rationalization of domination through the growth of bureaucracy. To the systems theorist, differentiation is the measure of the complexity and sophistication of a system.

These various terms give a flavor of the general thrust of the systems approach. It should be clear that the main emphasis is a relational one, in

[13]Katz and Kahn, p. 26.

which every element of a system is viewed as a member of a set. The set is itself held together by being (or at least appearing to be) oriented toward various goals and purposes.

Many proponents of general systems theory use organic or biological metaphors to express the relationships of the parts of a system to the whole. Few anymore do so with the literalness of Auguste Comte, the founder of sociology, who spoke of society as a living organism,[14] or of Herbert Spencer, who argued that "Society is an organism," and,

> Such, then, is a general outline of the evidence which justifies the comparison of societies to living organisms. That they gradually increase in mass; that they become little by little more complex; that at the same time their parts grow more mutually dependent; and that they continue to live and grow as wholes, while successive generations of their units appear and disappear; are broad peculiarities which bodies-politic display in common with all living bodies; and in which they and living bodies differ from everything else.[15]

Organic metaphors are now more often used by implication. Thus, Anthony Downs, a pre-eminent authority on bureaucracy, would be unlikely to embrace Spencer's "society is an organism," yet he talks of the "life cycle of bureaus," their "struggle for autonomy," and "the effects of age upon bureaus."[16] Likewise, the political scientist David Easton carefully distances himself from explicit use of the organic metaphor, yet at the same time uses language that draws from that source. For example, in his *A Framework for Political Analysis,* he summarizes his argument, saying that in

> ... the conceptualization being used here, our analysis will rest on the idea of a system imbedded in an environment and subject to possible influences from it that threaten to drive the essential variables of the system beyond their critical range. To persist, the system must be capable of responding with measures that are successful in alleviating the stress created.[17]

As metaphors, such images are often useful; however, they are also used at times to justify the idea that systems have a *natural* and *necessary* need to survive, to seek homeostasis and to increase negative entropy.

Like his structural/functionalist contemporaries, von Bertalanffy borrows heavily from metaphors in biology to help explain the nature of

---

[14]See Auguste Comte, *The Foundation of Sociology,* Kenneth Thompson, ed., (New York: John Wiley and Sons, 1975).

[15]Herbert Spencer, "The Social Organism", in *Essays: Scientific, Political, and Speculative,* vol. 1 (New York: D. Appleton, 1891), p. 306.

[16]Anthony Downs, *Inside Bureaucracy* (Boston: Little, Brown, 1966), pp. 5, 7, 18.

[17]David Easton, *A Framework for Political Analysis* (Chicago: University of Chicago Press, 1979), p. 33.

social systems. At the same time, however, he is cautious about taking such metaphors literally in explaining social activity. He warns against the "dangerous fallacies" resulting from the facile transfer of principles from one level of analysis to another."[18] In fact, he has been at the forefront of those systems theorists who have been most sensitive to the criticisms regarding the use of the organic metaphor to describe system behavior. Uncritically adopting such a metaphor in thinking about social systems, he argues, results from a misunderstanding of the purposes of general systems theory. Any search for similarities between systems across levels of analysis ("isomorphies") also reveals important dissimilarities:

> Analogies as such are of little value since besides similarities between phenomena, dissimilarities can always be found as well. The isomorphism under discussion is more than a mere analogy. It is a consequence of the fact that, in certain respects, corresponding abstractions and conceptual models can be applied to different phenomena. Only in view of these aspects will system laws apply. This is not different from the general procedures in science. It is the same situation as when the law of gravitation applies to Newton's apple, the planetary system, and tidal phenomenon. This means that in view of certain limited aspects a theoretical system, that of mechanics, holds true; it does not mean that there is a particular resemblence between apples, planets, and oceans in a great number of other aspects.[19]

His major target of criticism, however, is classical physics, whereas he sees considerable compatibility between the concepts of the biological and the social sciences. Such concepts as homeostasis, "the maintenance of balance in the living organism"[20] are central to understanding the organized complexity of social systems. Similarly, the idea of equifinality, "the tendency towards a characteristic final state from different initial states and in different ways"[21] von Bertalanffy finds useful in explaining the purposive, goal-directed, and evolutionary nature of social organizations. Feedback, a word now found in everyday parlance in organizations, more technically refers to the "homeostatic maintenance of a characteristic state or the seeking of a goal, based on circular causal chains and mechanisms monitoring back information on deviations from the state to be maintained or the goal to be reached."[22] The notions of homeostasis, equifinality, and feedback, although antithetical to classical physics with its conception of the world as fundamentally mechanical, are essential to the generic idea of organization in biology and social science. As von Bertalanffy notes,

[18]Von Bertalanffy, p. 34.
[19]Ibid., pp. 35–36.
[20]Ibid., p. 43.
[21]Ibid., p. 46.
[22]Ibid.

Characteristic of organization, whether a living organism or a society, are notions like that of wholeness, growth, differentiation, hierarchical order, dominance, control, competition, etc. Such notions do not appear in conventional physics.[23]

Even von Bertalanffy concedes, however, the limitations of biology for an accurate *empirical* understanding of the social world, as well as the potential normative dangers of the organic metaphor when used as the basis for moral/ethical judgments.

Organizations as Open Systems: Daniel Katz and Robert L. Kahn

If systems theory is currently the dominant school of thought in organization theory, then Daniel Katz and Robert Kahn's *The Social Psychology of Organizations* is the most comprehensive and important work representing that viewpoint. Initially published in 1966 and revised in 1978, their *magnum opus* comprehensively synthesizes the major ideas about organizations drawn from both structural/functionalism (especially Parsons) and general systems theory. The inclusion of "social psychology" in their title seems peculiar in the sense that their primary unit of analysis is the organization conceived holistically, with psychological and social-psychological considerations having secondary status. But they begin their work by noting the inadequacies of psychology for dealing with problems of the social world because of its

inability to deal with the facts of social structure and social organization. . . . The dominant tradition in psychology has included the implicit assumption that individuals exist in a social vacuum.[24]

Their objective is to develop a framework for organizational analysis that permits the merger of several levels of theoretical concern, from the micro (individual) level up through the macro (total organization in its environment) level. The open system perspective, in their view, is ideally suited to enable the integration of these various levels of analysis.

"Open system theory is rather a framework, a meta-theory, a model in the broadest sense of that overused term" (p. 752), they argue. This approach is especially applicable to the study of organizations, because it is an efficacious way of understanding the organization as "a recurrent

---

[23]Ibid., p. 47.
[24]Katz and Kahn, p. 2; in this section, all page references in parentheses are to this previously cited source; emphasis is in the original unless otherwise noted.

pattern of events, differentiated from, but dependent on, the larger stream of life in which it occurs and recurs" (p. 752). The approach postulates that organizations (the patterned activities of a group of individuals repeated within and bounded by space and time) have basic systemic properties of energic input, transformation, and energic output. With this, Katz and Kahn set aside any definition of organization that relies on identifying "goals" or "purposes," although they do allow that

> We may want to employ such purposive notions to lead us to sources of data . . . but not as our basic theoretical constructs for understanding organizations. (p. 20)

Thus, organizational functions or objectives are *not*

> . . . the conscious purposes of group leaders or group members but [are] the outcomes that are the energic source for maintenance of the same type of output.[25] (p. 21)

Organizational goals, they contend, are imbedded in the history, traditions, and protocols of the organization and must be understood in the context of the organization's own systemic framework of inputs, throughputs, and outputs, which may well diverge significantly from the current rational intent of any particular actor:

> Though the founders of the organization and its key members do think in teleological [i.e., rational, goal-directed] terms about organizational objectives, we should not accept such practical thinking, useful as it may be, in place of a theoretical set of constructs for purposes of scientific analysis. (p. 19)

Employing an input-output model (such as depicted earlier in Figure 7.1) as their framework of analysis, Katz and Kahn contend, provides a broader array of information about the important functions of organizations, especially those that, in a cumulative and historical sense, transpire independently of the conscious purposes of individual actors. In other words, they are not at all suggesting that the ideas that members have about the purposes of their organizations should be ignored; rather, they are emphasizing that these ideas are insufficient in themselves as explanatory notions about organizational behavior in the large.

As we saw above, open systems theory deals primarily with the prob-

---

[25]There would seem to be at least two problems with this formulation. One is the intentionality inherent in the word "function"; this is discussed in the text below. The second is that outcome as the source for maintenance does not allow for any organizational change except through a change in objectives. Explanation of how such change takes place is not, as we shall see, dealt with explicitly by Katz and Kahn.

lems of relationships, structure, and interdependence. In attempting to limit the application of the organismic analogy to organizations (and thereby avoid one of the more strident objections to system theory's tendency toward reification), the authors argue that organizations have unique properties as open systems, the most important of which is that they have no structure in the anatomical sense. Rather, because membership is not accidental and behavior of members is not random, the events of the organization (i.e., its members acting in purposive, patterned ways over time) constitute the structure; these assume dynamic forms called functions.[26]

"A human organization endures only so long as people are induced to provide those [organizational] inputs, including membership and role performance" (p. 754). Thus, it is necessary to distinguish two categories of inputs: *production inputs,* which are those energies and materials related to the work of the organization in turning out a product, and *maintenance inputs,* which are those energies and "information contributions" needed to hold members in the system and to persuade them to perform their activities as system members.

To relate the functioning of an organization as an open system to the activities of individuals in that organization, Katz and Kahn use the concept of *role,* relying on role theory to account for individual behavior. This is an important step of abstraction, for while an individual may fill a role, the person and role are not synonymous, each being slightly more than the other, like two overlapping circles in a Venn diagram. What is organized in an organization are acts—"the behavior of people acting on materials, acting on machines, but above all interacting with each other" (p. 183). An individual is located within this total set of activities by reference to an "office," which is a particular point in organizational space. *Space* is in turn defined "in terms of a structure of inter-related offices and the patterns of activities associated with them" (p. 188). Thus, *office* provides the relational quality to allow for the existence of roles, which require by their definition an assumption of relation.

Each office carries a set of activities and expected behaviors that constitute a role to be performed, while

> Role behavior refers to the recurring actions of an individual, appropriately interrelated with the repetitive activities of others so as to yield a predictable outcome. (p. 189)

---

[26]The "purpose of an organization as defined by its leaders," avoided earlier, crops up here in a slightly different guise. The term "function" carries several related meanings, including that of normal activity of an organism (such as the "procreative function"), or a duty or expected performance ("a teacher's function is to assist students"), or something that depends on and varies with something else ("crop yields are a function of the weather"). All three present the same difficulty as does assigning "purpose."

And, further,

> The enactment of roles always consists of individual behaviors, but the behaviors are primarily defined by system requirements and do not express the personality of the individual in significant ways. (p. 755)

Role episodes link the expectations of members of the role set to the behavior of the focal person (the individual whose office or role is under consideration). And, finally, the role system (i.e., the organization) is maintained by the confluence of three elements—task demands, shared values, and the observance of rules.

An organization, then, is an open system that develops

> the various functions of carrying on the work of the system, insuring maintenance of the structure, obtaining environmental support, adapting to environmental change, and coordinating and controlling activities [and thereby becomes] differentiated into appropriate subsystems. (p. 756)

The various functions can be seen in terms of generic organizational subsystems, which have a striking similarity to Parsons's functional imperatives outlined above. They are (p. 52):

1 production subsystems, concerned with the work that gets done;

2 supportive subsystems of procurement, disposal, and institutional relations;

3 maintenance subsystems for tying people into their functional roles;

4 adaptive subsystems, concerned with organizational change; and

5 managerial systems for the direction, adjudication, and control of the many subsystems and activities of the structure.

Three elements regulate the way in which these organizational subsystems operate. The *pattern of formal roles* determines an orderly and functional division of labor within the organization and across the subsystems. The *authority structure* decides and enforces how the management and control functions operate. And, finally, the *ideology* provides organizational norms supporting the authority structure.

Although Katz and Kahn regard bureaucracy as only one of several forms of social organization, their discussion of organizational role patterns and authority is highly reminiscent of Weber's outline of the ideal-typical bureaucracy, including its assumptions of rationality and impersonality. The authority structure is, for them, "the way in which the managerial system is organized concerning the sources of decision making and

and its implementation." As such, it is a property of the system and must be distinguished from "the dominance-submission patterns of individual personalitites" (p. 57). This conceptual separation between the individual and the organization leads the authors to legitimate the formal, impersonal authority of the bureaucratic model. This is an extension of the way in which Chester Barnard, in one of his few real-life example in *The Functions of the Executive,* approvingly tells the story of the switchboard operator who stays at her job (i.e., performing her formal role), while she watches her mother's house burn.

Katz and Kahn acknowledge the possibility of both democratic and authoritarian organizations. Democracy, however, is strictly limited to the "legislative (that is, policy-making) system," which they clearly distinguish from the "executive system," which is responsible for policy implementation. The latter is fundamentally authoritarian in nature, either by definition or practical necessity (it is unclear which). Thus,

> *The essential difference between a democratic and an authoritarian system is not whether executive officers order or consult with those below them but whether the power to legislate on policy is vested in the membership or in the top echelons.* (p. 58)

The distinction between the legislative and executive systems bears a strong resemblance to the means/ends separation of instrumental rationality evident both in Simon's work and in traditional public administration thought. After criticizing the naive rationalism of much of traditional management thinking, Katz and Kahn reinstate, via a different route, the spirit of that rationalism through their conceptual separation of legislative and executive systems. This separation is remarkably similar to the policy-administration dichotomy that served as the basis for the heavily rationalistic view of administrative ethics and decision making in the early public administration literature.

This distinction is also part of a later discussion of organizational models. After reviewing existing formulations and noting the deficiencies of each, Katz and Kahn conclude that insufficient attention has been given to the interplay of three motivational patterns: (1) compliance with rules, (2) responsiveness to economic returns and external rewards, and (3) value consensus and intrinsic rewards. The importance of focusing on these major forms of motivation is that "organizational design cannot be dictated solely by the seeming requirements of efficiency and effectiveness . . . Nor can the design of an organization be set once and for all" (p. 287). Motives are, for Katz and Kahn, the "direct ties between organizational requirements and individual motivations" (p. 289).

These three patterns are ideal types, and any organization contains some varying mixture of the three. Recognizing that discussions of motivation often commit the fallacy of equating the organization with the individual, the authors review the literature in these three areas with an eye to acknowledging the importance of, for instance, external rewards, while at the same time "acknowledging the complexities of individual and organizational behavior" (p. 324). In any case, the three motive patterns "are proposed as characteristic of organizations and as capable of producing the required behaviors in varying degrees" (p. 424).

"High levels of organizational effectiveness" require that members join and stay in the organization, perform their assigned roles in a dependable fashion, and *"engage in occasional innovative and cooperative behavior beyond the requirements of the role"* (p. 424). These generic requirements define organizational effectiveness at the individual level, which, the authors argue, is distinct from effectiveness at either the organizational or societal level. In addition, effectiveness is a concept—"a more inclusive and elusive concept"—than organizational efficiency, the latter merely being ratios of output to input.

Katz and Kahn argue that systems (particularly the bureaucratic type) also strive for expansion and growth through what they call the *maximization principle,* which marks a basic characteristic of social systems. Thus, the principle (p. 97):

> . . . can and frequently does override the maintenance dynamic for five basic reasons:
>
> 1 the proficiency dynamic [i.e., the tendency to produce technological improvements in the work process] leads to an increase in organizational capabilities;
>
> 2 expansion is the simplest method of dealing with problems of internal strain;
>
> 3 expansion is also the most direct solution in coping with problems of a changing social environment;
>
> 4 bureaucratic role systems in their nature permit of ready elaboration, and
>
> 5 organizational ideology encourages growth aspirations.

Katz and Kahn do not, however, regard the tendencies of organizations to grow and expand as an unqualified good. Their elaboration of the maximization principle is punctuated by terms such as "internal strain," "response to competitive pressures," and the "pretentiousness" of organizational ideology. They see organizational growth as seldom matched by commensurate increases in productivity. In fact, one gets the impression that growth, as they view it, is often pathological, irrational, and probably contrary to the long-term good of either the organization or the environment by which it is bound.

Critics have persistently argued that, by virtue of its preoccupation with problems of order and stability, structural/functional analysis has failed to deal adequately with social conflict. Katz and Kahn address this concern by arguing that the socially contrived character of organizations naturally renders them far less integrated than biological systems and therefore open to pervasive conflict. This lack of integration (and therefore the resulting social conflict as well) is exacerbated by the inherent antagonism between the imperatives of the formal organization's authority structure and the activities, norms, and types of support of the informal organization.

> The patterned relationships as the compromise outcome of antagonistic forces continue to reflect the essential conflicts which they have compromised. We have indicated that authority structure arises to maintain predictability but that informal structure inevitably arises to maintain the conflict between rules and regulation and human needs. We have also pointed out the fundamental cleavage in organizations based upon differentials in the hierarchical gradients of power, prestige, and reward. (p. 103)

They argue that conflict can be either functional or dysfunctional for the organization and are sensitive to the many pathologies of formal organizations. Nonetheless, they grant, as did Chester Barnard before them, *a priori* status and legitimacy to the organization; hence, "the nature of the built-in conflicts in a given organization should be studied for an adequate understanding of its present *functioning* and future *stability*." (p. 104, emphasis added).

Systems Theory and Organizational Rationality: James D. Thompson

Systems theorists are often criticized, after offering elaborate frameworks for analysis, for failing to provide testable hypotheses about how organizations will behave under particular conditions. Such hypotheses and tests that allow for their confirmation are the *sine qua non* of theory that enables prediction of the future and explanation of the past. James D. Thompson, most notably in his classic work, *Organizations in Action*, appears to be justifiably exempt from this charge by virtue of his systematic effort to use the open systems framework to explain strategies for organizational survival. He develops nearly one hundred propositions, each of which can presumably be restated as a testable hypothesis, about how organizations and individuals will act in particular circumstances. Collectively, the propositions comprise his theory, which, Thompson says, should be seen as the search for patterned variations in organizations.[27]

[27]James D. Thompson, *Organizations in Action* (New York: McGraw-Hill, 1967), p. vii; in this section, all page references in parentheses are to this source; emphasis is in the original unless otherwise noted.

He is particularly interested in two key variables that determine these patterned variations. The first is the kinds of *environments* to which organizations must (or at least choose to) respond; the second is the various *technologies* that serve as tools for organizations to accomplish their tasks.

Thompson extends the open systems assumptions and the work of Katz and Kahn in two important directions. First, he reinstates closed system concepts to a position of respectability, arguing that rational organizations must and do employ a combination of both open and closed systems strategies, which, though in tension with one another, are ultimately complementary. Second, he explicitly links the idea of rationality to the *means* by which organizations strive for efficiency and survival; in doing so, he blends together both the open and closed senses of rationality.

Thompson views organizations as "natural systems" (roughly equivalent to "open systems") by virtue of their dependency on their salient environment and the presence of an informal organization within the formal structures of authority. With respect to the informal organization, he sees that, in studying it,

> attention is focused on variables which are not included in any of the rational models—sentiments, cliques, social controls via informal norms, status and striving, and so on. It is clear that students of informal organization regard these variables not as random deviations or errors, but as patterned, adaptive responses of human beings in problematic situations. (p. 7)

These nonrational elements of open systems require that organizations develop searching and learning capabilities, in addition to rational decision-making capabilities. Given the uncertainties posed by their environments, organizations are typically limited to satisficing rather than maximizing strategies. System survival, "taken to be the goal" of organizations (p. 6), is achieved through mediating the tensions between their open and closed aspects. Thus,

> *We will conceive of complex organizations as open systems, hence indeterminate and faced with uncertainty, but at the same time as subject to criteria of rationality and hence needing determinateness and certainty.* (p. 10)

The essence of Thompson's picture of organizations is that decision makers prefer to follow closed system strategies, such as maximizing output by using rational measures of efficiency, but are often prevented from doing so because of uncertainties and contingencies in the environment that make such measures problematic to the organization's survival. This is analogous to the relationship between tame and wicked problems, which were used earlier in Chapter 1 to illustrate the kind of situations facing public administrators. Thompson argues, in effect, that because tame problems are more amenable to instrumentally rational solutions, decision makers tend to follow strategies that essentially assume the tameness of wicked problems. This can, however, be extremely hazardous, depending on the actual extent of the problem's wickedness.

Complicating this picture is the fact that closed system strategies of efficiency maximizing and open system strategies of boundary-spanning activities are performed by different sectors or levels of the organization. The *institutional sector* is responsible for the overall articulation of the purposes of the organization and the determination of what shall constitute its *domain*. (This is part of what Barnard classified as the "functions of the executive.") A domain consists of those "claims that an organization stakes out for itself in terms of [range of] products, population served, and services rendered" (p. 26). The domain also comprises the "points at which the organization is dependent on inputs from its environment" (p. 27). Thus, given the choices that organizations have in defining their domains, they are far from being passively at the mercy of their environments. In fact, those in organizations often actively and deliberately pursue strategies that enhance control over their environments. But, Thompson notes, establishing a domain is a two-way street, involving a consensus that defines "a set of expectations both for members of an organization and for others with whom they interact, about what the organization will and will not do" (p. 29).

Domain consensus includes agreement not only about goals, but also ideology. Because of this, it is useful to clarify the work of the organization by distinguishing between its organizational domain and its *task environment*. The task environment consists of those parts of the environment that are relevant to organizational goal setting and goal attainment; its relevant elements include customers, suppliers, competitors, and regulatory groups (p. 27). The task environment simultaneously enables and constrains the institutional sector in the definition and adjustment of the organization's domain. Thus, the task environment both provides resources to the organization and at the same time may pose barriers to the organization's successful control over, or adjustment to, its domain.

The *technical core* (or level) of the organization is primarily responsible for the efficient performance of tasks once they have been defined by the institutional sector. Although it is not, strictly speaking, a closed system, those working in the technical core prefer to act as though it *were* closed by pursuing rational maximizing strategies. Because such strategies are technologically more efficient (and more predictable), it behooves organizational leaders to create, to the extent possible, a closed system situation for the technical core. To do this, the boundary transactions between the task environment and the institutional sector must be handled such that the technical core is closed off from externally generated disturbances. This provides the technical core with an organizational equivalent of the economist's *ceteris paribus,* the assumption that all things are equal (and therefore stable). It allows those working in the technical core to make instrumentally rational assumptions on which to base their work and to offer instrumentally rational predictions about the outcomes of their efforts. Once again, this is an attempt to tame wicked problems by artificially bounding them. A useful analog is the way in which civil servants are traditionally divided into two groups, political appointees and the career positions. This division is based on the assumption that the latter constitute the technical core of the government bureaucracy and must be shielded from undue influence by the former.

Because of this need to shelter the technical core, tensions almost invariably develop between it and the institutional sector, given the differing problems and operating values of each. In addition, the technical core often generates its own imperatives as it increases in size and efficiency. Since it is typically in a hierarchically subordinate position, the tensions between it and the institutional sector are only further increased.

These tensions are mediated by the third organizational sector, the *managerial,* which

> *services* the technical sub-organization by (1) mediating between the technical sub-organization and those who use its products—the customers, pupils, and so on—and (2) procuring the resources necessary for carrying out the technical functions. (pp. 10–11)

It is this sector that controls the technical organization through administration. This means deciding on the scale and breadth of the technical process, its objectives and measures of success, the resources that will be allocated for its use, and, finally, the manner in which its outputs will be disposed of. To accomplish all of this, a prime responsibility of the managerial sector is to shield the technical core from environmental disruptions and instabilities. The predominant tool that the managerial sector has at its disposal is the application of organizational rationality to the problems that present themselves, both internally and externally.

Organizational rationality, for Thompson, has three aspects that correspond to Katz and Kahn's input-output model:

- Acquiring inputs from the task environment that may be "taken for granted by the technology" (p. 19);

- The use of the technology in the production of goods and services; and

- Dispensing the outputs back into the environment.

With respect to the boundary transactions between the organization and its environment,

> organizational rationality is some result of (1) constraints which the organiza-
> tion must face, (2) contingencies which the organization must meet, and (3)
> variables which the organization can control (p. 24)

Under "norms of rationality," as Thompson calls them, organizations try to buffer their technical cores from outside disturbances and, if this fails, they try to make adjustments to the task environments to which the technical core can then make its own accommodation. He sees these efforts to stabilize and reduce uncertainty as basic to the rational survival strategies of organizations.

Whereas the open system view generally sees organizations as dependent upon their environment, rational organizations, in Thompson's terms, are those that attempt to reverse this dependency by gaining power for themselves. Thompson advances a number of propositions in support of this idea. For example, rational organizations try to minimize the power of the task environment over them, to attain prestige, and to increase their power relative to those on whom they are dependent (pp. 32–34). Thompson casts these propositions neutrally by suggesting that

> an organization has power, relative to an element of its task environment, to
> the extent that the organization has the capacity to satisfy needs of that element
> and to the extent that the organization monopolizes that capacity. (pp. 30–31)

Though power may sometimes be granted to organizations by cooperative and satisfied clients, rational organizations regard cooperation with the task environment as a second-best alternative to control over it. This is because outcomes reached through cooperation are less predictable and therefore more likely to threaten the organization's prospects for survival.

Orderliness, predictability, control, and efficiency—values embraced by classical management thought and the bureaucratic model—are central to Thompson's open systems perspective as well. One important difference is that Thompson is more keenly aware of the problematic nature of realizing these values in competitive and uncertain environments. To the extent that they succeed in controlling or adapting to their environments, organizations can then proceed with the business of efficiently using their technologies to produce goods and services in order to achieve their goals.

Although his objective is to explain the behavior of organizations "in the round" (i.e., as collective wholes), Thompson devotes some attention to the actions of individuals, particularly managers, who act from their own norms of rationality. Broadly stated, his conclusion is that rational managers tend to play it safe. For example, "When the individual believes that his cause-effect resources are inadequate to the uncertainty [in the environment], he may seek to evade discretion" (p. 119). And, "Where alternatives are present, the individual is tempted to report successes and suppress evidence of failures" (p. 124). Norms of rationality, as they apply to individuals, would appear to be norms of self-interest (although Thompson does not explicitly concede this point), incorporating the same essential logic and values as organizational rationality, even though the two will often conflict with one another. Concern for survival, predictability, and control motivates both managers and organizations.

Thompson is aware of the limitations confronting individual managers in their efforts to secure both their own power within the organization and that of the organization relative to its environment. However, the sheer size of modern organizations means that power and expertise are widely dispersed, making unitary authoritarian control unrealistic. Thus,

> The basic function of management appears to be co-alignment, not merely of people [in coalitions] but of institutionalized action—of technology and task environment into a viable domain, and of organizational design and structure appropriate to it. (p. 157)

Hence, coalitions rather than individuals run organizations, with chief executives being those who manage or coordinate the dominant coalitions.

The Critique and Redirection of Systems Theory

Social theories whose explicit intent is to explain and predict behavior almost invariably carry with them certain beliefs about the kind of behavior that is good, desirable, or natural. This is certainly the case with systems theory, in which the assumed need of systems to survive puts a normative premium on behavior that conforms, in Parsons's terms for example, to the four functional imperatives of system survival. Pejorative labels such as "deviant" and "recalcitrant" describe human behavior that is at odds with organizational roles, which, if otherwise dutifully performed, would help to satisfy those functional imperatives. If system survival is taken as a given, as a natural orientation, then various individual behaviors are understandably interpreted (and implicitly evaluated) in terms of their "functional" contributions to that survival. Given its preoccupation with system needs, as opposed to individual ones, it is not surprising that the systems approach casts nonconformist behavior in such a negative light.

It is also not surprising that this perspective has evoked several lines of criticism. One of the strongest is that systems theory, when used to explain organizational events and individual actions within organizations, serves the interests of those at the top of the organization. It does this through its almost exclusive focus on stabilizing elements, which in turn highlight (usually in positive terms) those aspects of organizational action that contribute to survival. And it is those in power in the organization whose personal and role interests most directly depend not only on the survival of the organization, but also on the existing configuration of organizational power.

In addition to the normative criticism that it implicitly supports the interests of those currently in positions of power and authority, mainstream systems theory has also been criticized on empirical grounds. Critics such as David Silverman, for example, have argued that the organic metaphor (on which all mainstream systems theory relies at least to some degree) reifies organizations by attributing to them as collectivities human-like powers of thought, motive, and action.[28] By reifying organizations, organic systems theory ignores the idea that organizational action can only be fully understood in terms of meanings and intentions of individual actors. Moreover, these meanings and intentions, as well as values, of individuals are not naturally pregiven or determined by impersonal forces or system imperatives as suggested by the organic view. To the extent such forces exert power, they are always subject to interpretation in terms of individuals' values, goals, and situational definitions, all of which vary greatly and correspond only incidentally, if at all, with the "functional imperatives" of organizations.

The charge that functionalism and systems theory are deterministic insofar as they embrace the organic metaphor leads directly to an additional criticism, namely, that individual actors are not (or do not appear to be) responsible for their actions. Although Katz and Kahn and other mainstream theorists explicitly reject the extreme determinism implied by the organic metaphor, they nonetheless develop a model suggesting that the metaphor captures the essence of a natural (and implicitly a preferred) orientation of social systems. Even when stripped of its strictly deterministic implications, the organic metaphor ends up providing the basis for a conservative, survival-oriented normative theory in which the projects and needs of individuals are subordinated to the needs of the larger system. Several writers have attempted to rehabilitate systems theory in response to these criticisms, while generally maintaining the holistic, interrelated sense of "system." Three of these authors, Walter Buckley, Russell Ackoff, and Louis Gawthrop, are discussed below. First, however, the arguments of William Scott provide a useful prelude to further discussion of systems theory.

Systems and the Organizational Imperative: William Scott

Unlike Silverman, who objects to the organic model on empirical and methodological grounds, William Scott in effect accepts the organic met-

---

[28]See especially Chapter 3, "Structural-Functionalism," in Silverman, pp. 44–72.

aphor as capturing vividly and accurately the essence of what he calls the "organizational imperative," whose social consequences are pernicious and ultimately destructive of democratic values.

> The organizational imperative is a collectivistic social force based on two *a priori* propositions ... [which] state: what is good for man can only be achieved through modern organization; and therefore, all behavior must enhance the health of such modern organizations.[29]

Quite apart from the serious affront to the value and dignity of individuals that it represents, the organizational imperative has led to disastrous social and economic consequences in an era of diminishing economic and natural resources. Unlike Katz and Kahn, who see organizations as dependent on their environments, Scott sees the power relationship as reversed. Large organizations have proven to be so effective in the efficient use of their resources and in their ability to manipulate and control their environments that they have claimed as victims not only their own members, but also the publics that they presumably serve. Organizational values become, by necessity, everyone's values.

> Now modern organizations move with an inertia of their own, according to justifications of *their* making. We are overwhelmed by mammoth government, corporations, universities and other monoliths. Managers and ordinary citizens alike are entrapped within these multiple and overlapping systems, powerless to affect their direction. Thus, in order to persevere in this unprecedented milieu, it seems as if all must adopt the values required by organizations. Therein lie the problems. It seems almost too late to ask whether organizational values are satisfactory to individuals *qua* individuals. (p. 23)

The cumulative effect of the organizational imperative is especially dangerous to the survival of the larger social and economic system in an era of resource scarcity. As Katz and Kahn and Thompson note, social systems (including organizations) are naturally growthful and expansionistic. Given abundant resources in the environment to enable such growth, the social and economic consequences are at least tolerable. But when resources shrink, the organizational imperative to grow and expand necessarily means doing so at the expense of other organizations. As Scott notes,

> ... while giant organizations are essential up to a point for economic advancement, they are now partly responsible for the growing burden of national impoverishment. As more resources are diverted to the maintenance of vastly

---

[29]William Scott, "Organicism: The Moral Anesthetic of Management," *Academy of Management Review* 4:1(1979):23; in this subsection, all page references in parentheses are to this source; emphasis in original unless otherwise noted.

> complex and expensive administrative systems in a stabilized or declining environment, fewer products and services will be available for consumption. (p. 24)

Rational organizations, in Thompson's sense of the term, become very efficient predators. Their "need" to expand and thus grow is linked, through the organizational imperative, to the necessity of organizational survival. Operationally, this

> means that organizations must ingest those necessary elements in their environment that enable them to survive even if it means that they do so at the sacrifice of other organizations, which may not be as well adapted for survival. (p. 24)

Scott rejects as descriptively accurate the extreme determinism implied by a literal acceptance of the organic metaphor. He argues, however, that the survival imperative has nevertheless become operationalized in an implicit organizational ideology that public administrators adopt as the compelling motive force for their actions. Thus, the organic metaphor accurately describes modern organizations simply because those in organizations see little choice other than to act in accord with the ideology implied by it. When, in Katz and Kahn's terms, particular organizations efficiently transform energic inputs into outputs, the overall result for the economic system as a whole is suboptimization on a grand scale. Single organizations are rewarded on a short-term basis with survival for pursuing precisely those strategies that are ultimately exploitative and destructive for the environment as a whole (itself simply a larger system).

Scott is pessimistic about the chances of curbing the power of the organizational imperative. The organic metaphor on which is it based is objectionable for the reason that it describes with alarming accuracy the collective motives of organizations acting on what Thompson calls "norms of rationality." Scott calls for, at a minimum, a new management ideology that explicitly rejects the organic model of the open systems approach on normative as well as practical grounds. The new ideology should be predicted on assumptions of resource scarcity, individual dignity, and conflict. These should replace the organic model's assumptions of growth and abundance, systemic rationality, and consensus.

Systems as Self-Directed Entities: Walter Buckley

Systems theorists who are dissatisfied with the normative theory implied by the organic metaphor have found it necessary to develop systems frameworks more receptive to normative theories emphasizing conflict, change, and the legitimacy of those individual actions that may not accord with system imperatives. One of the more successful of these later systems theorists is Walter Buckley.

Not completely discounting the importance of the survival imperative of social systems, Buckley sees survival more as a dominant motive shared by individual actors than as a requirement dictated by the organic metaphor. He is explicit in his rejection of that metaphor and sees explanations of social systems as more properly based in the shared meanings among individual actors. Drawing from intellectual sources far removed from systems theory, such as symbolic interactionism (most notably G. H. Mead and Herbert Blumer), Buckley views social systems as "symbolically mediated" relationships among people. "The unit of dynamic analysis thus becomes the systemic *matrix* of interacting, goal-seeking, deciding individuals and subgroups, whether this matrix is of a formal organization or only a loose collectivity.[30] What is commonly referred to as "structure" is for Buckley simply a derivative of the matrix of relationships that the system comprises.[31] In rejecting the simplistic holism of earlier systems theory, he sees a system's structure as "only a relative stability of underlying, ongoing process.[32] By replacing the regulatory biases of the organic metaphor with a cybernetic model, social systems are seen as allowing for

not only self-regulation, but for *self-direction* or at least adaptation to a changing environment, such that the system may *change and elaborate its structure* as a condition of survival and viability.[33]

In view of the openendedness of available choices about directions to take, no particular direction is assumed *a priori* to be more "natural" or preferred than another. (Although system self-destruction does not appear high on Buckley's list of system choices, neither is it necessarily precluded.) Thus, deviation by individuals from the dominant norms and prescribed roles of the system is simply and neutrally labeled as a form of "variety" and is devoid of the negative connotation ascribed to "deviant behavior" by Katz and Kahn. Conformity by individuals to organizationally prescribed roles is neither determined, "natural," nor even normatively preferred. In support of the idea that people actively make choices, rather than their being determined in those choices by system imperatives, Buckley quotes Herbert Blumer approvingly:

[30]Walter Buckley, "Society as a Complex, Adaptive System," in Jong S. Jun and William B. Storm, eds., *Tomorrow's Organizations: Challenges and Strategies* (Glenview, Ill.: Scott, Foresman, 1973), p. 205.

[31]Ibid., p. 202.

[32]Ibid., p. 205.

[33]Ibid., p. 198, emphasis in original.

> The human being is not swept along as a neutral and indifferent unit by the operation of a system. As an organism capable of self-interaction, he forges his actions out of a process of definition involving *choice, appraisal* and *decision*. . . . Cultural norms, status positions and role relationships are only *frameworks* inside of which that process goes on.[34]

The nature of the social order, therefore, is not normatively specified in advance nor automatically maintained, as with Parsons and Katz and Kahn, "but is something that must be continually 'worked at,' constantly reconstituted."[35] The organizational order, then, is one that is sustained through continual negotiation.

Buckley retains much of the terminology of other systems theorists, yet the tenor of his writing differs greatly from, for instance, Katz and Kahn and suggests quite different criteria by which to measure the effectiveness of organizations. Although he does not explicitly offer a normative theory, Buckley's emphasis on the possibilities for individual choice clearly invites a normative stance compatible in some respects with Scott's normative concern with values of individualism, especially those suppressed by the organization imperative. Moreover, Buckley's concern with the symbolic negotiation of meaning and order leads him very close to a position congenial to schools of thought that traditionally have been most critical of the systems approach.

Among the major systems writers discussed here, only Buckley has contributed significantly to a conception of organizations as open systems that permits careful scrutiny of the motives of people, the normative choices available to them, and the manner in which order and stability are actively negotiated, and conflict is managed. These subjects are vital to comprehending the meaning of responsiveness and responsibility in public organizations. But in rehabilitating systems theory in this way, Buckley has had to alter fundamentally, if not reject outright, many of the most cherished assumptions and beliefs of his fellow systems theorists and embrace many of the ideas of their most vociferous critics.

Unlike Thompson, who outlines a comprehensive theory with the purpose of explaining and predicting behavior of organizations, Buckley's insistence on the open-ended, problematic, and highly variable nature of organizational values and contexts diminishes greatly the predictive power of this theoretical framework. Buckley instead ends up offering a framework for analysis that is potentially useful only for scrutinizing organizations on a case-by-case basis. In rejecting the determinism implicit in (although explicitly disavowed by) Katz and Kahn's approach, Buckley alerts us to the existence of a wide range of normative choices available to members of public organizations. The availability of real

---

[34]Ibid., pp. 206–7.
[35]Ibid., p. 211, emphasis in original.

choices, then, means that traditionally important normative issues in public administration, such as responsibility, the public interest, justice, and equity, are truly consequential rather than chimera. The optimism implicit in Buckley's approach, however, may itself be a chimera, if Scott's assessment of the organizational imperative is correct. We can hope, however, that Scott is a doomsayer who has overstated his case.

Systems Theory and Social Planning: Russell Ackoff

Those who object to mainstream systems theory's near–exclusive emphasis on values that instrumentally serve the end of organizational survival offer varying responses. The one proposed most often by normatively worried systems theorists such as von Bertalanffy and Buckley is to assert the importance of individual dignity and human choice as a warning against the spirit of instrumentalism produced by a literal (and scientistic) acceptance of the organic metaphor. Instead of fundamentally challenging the validity and usefulness of basic systems ideas, these efforts to "humanize" systems theory are intended to build into it countervailing values to the instrumentalism and determinism that the organic metaphor tends otherwise to generate.

A second response to the typically instrumental orientation toward values is evident in Russell Ackoff's *Redesigning the Future: A Systems Approach to Societal Problems.* His systems approach to thinking about macro social problems suggests strategies and social policies whose explicit intent in many cases is to realize, usually on a rather grand scale, values of the kind that are central to the practice of public administration. This kind of systems-theory-with-a-social-conscience seeks to link explicitly scientific explanation with strategic planning.

Ackoff emphasizes, for example, the complexities of contemporary social problems that result both from the myriad interdependencies among social units and technologies and from their changefulness. This appreciation provides the backdrop against which he advocates "interactive" planning, an approach to comprehensive social problem solving that stresses widespread participation, coordination, and integration on a continuous basis. Ackoff's is a heroic vision of social problem solving, one that combines most of the elements of what is ordinarily referred to as comprehensive or synoptic rationality with a strong dose of democratic process. The guiding values of his interactive approach to planning include:[36]

[36]Russell Ackoff, *Redesigning the Future: A Systems Approach to Societal Problems* (New York: John Wiley and Sons, 1974), pp. 18–19; in this subsection, all page references in parentheses are to this source; emphasis is in the original unless otherwise noted.

- self-control—as opposed to authoritative control;

- humanization—realized mainly through participative processes; and

- environmentalization—"serving the purposes of environmental systems more effectively."

Although Ackoff does not explicitly rely on the organic metaphor, his particular conception of systems thinking seems to embrace much of its spirit and meaning. He seeks to divorce his own thinking, however, from the determinism implicit in mechanistic or closed system thinking, in part by introducing two important "systems" ideas developed since 1940.

The first of these is *expansionism*, " . . . a doctrine that maintains that all objects, events, and experiences of them are parts of larger wholes" (p. 12). Ackoff uses this term in two quite different senses. In the first, expansionism is "another way of viewing things," that is, a consciously selected perceptual filter through which one views the objects of one's attention in terms of their relatedness with other objects. The second sense in which he uses the term is to describe how things actually are. That is, various objects *are* interrelated parts of wholes, a fact presumably independent of the observer's perceptual bias. Taken in either of these two senses, expansionism is important, Ackoff argues, because it provides a scientific approach to identifying problems related to "system performance" and, by implication, a frame of reference from which to work on solving problems.

The second important idea of systems thinking for Ackoff is *teleology,* "the study of goal-seeking and purposeful behavior ... [which] was brought into science and began to dominate our conception of the world" (p. 16):

> In mechanistic thinking, behavior is explained by identifying what caused it, never by its effect. In teleological thinking, behavior can be explained either by what produced it or by what it produces or is intended to produce. For example, a boy's going to the store can be explained either by his being sent there by his mother or by his wanting to buy ice cream. Study of functions, goals and purposes of individuals and groups—not to mention some types of machines—has yielded a greater ability to evaluate and improve their performance than did the study of them as purposeless mechanisms. (pp. 16–17)

While the notion of purpose is undoubtedly important in understanding organizational action, the failure to distinguish *whose* purposes are at issue and whether those purposes are consciously intended (as opposed to predetermined by impersonal forces) serves to confuse the meaning of "teleology" that Ackoff intends for it. In his use of the term, it seems apparent that those values associated with system survival, namely, efficiency, effectiveness, and adaptation are paramount. This is by implication rather than explicit declaration, but it is nonetheless a reasonable inference to make in view of the apparent "scientific" meaning of teleology and expansionism that Ackoff employs. That is, if objects and events are parts of larger wholes, and if the processes by which those parts interrelate are naturally directed toward some predetermined purpose, then particular values are legitimate only insofar as they instrumentally satisfy those system requirements. The assumption of teleology, then, only alters slightly the general metaphor of the system as a biological organism by replacing the more static notion of survival with a more dynamic one of direction or purpose. But this shift in orientation alters neither the primacy and "given-ness" of *system* needs nor the deterministic biases implied by the systems theorists' more typical use of the organic metaphor.

To be fair, we should note that Ackoff disclaims a deterministic view of system functioning and, in fact, espouses values relevant to the planning process that capture much of the essence of the fuller range of public administration values discussed earlier. There are, however, three objections to the manner in which he does this. First, it is not clear how he makes the transition from scientific explanation to normative prescription other than by simply equating one with the other. Secondly, to the extent that the social prescriptions that he offers serve the interests of "system performance," their desirability is contingent on their ability to satisfy instrumental values. And, finally, when Ackoff's recommendations about organizing and planning diverge from instrumental considerations of system performance, they often appear to be only incidentally related to his approach to systems thinking. Among his proposals, for example, are greater citizen participation in the decisions of both public and private organizations, proportional representation in legislative bodies based on interest, and the creation of neighborhood governments.[37] Whatever the merits of these ideas, Ackoff does not make evident why systems theory is either necessary or even useful in advocating or justifying them. And once these programs are in place in an organization, legislature, or neighborhood, one intuitively senses that systems theory may well help in understanding their dynamics, except that Ackoff does not indicate how.

Systems Theory and Public Ethics: Louis Gawthrop

The verb "to reify" is not the average man-in-the-street sort of word, but it represents an idea that is crucial to any serious thinking about orga-

[37]Esp., Chapter 3, "The Humanization Problem," pp. 34–53.

nizations, particularly public ones, and their effects on society.[38] The notion is a simple one: To reify means to look upon a nontangible human creation, such as an action, an idea, or an organziation, as though it has a life of its own, one quite apart from its human creators. This particularly happens when we spend time in and around organizations, for the word "organization" is one of the more consequential reifications of modern life.

In a sense, reification may be salutary insofar as it produces stability, which in turn enables realistic predictions over time about outcomes of organizational action. The negative side is that individuals may well be blinded to creative, innovative solutions, particularly insofar as they perceive that they have no responsibility for organizational direction or action. The moral consequence of reifying organizational activity is the very real possibility, reinforced by organizational structures, that the individual will lose sight of his or her personal responsibility in acting organizationally. Speaking, deciding, writing, declaring "in the name of" all create a high potential for dissonance between personal standards of responsibility and the consequences of organizational actions. This is particularly troublesome in public administration, where a significant amount of organizational action is likely to have negative consequences for the recipients of that action.

A degree of reification, at least, characterizes most theoretical and practical discussions about organizations. Systems theory, especially, has received more than its share of criticism in this regard by virtue of its reliance on the natural science metaphor of the biological organism. In a broader sense, however, it is our language that gets in the way: In English, nouns may make "things" out of processes, such that they seem to take on a reality of their own, independent of human action. This is frequently evident in discussions of organizations, when one talks about their "purposes," their "goals," and their "plans," as if organizations, themselves, had a kind of consciousness. Attributing purposes to organizations tends to make us forget that it is human beings that constitute those organizations; yet, because the human beings come and go while the "organization" perseveres, we are at a loss as to how to proceed if we are to be at all conscientious and responsible. The dilemma, particularly for those in public organizations, is acute: How do we meaningfully acknowledge our individual responsibility as organizational actors, yet also acknowledge that "purpose" has some meaning in terms of the collective activity that an organization comprises?

---

[38]The substance of this subsection appeared as a book review by Richard T. Mayer of Louis Gawthrop, *Public Sector Management, Systems, and Ethics* (Bloomington, Ind.: Indiana University Press, 1984), in the *New England Journal of Human Services* 5:1(1985):46–47.

Louis Gawthrop, in *Public Sector Management, Systems, and Ethics,* confronts, and proposes a way out of, the dilemma of organizational purposiveness. His intent is to bring the notion of purpose back into the discussion of organizations by offering a legitimate way of talking about organizational purposes without either rendering them as reified abstractions or creating meaningless circumlocutions.

His book takes its title from his thesis:

> ... if fundamental change in public sector organizations in the United States is needed, then the notions of management, systems, and ethics must themselves be viewed collectively as an integrated megasystem.[39]

The core of his view is that public organizations need to be designed and *re*designed in order to cope effectively with their environments. These environments are more porous, more heterogeneous, and more complex than ever before, requiring for public managers "an institutional environment wherein [they] are expected to think independently, critically, and constructively" (p. 6).

The core of Gawthrop's message is that organizational design should be couched in terms of an ontological construct as the basis for thinking about and performing organizational action. An "ontological construct" is the framework that individuals use in sorting out the variety of the external world; it is what we use to make sense of what we see around us. The elements of this framework are "a defined sense of identity (What do I stand for?) and a defined sense of faith (What do I hope for?)" (p. 32). Gawthrop emphasizes these because he wants to use them as a link to the idea of "critical freedom" as the base for both organizational design and ethical conduct within public organizations. To get there, however, requires a clearer sense of his use of the idea of ontological construct.

Ontology is a fundamental notion that embodies our sense of history, of purpose, of consequence, and of order:

> To the extent that an individual human being becomes even minimally aware of questions that touch deeply on the purposefulness of life, the consequences of one's acts, the historical linkages between past, present, and future, and the orderliness of phenomena, the individual must be viewed as an ontological self. At the very least, these concepts ... provide the individual with the ability to transcend the emptiness of an otherwise helpless existence. (p. 32)

It is in this sense of oneself as an ontological being that one can begin to exercise one's sense of critical freedom to create what Paul Ricoeur calls "a delicate consciousness." Critical freedom is more than merely the

---

[39]Gawthrop, p. 7; in this section, all page references in parentheses are to this previously cited source; emphasis is in the original unless otherwise noted.

freedom to speak one's mind, and it is considerably more than our usually narrow idea of indivdual rights. Critical freedom is in part embodied in the now-popular idea of critique, but it goes beyond criticism alone by questioning society and its institutions, questioning them in the ontological terms of history, purpose, order, and consequence. It is only with the development of critical consciousness and the exercise of critical freedom that public administrators can properly appreciate the problems of public policy: "[T]he public policy problems of the future are certainly technical and logistical (as well as conceptual) in nature, but they are also political and ethical in nature" (p. 35).

Gawthrop is concerned with change and how organizations, and therefore managers, deal with it. He describes two opposing philosophical stances regarding change: "Either the future is seen as a projection of the present, which, in turn, is based on the past; or the future is seen as that state of being where one can change the patterns of the present and undo the negatives of the past" (p. 48). The first is reactive and the second is anticipatory. "Reactive" and "anticipatory" are characteristics not only of managerial attitudes but of the value premises embedded in the organizational structures within which they work. These latter become a "latent network of reinforcing value premises that, in fact, shapes the individual's perspective of change and changing" (p. 49).

In order to bring home his concern for the relationship between these reinforcing value premises and organizational structures, he draws a comparison betwen two ideal-typical organization structures, Network X and Network Y. These embody the general characteristics of vertical and horizontal, reactive and anticipatory. Their utility lies in etching clearly the contrast he makes between the world now and the world as it could be.

At first glance, his two models appear to be no more than an organizational restatement of Douglas McGregor's famous Theory X and Theory Y, in which the former embodied the conventional theory ("management by control") and the latter the more "enlightened" theories of human relations (e.g., "management by objectives"). There is, however, an important difference. Gawthrop's discussion focuses on the substantial ontological and valuative differences between the two networks (See Table 7.1).

The "value components" in Table 7.1 are the ontological elements that were discussed earlier; the adjectives attached to each network ("reactive," etc.) are Gawthrop's descriptors for the response patterns likely to be supported within that network. As he points out:

> In the most immediate and direct sense, these two networks of value patterns shape public organizations' and managers' perspectives of change . . . However, in an indirect manner, their importance becomes even more significant. . . . [P]erceptions of change applied to specific instances determine, or at least influ-

Table 7.1
Two Ideal-Typical Structures

Network X	Value Components	Network Y
(reactive/consolidative/ incremental)		(anticipatory/innovative/ systems)
Ateleological	Purpose	Teleological
Atomistic	Consequence	Holistic
Spatial	History	Temporal
Vertical	Order	Horizontal

Source: Louis C. Gawthrop, *Public Sector Management, Systems, and Ethics,* (Bloomington, Ind.: Indiana University Press), 1984, p. 56.

ence significantly, the actual behavioral patterns and roles assumed by public managers and organizations confronted with the forces of change. (p. 57)

As dense as the terms in Table 7.1 may appear to be, they in fact point out some useful contrasts. Take for example the two "value components" of purpose and consequence. As noted earlier, Gawthrop is arguing that these are two important ontological elements that help" ... provide the individual with the ability to transcend the emptiness of an otherwise helpless existence," and the way in which an organization is structured reinforces an orientation toward these values. It does this by erecting boundaries (as all organizations do) that circumscribe the limits of appropriate action by individuals.

Network X is what we tend to think of as the traditional bureaucracy. As an organization, it is structured such that any sense of purpose *for the organization* (i.e., teleology) is centered only on the immediate present: "Will this work now?" This also means that organizational actions are seen as discrete, both in their occurrence and in their effect. There is, in other words, a tendency to view decisions and solutions to problems as being linear, that is, as not being significantly related to other decisions and solutions around them nor having discernible consequences beyond the immediate target.

In terms of Network Y, the orientation around these two value components is appreciably different. Sense of purpose pervades the structure: "Notions of purpose and purposeful behavior constitute the basic essence of a network Y orientation" (p. 55). Managers would be allowed (presumably encouraged) to act purposefully in their work. In terms of the consequences of this work, the effects are viewed in a systemic fashion, that is, in relationship to other decisions and solutions that also are being created and to the second- and third-level consequences of those decisions and solutions.

A significant portion of the book is given over to describing what a *re*designed organization would look like. The rationale for this is clear: "A thinking government demands thoughtful and reflective systems management because it is the executive organization network that links the body politic most directly to public policy programs" (p. 118). But Gawthrop's main thrust is found in the final chapter. It is here that we find the principal message that he has been leading up to all along:

> The true deputyship of public management must be built around a mature critical consciousness, and the individual administrator must be prepared to assume the full burden of responsibility for actions and decisions taken in the name of the organizaton. No collective organizational imprimatur can absolve the individual public manager from this responsibility.... Loyality and obedience to organizational values and directives can be demanded up to the point that such demands are related to purposeful and ethical ends for enhancing the qualitative goodness of the daily lives of the body politic. (p. 156)

Systems Theory and the Public Administration Framework

Early in the twentieth century, Max Weber wrote about the internal structuring of bureaucracy at the time when those organizational behemoths were coming into their own. Chester Barnard, while trying to loosen what he characterizes as an emphasis in the literature on structure, only incidentally helps us see beyond the immediate borders of the organization's chain of command (and then only from the perspective of the executive). This deemphasis on formal organizational structure was reinforced by the findings of the Hawthorne Experiments, with their recognition of the role of small, informally organized groups within the larger organization. It was not until after World War II, however, that the full importance of this shift in thinking was fully realized, i.e., with the systems theorists' description of the interaction of large-scale social units as they are intimately connected with a larger social world. In large part, one could reasonably argue, this is because reality itself made this necessary. Organizations of a size, scope, and complexity of task not experienced before were created to tame the growing wicked problems of postwar America.

With systems theory came an articulation for public administration of the interplay of the organizational arenas that was unavailable before. Both "equilibrium" (in the sense of a balancing of forces) and then "homeostasis" help make intelligible the connections between the roles of the public administrator in the person, for instance, of the welfare case worker:

- As an agent of the local welfare department, as well as of the county, state, and federal governments, the worker interacts with other agents of other departments and agencies to negotiate appropriate benefits and services for clients. (The *inter–organizational* arena)

- As an employee of the welfare department, the worker interacts with other workers, supervisors, and administrative staff in managing the flow of work and working conditions. (The *intra–organizational* arena)

- As representative of the state, the worker interacts with the client in interpreting and applying regulations in order to make decisions on the basis of rules that determine the level of assistance to be provided, if at all. (The *organization-to-individual* arena)

Thus, systems theory, with its emphasis on the concept of role, enables one to articulate these different relationships that the welfare case worker maintains as part of his or her public administration work.

While providing a framework for analyzing the interplay of the three organizational arenas, most of the systems theory literature tends to cast that interplay benignly, as evidence of adaptation processes. What mainstream systems theory has generally failed to come to terms with, however, is Charles Perrow's warning that organizations *control* their environments at least as much as they adapt to them.[40] Thompson, for example, is certainly aware that rational organizations *attempt* to control their environments, with cooperation and adaptation being only second-best strategies. But Perrow, similar to William Scott, suggests that the phenomenal success of organizations in their efforts at controlling their environments is precisely the reason why we should be alarmed. Even though growth and expansion may be tolerable and in some respects salutary when energy and economic resources are abundant, a time of resource scarcity and cutback management in government requires that rational organizations become predators that thwart rather than serve the larger public interest.

The concerns voiced by Perrow and Scott are especially salient to the normative assessment of public organization, to which systems theory has paid far less attention than it has to organizations in the private sector. The expectation that public organizations should be responsive and accountable to the publics they serve implies a normative theory that is inconsistent with the control orientation dictated by Thompson's norms of rationality. Even if the power of large organizations relative to their environments was considerably less than that suggested by Scott, it is by no means certain that the "adaptive" strategies pursued by rational orga-

---

[40]Charles Perrow, *Complex Organizations: A Critical Essay,* 2nd ed. (Glenview, Ill.: Scott, Foresman, 1979), especially Chapter 6, "The Environment."

nizations would necessarily be compatible with the needs of the larger environment. Since organizations use adaptation strategies in the interest of their own survival, it is doubtful that adaptation is the equivalent of responsiveness in a broader sense. Adaptation, even in the presumably enlightened open system view, is governed by norms of instrumental rationality that in substance differ little, if at all, from the instrumental values implicit in the machine metaphor of the earlier closed system model of organization.

The Normative Vectors of Public Administration

Systems theory can be helpful in clarifying the relationship of efficiency and effectiveness to organizational adaptation and survival, but it provides little illumination of the other two normative vectors of the public admin- istration framework: individual rights and the adequacy of organizational processes, and representation and the control of discretion. These two vec- tors, each of which concerns the interests of individuals more than those of institutions, are accorded at best secondary normative status in the mainstream systems view. Frederick Thayer makes this point in even stronger language when he says that

> . . . organizational survival tends to emphasize the integrity of the single orga- nization, and it introduces a determinism which inevitably reduces the individ- ual to a position of lesser importance. Given their addiction to the hierarchical ordering of systems, [general systems theory] proponents almost inadvertently have sacrificed the individual for the sake of the larger system, . . .[41]

Support for Thayer's concern is evident from further scrutiny of the "norms of rationality" that underlie James D. Thompson's explanation of organizational action. Those norms are not only narrowly instrumental, they are also instrumental only toward a single end, that of survival of the organization through stabilization of its environment (both internal and external). This is not surprising if one remembers that, from Thompson's perspective, the "rational organization" sees cooperation with its task environment as a second-best alternative to control over it. Both the rec- ognition of rights (e.g., of clients in relation to the organization) and rep- resentation (e.g., of "the public interest") are based on an assumption of necessary cooperation with other parties in the task environment. To rec- ognize the legitimacy of either of these vectors requires, however, that we accept as necessary and legitimate the very thing that, according to

---

[41]Frederick C. Thayer, "General System(s) Theory: The Promise That Could Not Be Kept," *Academy of Management Journal* 15:4(1972):485.

Thompson, rational organizations will try to avoid, deny, or suppress: unpredictability.

There are two ways to look at this in terms of the public administration framework. First, assume that Thompson is correct in saying that the efforts of administrators to stabilize and reduce uncertainty are the logical outcomes of their organizations pursuing rational survival strategies. If this is the case, then the public administrator who adopts such a strategy might well do so at the cost of ignoring normative concerns about rights and representation, since they tend to decrease predictability and control. This suggests a crucial limitation that the term "norms of rationality" brings to the understanding of public organizations. It is a term that is descriptively useful only insofar as one assumes that *the* objects of a rational strategy are stability, predictability, and control. That this is the objective of a considerable amount of organizational behavior in public organizations is without question; that it is the sole or even the primary objective of organizational behavior is, however, far from clear. Put another way, Thompson's hypotheses are useful for understanding organizational behavior *when that behavior has the purpose of reducing uncertainty.* This unfortunately begs the question of how one determines whether that is, or should be, the principal purpose for either the organization or the individual in any particular setting.

Secondly, when a premium is placed on reducing uncertainty, any concerns about rights and representation that do surface will be treated as merely procedural issues, in which the chief criterion governing their disposition is efficiency. Using the efficiency criterion, matters of individual rights and representation are handled in public organizations by imposing rules and regulations. This would suggest an addition to Thompson's list of hypotheses: under norms of rationality, an organization will respond to questions of equity (for instance) by defining them as ones of procedural equality to be handled through rules generated and maintained by the organization; likewise, it will consider claims that do not fit established procedural categories as illegitimate.

Bureaucratic structuring nicely fits the bill as a means for containing rational organizational behavior and for generating rules to quell uncertainty. Likewise, bureaucratic structuring emphasizes, as do the systems theorists, the primacy of the normative vector of efficiency and effectiveness.

Conclusion

Systems theory has been the dominant perspective in American organization theory for more than a quarter of a century. In its more conservative form, organizational systems theory projects an image of public organizations in which organizational roles and environments are naturally stable, predictable, and congruent with one another. Efficiency and effectiveness provide the normative criteria by which efforts to sustain that image are ultimately judged. The other two normative vectors of individual rights and the exercise of discretion either do not intrude themselves or are sufficiently rule-bound and regularized so that organizational action can be predicted and controlled. For public administrators whose organizational roles and environments fit this image, systems theory may provide a useful framework for understanding the organizational behavior around them. It would appear, however, that for a good many (and, some would argue, an increasing number of) public administrators their world is not like that at all. It is not readily predictable, and it frequently requires the exercise of discretion as well as a constant attention to unique circumstances not covered by existing rules and procedures. Systems theory, at least as it is traditionally framed in the works of writers such as Thompson and Katz and Kahn, has severely limited utility for these public administrators.

Buckley, Ackoff, and, especially, Gawthrop present far more appealing images of what public organizations might become, inasmuch as their theoretical frameworks explicitly encourage a concern with normative issues involving individual rights, representation, and administrative discretion. These efforts have paved the way for transforming systems theory from a theory of prediction and authoritative control to one of change and democratic control. But in so doing, and without explicitly acknowledging it (or possibly even being aware of it), they have also done something much more. They have in effect abandoned general systems theory as a comprehensive framework for the *scientific* explanation of the social world and in its place have proposed the beginnings of a *social philosophy* called by the same name. It is certainly true, or at least few would now contest, that social science and social philosophy are very much related enterprises, but there are nonetheless significant differences between the two, as well as very different forms of argumentation required for their defense. By failing to differentiate social science from normative social philosophy, the new general systems writers make even more ambiguous both the meaning of theory as well as the uses to which it can and should be put.

8

Later Human Relations Theory: Integrating Individuals and Organizations

With each perspective discussed thus far, the primary normative thrust has been that of efficiency. This has been expressed in systemic terms (a la James D. Thompson), decisional terms (Herbert Simon), organizational terms (Chester Barnard), productivity terms (Frederick Winslow Taylor), and bureaucratic terms (Max Weber). That this should be the case is not surprising given the history of the increasing bureaucratization of society. The dominant rationalizing, instrumental logic of organizational activity, predicted so clearly in Weber's work, has focused societal efforts on manipulating the malleable physical and social environment. The assumption underlying this logic is that rationality holds the key to creating a progressively better world. Again and again for organization theorists, the question was clear: how can human activity best be organized to achieve given societal goals in an efficient and effective manner? The answers to this question, as we have seen so far, have a striking similarity.

Their similarity lies not only in an emphasis on efficiency, but, more importantly, in an emphasis on the organization as logically, morally, and socially prior to the individual who inhabits it. For each perspective so far, it is the organization (as the embodiment of social purpose) that defines a social situation, rather than the particular individuals who happen to populate it at a given moment. This was well characterized by the systems theorists as they explored the question of how an organization continues to function in relatively stable fashion despite the constant movement of different individuals through it. In each of the other perspectives, the condition of organizational stability is similarly taken as a given. In all cases, this results in a presumption that any conflict between organization and individual is most likely the result of some weakness in the latter and should therefore generally be decided in favor of the former, usually by adapting the individual in some fashion to the dictates of the organization. Thus, one sees the work coming out of the Hawthorne Experiments as generally oriented to understanding how to manipulate the behavior of small groups in order to further larger organizational purposes. Or, in the decision–perspective, how individual rationality is defined as necessarily isomorphic with organizational rationality. Or, for Chester Barnard, how the personal code of the executive is presumed to be coterminous with the moral code of the organization.

By the mid-1960s, a profound questioning of this rationalizing presumption surfaced all across the social sciences. In organization theory and in public administration, critics voiced increasing dissatisfaction with the way in which such democratic values as individual freedom and choice were handled both in the academic literature and in organizations themselves. There was a growing realization—inspired in part by the outcomes of the Hawthorne Experiments—of a potentially strong relationship between long-term organizational efficiency and the manner in which employees are treated. Finally, a growing suspicion was voiced that organizations built solely on efficiency lines, particularly in the public sector, were likely to deny the very political process values of representation and rights that they were established to further in the first place.

Put another way, in the field of public administration there was growing realization of the profound tensions *between* the normative vectors that make up the public administration framework outlined in Part I. During this time, there were continuing explicit and systematic attempts to further rationalize the administrative process. This was the primary purpose, for example, of programmatic efforts such as the Planning, Programming, and Budgeting System (PPBS) initiated in the Department of Defense. The critics of such rationalistic organizing attempted to chart the effects of these efforts on the personal and social lives of individuals in those organizations.

Prior to the early 1960s, the subordination of the individual in the interest of organizational rationality went, with rare exceptions, largely unchallenged. It was not until the development of what we are calling here the later human relations perspective that these misgivings and concerns took on any articulated voice.[1] Although there are numerous quar-

---

[1] Dissatisfaction with bureaucracy was not new to the generic organization literature. In 1940, Robert Merton argued that the potential for severe dysfunction in bureaucracies led ultimately to inefficiencies rather than to efficiency. See Robert K. Merton, "Bureaucratic Structure and Personality," *Social Forces* 18(1940):560–68. This was the beginning of a solid tradition of antibureaucratic writings. In each case, however, the writers stood with their

rels with the specifics of this perspective, as we will see in this chapter, its basic argument of injecting human values and individual development into organizational activity has left a significant mark on the study of organizations.

Introduction

It is often intellectually easier when studying the development of a field such as organization theory to contrast ideas as though they represent polar opposites, even though such dichotomous states rarely exist in so clear-cut a fashion. However, to understand the development of the later human relations tradition, such comparisons are no mere pedagogical device; they are, rather, a necessity because of the fundamental challenge that this perspective brought to the field of battle. In a nutshell, these theorists argued that the rationalistic, organization-dominant view of organizational behavior, by effectively ignoring the rights, values, and personal development of individuals in organizations, causes serious damage both to the individuals involved and to the larger society. Their opponents— and the fundamental nature of this debate requires seeing them as opponents—argued, simply, that such concerns about individual matters, while perhaps well-intentioned, seriously undermine the social charge of the organization. If taken too seriously, these concerns would threaten the very structure of society and government.

Both the intellectual animosity and the intellectual stakes involved are succinctly captured in a 1973 exchange of articles between Chris Argyris and Herbert Simon in the *Public Administration Review*. An examination of this interchange serves to introduce the basic issues that were (and still are) debated between the later human relations theorists and the mainstream perspectives in organization theory.

Following this is a review in some depth of the intellectual challenge to the mainstream perspectives in organizational theory made by several of the later human relations theorists. Initially, the focus centers on Abraham Maslow, whose humanistic psychology emphasized the needs and characteristics of mentally healthy (or self-actualizing) people. Although Maslow, himself, was not mainly concerned with organization and management, his writings profoundly influenced, beginning in the 1950s, the work of the major organizational psychologists of that era, including Douglas McGregor, Chris Argyris, Warren Bennis, Rensis Likert, and

---

feet firmly planted in a more general perspective—most often, like Merton, that of functionalism. It was not until this later period that theorists began to question the relationship between bureaucratic organization and issues such as representation and rights.

Frederick Herzberg. The later human relations writers, especially Likert[2] and Herzberg,[3] are interested in empirical questions about the relationship of participative strategies and job enrichment to organizational effectiveness. At the same time, this perspective is also characterized, not surprisingly, by a strong normative commitment to the project of individual growth and development.

Influenced heavily by Maslow's notion of self-actualization, these organizational psychologists confronted the question of whether the normative image of the healthy, self-actualizing individual was compatible with the organizational need for efficient goal attainment. The works of McGregor, Argyris, and Bennis are represented here because of the different answers they provide to this question. During the approximately two decades since the appearance of many of their major contributions, a great deal of research has built upon, modified, and even challenged their ideas. Thus, while some of their writings might now appear to be somewhat dated, the early thinking of McGregor, Argyris, and Bennis has nevertheless proved to have had a remarkable staying power. This is chiefly because each of these three writers has contributed significantly to a general understanding of the individual in relation to the organization so as to provide an enduring normative context for much of the later research in organizational psychology.

More than any other psychologists, Maslow, McGregor, Argyris, and Bennis have profoundly influenced public administration discourse on the role and meaning of democracy in public organizations, a subject taken up in the second half of the chapter. This is reflected, for example, in their influence, as well as that of other human relations theorists, on the so-called "New Public Adminstration" movement of the late 1960s and early 1970s. The overall relevance of the later human relations perspective to public organizations is dealt with in the concluding section on the public administration framework.

There are five principal propositions reflected in the writing of the newer human relations theorists and discussed in this chapter:

1 Later human relations theory challenges the underlying assumptions about human nature and the essential purposes of social organization implicit in mainstream organizational theories. At issue is the nature and normative importance of rationality as it applies both to individual motivation and the collective attainment of organizational purposes.

---

[2]See Rensis Likert, *New Patterns of Management* (New York: McGraw-Hill, 1961); Likert, *The Human Organization* (New York: McGraw-Hill, 1967); and Likert and J. G. Likert, *New Ways of Managing Conflict* (New York: McGraw-Hill, 1976).

[3]See Frederick Herzberg, *Work and the Nature of Man* (Cleveland: World, 1966), and Herzberg, "One More Time: How Do You Motivate Employees?" *Harvard Business Review* 46:1(1968):53–62.

2 Later human relations theory is guided by the belief that a fundamental tension exists between the needs of healthy individuals and the needs of formal organizations. The chief task of management is to integrate—or alternatively to negotiate a reasonable balance between—the needs of these two levels.

3 Although differing greatly in their reasons for doing so, later human relations theorists have championed the idea of organizational democracy. Fundamental to their particular conception of democracy is the idea of participative management. Notably absent in the human relationists' arguments for organizational democracy is any serious consideration of its relationship to the idea of *political* democracy.

4 Important tensions exist between later human relations theory and more orthodox theories of public administration. These tensions can be traced to conflicting conceptions of democratic administration. While providing an incomplete conception of democracy for public administration, later human relations theory has significantly altered public administration discourse about this subject.

5 On balance, the principal later human relations theorists are guided by an implicit faith in the intrinsic virtue of democratic organizations, rather than by instrumental considerations such as greater efficiency, effectiveness, or productivity. That they have often not been explicit about this value commitment (and indeed have often seemed to be genuinely ambivalent about it) has seriously confused and limited the value of their contributions to the field of public administration.

The Argyris/Simon Debate

Organizational theory in public administration may be undergoing an important transformation. The new critics find much administrative descriptive theory to be nonrelevant to many critical problems of organization. They suggest that the present theories are based on a concept of man, indeed a morality, that leads the scholar to conduct research that is, intentionally or unintentionally, supportive of the status quo. . . . The newer, critical writings are also concerned with individual morality, authenticity, human self-actualization. The scholars are not only asking what makes organizations more effective; they are concerned with the issues: For whom are organizations designed? How humane can organizations become and still be effective?[4]

[4]Chris Argyris, "Some Limits of Rational Man Organizational Theory," *Public Administration Review* 33:3(1973):253.

So begins a 1973 article by human relations theorist Chris Argyris in the *Public Administration Review*. The trouble, he goes on to argue, is that "rational-man organization theorists" such as Herbert Simon (in other words, those described in Chapter 6 as sharing in the decision-set perspective) exclude important variables about organizational settings and cannot, therefore, make adequate predictions about organizational events. The source of the difficulty is that rational-man theories, by virtue of their implicit and explicit assumptions about human nature, systematically deny the validity of nonrational elements in organizational settings.

In the very next issue, Herbert Simon responded in an article entitled "Organization Man: Rational or Self-Actualizing?" There he summarizes what he sees as their polar opposite views:

> In Argyris' Dionysian world, reason is one of the shackles of freedom. The rational man is cold, constrained, incapable of self-actualization and "peak experiences." Man must throw over his reason, must respond to impulse in order to release the swaddled Real Person within.
>
> In my Appolonian world, reason is the handmaiden of freedom and creativity. It is the instrument that enables me to have peak experiences unimaginable to my cat or my dog. It is the instrument that enables me to dream and design. It is the instrument that enables me and my fellow men to create environments and societies that can satisfy our needs, so that all of us—and not just a few—can experience some of the deeper pleasures of sense and mind. And because we depend so heavily upon reason to create and maintain a humane world, we see the need to understand reason better—to construct a tested theory of reasoning man.[5]

Also in that issue of the journal, Argyris rejoined in an article entitled "Organization Man: Rational *and* Self-Actualizing":

> Reason, for me, is not, and never has been, a shackle of freedom.... It is the design and administration of organizations that do not encourage the discussion of emotions and emotionally loaded substantive issues (when they are relevant) that is the shackle.[6]

While these three articles contain some of the usual academic sniping, hair-splitting over definitions, and claims of misquotation, they highlight two essential aspects of the intellectual currents of the times, two aspects that are reflective of the challenge that the later human relations theorists such as Argyris threw down in front of orthodox organization theory. The first of these is the idea that the theorist has a social responsibility for the theories that he or she develops, researches, and presents, because theories

---

[5]Herbert A. Simon, "Organization Man: Rational or Self-Actualizing?" *Public Administration Review* 33:4(1973):352.

[6]Argyris, "Organization Man: Rational *and* Self-Actualizing," *Public Administration Review* 33:4(1973):356.

about social conditions are based on a particular model of man. This model, whatever its content, then effectively determines what the theorist sees as legitimate and illegitimate behavior in the organization, which in turn prescribes and proscribes the available options for organizational change. In other words, in being "merely descriptive," the theorist presents a view of the organization to its members that validates (whether this is the intention or not) the then-current view of power and relationships in that organization.

As we have seen, both organization theory and organizational action had up to this point stressed the rationalizing of social reality as both a *pragmatic* and *theoretical* necessity. An important consequence of this, as Max Weber clearly pointed out, is the almost exclusive use of instrumental rationality in dealing with organizational problems. Instrumental rationality, in turn, stresses and reinforces the impersonality of relationships both within the organization and between the organization and its environment. This is the second essential aspect brought out in this debate: the role of the nonrational (actually, the noninstrumentally rational) aspects of organizational behavior in understanding, describing and, therefore, changing organizations. Clarifying this role was a primary project of the later human relations theorists.

These two aspects—the social role of theory and the relationship of the rational and nonrational—separate not only the later human relations perspective from the decision-set perspective, but also all those perspectives presented thus far from all those to follow. Their surfacing at this time marks a kind of intellectual watershed for organization theory, particularly as it applies to public administration.

The Individual as Self-Actualizer: Abraham Maslow

In *The Functions of the Executive*, Chester Barnard affirmed the view of organizations as naturally cooperative systems. The cooperativeness of organizations, however, simply reflected the essential cooperativeness of individuals, who, to Barnard, could realize both their rational as well as moral purposes only through social, especially organizational, contexts. The ethos of cooperation evoked a benign image of organizational life, yet it was nevertheless one in which the organization was seen as morally superior to the individual, whose own goals and purposes derived from the collectivity of which he or she was a member. It is only a short step from here to the concomitant belief that the individual's actions should ultimately be evaluated in terms of their contributions to the health of the organization.

Barnard's belief in the moral supremacy of the organization over the individual reinforced an essentially functionalist view that was later embraced, as we saw in Chapter 7, by the mainstream systems theorists. So, while Barnard claimed that organizational authority flowed from the bottom to the top of the organization, this apparently democratic interpretation seems ironic, if not disingenuous, in light of his belief in the moral supremacy of organizations as collectivities—led, of course, by wise and benevolent executives.

Barnard's writings marked the culmination of the early human relations movement, which was initially inspired by the Hawthorne Experiments and later interpreted by Elton Mayo and F. J. Roethlisberger within a functionalist framework.[7] Even though attention was given to the individual's "needs," these were chiefly important insofar as they could be manipulated in service of the organization's need to maintain social "equilibrium." For Barnard, as for the early human relationists, the primary unit of analysis, as well as the principal object of his own loyalties, was the organization as a whole.

The great turning point in the human relations movement may be seen essentially as a shift in loyalties from the organization to the individual. This shift in loyalties was more implicit than explicit and was in many ways incomplete, ambiguous, and contradictory. Most importantly, at least in its influence on the study of public administration, the broadly humanistic sentiments of the later human relations literature brought a new, as well as a highly controversial, meaning to the idea of democracy in and for public organizations.

The chief source of inspiration to the later human relations writers was Abraham Maslow, a psychologist whose interests lay mainly in areas other than organizational psychology. Only relatively late in his career did Maslow write directly about organizations, publishing, in 1965, *Eupsychian Management*.[8] Rather, Maslow's writings dealt with psychology at the level of the individual. In particular, his project was to synthesize a melange of psychological theories that depicted in developmental terms the individual as naturally oriented toward growth, maturity, autonomy, and the realization of an inherent potential for freedom. Maslow was a cheerful existentialist, eschewing both the dark pessimism of Freudian theory and the stark scientism of behaviorist psychology, who proposed instead a humanistic "third force" in psychology predicated on an underlying belief in the individual's potential for goodness.

---

[7]F. J. Roethlisberger (see Chapter 5) deserves recognition for anticipating many of the dilemmas subsequently grappled with by the later human relationists, most notably Chris Argyris. Although Roethlisberger's systems framework reflects a fairly clear functionalist (and therefore conservative) orientation, he was well aware of the serious tensions between the opposing logics of efficiency and "sentiments." See especially Chapter 24, "An Industrial Organization as a Social System," in F. J. Roethlisberger and William J. Dickson, *Management and the Worker* (Cambridge: Harvard University Press, 1939) pp. 551–68.

[8]Abraham Maslow, *Eupsychian Management* (Homewood, Ill.: Richard D. Irwin, 1965).

To call Maslow an empirical scientist would be to take some liberties with the term. His writings are filled with a purple prose that often anticipates, rather than draws from existing, scientific documentation. For example:

> There is now emerging over the horizon a new conception of human sickness and of human health, a psychology that I find so thrilling and so full of wonderful possibilities that I yield to the temptation to present it publicly even before it is checked and confirmed, and before it can be called reliable scientific knowledge.[9]

This passage, like many found in his writings, highlights at the outset that the force of Maslow's thinking derives principally from romantic, and only secondarily scientific, sentiments.[10] They are romantic in the sense that they reflect a set of beliefs about human nature based more on faith—in a sense, a spiritual commitment—than on dispassionate observation and analysis. Thus, while many who have commented on his work are correct in noting that Maslow's depiction of human motivation is more "complex" than the "social man" of the early human relationists, more significant is his optimism that the individual's natural developmental orientation is toward self-realization and autonomy. To Maslow, the natural *goodness* of man is more significant even than his complexity.

Maslow's works, in addition to offering a psychology that takes account of the complexity of motivation, also provide the basis for a theory of social, and, by extension, organizational values. As Maslow puts it,

> Humanists for thousands of years have attempted to construct a naturalistic value system that could be derived from man's own nature, without necessity of recourse to authority outside the human being himself. . . . [I]t is my belief that certain developments in the art and science of psychology, in the last few decades, make it possible for us for the first time to feel confident that this age-old hope may be fulfilled. . . .[11]

In particular, it is a value theory that, unlike Barnard's, sees the needs of healthy individuals as often at odds with those of organizations.

---

[9]Maslow, *Toward a Psychology of Being* (Princeton, N. J.: D. Van Nostrand Company, Inc., 1962), p. 3.

[10]For a provocative exploration of the essentially romantic basis from which the modern organizational behavior movement draws its intellectual energy, see Peter B. Vaill, "Integrating the Diverse Directions of the Behavioral Sciences," in Robert Tannenbaum, Newton Margulies, and Fred Massarik, eds., *Human Systems Development: New Perspectives on People and Organizations* (San Francisco: Jossey-Bass, 1985 pp. 547–77).

[11]Maslow, *Toward a Psychology of Being*, p. 141.

The Hierarchy of Psychological Needs

The most familiar and most influential feature of Maslow's theory of motivation is his notion of a hierarchy of human need ordered according to their prepotency. "Prepotency" refers to the urgency of the satisfaction of a particular need.[12] The basic idea is that a "lower" or more primitive need must be satisfied before a higher need becomes relevant to the person as a source of motivation. Relatedly, a satisfied need is no longer a motivator. The five levels of the need hierarchy are:

1 *Physiological.* Chiefly food and shelter.

2 *Safety.* Freedom from physical harm and deprivation.

3 *Love.* The desire for affectionate and supportive relationships with family, friends, and associates.

4 *Esteem.* The recognition by others of one's competence, achievements, and overall personal worth.

5 *Self-actualization (or self-realization).* The need to realize one's inherent potential, one's creative abilities, "to be everything one is capable of becoming."[13]

The need hierarchy represents a series of developmental stages that reflect the individual's natural "impulse toward growth."[14] Frustration at the four lower levels, which Maslow calls "deficiency needs," impedes movement toward the highest level, that of self-actualization, which he terms a "being need." Although people operating at this level may also experience psychological pain, it is of a different order from neuroses associated with the first four levels.

The now-famous need hierarchy and, especially, the notion of self-actualization, have sometimes been interpreted by management theorists in ways in which many of Maslow's followers, such as Douglas McGregor, would probably have disapproved. Modern contingency theory, for example, regards the need hierarchy as a device for identifying,

---

[12]Just how literally Maslow intended his readers to take the idea of the psychological need hierarchy is unclear. Empirical evidence of its existence is shaky at best. See Mahmoud A. Wahba and Lawrence G. Bridwell, "Maslow Reconsidered: A Review of Research on the Need Hierarchy Theory," *Proceedings of the Academy of Management* 1973:514–20. Moreover, David Silverman goes so far as to question even the logical possibility of empirically verifying the existence of psychological "needs," whatever their particular content and order of prepotency. See David Silverman, *The Theory of Organisations* (New York: Basic Books, 1971), pp. 81–82. Although defenders of Maslow might rejoin that he intended the need hierarchy merely as a "heuristic device," the confident tone in which Maslow wrote seems to belie that more modest intent.

[13]Maslow, *Motivation and Personality* (New York: Harper and Brothers, 1954), p. 82.

[14]Maslow, *Toward a Psychology of Being*, p. 21.

by means of objective indicators, the many differing factors that motivate various employees in order to match those factors with appropriate styles of management and inducements for effective performance.[15] The current need level of the employee is taken as a given, to which management may adjust its tactics in the interest of organizational effectiveness and goal attainment. Knowledge of employee needs, in other words, serves the instrumental needs of the organization, rather than the developmental needs of the employee.

The humanists of the later human relations movement would object to this approach because of their normative commitment to self-actualization for its own sake. Knowledge of the employee's currently prepotent need level, presuming that such knowledge could be reliably obtained, only serves the diagnostic purpose of identifying, one hopes, temporary barriers in the natural development of the employee toward self-actualization. To Maslow, the fullest opportunity of the individual to realize the potential for self-actualization constitutes a virtual political right that implies a corresponding obligation on the part of the organization to promote it. Even while he believed that organizations would inevitably benefit from the efforts of increased numbers of self-actualizing employees, Maslow, as a humanist, was principally concerned with the well-being of the individual and only secondarily with that of the organization.

From Maslow's perspective, self-actualization in organizations requires, among other things, participation by employees in managing their organizations, in contrast to the authoritative management typical of traditional formal organizations. Participation and self-actualization are for Maslow synonymous with his conception of organizational democracy, which is not restricted to democracy *within* organizations. His particular version of the democratic ideal also carries over into the political arena, in which opportunities for self-actualization in organizations are political rights, rather than (at least chiefly) functional requirements for organizational effectiveness. Maslow went so far, for example, as to propose a system of taxation, a "moral accounting scheme," in which corporations would be rewarded according to their contribution to the mental health of their employees. Moreover,

> Some kind of tax penalty should be assessed against enterprises that undo the effects of a political democracy, of good schools, etc. etc., and that make their people more paranoid, more hostile, more nasty, more malevolent, more destructive, etc. This is like sabotage against the whole society. And they should be made to pay for it.[16]

---

[15]See, for example, Fred Luthans, *Introduction to Management: A Contingency Approach* (New York: McGraw-Hill, 1976).

[16]Maslow, *Eupsychian Management*, pp. 59–60.

The need hierarchy and its implied stages of development toward self-actualization are the primary link between Maslow and the generation of humanistic psychologists and younger organization and management theorists who would later press the case for humanizing the rational organization. Ironically, however, in Maslow's writings (his later ones in particular) there is clearly an elitism that qualifies both his apparently unabashed belief in the essential goodness of human nature and his support for participative democracy in organizations. In a now-famous article titled "The Superior Person," Maslow chides his contemporaries for naively assuming that an attitude of trust and a commitment to participation are universally appropriate. In that article, Maslow wrote:

> The unselected differentiated population at large has a fair proportion of very sick people, very incompetent people, very psychopathic people, insane people, vicious people, authoritarian people, immature people. Any reasonably intelligent personnel policy will exclude many of these diminished and inadequate people that one finds in any larger society. Even within this selected environment, the human relations techniques under discussion here refer exclusively to executive personnel; for example, top management vis-a-vis middle management. . . .
>
> The writers on the new style of management have a tendency to indulge in certain pieties and dogmas of democratic management that are sometimes in striking contrast to the realities of the situation. Robert Tannenbaum in *Leadership and Organization* says, for instance, "Managers differ greatly in the amount of trust they have in other people," as if trust depended entirely on the character of the manager. Surely trustfulness depends also on who the manager is dealing with. To trust psychopaths or paranoiacs is not generous but foolish. Any outlook which encourages us to trust everybody is an unrealistic dogma.[17]

Not only are *inferior* people to be excluded from the *benefits* of participation, but *superior* people, says Maslow, are justifiably exempt from the *burdens* that it entails. The "very superior boss," for example, should be allowed to operate "without any obeisance at all to democratic dogma"[18] by doing "what pleases him most and by getting rid of what irritates him most,"[19] including, one presumes, recalcitrant employees. Just how these superior bosses are identified in the first place Maslow does not say. He did, however, qualify his remarks about inferior and superior persons by asserting that he was not suggesting

> a rejection of what human relations theory has to say about management. The facts *do* tend to support participative management insofar as the culture is good

---

[17]Maslow, "The Superior Person," in Warren G. Bennis, ed., *American Bureaucracy* (Hawthorne, N. Y.: Aldine, 1970), pp. 31–32.

[18]Ibid., p. 33.

[19]Ibid., p. 34.

enough, the people involved are psychologically healthy, and the general conditions are good.[20]

Despite this disclaimer, however, the organizational humanists inspired by other aspects of his work probably wished that Maslow had confined his attention to psychology, leaving questions about management and politics to those having more temperate and informed sensibilities. Douglas McGregor was among the most influential of those theorists who extended Maslow's humanistic psychology—notably his self-actualization scheme, rather than his observations on organizations—to the "human side of enterprise."

The Human Side of Enterprise: Douglas McGregor

For Douglas McGregor, the natural development of the individual toward self-actualization logically conflicts with the traditional practice of management in formal organizations. Although the resulting struggle may temporarily abate, it continually reasserts itself and requires special effort to cope with it effectively.[21]

Like Maslow, McGregor, though in many ways disillusioned in later life, was essentially optimistic about people's capacity for self-fulfillment, a belief sustained by his reading of Maslow's earlier work. McGregor's optimism about human nature extended also to an optimism about the possibilities for merging individual and organizational needs in ways that would satisfy both. McGregor sees no necessary conflict between individual and organizational goals, arguing that it is through enlightened management that the goals of both may be satisfied. Thus, McGregor appears to take a middle ground position between Barnard's functionalism, in which individual goals derive *from* the organization, and the generally Marxian-Freudian (and Weberian) position of the critical theorists, who regard formal organizations as instruments of social domination (see Chapter 10). McGregor's intermediate stance on this issue has evoked, especially from the critical organizational theorists, the charge that he waffles badly on the matter of where, ultimately, his loyalties lay: with the individual or with the organization. Logically, however, there is no necessary reason to "take sides," if in fact individual and organizational goals

[20]Ibid., p. 36.
[21]His principal works include: Douglas McGregor, *The Human Side of Enterprise* (New York: McGraw-Hill, 1960); *Leadership and Motivation: Essays of Douglas McGregor*, Warren G. Bennis and Edgar Schein, eds. (Cambridge, Mass.: MIT Press, 1966); and *The Professional Manager*, Warren G. Bennis and Caroline McGregor, eds. (New York: McGraw-Hill, 1967).

can be integrated. On the other hand, McGregor does seem to gloss over the difficulty of such an integration through a rather forced conjunction of Maslovian humanism and "bottom line" preachments.

Theory X and Theory Y

McGregor's name is most commonly associated with two contrasting sets of beliefs about management, which he calls Theory X and Theory Y. The former is summarized in three basic propositions:[22]

1 Management is responsible for organizing the elements of productive enterprise—money, materials, equipment, people—in the interest of economic ends.

2 With respect to people, this is a process of directing their efforts, motivating them, controlling their actions, modifying their behavior to fit the needs of the organization.

3 Without this active intervention by management, people would be passive—even resistant—to organizational needs. They must therefore be persuaded, rewarded, punished, controlled—their activities must be directed. This is management's task. We often sum it up by saying that management consists of getting things done through other people.

For McGregor, Theory X is the conventional theory of management and is implicitly predicated on the following assumptions about workers:[23]

1 The average man is by nature indolent—he works as little as possible.

2 He lacks ambition, dislikes responsibility, prefers to be led.

3 He is inherently self-centered, indifferent to organizational needs.

4 He is by nature resistant to change.

5 He is gullible, not very bright, the ready dupe of the charlatan and the demagogue.

The central element of Theory X is the conventional belief that management chiefly consists of direction and control. It may be either "hard," in which managers use threats of coercion to achieve organizational objec-

---

[22]McGregor, "The Human Side of Enterprise," in Walter Nord, ed., *Concepts and Controversy in Organizational Behavior* (Pacific Palisades, Calif.: Goodyear, 1972), p. 53; originally published in *Management Review* 46:11(1957):22–28.
[23]Ibid.

tives, or "soft," where in the interests of harmony managers employ a permissive style to achieve those same ends. McGregor's work is often misread as equating Theory X with "hard" management and Theory Y with "soft." For McGregor, however, "hard" and "soft" management are simply two variations of Theory X, both of which are unsatisfactory. Regardless of whether it is manifested in its hard *or* its soft variety, the Theory X assumption that management consists of directing and controlling inevitably violates, in Maslow's terms, the higher-level psychological needs of employees. With respect to worker's social needs (such as love and self-esteem), for example, McGregor states that,

> [M]anagement, fearing group hostility to its own objectives, often goes to considerable lengths to control and direct human efforts in ways that are inimical to the natural "groupiness" of human beings. When man's social needs—and perhaps his safety needs, too—are thus thwarted, he behaves in ways which tend to defeat organizational objectives. He becomes resistant, antagonistic, uncooperative. But this behavior is a consequence, not a cause.[24]

And regarding self-esteem:

> The typical industrial organization offers few opportunities for the satisfaction of these egoistic needs to people at lower levels in the hierarchy. The conventional methods of organizing work, particularly in mass-production industries, give little heed to these aspects of human motivation. If the practices of scientific management were deliberately calculated to thwart these needs, they could hardly accomplish this purpose better than they do.[25]

Most especially, however, McGregor sees the conventional Theory X approach to management as stifling the individual's impulse toward self-fulfillment (in Maslow's terms, self-actualization). He regards these as relatively weak needs, which typically lie dormant by virtue of the individual's struggle to deal with deprivations at the lower need levels.

To undo the motivational damage produced by Theory X management, McGregor introduces four propositions that describe his preferred alternative, which he calls Theory Y:[26]

1 Management is responsible for organizing the elements of productive enterprise—money, materials, equipment, people—in the interest of economic ends.

2 People are *not* by nature passive or resistant to organizational needs. They have become so as a result of experience in organizations.

---

[24]Ibid., p. 55.
[25]Ibid.
[26]Ibid., pp. 57–58; emphasis in original.

3 The motivation, the potential for development, the capacity for assuming responsibility, the readiness to direct behavior toward organizational goals are all present in people. Management does not put them there. It is a responsibility of management to make it possible for people to recognize and develop these human characteristics for themselves.

4 The essential task of management is to arrange organizational conditions and methods of operation so that people can achieve their own goals *best* by directing *their own* efforts toward organizational objectives.

Although the first proposition of Theory X and Theory Y are identical, the remaining ones of the latter explicitly contradict those of the former, both with respect to the underlying philosophy of management and the motivational assumptions on which they are based. Rather than management by direction and control, Theory Y portrays the function of management as creating the conditions in which workers may control their own activities in the achievement of organizational goals. To assume that such self-direction will ultimately produce actions consistent with organizational goals obviously requires a set of beliefs about individual motivation far different from, and much more optimistic than, those of Theory X.

McGregor cites several management practices that conform in spirit to Theory Y assumptions. Delegation and decentralization, increased worker participation in making managerial decisions, enlargement of jobs in order to tap workers' creative potential, and performance appraisal geared to the achievement of objectives that individuals set for themselves head the list of McGregor's suggestions. But the thrust of McGregor's thinking is not mainly to provide a laundry list of management "techniques" intended to increase organizational effectiveness. Instead, his purpose is to offer managers a new way of thinking about management and workers. Thus, while McGregor continually refers to the "science-based" character of Theory Y management, these allusions sometimes confuse rather than clarify his more important message, which is far more value-based than science-based.

Theory Y is a *normative philosophy* of management, one whose validity is not ultimately testable by the neutral methods of science. Management assumptions, whether they be of the Theory X *or* the Theory Y variety, are in effect self-fulfilling prophecies: They become "true" by virtue of our implicit and even unconscious commitment to them. The manager in other words, evokes the kind of behavior in subordinates that conforms to his or her unconscious projections about their motivations.

McGregor's insistence that Theory Y cannot be reduced to a set of techniques to be used to motivate employees stems from his belief that people are by nature active rather than passive. That is, people are intrinsically motivated, which is to say that they possess psychological energy; they are not passive beings needful of external sources in order to motivate them. If motivation is primarily intrinsic rather than extrinsic, the task of management is to *channel* worker energy, not to try to create it by means of external sanctions and rewards. Sanctions and rewards still have a place, but one limited merely to fulfilling the more basic needs and, in some situations, to providing recognition of social needs.

Integrating the Individual and the Organization: Chris Argyris

Chris Argyris, a contemporary of McGregor, has also grappled with the problem of the individual's relationship to the organization.[27] Apparently less explicitly influenced by Maslow than was McGregor, Argyris regards the tension between the individual and the organization as more a product of the formal organization's requirements for rationality and specialization than of its usual authoritarian management practices. In this regard, Argyris is more of an *organization* theorist than was McGregor, who, more properly regarded as a management theorist, takes the organization's logic as a given. This admittedly fine distinction calls attention to Argyris's concern with the imperatives implicit in the logical structure and the functional requirements of formal organizations. This results in a view of organizational effectiveness in some respects not dissimilar to that of the mainstream systems theorists. Unlike them, however, Argyris evinces a far greater concern for, and indeed uses as his starting point of analysis, the characteristics of mature individuals and the processes entailed in their development toward maturity. In his most important early work in organizational behavior, *Personality and Organization*, Argyris identifies four imperatives for the development of the healthy individual as they bear on his or her relationship to the formal organization:[28]

1 To decrease his feelings of dependence, submissiveness, subordination, and passivity toward management.

2 To decrease the probability that he is subject to arbitrary unilateral action by the people in power, thereby increasing the possibility that he can find opportunity to be self-responsible.

---

[27]This section heading is borrowed from the title of one of Argyris's most influential books. See Chris Argyris, *Integrating the Individual and the Organization* (New York: John Wiley and Sons, 1964).

[28]Chris Argyris, *Personality and Organization* (New York: Harper & Row, 1957), p. 230.

3 To express his pent-up feelings ranging from outright aggression and hostility to passive internalization of tensions that are caused by the formal organization, directive leadership, management control, and pseudo human relations programs.

4 To create his own informal world with its own culture and values in which he can find psychological shelter and firm anchor to maintain stability while in the process of constantly adjusting and adapting to the formal organization (and directive leadership). By creating the informal world he can also take an active role in influencing the formal organization.

Somewhat reminiscent of Weber, Argyris cites several characteristics of formal organization[29] that are logically incompatible with the requirements of the mature individual. Specialization, for example,

> requires a person to use only a few of his abilities, and the more specialized the task the simpler the ability involved. This goes directly counter to the human tendency to want more complex, more interesting jobs as he develops.[30]

Similarly, hierarchical authority stifles the needs for autonomy and self-direction characteristic of mature individuals. The informal organization, while susceptible to its own pathologies, serves as the refuge for sanity within which individual members may strive to satisfy their developmental needs.

Unlike Weber, Argyris sees formal organizations as not being inextricably bound by the theory of management that has given rise to them. Thus, while he sees a "lack of congruency between the needs of healthy individuals and the demands of the formal organization,"[31] management may consciously alter those demands in order to make them more congruent with the needs of healthy individuals. This, in fact, is a principal task of management and can take the form of job enlargement, greater employee participation in making organizational decisions, and other such practices usually associated with, for example, McGregor's work.

Through enlightened effort, the needs of the individual and the organization can, therefore, be integrated. It is only the *theory* that typically drives the formal organization, not the *fact* of formal organization, that inhibits healthy individual development. As human inventions, theories may be deliberately changed, if only we possess the wit to do so. In this

---

[29]Although Argyris does not often use the term "bureaucracy," his description of "formal organization" bears strong resemblance to the former.

[30]Argyris, "Being Human and Being Organized," in Bennis, ed., *American Bureaucracy*, p. 22.

[31]Argyris, *Personality and Organization*, p. 233.

regard, Argyris provides a far more optimistic picture of what organizations might become than does, for example, William Scott (see Chapter 7), who sees the individual as already pretty much doomed by the "organizational imperative," or the critical theorists, discussed in Chapter 10, who hold that organizations are inherently oppressive. Argyris thus takes a middle-ground position between the sometimes gloomy pessimism of these writers and the benign image of organizational life evoked by Barnard and the systems theorists who followed in his wake.

Organization Development

If Argyris's analysis of the conflict between formal organization and the developmental needs of the individual is correct, then what, as a practical matter, can be done about it? How, in other words, may greater congruence be achieved between the organization's stated objectives and the needs of individuals for autonomy, self-esteem, and authentic relations with others? Argyris generally endorses Theory Y managerial practices; at the same time, he has also been a leading figure in an effort to develop methods and strategies by which professionals may effectively "intervene" in the process of organizations.

Collectively, these intervention strategies have been identified by a variety of labels, the most common of which are "process consultation" and "organization development" (or OD). An underlying assumption of OD activities is that achieving greater congruency in organizations is often unattainable by simply exhorting managers to read the collected works of McGregor, Argyris, and others—and then to act accordingly. Rather, because of distorted communication, hidden agendas, psychological defenses, and preoccupation with substantive tasks, people in organizations are often oblivious to the pathologies imbedded in the ways in which they act toward one another, pathologies that are reinforced by the rational organization. These have profound and long-lasting effects on organizational performance, for which expert and disinterested assistance is needed in order to undo the damage they cause.

The interventions that Argyris and other OD practitioners propose are deducible in part from the formal theories they write about, but they have also been greatly informed by the laboratory education and sensitivity training movements. OD, in fact, is sometimes offhandedly referred to as "applied sensitivity training." This is at best an oversimplification, but OD and sensitivity training both share a common commitment to the idea that group process and personal feelings are vitally important to the health of organizations and people. Sensitivity training (or T-groups, as they are often called) still forms an integral part of many formal OD efforts, the belief being that personal learnings from T-group experiences better prepare participants for subsequent interventions that constitute the overall organization development process.[32]

As *process* interventionists, OD consultants assiduously avoid giving advice to their clients, the assumption being that the clients are the experts on matters of substantive knowledge about job tasks. (If they aren't, then a different kind of consultant is probably needed.) Even with respect to "process" issues, such as those involving the interpersonal dynamics of work relationships, giving advice is discouraged for the simple reason that it is almost always rejected. Rather than tell their clients how they should behave, Argyris says that the role of the OD consultant is to assist the client organization in generating valid information, which is to say, information about both substance and process that participants can intersubjectively agree upon.[33] The purpose in generating valid information is to provide organization members with a more realistic basis from which to make free and informed choices, which, in turn, will produce a higher level of commitment to the collective projects of the organization. This is a difficult, but crucially important, task since group mores, distrust, and varying definitions of what is going on produce wide discrepancies of opinion.

To skeptics, especially those who see organizations as inherently alienating, this may appear to be an excessively optimistic scenario of what does or even can occur in OD efforts. In describing the essentials of the OD process in this way, however, Argyris is simply being consistent with his early theorizing, which grants the possibility, and even the likelihood, of meshing the needs of healthy individuals with an enlightened view of what is good for the organization.

Organizational Learning

Argyris's thinking has more recently evolved in the direction of a theory of organizational learning. In his work with Donald Schön, in particular, Argyris has advanced the notion that the generation of valid information in order to enable free and informed choice is made difficult by discrepancies between the individual's "espoused theory" and his "theory-in-use." Briefly, the former comprises the person's consciously held beliefs about how he prefers to see himself, whereas the latter explains what he

---

[32]This was the rationale behind Argyris's use of T-groups in the initial stages of an OD effort with the United States Department of State during the mid-1960s. For a history of that effort, see Michael M. Harmon, "Organization Development in the State Department: A Case Study of the ACORD Program," *Report of the Commission on the Organization of the Government for the Conduct of Foreign Policy*, Volume 6 (Washington, DC: U. S. Government Printing Office, June 1975), pp. 65–78.

[33]Argyris, *Intervention Theory and Method: A Behavioral Science View* (Reading, Mass.: Addison-Wesley, 1970), pp. 17–20.

actually does, at least as seen by others. As Argyris and Schön explain:

> When someone is asked how he would behave under certain circumstances, the answer he usually gives is his espoused theory of action for that situation. This is the theory of action to which he gives allegiance, and which, upon request, he communicates to others. However, the theory that actually governs his actions is his theory-in-use, which may or may not be compatible with his espoused theory; furthermore, the individual may or may not be aware of the incompatibility of the two theories.[34]

For both individuals and organizations, the role of the consultant is to enable actors to perceive discrepancies between their espoused theories and their theories-in-use in order that these might be brought into greater harmony. This involves "double-loop" learning, which means learning "to be concerned with the surfacing and resolution of conflict rather than with its suppression."[35] For Argyris and Schön, the internalization of the processes of double-loop learning enables people to learn how to learn.

Otherwise sympathetic readers of Argyris's work have expressed misgivings about whether, in the final analysis, he confronts some very real issues regarding power and vested interests in organizations. Robert Denhardt, for example, poses the following dilemma implicit in Argyris's theory of learning:

> The manager is not a disinterested party but rather has a personal interest in the life of the organization. Moreover, the manager, being in a position of some power, has a stake in the status quo, a vested interest in maintaining the structure of power as it is. Where learning occurs that is critical of the existing normative structure of the organization, the manager must either choose to act authoritatively to preserve the organization as it is or to act democratically to assist in altering the group's norms. Obviously, a full commitment to double-loop learning would require the latter, yet Argyris is ambiguous on the point.[36]

Nor are such doubts likely to be allayed by Argyris's convictions that the pyramidal, bureaucratic organization will be with us indefinitely and that OD efforts, in order to be effective, must be managed from the higher echelons of the organization, where motives of power and self-interest may lead to the use of OD for manipulative purposes.

---

[34] Argyris and Donald Schön, *Theory in Practice: Increasing Professional Effectiveness* (San Francisco: Jossey-Bass, 1974), pp. 6–7. Also see Argyris and Schön, *Organizational Learning: A Theory of Action Perspective* (Reading, Mass.: Addison-Wesley, 1978); Argyris, *Reasoning, Learning, and Action: Individual and Organizational* (San Francisco: Jossey-Bass, 1983). For a complementary perspective on organizational learning, see Donald N. Michael, *On Learning to Plan—and Planning to Learn* (San Francisco: Jossey-Bass, 1973).

[35] Argyris and Schön, *Theory in Practice*, p. 19.

[36] Robert B. Denhardt, *Theories of Public Organization* (Monterey, Calif.: Brooks/Cole, 1984), pp. 100–101.

"Democracy is Inevitable": Warren Bennis

Chris Argyris is ultimately hopeful regarding the possibilities of reconciling the needs of healthy individuals with those of organizations and is generally accepting of the permanence of formal, hierarchical organizations. By contrast, one of his contemporaries, Warren Bennis, is more dubious about such a reconciliation, but sees reason for hope in the "inevitable" demise of bureaucratic organizations, which will be replaced by democratic ones.

On the matter of reconciling needs at the individual and organizational levels, Bennis criticizes what he terms Argyris's "utopian solution" to this issue, a solution that derives from a reliance on Maslow's idea of self-actualization. Bennis argues that "self-actualization" is inherently fuzzy and that individual motivation is in truth far more complicated owing to situational factors that cannot be anticipated by the theory. As Bennis puts it:

> As for my own belief, I, like Machiavelli, hold that man is both good and evil and that certain conditions in the organization will accentuate the expression of one or the other. Man's goodness and/or badness, this ambivalence, is part of the human condition and, as such, has to be considered in any theory of organization.[37]

Bennis's disagreement with Argyris's optimistic vision of human nature leads him to endorse what he regards as Douglas McGregor's "tragic view," namely, that the best one can hope for is to acheive a satisfactory resolution between the competing claims of the individual and organizational levels. To Bennis, McGregor's position is the more realistic of the two, especially in his later writings, which reveal considerable disillusionment with a management role that is largely facilitative rather than authoritative. In chiding Argyris for advocating the usual participative management and job enrichment practices spawned mainly by humanistic sentiments, Bennis urges favorable consideration of McGregor's "'tragic view' because it . . . recognizes the trading, negotiations, and accommodations necessary to realize a true integration."[38]

More significant in Bennis's disagreement with Argyris is what appears to him to be an excessive optimism about human nature. Yet, in Argyris's defense, it could be argued that his normative vision of the *possibilities* of

---

[37]Warren G. Bennis, *Changing Organizations* (New York: McGraw-Hill, 1966), p. 74.

[38]Ibid., p. 77. On re-reading Argyris's works, however, one suspects that Bennis has overdrawn their differences, since the similarities of McGregor's and Argyris's proposals for improving management practices far overshadow their differences. For example, both urge collaborative practices to iron out differences between organizational levels, while participative and job enrichment practices seem to be almost equally prominent in their works. Bennis, in short, could have chosen a better foil for Argyris than McGregor.

individual development in no way denies the reality of severe difficulties, both psychological and organizational, in realizing those possibilities. What really seems to separate the two theorists is the question, once again, of where their principal loyalties lie.

During the late 1960s and early 1970s, organizational democracy was a matter of keen interest to academic public administrationists, many of whose views on this subject were greatly influenced by the writings of the later human relationists. Significant among the latter were Argyris and Bennis, both of whom may be fairly regarded as "organizational democrats." But, where Argyris's democratic leanings are attributable mainly to humanistic sentiments associated with the self-actualization ideal, Bennis sees democracy as a practical imperative for organizational survival. Writing with Philip Slater, Bennis summarized his argument by saying that "Democracy becomes a functional necessity whenever a social system is competing for survival under conditions of chronic change."[39] In rejecting the benign sentiments that have traditionally inspired advocates of organizational democracy, Bennis and Slater argue that democracy is the most efficient form of social organization for assuring survival in a rapidly changing, technological age. By democracy, they refer to a "climate of beliefs" that includes the following:[40]

- Full and free communication, regardless of rank and power;

- A reliance on consensus, rather than on the more customary forms of coercion or compromise, to manage conflict;

- The idea that influence is based on technical competence and knowledge rather than on the vagaries of personal whims or prerogatives of power;

- An atmosphere that permits and even encourages emotional expression as well as task-oriented acts;

- A basically human bias, one which accepts the inevitability of conflict between the organization and the individual, but which is willing to cope with and mediate this conflict on rational grounds.

The triumph of these democratic values, say Bennis and Slater, is inevitable by virtue of the emergence of three organizational conditions that render the traditional bureaucratic form obsolete. First, the newer democratic values, and the mode of organizing suggested by them, are better suited for adapting to the rapidly changing demands and uncertainty of organizational environments than is the rigid, military model implicit in

[39]Ibid., with Philip E. Slater in Chapter 2, "Democracy Is Inevitable," p. 19.
[40]Ibid., p. 19.

traditional bureaucracies. Second, in view of the technological complexity of the problems that confront modern organizations, a "scientific attitude" is required that is far more compatible with a democratic model of organizing than a bureaucratic one. As Bennis and Slater state:

> The processes of problem solving, conflict resolution, and recognition of dilemmas have great kinship with the academic pursuit of truth. The institution of science is the only institution based on, and geared for, change. . . .
>
> In order for the "spirit of inquiry," the foundation of science, to grow and flourish, there is a necessity for a democratic environment. Science encourages a political view which is egalitarian, pluralistic, and liberal. It accentuates freedom of opinion and dissent. It is against all forms of totalitarianism, dogma, mechanization, and blind obedience.[41]

Finally, the adaptive and scientific attitudes are, happily, reinforced by the values embraced by the cadre of professionals who are rapidly replacing the "organization men" of the earlier bureaucratic era. Thus, Bennis and Slater conclude:

> These new professional men are remarkably compatible with our conception of a democratic system. For like these new men, democracy seeks no new stability, no end point; it is purposeless, save that it purports to ensure perpetual transition, constant alteration, and ceaseless instability. It attempts to upset nothing, but only to facilitate the potential upset of anything. Democracy and our new professional men identify primarily with the adaptive process, not the "establishment."[42]

Although Bennis shares with other later human relationists many of the same humanistic sentiments, his position is more correctly viewed as allied with the functionalism of the systems perspective discussed in Chapter 7. Like most systems theorists, Bennis's loyalties lie chiefly with the organization rather than with the individual, and these loyalties profoundly affect the substance of his argument for organizational democracy. It is not an argument based on a set of normatively preferred values (e.g., freedom, equality, self-realization), unless one accepts the highly arguable notion of organizational survival itself as an *a priori* normative good. Even if, for the sake of argument, one accepts such survival as an overarching normative value, then the justification of Bennis's version of democracy depends chiefly on empirical, rather than philosophical, support for it. That, in the years following his pronouncement (as early as 1964), bureaucracy has not noticeably given way to a more democratic successor suggests on its face good reasons for doubting the empirical

---

[41]Ibid., pp. 20–21.
[42]Ibid., p. 25.

basis of Bennis's argument. Moreover, many of those reasons were already known during the time that Bennis wrote, including some that were anticipated by Weber more than fifty years earlier.

Take, for example, Bennis's claim that organizational democracy is required for purposes of adaptation in a technological age. This seems to ignore the fact that modern bureaucracies, in part by virtue of their concentrations of technological expertise, are potent social forces in their own right, which *control* their environments as much as, if not more than, they adapt to them. In Chapter 7, we noted in this regard James D. Thompson's proposition that *rational* organizations attempt to do precisely that, using adaptation strategies only as second-best expedients when attempts to control fail. Moreover, according to William Scott, bureaucratic organizations have been phenomenally successful in their efforts at such control, driven as they are by the "organizational imperative."[43] The social consequence of technology, rather than democratizing organizations as Bennis claims, may simply cement, as Weber contended, the rationalizing power of bureaucracy into an efficient instrument of social domination.

Although Bennis might argue that all this is changing because of the "democratic" scientific attitude in organizations, there is reason to suspect that his is an extremely idealized view not only of scientific practice, but also of an attitude that pervades problem solving in modern organizations. The logic of the scientific method, as Bennis rightly suggests, is grounded in sentiments congenial to democratic values, yet that logic is easily subverted in practice. The scientific attitude, especially as it is affected by the growing professionalization of the organizational work force, might just as easily produce new positions of power and privilege that replace older ones based on formal authority.[44] If there is any truth in George Bernard Shaw's assertion that all professions are conspiracies against the laity, then Bennis might well be suspected of painting an unrealistically benign—indeed utopian—future for organizations.

Most conspicuous about Bennis's as well as the other later human relationists' arguments about democratic organizations is the absence of any reference to political power and political legitimacy, issues of great moment to citizens as well as to public administrationists and political scientists. As David Silverman says of Bennis:

> To show that he is aware of the difficulties ahead he concedes that, in a full view, " ... the distribution of power ... [will] have to be considered." But

---

[43]See Chapter 7 above; also, William G. Scott and David K. Hart, *Organizational America* (Boston: Houghton Mifflin, 1979), especially Chapter 2.

[44]This in fact is very close to the critique of bureaucracy made by the critical theorists discussed in Chapter 10.

apparently it will have to be considered by somebody other than Bennis who devotes no further time to it. Having begun in a tradition which stresses the needs of Man, Bennis has moved over to a primary concern with the needs of the Organisation.[45]

As organizational psychologists, Bennis, Argyris, and McGregor seldom focus on the issues of political power and legitimacy that have traditionally occupied the attention of public administration scholars. These issues nevertheless invite analysis from the standpoint of their otherwise very important contributions to the ideas of organizational democracy and democratic administration. The next section examines the later human relations perspective as it bears on these issues and, more generally, on the normative and political context of public administration.

Later Human Relations Theory and Democratic Administration

To the humanists of the later human relations tradition, employee participation was a virtual synonym for organizational democracy. Notwithstanding Maslow's perhaps intemperate suggestion of a government-administered "moral accounting system," however, most of the later human relationists confined their democratic visions to the *internal* management of organizations. The implications of organizational democracy for *political* democracy were not of serious concern to these writers, whose disciplinary commitments lay mainly in psychology and business management rather than in public administration and political science. For these latter two disciplines, however, the role of administration in political democracy had long been an important subject of controversy. But, beginning in the late 1960s, the idea of democratic administration took on a new meaning, owing to the influence of Maslow and his followers on the so-called "New Public Administration."

Although the vast majority of American public administration writers have historically considered themselves democrats, the meanings of democracy are sufficiently varied that no single conception of the role of administration in a democratic society has prevailed. In its early years as a self-conscious field of study, however, there was fairly uniform agreement that *political* democracy precluded democracy *within* administration. As Dwight Waldo has commented:

> [T]he early "public administrationists"—Woodrow Wilson, Frank Goodnow and Charles Beard, to name but a few—accepted democracy as the central meaning and principle of the American political system. The concern of such

---

[45]Silverman, pp. 91–92.

men was not, of course, with public administration in any narrow sense; on the contrary, they made the whole complex of political institutions their province. Yet curiously, these early students laid the foundations for a pattern of thought according to which democracy was for a generation to be a political principle external to the field of professional interest in public administration. In fact, the later students not only came to see democracy as external to their field of professional interest, but frequently regarded it as hostile to their central principle, efficiency. They became ambivalent, schizoid, seeking ardently to advance democracy by denying its relevance to the administrative process.[46]

The centrality of the notion of efficiency in public administration was upheld, of course, by the idea of a strict separation of politics from administration. The politics-administration dichotomy was logically sustained by analogous dichotomies between ends and means, value and fact. According to this view, politics concerned decisions about ends inferred from collective values, whereas administration involved the (presumably efficient) means by which factual premises, to use Simon's term, were applied in the attainment of those ends. Paralleling early public administration's belief in efficiency was Wilson's conviction that democratic government required a unitary center of power. According to Waldo, Wilson

found democracy actually endangered by too widespread a distribution of power: [quoting Wilson] "There is no danger in power, if only it be not irresponsible. If it be divided, dealt out in shares to many, it is obscured; if it be obscured, it is made irresponsible."[47]

Wilson reasoned that if political power were fragmented, the lines of political accountability would be blurred, especially as they extended down through the administrative apparatus. The result would obscure the ends that administrators were responsible for efficiently attaining. If those ends are obscured, the criterion of efficiency, in Wilson's view, has no operational meaning, since efficiency presupposes clarity about ends. Thus, the idea of democracy *within* administration was out of the question, since it would inevitably lead to ever–greater fragmentation of authority, further obscuring the ends for which administrators were accountable. From this view, efficiency as an adminstrative value is derived from the superordinate political value of accountability, which precludes democracy (read "fragmentation") within administration. As Waldo has summarized, the maxim implicit in the early public administration orthodoxy was "Autocracy during hours is the price of democracy after hours."[48]

[46]Dwight Waldo, "Development of Theory of Democratic Administration," *American Political Science Review* 46:1(1952):85.
[47]Ibid., p. 86.
[48]Ibid., p. 87.

Prior to World War II, the doubtful status of democratic administration drew intellectual support from other sources as well. Weber, for example, ruefully acknowledged not only that bureaucracy excluded the possibility of democracy *within* administration, but that the machine-like efficiency of bureaucracy, a potent social force in its own right, threatened to displace politics (democratic or otherwise) as the primary arbiter of public values. Similarly, in the United States, the mainstream literature of business management was distinctly undemocratic, wedded as it was to capitalist free enterprise and the sanctity of private property. That workers were *instruments* of production was seldom questioned.[49] Even the early human relations movement, for all its concern for the "social needs" of workers, did little to alter the implicit authoritarianism of early organizational and administrative thought toward a more democratic direction. Quoting Dwight Waldo again:

> The "softening" of private administration theory is not, of course, to be equated with the growth of "democratic administrative theory." There is a significant distinction between the most benevolent paternalism and a healthy, functioning democratic system. Obviously some of the "softening" has come about for reasons quite unrelated to democracy or even to humane sentiment, i.e., to achieve higher output or to forestall corrective political action. Yet even if we discount entirely any democratic motives on the part of private administration, the movements toward an enlightened paternalism may nevertheless have created conditions out of which democratic administration can grow—can grow more easily, at least, than it could have grown a generation or two ago.[50]

After decades of languishing as a distinctly minority perspective, the notion of democracy within administration emerged in the 1940s and 1950s as an idea in good currency.[51] The chief reason for this was the widespread recognition that any strict dichotomy between politics and administration simply could not be meaningfully sustained in practice. The activities of one necessarily intruded into the domain of the other, a fact made especially difficult to deny as government, in the years following World War II, grew larger and more complex, while the specialized expertise of bureaucracy increasingly influenced decisions about public policy. Necessity thus required that some version of democratic administration be made into a virtue in order to legitimate what was, in any case, inevitable.

[49]This can be seen clearly in the work of Frederick Taylor and Chester Barnard; see Chapter 5 above. A notable voice of dissent from this view in the first half of the century was Mary Parker Follett, whose ideas are discussed at some length in Chapter 11.

[50]Waldo, p. 84.

[51]This paralleled the emergence of the public organization as a respectable subject for theoretical inquiry; see Chapter 2 above.

The particular meaning of democratic administration that resulted from the breakdown of the dichotomy was in some respects, however, a limited one. Democratic administration typically referred to participation by administrators in the policy-making process within the already existing governmental-bureaucratic context. Few public administration theorists during this period urged *more* such participation by administrators, only that its current presence be recognized, legitimated, and then explicitly guided by a general commitment on the part of administrators to the broader values of political democracy. Such a conception of democratic administration did not include, to be sure, partisan advocacy of government policies. Even more significantly, its justification was seldom based on any belief in the positive benefits, for example in the form of better policies or more effective administration, that might accrue from increased involvement by administrators in the formulation of policies. And least of all was this conception of democratic administration defended on the ground that it was good for the public administrator's mental health. If bureaucrats wanted to self-actualize, they could do so on their own time. Whatever the particular form that the idea of democratic administration might take, its purpose was most assuredly to serve the larger interests of political democracy as traditionally understood and *not* to promote the psychological betterment of government employees.

Organizational Humanism and the "New Public Administration"

As public administration struggled to reconcile democratic administration with democratic political theory, the later human relations theorists contributed a new and radical dimension to that discussion. Writing from a vantage point removed from the constraints imposed by constitutional democratic theory, the humanists who followed Maslow's lead urged a particular form of internal organizational democracy based on a combination of ethical and human development grounds. Because the writings of McGregor, Argyris, and the other organizational humanists deal mainly with private-sector enterprises, the possible conflicts between the outcomes of internal organizational participation and the politically mandated goals of constitutional democracy were neither immediately apparent nor of overriding concern to them. Democracy's primary value, *participation*, should be carried into organizations. To the public administration traditionalists, on the other hand, democracy required *accountability* within the organization insofar as adminstrators were concerned.

Within the public administration academic community, relatively little direct confrontation between these two conflicting stances was evident until the late 1960s. Up to that time, "organizational behavior" had remained on the periphery of the principal intellectual debates among academic public administrationists. Courses on (and professors of) organizational behavior in the Maslovian tradition occupied only marginal status in the discipline, but were tolerated so long as their principal conclusion *appeared* to be that participation within organizations effectively served politically pregiven ends.

At least two developments thrust the ideas of the organizational humanists into the center of the intellectual fray about democratic administration. The first was a rising chorus of dissent from within the discipline of political science, which questioned the adequacy of existing democratic political and administrative institutions to realize the values they were ostensibly designed to promote. The then-dominant tradition of pluralism in political science was subjected to a barrage of criticism, the gist of which was that the prevailing politics of pluralistic competition among interest groups served the interests of the rich, while leaving the poor and minorities politically disenfranchised.[52] The critique of political pluralism and democratic politics-as-usual extended to administrative institutions, as well, with public bureaucracy emerging as one of the chief villains.

Significantly, the alternative conception of democracy that emerged from the dissenting political scientists bore a strong resemblance to that of the organizational humanists. Peter Bachrach, for example, argued for a "self-development" theory of political democracy, proposing that the primary criterion of a democratic society was the extent to which its citizens participated in cooperative activity.[53] Participation, in his view, is not simply a political right that assures each citizen a fair opportunity to pursue self-interested ends; in addition, participation, as a social process, is an intrinsic part of the citizen's quest for maturity and self-realization. Thus Bachrach, whose writings were fairly representative of the newer political scientists' critique of existing democratic politics, embraced a line of reasoning strikingly similar to McGregor and Argyris's arguments for participative organizations.

Symbolizing the attempt to merge the political and organizational conceptions of democracy was the literature spawned by the New Public

---

[52]The critique of political pluralism had a conservative variant, as well, perhaps best represented by Theodore Lowi's *The End of Liberalism* (New York: Norton, 1969). Lowi argues that "interest group liberalism," his term for political pluralism, undermines the sovereign authority of the state as represented by the Congress. Public bureaucracies are intimately involved as political actors in the struggle (but even more dangerous, in the collusion) between partisan interests. To Lowi, this illegitimate exercise of political power could be curbed by, among other things, severely limiting administrative discretion and other forms of administrative involvement in the policy process.

[53]Peter Bachrach, *The Theory of Democratic Elitism: A Critique* (Boston: Little, Brown, 1970). For a series of critical essays in much the same vein, see Philip Green and Sanford Levinson, eds., *Power and Community: Dissenting Essays in Political Science* (New York: Pantheon Books, 1969).

Administration movement of the late 1960s and early 1970s. Several younger public administration scholars who had been exposed to both sides of the debate sought, albeit with only partial success, to forge a new synthesis for public administration, drawing from both the public administration traditionalists and the organizational humanists. In *Toward a New Public Administration: The Minnowbrook Perspective*, a compilation of essays from a 1968 conference at Syracuse University's Minnowbrook conference site, the book's editor, Frank Marini, identified five major themes that permeated the conference papers and the discussion they generated.[54]

The first theme dealt with a widespread concern about the relevance of public administration teaching to the then-turbulent political climate engendered by the civil rights movement, the United States involvement in the Vietnam War, the recent assassinations of Robert Kennedy and Martin Luther King, and the Johnson administration's "War on Poverty." Especially strong criticism was directed at teaching that reinforced the ethic of value neutrality for administrators. Ethical neutrality, it was argued, is both unrealistic as a practical matter and normatively indefensible in the face of the pervasive inadequacy of the political activism among public administration academics and practitioners that, arguably, could obliterate the already tenuous distinction between politics and administration. It is within this context that social equity was vigorously advocated as a guiding value, mainly by George Frederickson[55] and later by David K. Hart.[56]

A second prominent theme, loosely referred to as "post-positivism," concerned the growing disenchantment with the underlying theoretical premises of mainstream social science research. Already under severe attack in related disciplines such as political science and sociology, the notion of a value-free social science was roundly condemned. Although much of this criticism at the conference was polemical in its tone, the Minnowbrook volume included some serious and sophisticated analyses of the limitations of behavioralist, and more generally positivist, social science.[57]

The third theme, identified under the heading "Adapting to Turbulence

---

[54]See Frank Marini, "The Minnowbrook Perspective and the Future of Public Administration," in Marini, ed., *Toward a New Public Administration: The Minnowbrook Perspective* (Scranton, Pa.: Chandler, 1971), pp. 346–67.

[55]H. George Frederickson, "Toward a New Public Administration," in Marini, pp. 309–31; and Frederickson, ed., "A Symposium: Social Equity and Public Administration," *Public Administration Review* 34:1(1974):1–51.

[56]David K. Hart, "Social Justice, Equity, and the Public Administrator," *Public Administration Review* 34:1(1974):3–11.

[57]The most prominent of these was Larry Kirkhart's "Public Administration and Selected Developments in Social Science," in Marini, pp. 93–121, which summarizes some of the major criticisms of behavioralist social science. Kirkhart presented, for the first time in the United States public administration literature, the basic elements of a phenomenological alternative grounded in the writings of Max Weber and Alfred Schutz (see Chapter 10 below).

in the Environment," reflected a merging of three elements: (1) the previously mentioned concern about the relevance of contemporary public administration to the pressing social and political issues of the day; (2) concerns raised in the organization development and organizational change literature, whose most visible contributors at that time were Chris Argyris and Warren Bennis; and (3) the issues raised in the open systems literature (not otherwise noteworthy for grounding theories of social and political activism) that grew out of general systems theory, socio-technical systems, cybernetics, and functionalist sociology. One implication of the combination of these elements was that public organizations could not rely solely on the existing political apparatus in order to respond adequately or effectively to the rapidly changing needs and demands of their relevant constituencies and the public at large.

The fourth theme, "New Organizational Forms," was inspired by the already familiar criticisms of the bureaucratic form of organization. Warren Bennis's notion of the "temporary organization"[58] and Kirkhart's "consociated model" of organization[59] were cited as preferred alternatives to Weber's bureaucratic model.

The final theme, "Client-Focused Organizations," drew its inspiration mainly from two sources, the first being the citizen participation movement fostered in part by the War on Poverty, and the second being humanistic psychology, principally the writings of Abraham Maslow. The client focus, in addition to reflecting the Minnowbrook emphasis on equity and social justice, also included more subjective and qualitative concerns that were informed more by the discipline of psychology than by political science.

The one paragraph from *Toward a New Public Administration* that best summarizes the overall sentiment of the Minnowbrook conference was provided by Todd LaPorte, who explicitly linked an emerging conception of political democracy with the later human relationists' proposals for internal organizational democracy. LaPorte argued that

> our primary normative premise should be that *the purpose of public organization is the reduction of economic, social, and psychic suffering and the enhancement of life opportunities for those inside and outside the organization.* Translated into more detailed sentiments, this statement means that public organizations should be assessed in terms of their effect on the production and distribution of material abundance in efforts to free all people from economic deprivation and want. Furthermore, it means that public organizations have a responsibility to enhance social justice by freeing their participants and the citizenry to decide their own way and by increasing the probability of shared

[58]Bennis, *Changing Organizations.*
[59]Kirkhart; see especially, pp. 158–64.

political and social privilege. Finally, it means that the quality of personal encounter and increasing possibilities of personal growth should be elevated to major criteria of organizational assessment.[60]

To the degree that LaPorte's statement was representative of the thinking at Minnowbrook, the New PA was probably guilty of glossing over the potentially conflicting requirements of public authority, on the one hand, and the humanists' demands for internal organizational democracy, on the other. Anticipating the dilemma posed by these competing pressures, Frederick Mosher cogently stated the traditionalist position shortly before Minnowbrook:

> [T]here has already developed a great deal of collegial decision-making in many public agencies, particularly those which are largely controlled by single professional groups. But I would point out that *democracy within administration*, if carried to the full, raises a logical dilemma in its relation to *political democracy*. All public organizations are presumed to have been established and to operate for public purposes—i.e., purposes of the people. They are authorized, legitimized, empowered, and usually supported by authorities outside of themselves for broad purposes initially determined outside of themselves. To what extent, then, should "insiders," the officers and employees, be able to modify their purposes, their organizational arrangements, and their means of support? It is entirely possible that internal administrative democracy might run counter to the principles and objectives of political democracy in which the organizations of government are viewed as instruments of public purpose.[61]

To date, there has been no satisfactory resolution of these two competing conceptions of democracy in and for public administration. Nor is it likely that such a resolution will or even should be forthcoming. Democratic theory has historically depicted a tension among competing values (e.g., liberty and equality), rather than offering up utopian formulas free of tension and conflict. The contribution of the New PA appears to have been consistent with that tradition by having introduced a healthy degree of tension between the ideas of the organizational humanists and the older political science tradition of public administration. It is probably true that the Minnowbrookers, on the whole, erred by siding too much with the former, while occasionally sidestepping important issues of administrative accountability to legitimate public authority. The New PA, however, in a variety of (not always consistent) ways, forced the discipline to consider the reality that the most important normative questions of administration are not always reducible to political accountability. If indeed there is no

---

[60]Todd R. LaPorte, "The Recovery of Relevance in the Study of Public Organization," in Marini, p. 32; emphasis in original.

[61]Frederick C. Mosher, *Democracy and the Public Service* (New York: Oxford University Press, 1968), pp. 18–19; emphasis in original.

clear dichotomy between politics and administration, then normative theories must appreciate the tension between them. The literature growing out of Minnowbrook, if sometimes only implicitly, helped to produce and clarify that tension.

Later Human Relations Theory and the Public Administration Framework

In assessing the contributions of the later human relations theory to the field of public administration, it is important to distinguish, but also to bear in mind the relationship between its underlying philosophy and the techniques and interventions that have sprung from it. That the later human relationists have often been ambivalent, at least in their public presentations, as to where their philosophical commitments lie, however, complicates an assessment of their strategies for improving administrative practice. Nowhere is their ambivalence more evident than in terms of public administration's historical commitment to the values of efficiency and effectiveness.

Efficiency and Effectiveness

Mother Teresa, who won the Nobel Peace Prize for her work with the poor and dying in Calcutta's slums, was once asked by Senator Mark Hatfield, "don't you get awfully discouraged when you see the magnitude of the poverty and realize how little you can really do?"—to which she replied: "God has not called me to be successful; He has called me to be faithful."[62]

The later human relations tradition challenged orthodox thinking about organizational behavior in a way that is as profound—metaphorically, if not spiritually—as the challenge of faith is to the quest for success. The Senator and Mother Teresa, in other words, have their counterparts in the history of organization theory. In organizations, success is typically measured almost solely by the normative vector of efficiency and effectiveness, which assumes an instrumental, external standard by which to judge organizational action. Whereas in private organizations, efficiency and effectiveness are presumed to promote higher profits, a larger share of the market, or simply continued organizational survival, in public organizations

[62]Phyllis Theroux, "Amazing Grace," *Washington Post Magazine*, October 18, 1981, pp. 34–35.

these two normative criteria are linked to the attainment of publicly mandated goals. In the latter, success is defined by the force of public authority as *the* legitimate basis from which to judge management practice.

Against this backdrop, the organizational humanists have struggled mightily to maintain their faith in the intrinsic virtue of participatory democracy. At the same time, they have acquiesced to demands to demonstrate to political authorities that their techniques will bring success. Indeed, most, if not all, empirical research on the effects of participative management practices on organizational productivity is undertaken on the hopeful but arguable assumption that success and faith may amicably coexist. While John Calvin might cast an approving eye, Mother Teresa would likely raise a disapproving eyebrow.

The strained relationship of success and faith as the twin forces that have driven the later human relations movement seems symptomatic of the confusion around the meaning and purpose of the various organizational practices that it recommends. To regard participative management, organization development, sensitivity training (or any of the other practical activities associated with organizational humanism) principally as *techniques* ultimately subordinates faith to success. The enterprise of empirical research, by and large, serves as the intendedly neutral arbiter to tell us which techniques are successful—that is, efficient and effective—and which are not. For the record, the evidence of their degree of success is decidedly mixed, a conclusion even further muddled by conflicting opinions not only about appropriate methodology, but also about the meaning and relevance of science to an understanding of the social world.[63]

More significant than the ambiguous *results* of empirical research on the effectiveness of organizational participation is that we should expect, at the outset, that research might provide definitive guidance to managers. Just as the organizational humanists are moved more often by faith than by evidence, so too are practicing managers persuaded more by the intuitive appeal of particular theories and (if one insists) techniques than by the weight of research findings that might or might not support them.[64] As professors of organization behavior know from their experiences in the classroom, a student's demand for proof that, for example, participative management "works" is, as often as not, a code for expressing disbelief that it does or can.

Even though, as a collectivity, theorists and practitioners of organiza-

---

[63]For a discussion of the assumptions underlying various research strategies in public administration, see L. Vaughan Blankenship, "Public Administration and the Challenge to Reason," in Waldo, ed., *Public Administration in a Time of Turbulence* (Scranton, Pa.: Chandler, 1971), pp. 188–213.

[64]The persuasiveness of intuitive appeal is, of course, hardly limited to the theories of the human relations perspective.

tional behavior appear ambivalent about the relative priority of faith and success, many as individuals have clearly taken their stand on one side or the other. On the side of success stand, for instance, the proponents of contingency theory. By declaring "effective goal attainment" as their standard of the good and the right, the contingency theorists are content to take their chances on whatever the research shows, apparently confident that, under some circumstances at least, participation will prove cost effective. On the side of faith stand those (for whom we know of no label) whose Kantian or religious sensibilities preclude arbitration by the scientific method. Representative of this viewpoint is Jerry Harvey, who observes that

> it is clear to me that competent interveners always base their actions on faith and not consequence. If they don't, they are inevitably overcome by the ravages of caution. Less euphemistically, they lose their courage. For that reason, I have the uncomfortable feeling that the ultimate question facing all interveners is whether their faith is based on anything of transcendent importance.[65]

Whether Harvey and those who share (secretly or otherwise) his point of view have embraced the *right* faith is, of course, open to question. One thing is sure, however, and it is that social science research cannot provide us with the answer.

Rights and the Adequacy of Process

A chief contribution of the later human relationists to the study of public organizations has been to elevate the idea of individual participation in organizations to the status of a moral right. This is clearly evident in Maslow, who argued for such participation as an ethical matter, whereas McGregor and Argyris mainly stress the merit of participation on psychological grounds. Although all three are cognizant of the frequent conflicts between the needs of healthy individuals and needs of organizations, they are nevertheless confident of the possibility of synthesizing the two. This optimism is based partly on the belief, implicit in their psychologies, that mentally healthy individuals are also socially responsible; the consequences of their actions will, within limits, largely be congruent with both organizational goals, as well as those of a democratic society.

The contribution of public administration scholars who share a similar humanistic orientation has been to try to reconcile the predominantly

---

[65]Jerry Harvey, "On Tooting Your Own Horn: or, Social Intervention as the Process of Releasing Anal Flatus in the Confines of Religious Institutions, by Bobby Lee Bemus, Blue Point College, Blue Point, Texas, As Told to Jerry B. Harvey," The George Washington University, Washington, DC, unpublished manuscript, 1984, pp. 8–9.

psychological orientation of the later human relationists with the basic tenets (as they see them) of political democracy and American social values. We have already noted the position of the "New Public Administration" in this regard. A prime example is LaPorte's contention that rights of participation in the activities of public organizations and opportunities for personal growth should extend to the citizenry at large, as well as to the members of such organizations. Robert Golembiewski develops a somewhat different but generally compatible argument derived from his understanding of the Judeo-Christian ethic. To Golembiewski, the psychologically based arguments for participation made by the later human relationists are but a reflection of the larger socio-religious ethic that historically has grounded American conceptions of work and economic life. In *Men, Management, and Morality*, he lists five values associated with the Judeo-Christian ethic:[66]

1 Work must be psychologically acceptable to the individual. . . .

2 Work must allow man to develop his own faculties. . . .

3 The work task must allow the individual considerable room for self-determination. . . .

4 The worker must have the possibility of controlling, in a meaningful way, the environment within which the task is to be performed. . . .

5 The organization should not be the sole and final arbiter of behavior; both the organization and the individual must be subject to an external moral order.

Golembiewski's stated intent is "to enlarge the area of discretion open to us in organizing and to increase individual freedom."[67] Although the first four values of the Judeo-Christian ethic that he cites are familiar to readers of Maslow and McGregor, the fifth directly confronts, but does not ultimately resolve the crucial political question of what to do when the imperatives of public organizations collide with the psychological needs of the individual. To say that the "organization should not be the final and sole arbiter of behavior" raises some thorny questions when one is talking about *public* organizations, whose existence, not to mention their legitimacy, presumes that they have been created to serve the very values that Golembiewski associates with the Judeo-Christian ethic. If public organizations are guilty of violating the fundamental social values that they are designed to further, clearly a more radical alternative is

---

[66]Robert T. Golembiewski, *Men, Management, and Morality* (New York: McGraw-Hill, 1965), p. 65.
[67]Ibid., p. 305.

needed than the timid cure that Golembiewski offers. As Robert Denhardt has observed,

> rather than confronting the task of building a sociopolitical ethic based on democracy, socialism or whatever, Golembiewski . . . chooses instead to discuss the issue of centralization and decentralization in organizations, positing decentralization as the answer to "the central moral question." . . . Presumably, individuals in decentralized organizational structures would have greater moral latitude. Although this might be true, the ethic of the organization would still assert itself, especially since "freedom to act in a decentralized structure is paid for by adherence to corporate policies." The freedom of the individual would still be defined by the organization; there would be no external moral order to which both the individual and the organization could be held accountable.[68]

Trusting the Process The concern for promoting individual rights to participation and personal growth for public administrators has long posed a dilemma for those who share an equal concern with insuring that those same administrators be held politically accountable for the results of their actions. Mosher's remarks on the logical dilemma between the humanists' notion of internal organizational democracy and political democracy were noted earlier in this regard. A not-implausible response to the dilemma is simply to accept it, shrugging philosophically that democratic government necessarily entails the clash of opposing principles. This suggests that while opposing principles may, perhaps, be mediated on an *ad hoc* basis, they can never be definitively resolved. Instead, they must be continually re-solved.

In subsequent chapters, we review several points of view that are more ambitious in their attempts to resolve this dilemma. From the perspectives discussed in this chapter, however, the seriousness of the dilemma, as posed by the public administration traditionalists, may have been greatly overstated, if not misconceived. A clue to why this may be the case lies in an implicit organizational humanist injunction to "trust the process." This is an injunction whose full implications were never fully articulated, nor even understood, by the organizational humanists themselves. As Peter Vaill has described it:

> To trust the process as an injunction to the trainer/leader is to free one from the need to *make* anything in particular happen in the training setting. To trust the process as an injunction to the learner is to free one from the need to learn anything in particular from the experience, that is, to free oneself from the mind-compressing question: What am I *supposed* to be learning here?
>
> . . .
>
> Behind this rule of thumb, as it were, was far deeper wisdom and faith about human interaction. This deeper wisdom was about the inherent capacity of the

---

[68]Denhardt, p. 103.

human being to trust, to cherish, to share, to rage at silliness and shallowness and bankrupt values, to be honest, to be helpful, to reach out and to be supportive of one's fellow group members as they struggled with the dilemmas of their existence. One did not need to make these things happen; one did not need to exhort oneself and others of the virtues of these qualities, as preachers have done for ages from pulpits. To trust the process was to know that these qualities would emerge if one would just sit down in a sensitivity training group.[69]

Vaill's intent is not merely to establish the point that trust in the process was central to the humanists' commitment to the sensitivity training movement. Rather, he is concerned to point out that the leaders of that movement understood neither the power nor the implications of that injunction for a broader assessment of organizational life. In the context of this chapter, the injunction to trust the process is one that is based on faith rather than on success. This injunction of faith, however, has decidedly practical implications, as well, inasmuch as the usual criteria by which success is presumably determined are so illusory and ambiguous that faith (or trust) in humane organizational processes provides a more sensible basis for assessing organizational performance. To trust the process means in effect to suspend one's immediate concern with identifying goals and objectives by which to judge group or organizational effectiveness.

Still, one might well respond, government organizations are not the same as sensitivity groups. Even if we should trust the process in the latter, does that suffice as a reason to be similarly trustful of it in the day-to-day administration of government programs? Success, in the sense of goal attainment, may not be relevant to sensitivity trainers, but is it not vital for public administrators, especially in a political democracy in which they are held accountable to their political masters? Organizational humanists typically do not engage these questions directly, yet there is some reason to suspect that the practical value to trusting the process *does* extend beyond sensitivity groups at least to the daily activities of often-perplexed managers. Since the evidence is necessarily anecdotal, managers must judge that evidence solely on its intuitive resonance for them. Based on their own experience, they must judge whether Vaill's conclusion about his own managerial role (and *not* his role as sensitivity trainer) helps to explain their own difficulties in achieving, or even recognizing, success:

Maybe the accomplishment of a process is about all we can really ask for in the managerial role—to be able to tell ourselves that we have acted in a way that meets our standards for an effective performance. I say this because after only relatively brief experience in my little pressure-cooker job [as a university

[69]Vaill, pp. 561–62, emphasis in original.

dean], I concluded that results are always ambiguous and equivocal. For every fact that I can produce to prove that something worked, I or someone else can produce another fact that proves it didn't. *If results are always ambiguous, then process accomplishment is much more real and holds more promise for developing a sense of closure.*[70]

If Vaill is correct in arguing that results are always ambiguous, and if his observation applies to the development and implementation of government programs as well as to other arenas of management, then the traditionalists' belief in accountability as the pre-eminent value for public administration would appear, as a practical matter, to rest on a less than solid base. Accountability presupposes not only clarity about ends, but also relatively clear and unambiguous measures of the success of their attainment. Even though there is good reason to demand accountability from administrators in a democratic society, there is also wisdom in recognizing the limits beyond which those demands become increasingly unrealistic. For all its virtues, the idea of accountability may also become a fetish, something often demanded from administrators in inverse proportion to the public's knowledge of what it wants them to do. Through their injunction to trust the process, the organizational humanists seem to be telling us that, at the very least, faith is a practical substitute when success is either undefinable or impossible to measure. Nor, from an alternative conception of democracy, is the humanists' trust in the process even inconsistent with democracy. American pragmatists, especially John Dewey and Mary Parker Follett, conceived of democracry as almost synonymous with experimentation and discovery. It was a conception of democracy rooted more in their faith in the process than in their certainty of the product.

Representation and the Control of Discretion

Without intending to, the later human relationists have provided public administration with more dilemmas than answers. The effect of their influence has been to complicate, but also to enrich, public administration's self-understanding of its appropriate role in a democratic society. In part, this has resulted from the meaning of democracy that they adhere to, one that in turn profoundly alters the meanings of other normative issues in public administration, including those of administrative discretion and the representation of interests.

The meanings of these terms to the later human relationists derive significantly from two prominent themes that pervade their writings: the ten-

[70]Vaill, "Management as a Performing Art," *Personnel* 53:4(1976):19; emphasis in original.

sion between the needs of individuals and organizations, and the injunction to trust the process. With regard to the first of these themes, it is
evident that the organizational humanists harbor serious doubts that formal organizations are, by their nature, capable of representing the most
basic of their members' interests, which are chiefly psychological ones.
Although McGregor and particularly Argyris argue for the importance of
integrating individual and organizational needs, both are also mindful of
the enormous difficulties of doing so. To enable that integration, Argyris,
as well as Golembiewski, have proposed organization development strategies as the practical means by which its attainment might have a fighting
chance.[71] In counterpoint to their restrained optimism that enlightened
thinking and hard effort might enable that integration, however, is William Scott, who contends that the imperatives of formal organization have
pretty much won the struggle already, leaving resistance as the final
recourse of the individual.[72]

Scott, as well as the public administration scholars who have been influenced by the organizational humanists, however, are concerned not only
with the struggle of individuals *within* organizations, but the capabilities
of public organizations to represent (or, as they usually put it, to be
responsive to) the needs of citizens. To many of the New Public Administrationists, the problem was not so much that bureaucracy was inefficient
in performing its official tasks; rather, by virtue of its efficiency, bureaucracy precluded individual citizens from cooperatively determining their
destinies. However efficient bureaucracy may be in representing citizens'
interests when they are construed as pregiven *ends*, it fails insofar as interests are defined in process terms. To political theorists such as Bachrach,
however, political and administrative institutions in a democracy must
represent both of these kinds of interests. He concludes

> that a theory of democracy should be based upon the following assumptions
> and principles: the majority of individuals stand to gain in self-esteem and
> growth toward a fuller affirmation of their personalities by participating more
> actively in meaningful community decisions; people generally, therefore, have
> a twofold interest in politics—interest in end results and interest in the process
> of participation; benefits from the latter interest are closely related to the degree
> to which the principle of equality of power is realized.[73]

Bachrach thus echoes the later human relationists' maxim not only to

---

[71]In addition to Argyris's works cited earlier, see Golembiewski, *Public Administration
as a Developing Discipline: Part II* (New York: Marcel Dekker, 1977); and Golembiewski
and William Eddy, eds., *Organization Development in Public Administration: Part I* (New
York: Marcel Dekker, 1978).
[72]See Chapter 7 above.
[73]Bachrach, p. 101.

trust the process of cooperative activity, but also to encourage it. This is sometimes read to mean allowing for greater discretion by administrators in interpreting and implementing organizational policies. It may not *necessarily* be inconsistent to argue for both of these; they are by no means the same thing and may in particular cases even be at odds with one another. Although greater administrative discretion is often proposed as a means for promoting democratic administration, the recipients of unilateral discretionary judgments may frequently fail to discern in them anything that is democratic.

In this sense, then, discretion may contradict the notion of trusting the process, which by definition is a social one. Indeed, trusting the process seems far more consistent with the democratic ideal of self-development upon which both Bachrach and the later human relationists themselves claim to ground their theories. The later human relationists often describe this process of development in highly individualistic terms, invoking, for example, Maslow's idea of self-actualization. Yet, their practical contributions, in particular the interventions taken under the heading of organizational development, have a far more social cast to them. Organizational development practitioners, most of them at any rate, are mainly facilitators of organizational, and sometimes even community, processes. To the extent that "self-development" occurs as a result of OD interventions, it is mainly a residue of the social processes that those interventions generate. In order to be consistent with the later human relationists' injunction to trust the process, the notion of discretion requires a far greater *social* connotation than it is presently given.

Conclusion

In no small measure, the intellectual vitality of public administration might well be attributed to the apparent ease with which other disciplines have intruded upon its academic turf. Indeed, it is arguable that public administration is not a discipline at all, but a collection of disciplines, each focusing in a distinctive way on a common concern—the effective management of government. Despite its variegated composition, however, the field has historically sustained a degree of internal coherence by virtue of its commitment to the idea of democracy. During the last two to three decades, that commitment has not wavered, but the meaning of the idea of democracy *has* changed, if in no other way than by being revealed as vastly more complicated than the public administration traditionalists ever anticipated.

As an important contributing discipline to the field of public administration, organization theory has also managed, despite *its* internal differences, to sustain coherence around a core belief: namely, that the ends of the organization take analytical and moral precedence over the individuals who make up the organization. This was the case, that is, until the later human relations theorists made their influence felt on organization theory and, eventually, on public administration. The later human relationists disputed the primacy of efficiency as an *organizational* value, and challenged, though inadvertently at times, the notion of accountability as the overriding value of political democracy. In both instances, these challenges are traceable to the normative commitment that the later human relationists have placed on values associated with individual development.

Owing largely to their own ambivalence about how far to press that commitment, and whether it derives chiefly from faith or from a concern with success, these theorists have raised far more questions than they have answered. Nevertheless, the internal tensions in the later human relations perspective about what is rightfully God's and what is Caesar's have forced theorists of public organizations to ponder those same questions. The theory of public organization has been greatly enriched as a result.

As we shall see in the remaining chapters, a primary commitment to the individual is not limited exclusively to the later human relations theorists. Allegiance to the individual as the moral and analytical beginning point may itself encompass radically differing opinions about what is the most essential interest of the individual. Faith, in other words, may take many forms, and to date there is little agreement in organizational theory about which form is correct.

9

Market Theories: Organizing as Revealed Self-interest

Used here as a loose umbrella term, the term "market theories" encompasses several contributions to the theoretical understanding of organizational processes made either by economists or by scholars deeply influenced by that discipline. Although the literature discussed in this chapter is not usually considered to be organization theory as such, it has much to offer in the way of enriching our understanding of organizational processes. This is especially true with respect to public sector organizations, since market theories of organization typically deal with political and governmental concerns.

Any theory about organizing begins with a claim regarding the proper starting point, or primary unit of analysis, from which to proceed with the development of its overall framework of description and explanation. This claim is typically accompanied by a set of assumptions underlying the unit of analysis. Although not always explicit, these assumptions bear on such matters as the primary unit's ontological standing (if any) and its methodological strengths (and limitations) in predicting behavior. They also reflect beliefs about human and social values that are supported by the primary unit and the philosophical and historical antecedents that give it credence. Finally, these assumptions underpin the practical value of the primary unit of analysis as a basis from which to offer advice for understanding and improving organizations.

The two earlier chapters on systems theory and human relations theory, for instance, employed as primary units of analysis, respectively, the system (conceived metaphorically as an organism) and the affective individual. Each of these calls attention to the social dynamics that influence organizational functioning, but from differing perspectives. Various theorists within each of those two traditions differ in the strictness with which they adhere to the assumptions and implications of their respective primary units of analysis; at the same time, each tradition offers, on the whole, a fairly coherent image of organizational life.

The present chapter about market theories of organization provides yet another view of organizing, one that is as distinct from the other two as they are from one another. The distinctive character of market theories is attributable to their primary unit of analysis, namely, the self-interested individual seeking to maximize his or her utility through the exercise of rational choice. This assumption of rational self-interest explicitly and profoundly influences the scientific approach and the value basis, as well as the practical implications of the market theories. In addition, it provides the ground for both an explicit opposition to organic system theories, on the one hand, and an apparent indifference to the possible merits of human relations theory, on the other.

Introduction

Like Western economics generally, market theories of organization owe a major debt to the philosophy of utilitarianism in shaping their tone, substance, and method. Utilitarianism was probably the most influential school of political thought in Britain and America during the nineteenth and, arguably, the twentieth centuries. Initially inspired by the deep pessimism of Thomas Hobbes, utilitarianism was founded by the great conservative Scot, David Hume, and developed to maturity in the writings of Jeremy Bentham and John Stuart Mill.

Reacting against the natural rights and social contract theories of the Enlightenment, the utilitarians held in disdain the idea of the existence of *a priori* moral principles discoverable through reason. The role of reason is instead limited, especially for Hume, to directing people's actions, which are fundamentally governed by their passions. Reason, to Hume,

> may be employed to show logical relationships; it cannot demonstrate existence (facts) or values (tenets of the natural law). Human values are determined by "passion" or feeling. Reason may be helpful in directing action toward the attainment of values, but its role is secondary. It is an instrument.[1]

[1] M. Judd Harmon, *Political Thought: From Plato to the Present* (New York: McGraw-Hill, 1964), p. 139.

As realists, the utilitarians held that experience, rather than abstract reflection, revealed people's interests. However, with John Stuart Mill the notable exception, they were usually less optimistic than the contemporary market organization theorists about the ability of the masses to recognize their true interests and to act in ways consistent with them. The utilitarians' aversion to abstract speculation is bolstered by their commitment to empiricism and their belief in the benefits of a scientific approach to understanding human affairs. Nowhere in modern social science is a similar commitment more evident than in contemporary Western economics, the most immediate intellectual antecedent of market organization theories.

Finally, the utilitarians, in view of their preoccupaton with individual interests, pleasures, and happiness, were decidedly scornful of the social and communitarian values embodied in such terms as "civic duty," "moral virtue," and "personal development." Indeed, to Bentham,

> The community is a fictitious *body,* composed of the individual persons who are considered as it were its *members.* The interest of the community then is, what?—the sum of the interests of the individual members who compose it.[2]

Although social collectivities did occasionally produce people of civic virtue motivated by altruism, such individuals were hardly in sufficient supply (nor were they really necessary) to predicate systems of philosophy and institutions of government on their presence. In this respect, utilitarianism was equalitarian, since many could at least discern their own interests, even if only few were able to comprehend concepts of moral virtue. Given the time that has elapsed between the emergence of utilitarianism and the appearance of market theories of organization, the influence of the former on the latter is often only implicit and indirect. Yet, the task of government, according to the utilitarians, was to invent the means to calculate the greatest happiness for the greatest number and to construct the institutions necessary to administer the policies implied by those calculations. This, in essence, is also the project of contemporary market theories of organization.

There are five basic insights deriving from the self-interest assumption that, collectively, provide a composite view of market organizing theory:

1 Individual choice is, at bottom, the basis for organizational or collective action. That is, what is usually thought of as collective action is, in reality, the aggregation of individual choices.

---

[2]Jeremy Bentham, *The Principles of Morals and Legislation* (New York: Hafner, 1948), chap. 1, sec. 4; quoted in Harmon, p. 372, emphasis in original.

2 Individual choices are expressions of individual preferences, which differ from and conflict with one another. Conflict is, therefore, inherent in social life, and organizing is the means for managing (though not necessarily resolving) that conflict.

3 Rules are needed to adjudicate among conflicting preferences. These rules serve to simplify and bring order to those situations in which collective decisions are required.

4 Differences in individual (and group) preferences, as well as limitations of time, information, and resources, tend to produce satisficing, rather than maximizing, strategies by decision makers.

5 Organizationally, these satisficing strategies result in decisions that typically differ only incrementally, rather than fundamentally, from earlier decisions and states of affairs.

Despite their common economics background, the theorists in this chapter by no means offer a unified theoretical perspective. The next sections, for example, review two principal works on public choice theory, James M. Buchanan and Gordon Tullock's *The Calculus of Consent* and Vincent Ostrom's *The Intellectual Crisis in American Public Administration*. The discussion of public choice theory is followed by a summary and analysis of what is commonly termed the "incrementalist" perspective, as presented in David Braybrooke and Charles Lindblom's *A Strategy of Decision*. Public choice and incrementalist theory share a similar skepticism about the benefits of bureaucratic organization and centrally coordinated organizational decision making. At the same time, they differ both in the strictness with which they adhere to some of the basic assumptions long cherished by economists, as well as in the recommendations they offer regarding the effective functioning of public organizations.

The next part of the chapter reviews some ideas about organizations developed by another economist whose point of view is less susceptible to a convenient label. Albert O. Hirschman's writings have mainly dealt with the processes of economic development in third-world countries, but of primary interest to the present discussion is his *Exit, Voice, and Loyalty*. Here he synthesizes economics and politics to explain the strategies used by organizations to cope with "repairable lapses" in both productivity and responsiveness to member and client demands. The chapter concludes with an overall analysis of the strengths and limitations of the various market theories from the standpoint of the public administration framework.

Democracy and Political Organization: James M. Buchanan and Gordon Tullock

Public choice theory, the subject of this and the next two sections, has been defined as "the ecomonic study of non-market decision-making, or simply as the application of economics to political science."[3] As reflected in the writings of its most prominent exponents, public choice theory has put forth an exceedingly ambitious agenda. As evidenced in the works reviewed here, it offers far more than a series of specific proposals for governmental reform; it seeks to provide a comprehensive theoretical basis for the creation and preservation of democratic government, paying considerable attention to issues of effective and efficient administration.

In pursuing their project, public choice theorists adhere tenaciously to a particular set of assumptions and values. Their primary methodological assumption is that political action must be understood as the outcome of the actions of motivated, atomistic *individuals,* whose particular interests typically differ, for good reason, from one another. Thus, they argue, any methodology that seeks to explain and predict political action must be premised on the assumption of rational individuals pursuing their own interests. Hence, the term "methodological individualism," which pervades the public choice literature.

But the assumption of individualism is more than simply methodological, for it also provides the basis for public choice theory's philosophical commitment to certain political values. Inherited in large part from utilitarianism and the American liberal tradition, these include the promotion of free individual choice, maximization of individual utility, and cooperation rather than coercion in those instances that require collective action. Even while public choice evinces a commitment to orderly and efficient institutions of government, its defense of these "collective" values is not based on a concern with system survival, as is the case, for example, with mainstream systems theory. Rather, order is simply a prerequisite to enable free individual choice within a relatively stable context, and efficiency is a measure of the equation by which net individual utility is calculated. Value criteria to judge the goodness of institutions are, in short, determined by the extent to which they promote freedom and utility among aggregates of individuals.

A persistent issue in the evolution of Western political values has been the tension between individual liberty and the stability of the social order. Though there is not necessarily an irreconcilable conflict between the two, various philosophical writings inevitably lean toward one or the other as having primary philosophical status. Public choice theory clearly places a normative premium on individual liberty. However, in doing so, it has had

[3]Dennis L. Mueller, "Public Choice: A Survey," *Journal of Economic Literature,* 14:2(1976):395.

to contend with the problem of explaining the origins of and require-ments for a stable social order sufficient to protect individual liberty and enable collective action. This is the project of James M. Buchanan and Gordon Tullock in *The Calculus of Consent,* published in 1962.

Their aim is to explain the initial conditions under which a democratic political order is made possible. Those initial conditions, which they call the "constitutional" requirements of political organization, are the rules that people could agree upon in advance to construct political institutions. It is important to be clear about what they are arguing for here. Buchanan and Tullock are not, for instance, describing the historical development of these "constitutional requirements"; rather, they are making a philo-sophical argument that begins with the following question:

> If the people in this society could all get together and decide what was to be the basis of their political system, what rules would be consensually agreed upon?

This is the same form of the exercise that John Rawls conducts in his *A Theory of Justice* and that Robert Nozick develops in his rebuttal, *Anar-chy, State, and Utopia.*[4] In all cases, the authors join a long tradition of ethical and political discourse that has its roots with the early Greeks. However, as Bertrand Russell notes in a discussion of the development of mathematics, the history of arithmetic is significantly different from and of little consequence to the study of arithmetic as a logically connected science. Even though it may have developed the way it did because humans have ten digits, we now use it as a tool in ways that take no account of the number of fingers on our hands. The requirements for such a system, be it arithmetic or political, are logical and philosophical, not historically empirical. Similarly, the constitutional requirements, which are a function of the public choice unit of analysis, must be logically con-nected to and derived from their stipulated assumptions about human motivation. Without this logical connection, any edifice of political orga-nization would be built only on sand. It is necessary, therefore, to examine the basic assumption about human motivation on which public choice theory rests before reviewing the rudiments of its theory of political organization.

The Assumption of Individual Self-Interest

The "individualistic postulate" is the linchpin of public choice theory. It is most understandable by comparison with what it is *not.* It rejects, for

[4]Cf., John Rawls, *A Theory of Justice* (Cambridge: Harvard University Press, 1971), and Robert Nozick, *Anarchy, State, and Utopia* (New York: Basic Books, 1974).

example, those organic views of social and political organization that value individuals merely in terms of their functional contributions to the fulfillment of system needs. Such organic views of the state, Buchanan and Tullock argue, are "essentially opposed to the Western philosophical tradition in which the human individual is the primary philosophical entity."[5] Also, following Bentham, they take a dim view of concepts and terms that ostensibly embody such communitarian values as the "public interest" and the "general will," labeling them "mystical notions" (p. 12). Likewise, the Marxian idea of class domination is abruptly dismissed as being "foreign to our purposes" (p. 12).

The postulate of individualism, for Buchanan and Tullock, is, at least on the surface, a relatively simple idea derived from economics:

> Reduced to its barest essentials, the economic assumption about [human motivation] is simply that . . . when confronted with real choice in exchange, [individuals] will choose "more" rather than "less." (p. 18)

However, because their interests are not the same, different individuals will not necessarily each choose more of the same thing. This happens "for reasons other than ignorance" (p. 4), because individuals are both generally able to discern what is good for them individually and capable of acting in ways consistent with their interests. For public choice theory, the rational bases for voluntary cooperation are deducible from, to put it baldly, people's selfish nature.

Buchanan and Tullock qualify somewhat their endorsement of the self-interest assumption by noting that people are not always narrowly hedonistic and that a few individuals do exhibit "Kantian scope" in exercising moral restraint (pp. 305–6). Occurences of the first and the numbers of the second, however, are sufficiently few so as to discourage the construction of a political system based on any assumption of their pervasive presence. Moreover, "economic theory does not try to explain all human behavior, even that which might be called 'economic' in some normally accepted sense of this term. . . . [It] requires only the existence of the economic relation to a degree sufficient to make prediction and explanation possible" (p. 18).

Buchanan and Tullock's adoption of the individualistic postulate, however, goes beyond the scientific concerns of prediction and explanation because it influences their theory of values, as well. The individual is the "primary philosophical entity," and because individual values and preferences differ, no moral proposition about "the good society" can provide the goal toward which collective political action should be directed. The

---

[5]James M. Buchanan and Gordon Tullock, *The Calculus of Consent: Logical Foundations of Constitutional Democracy* (Ann Arbor, Mich.: University of Michigan Press, 1962), p. 11; in this section, all page references in parentheses are to this source; emphasis is in the original unless otherwise noted.

important values, they argue, are not found in moral codes and philosophies, but are instead synonymous with the private wants or interests of individuals. Insofar as collective values can even be considered, they are derived from the coincidence of people's shared interests. These are empirically identifiable, rather than postulated in advance on the basis of metaphysical speculation. Thus,

> institutions and legal constraints should be developed which will order the pursuit of private gain in such a way as to make it consistent with, rather than contrary to, the attainment of the objectives of the group as a whole. (p. 27)

This is the overriding concern of Buchanan and Tullock's theory of how best to organize human activity so as to take fundamental account of the self-interest assumption.

The Costs of Collective Action

In addition to preserving individual liberty by limiting coercive collective action, Buchanan and Tullock are also concerned with the problem of minimizing the costs that collective action entails. People want to maximize their utility with minimal intrusion on their liberty; they also want to maximize it as cheaply (or efficiently) as possible. Decision making, especially that which requires time and resources in dealing with others, is expensive. Other things equal, the rational individual will prefer to make decisions privately (alone) and therefore avoid the expense (the costs) of cooperative endeavor. On the other hand, collective action, despite its costliness, may both produce benefits not otherwise attainable through private action, as well as mitigate the negative effects or costs to one individual that result from the private acts of other individuals. Thus,

> the choice between voluntary action, individual or co-operative, and political action which must be collective, rests on the relative costs of organizing decisions, on the relative *costs of social interdependence*. (p. 48)

The Unanimity Rule and Its Alternatives

In those cases where the external costs of private actions are too great, or where benefits are simply not achievable by acting alone, some sort of collective action is then required, despite the organizing costs that it entails. In organizing for collective action, the objective is to construct decision-making arrangements—which is to say, organizations—that produce the least possible infringement on individual liberty and hold the organizing costs to a minimum, and at the same time produce results with which everyone involved can live. Ideally, the best rule for collective decision making is that of unanimity, "since it is only through this rule that the individual can insure himself against the external damage that may be caused by the action of other individuals, privately or collectively" (p. 81). Further, unanimity, by definition, implies the absence of coercion and therefore does not violate Buchanan and Tullock's commitment to the value of individual liberty.

Although the unanimity rule is preferred as an ideal, it is typically unattainable because the costs, usually of time, are regarded by participants as too high.[6] Departures from the unanimity rule are then required. Alternative rules cannot be selected on the basis of which rule would lead to the best decision, since there are no independent standards to determine what a "best" decision would be. Similarly, individual utility (defined in terms of satisfaction) cannot be measured directly, but only through a calculus of what people forego in order to obtain something else. No single alternative to the unanimity rule is better in a general sense than any other; and choices among alternatives should depend "on the individual's own assessment of the expected costs" (p. 81). Majority rule, for example, is simply one of many alternative rules that people might consider in particular cases and should not, Buchanan and Tullock caution, be accorded the lofty status it has traditionally possessed in democratic theory (p. 81).

The selection of a decision rule should be based on a consideration of its costs to participants and on whether it is likely to result in mutual gains to them, rather than on an authoritative moral principle. The problem, then, is to construct a decisional framework that will produce decisions that are regarded as fair by all participants (that is, produce mutual gains)—and do so efficiently.

Buchanan and Tullock assert that the means by which such agreements may be reached is through *trading*. Specifically, if a particular proposal is regarded as good by some and bad by others, those who would gain from the proposal could reimburse those adversely affected by it in order to compensate them for their losses. If agreement could not be reached through this kind of compensatory trading, then the proposal would fail. Precisely because of this failure to reach agreement, the proposal would (and should) be considered bad. In effect, trading produces decisions that satisfy most of the requirements of the unanimity rule by taking account of the preferences of all participants and by avoiding coercive means for reaching agreement.[7]

---

[6]It is interesting to note that the main limitation is time. This implies that individual interests are not likely to be irreconcilable; rather, there may just not be enough time to find the other person's price. This is at odds with a main theme of political pluralism, for instance, that assumes interests have a limit beyond which they cannot be noncoercively bargained away. The importance of this point lies in how it colors the choice of departures from the unanimity rule.

[7]"Trading" here is individual to individual and should not be confused, in the way they use it, with "political bargaining." The latter describes negotiations between politically defined interest groups, and usually implies the notion of moving incrementally, from either party's point of view, away from an existing social ill. When Buchanan and Tullock talk of trading, it always carries a sense of tangible, immediate satisfaction on the part of the traders, usually in terms of money or services rendered.

By employing the market-like process of trading, rather than the problematic and time-consuming effort of trying to persuade others through
moral-ethical argument, decisions will be arrived at more efficiently. And
trading is not only more efficient in most instances than unanimity
through consensus-building processes; it is also more realistic.[8] It should
be remembered that Buchanan and Tullock believe not only that people's
perceptions of their own interests differ from one another, but that they
differ for good reason. These differences, then, are more than just a fact
of political life; they are also assumed to be morally legitimate. In view of
both the reality and the legitimacy of such differences, trading is typically
more practical than unanimity and normatively preferable both to coercion and the "partisan struggle of winners and losers" (p. 266).

Trading Social Services: An Example

A hypothetical example described by Buchanan and Tullock is useful
to show how the idea of trading may be applied to the administration of
social service agencies. The example deals with the distribution of a limited number of public housing units among families eligible to receive
them. It illustrates the purported advantages of trading over more traditional bureaucratic procedures, which Buchanan and Tullock regard as by
definition coercive.[9]

A local public housing official is confronted with the task of allocating
six housing units among ten eligible families who have applied for them.
Since not all of the ten families, obviously, can fit into six units, the question arises as to how a decision can be reached in which all of the families
will be better off then they were before. Further, since the decision should
be noncoercive, each family should participate in the decision. Because all
of the families are presumed to be utility maximizers looking out for their
own interests, altruism and sacrifice cannot be counted upon as motives
to guide their bargaining strategies.

A public choice process for arriving at a decision under these conditions would have the housing official create six vouchers, each representing one housing unit; and each voucher is divisible into tenths. Each eligible family is provided with six-tenths of a housing voucher that can be
used as currency, along with that family's other resources (such as money,
skills, and possessions), to be traded with the other families. The family
may trade either its own resources to get additional voucher portions or
trade its voucher portions to get enough of other families' resources so
that it can afford rental of private housing of comparable quality. The

---

[8]However, for anyone who has been involved in a serious trading situation, Buchanan
and Tullock's presumption about the ease and efficiency of such activity is likely to appear
highly glamorized. It is not clear that the costs of trading are as minimal as they suggest.

[9]The example below generally follows Buchanan and Tullock, pp. 277–79.

decision process is regarded as complete when six families each have an entire voucher (ten-tenths) and the other four have enough resources, by virtue of trading their voucher portions, to do as well in the private market.

For this process to work, of course, requires among other things that the amount of "slack" resources among the ten families as a whole is sufficient to pay the rental for four private housing units of at least comparable quality to the public housing units. (It also requires that the cost of the public and private units be comparable.) Notwithstanding practical difficulties that may arise, this process has in principle at least three important benefits. First, all ten families are better off than they were before; there are no losers. Second, the differing preferences (that is, "definitions of utility") are accounted for by the market-like decision process in a way that standardized solutions employed by bureaucratic organizations cannot. And finally, the families participated in determining their own fate rather than having it decided for them.[10]

Public Choice and Decentralization

Trading is the primary, but by no means the sole, practical suggestion following from Buchanan and Tullock's theory. Trading derives from a more general commitment to the idea that decision-making authority should be dispersed and differences in individual preferences accounted for in decisional processes. It should not be surprising, therefore, that Buchanan and Tullock also argue at some length for the merits of governmental decentralization, a topic of perennial interest to students of public administration. However, because of their attachment to market notions of trading and competition, the particular slant taken by public choice theorists departs from that of most other proponents of decentralization. Thus, whereas other advocates tend to center their arguments around such notions as "bringing government closer to the people," Buchanan and Tullock see decentralization as an opportunity to promote competition among government agencies. Among the advantages to be derived is the introduction of

marketlike alternatives into the political process. If the individual can have available to him several political units manufacturing the same collective activity, he can take this into account in his locational decisions. This possibility of individual choice among alternative collective units limits both the external costs imposed by collective action and the expected costs of decision-making.... In concrete terms this suggests that the individual will not be forced to suffer unduly large and continuing capital losses from adverse collective deci-

---

[10]This example is based, as was the earlier discussion, on the assumption that individual interests are not irreconcilable. The methodology offers no help should that not be the case.

sions when he can move freely to other units, nor will he find it advantageous to invest too much time and effort in persuading his stubborn fellow citizens to agree with him. (p. 114)

Thus, the greater the diversity (via decentralization) of municipal services within a geographical area, for example, the greater the opportunity for citizens to "vote with their feet" by moving to localities where the range and costs of services are better suited to their particular needs.[11]

Public Choice and Public Administration: Vincent Ostrom

A theoretical perspective's definition of "organization" bounds its view of the role of the individual. For the market theorists in general and Vincent Ostrom in particular, this view is intimately tied to the ways in which individuals are seen as making decisions in organizations. Thus, in *The Intellectual Crisis in American Public Administration*, Ostrom argues that

> Organizational arrangements can be thought of as nothing more or less than decision-making arrangements. Decision-making arrangements establish the terms and conditions for making choices.[12]

Moreover, Ostrom explicitly rejects at a very basic level any distinction between political decision making, which occupied the attention of Buchanan and Tullock, and administrative decision making, which, he argues, is inherently political and not simply technical in nature.

Ostrom's project is to construct a theory of democratic administration using as a foundation the basic assumptions of public choice theory, or, as he refers to it, the works of the "contemporary political economists." His aim is an extremely ambitious one, for it entails the formulation of a paradigm for an entire field, one that would reshape the theoretical assumptions and modes of organizational practice in public administration.[13] Successful completion of even the basic outlines of this project

---

[11]As will be seen later in the discussion of Hirschman's *Exit, Voice, and Loyalty*, however, these market processes also exact social and political costs of a kind that do not figure prominently in the calculations of most economists. These attendant costs are most likely to affect the degree of equity with which services are in fact provided and the quality with which they are likely to be delivered.

[12]Vincent Ostrom, *The Intellectual Crisis in American Public Administration*, rev. ed. (University, Ala.: University of Alabama Press, 1974), p. 3; in this section all page references in parentheses are to this source; emphasis is in the original unless otherwise noted.

[13]Like Buchanan and Tullock, Ostrom's intent is in fact philosophical rather than descriptive, despite disclaimers otherwise. He too attempts a logical construction that will ground a particular ethical and philosophical stance in organizing. Even more than with Buchanan and Tullock, Ostrom's attempt to construct a "scientific theory" often clouds this point.

requires not only a compelling case for the merits of the new theory, but also convincing reasons why the old one—for Ostrom, the so-called "classical paradigm"—should be regarded as inadequate.

Ostrom's Critique

Ostrom devotes fully half his book to a thoroughgoing critique of the ideas of the principal contributors to the classical paradigm, particularly the ideas of Woodrow Wilson, Max Weber, Luther Gulick, and Herbert Simon. (The remainder of his book is given over to his own proposals.) To understand his project, however, it is necessary to review in some detail his critique of this classical paradigm, a critique that is perceptive even if one is not drawn to the same ultimate conclusions.

Woodrow Wilson and Unitary Power   Ostrom begins by questioning a central assumption of the classical paradigm made by Woodrow Wilson, generally acknowledged as the intellectual founder of American public administration. Wilson's key assumption is that in all governments, whether democratic or autocratic, there must always be a single center and source of power. Concomitantly, "the more power is divided, the more irresponsible it becomes" (p. 25). For Wilson, the center of political power in the United States government was appropriately lodged in the Congress; however, irrespective of where the power center is located in any particular government or political regime, the principles of effective administration would be essentially the same. Although many, if not most, of those principles still awaited discovery, they would derive from the premise that administration is separate from and subordinate to politics. Because administrative authority is derived from and accountable to political authority, it is oriented in its work by values quite different from those governing the political sphere. Wilson's intent was to build a *science* of administration; Ostrom's summary of the basic propositions of this science appear in the accompanying box.

The sixth and seventh propositions regarding the necessity for hierarchical ordering to maximize efficiency are perhaps most basic to Ostrom's critique of the classical public administration paradigm, since they deal most directly with the assumption of hierarchy as the primary structural element of organization. Ostrom, while also espousing the value of efficiency, questions the belief that hierarchy is necessarily the most efficient form of organization. Moreover, he is optimistic that democratic decision making and efficiency *within* public organizations are not necessarily incompatible values. Indeed, for Ostrom, democratic administration is to be valued precisely because it is the most efficient form of administration. As we shall see later, however, Ostrom's definition of efficiency departs substantially from the ordinary bureaucratic meaning of the term.

THE BASIC PROPOSITIONS OF WILSON'S "SCIENCE OF ADMINISTRATION"

1 There will always be a single dominant center of power in any system of government; and the government of a society will be controlled by that single center of power.

2 The more power is divided the more irresponsible it becomes; or, alternatively, the more power is unified and directed from a single center the more responsible it will become.

3 The structure of a constitution defines and determines the composition of that center of power and establishes the political structure relative to the enactment of law and the control of administration. Every system of democratic government will exalt the people's representatives to a position of absolute sovereignty.

4 The field of politics sets the task for administration but the field of administration lies outside the proper sphere of politics.

5 All modern governments will have a strong structural similarity so far as administrative functions are concerned.

6 Perfection in the hierarchical ordering of a professionally trained public service provides the structural conditions necessary for "good" administration.

7 Perfection in hierarchical organization will maximize efficiency as measured by least cost expended in money and effort.

8 Perfection of "good" administration as above defined is a necessary condition for modernity in human civilization and for the advancement of human welfare.

—From Vincent Ostrom, *The Intellectual Crisis in American Public Administration*, rev. ed. (University, Ala.: University of Alabama Press, 1974), pp. 28–29.

Max Weber and Hierarchy   Since a hierarchical ordering of offices is the defining element of bureaucratic organizations, it is not surprising that the writings of Max Weber, who most succinctly summarized the main elements of bureaucracy and the social conditions giving rise to it, are subjected to Ostrom's scrutiny. Even though presenting Weber as perhaps more sympathetic to the merits of bureaucratic organization than is warranted by a careful analysis of his writings, Ostrom does note Weber's cognizance of the pathological social consequences of bureaucracy in its fully developed form. Regardless of Weber's normative disapproval of bureaucracy, however, the social and organizational values implicit in it are, as Ostrom rightly contends, "fully congruent" with much of Wilson's prescription for a science of administration predicated on a radical separation of politics and administration. In essence, the politics/administration dichotomy constitutes a variant on the more generic distinction between ends and means. Bureaucracy takes as given those ends that are authoritatively (especially politically) defined and seeks to attain them rationally, efficiently, and impersonally.

By virtue of its machine-like character, bureaucracy is technically superior, Weber said, to any other form of organization. But, owing in part to its own perfection, bureaucracy inexorably creates a social and political imperative that both captures its own members and renders its political masters powerless. On this point, Ostrom quotes Weber as saying:

> The individual bureaucrat cannot squirm out of the apparatus in which he is harnessed. [The] professional bureaucrat is chained to his activity by his entire material and ideal existence. [He] is only a single cog in an ever-moving mechanism which prescribes for him an essentially fixed route of march. ... The individual bureaucrat is thus forged to the community of all the functionaries who are integrated into the mechanism. (pp. 31–32)

In the face of bureaucracy's monopoly on technical expertise and knowledge, political authorities become impotent "dilettantes" who are controlled by, rather than themselves controlling, the monolithic instrument of social control. The consequence is that administration replaces politics as the paradigm of government, and efficiency becomes an end in itself, rather than a measure of how well organizations attain those ends with which they are charged.

Ostrom's arguments concerning the pathologies of bureaucracy, however, subsequently extend in a different direction than Weber's. Quite apart from the threat to democratic government that bureaucratic organizations represent, they are likely to be inefficient as well. Ostrom notes that little empirical evidence supports the classical paradigm's hypothesis that bureaucracy is more efficient than alternative organizational forms. Moreover, the underlying logic of the bureaucratic form contains inconsistencies that serve to explain the absence of such evidence. Here Ostrom's target of criticism is neither Wilson nor Weber, but Luther Gulick, who served on and summarized the findings of President Roosevelt's Committee on Administrative Management in 1937.

Luther Gulick and Organizational Principles   In spirit, if not wholly in substance, Gulick's writings appear to reaffirm both the central tenets of the Wilsonian orthodoxy and the logic of the bureaucratic model of organization. The Committee's report, and especially Gulick's contribution to it, gave credence to this tradition by supporting the idea that

> Such concepts as unity of command, span of control, chain of command, departmentalization by major function, and direction by single heads of author-

ity in subordinate units of administration are assumed to have universal applicability in the perfection of administrative arrangements. (p. 35)

Ostrom points out, however, that Gulick may have unwittingly laid the groundwork for rejecting the traditional principles by demonstrating their incompatibility with one another. In particular, what Gulick calls the "homogeneity principle" may fundamentally conflict with the hierarchical notions of a single center of administrative authority and chain of command. As Ostrom notes,

The principle of homogeneity implies that the means must be instrumental to the accomplishment of a particular task. Associating two or more non-homogeneous functions would sacrifice technical efficiency in administration by mixing factors of production which would have the effect of obstructing or impairing the net social product.... Public welfare administration [for example] should ... be separated from police administration.... The functions are too heterogeneous to be combined in a single agency.

... If there are limits on the grouping of agencies which would impair technical efficiency, then the central precepts in Wilson's theory of administration comes tumbling down. Efficiency in administration measured in the accomplishment of work at least cost is not necessarily attained through perfection in hierarchical organization. There may be circumstances where hierarchical organization will violate the principle of homogeneity and impair administrative efficiency. (p. 37)

The competing requirements of the homogeneity principle and hierarchical organization thus led Gulick to abandon the idea of a single structure of authority, which

had somehow dissolved into a "fabric of organizational interrelations" with multiple networks of cross-departmentalization. The symmetry of a hierarchical pyramid was abandoned for the tangled lattice-work of a "jungle gym." (p. 39)

While it was possible and perhaps necessary for this lattice-work to be under the direction of a single chief executive, the organizational structure implied by Gulick was only a remote facsimile of the bureaucratic form typically associated with the classical paradigm inspired by Wilson and explicitly sanctioned by Gulick.

Herbert Simon and Internal Structure In the 1940s, Herbert Simon identified the contradictions implicit in Gulick's analysis by explicitly challenging "the presumption that perfection in hierarchical organization is synonymous with efficiency," the defining criterion of good administration (pp. 45–46). He labeled the traditional principles of administration as mere "proverbs," whose validity, far from being universal, depended very much on the particular context within which they were applied. Given both a commitment to the idea of rational choice (governed by the criterion of efficiency) and a recognition of the cognitive and psychological limits to its effective exercise, Simon argued, organizations are most accurately characterized "as being an equilibrium maintained within areas of acceptance established by the different constituent elements of an organization" (p. 44). Instead of conforming to Wilson and Gulick's principles of administration, administration (as Ostrom interprets Simon) "becomes the management of interdependencies among constituent elements within an organization in relation to opportunities and threats in a dynamic environment" (p. 45).

Ultimately, however, Simon backs away from the radical implications of his analysis by accepting the inevitability of hierarchy as an organizing principle and by limiting his attention to the *internal* structure of organization, rather than to interorganizational relationships. In doing so, Simon thus retreats from the full implications of his commitment to efficiency and ends up by reaffirming the dichotomy between politics and administration, the keystone of Wilson's paradigm. Ostrom concludes that,

> By bounding his own theory of organization with a preoccupation for intra-organizational arrangements, Simon reduced the theoretical impact of his challenge. By leaving legislatures in the position of being the principal designers and ultimate arbiters of institutional arrangements, the dichotomy of politics and administration is sustained. The criterion of efficiency becomes a tool for suboptimization. (p. 47)

Democratic Administration

Following this critique of the classical paradigm, Ostrom outlines a theory of democratic administration. His theory is essentially an amalgam of Western economic theory and an interpretation of various thinkers who have contributed greatly to the American political tradition. Principal among these are Madison, Hamilton, and de Tocqueville. There are four basic elements of that theory.

First, in view of the corruptibility of political decision makers, authority should be divided so as to limit and control the exercise of political power. Second, because administrative rules are "*not* a matter of political indifference to the users of public goods and services" (p. 63), no presumption should be made that administration is separate and distinct from politics. Third, multiorganizational arrangements stimulate healthy (and democratic) competition among government agencies, in contrast to Wilson's belief in the necessity of a single center of power controlling an administrative apparatus structured along hierarchical lines. In Ostrom's terms, political and administrative structures built on these elements would be characterized by "polycentricity," rather than "monocentricity" (p. 81). Fourth and finally, the purpose of democratic administration is to "maximize efficiency as measured by least-cost expended in time, effort, and resources" (p. 112).

The meaning of efficiency, however, is far different for Ostrom than it is for the adherents of the classical paradigm. He argues that it should be viewed in terms of a "cost calculus" (p. 48), which takes account of the diverse preferences of consumers:

> If public agencies are organized in a way that does not allow for the expression of a diversity of preferences among different communities of people, then producers of public goods and services will be taking action without information as to the changing preferences of the persons they serve. Expenditures will be made with little reference to consumer utility. *Producer efficiency in the absence of consumer utility is without economic meaning.* (p. 62)

These remarks should strike a familiar note in view of the above discussion of Buchanan and Tullock's individualistic postulate. Ostrom, too, employs that postulate as the basis for his theory of democratic decision making. His particular version of it, which he refers to as "methodological individualism," is based on five interrelated assumptions about individuals, namely that they (p. 51):

- are motivated mainly by considerations of self-interest,
- are rational in the sense that they are able to rank alternative choices known to them,
- have varying amounts of information regarding the probable consequences of pursuing those alternatives,
- prefer an orderly context within which to engage in those pursuits, and
- will choose strategies that will maximize their interests.

Individual interests are given *a priori* legitimacy; they also are the criteria by which to assess whether outcomes of public decision making are both democratic and efficient.[14] Bearing in mind that "decision-making arrangement" is synonymous with "organization," Ostrom concludes that,

> The essential problem in the theory of organization is to (1) anticipate the consequences which follow when (2) self-interested individuals choose maximizing strategies with (3) particular organizational arrangments when applied to (4)

---

[14]As Ostrom defines them, democracy and efficiency are not simply closely related notions but are virtually synonymous.

particular structures of events. The optimum choice of organizational arrangements would be that which minimizes the costs associated with institutional weakness or institutional failure. (p. 55)

Although Ostrom argues that this is essentially an empirical problem and that "No single form of organization is presumed to be 'good' for all circumstances" (p. 55), there is little doubt as to where his own preferences lie. Like Buchanan and Tullock, he urges a sympathetic hearing both for market-like organizational arrangements internally and for competition among those agencies and jurisdictions providing public services the use or consumption of which is divisible among individual members of the public. The primary benefit of such proposals is that " ... overlapping jurisdictions and fragmentation of authority can facilitate the production of a heterogeneous mix of public goods and services in a public service economy" (p. 74).

Ostrom does not categorically oppose the bureaucratic form of organization, which on occasion may reduce some of the costs of individual choice. On balance, however, his analysis amounts to a denunciation of bureaucracy as the primary mode of public organization:

The very large bureaucracy will (1) become increasingly indiscriminating in its response to diverse demands, (2) impose increasingly high social costs upon those who are presumed to be the beneficiaries, (3) fail to proportion supply and demand, (4) allow public goods to erode by failing to take actions to prevent one use from impairing other uses, (5) become increasingly error prone and uncontrollable to the point where public actions deviate radically from rhetoric about public purposes and objectives, and (6) eventually lead to a circumstance where remedial actions exacerbate rather than ameliorate problems. (p. 64)

Administrative Ethics

Ostrom not only provides a radical vision for restructuring governmental institutions, but is also explicit about the transformation of administrative ethics that would derive from it. The classical public administration paradigm, by virtue of its separation of politics from administration, is centered on the uncomplicated notion that obedience to higher authority is the defining characteristic of responsible administration. Ostrom's rejection of that separation and the related idea of a single center of power shifts the locus of administrative responsibility from a single master to fragmented and multiheaded authority structures and even to citizens directly. As Ostrom puts it:

The practitioner of American public administration, if he is to contribute to the viability of a democratic society, must be prepared to advance and serve the interests of the individual persons who form his relevant public. His service is to individual persons as users or consumers of public goods and services and not to political masters. . . . While he is obliged to respect governmental authority, [the public official] in a democratic society is not a neutral and obedient servant to his master's command. . . . Each public servant in the American system of democratic administration bears first the burden of being a citizen in a constitutional republic. (p. 131)

These are obviously strong words, especially in view of the complex mechanisms that by implication would be required for determining to whom administrators are in fact accountable under Ostrom's approach. In many cases, administrative accountability would be insured (or even made irrelevant) by the effective functioning of market-like processes that remove a monopoly on decision-making authority from the hands of a single public official. But since Ostrom does not go so far as to propose the outright elimination of hierarchical organizations, the inevitable tensions between hierarchical and market-based authority raise some unresolved questions about who should be the final arbiter when the two collide. Whereas market arrangements may mediate competition among individual interests, the single center of authority that the bureaucratic organization ostensibly serves must assume the existence of a general public interest that is more than a simple amalgam of individual interests.

Certainly there may be better organizational forms than bureaucracy by which to administer the public interest. Nevertheless, simply describing, however convincingly, the pathologies of bureaucracy does not obviate the need to grapple with the difficult problem of how alternative organizational structures would affect the manner in which the general interest is identified and realized through administrative action. Public choice theory, by narrowly viewing the public interest as the efficient maximization of aggregate utility, chooses not to address the problem directly; rather it, in effect, defines it away.

A Critique of Public Choice Theory

Underlying all public choice theory is the central assumption that individuals are motivated by self-interest and will choose courses of action that maximize their utility. Using this assumption, public choice theory, as represented by Buchanan, Tullock, and Ostrom, makes three essential claims:

1 The basic assumptions of public choice theory provide the necessary underpinnings for the scientific study of political and administrative decision making, thus enabling rigorous explanation of the past and present, as well as prediction of the future.

2 Its basic assumptions also offer a reasonable conception of human motivation from which may be derived a preferred theory of values.

3 This value theory suggests prescriptions for improving the performance of government. "Improving," in public choice theory, means making government both more democratic and more efficient.

These are formidable claims, since, taken together, they form the basis of an overall theory (or, to Ostrom, a paradigm) for the study and practice of public administration. If sustained, they also become the basis for a theory that presumably offers the most cogent explanation of organizational action.

The Principle of Self-Interest

The self-interest/utility-maximizing assumption is central to the first two claims of public choice theory. That assumption is, first of all, methodological. It stipulates in advance the dominant motive that presumably explains any observations of individual and collective behavior in decision-making contexts. The first question that arises, therefore, is whether there is an empirical basis for this principle. Buchanan and Tullock, for instance, make much of the fact that their theory of collective action, including its implied prescriptions for public decision making, requires neither a theory of ethical and moral values nor the actual presence of people motivated by anything other than a concern for their own utility. They explain the absence of a need for ethical theory on the ground that their project is principally *scientific,* that is, the development of empirically testable theory. Hence, they note, "The ultimate defense of the economic-individualist behavioral assumption must be empirical" (p. 28).

This presumed empirical base of the individualistic postulate is troublesome in a number of respects. First, one may legitimately question the seriousness of Buchanan and Tullock's commitment to actually testing their basic assumption empirically. In *The Calculus of Consent* they construct a fairly comprehensive theory of political decision making that yields prescriptions that necessarily presume the empirical validity of the individualistic postulate. Yet, if this basic assumption is indeed as empirically problematic as they appear to concede in some instances, then it is curious that they have forged ahead with such apparent confidence. Although Buchanan and Tullock do allude, albeit in a cursory fashion, to some impressionistic indicators of their key assumption's plausibility, these are a far cry from the sterner empirical tests of it that they themselves say are required.

Second, and perhaps even more troublesome, is whether the individualistic postulate, as Buchanan and Tullock formulate it, is really empirically testable at all. Without reducing the considerable ambiguity surrounding public choice theory's use of the self-interest idea, its empirical testability is highly doubtful, at best. Public choice theorists, often in the same breath, use the term to mean two quite different things, apparently unaware of the significance of that difference. Each meaning has its limitations, which puts public choice theorists, as Robert Golembiewski has pointed out, "between the analytical rock and a hard place."[15]

The first approach is to describe self-interest narrowly and concretely by identifying empirical indicators of what characterizes self-interested behavior (e.g., economic gain) and what does not (e.g., subordinating one's own economic advantage to the good of others). Leaving aside the practical methodological problems of actually employing these indicators in research, this approach would seem to have the advantage of enabling researchers to determine empirically the extent to which and conditions under which the self-interest assumption, in comparison with alternative assumptions, may in fact explain and predict behavior.

Useful as this may be in the conduct of empirical research, it immediately reveals a limitation of the self-interest assumption as an *a priori* basis for the construction of a comprehensive theoretical paradigm for an entire field of study. The problem is simply that research and analysis may reveal that self-interest ranks relatively low on a list of motives that guide political behavior. Even if it ranks very high on such a list, self-interest would nonetheless have little predictive value unless its use were restricted to those areas of political behavior where it could be shown to be a nearly exclusive motive. Its highly problematic status as an empirically warranted assumption, therefore, renders self-interest as a shaky basis indeed on which to build a comprehensive paradigm.

Ostrom attempts to solve this problem by using a second approach to defining the term. He enlarges the permissible meaning of self-interest to include such motives as altruism, as well as the usual, narrower hedonistic meaning typically associated with the term. Despite the surface appeal of an enlarged definition of self-interest, the consequence is to eliminate whatever predictive (i.e., scientific) value it might otherwise possess. When it is broadly defined to include a wide range of motives,

> the self-interest assumption is too general to be adequate as an explanation of behavior. Because self-interest can be used *post hoc* to "explain" *any* individual choice, then by definition it cannot be falsified. If self-interest "explains" all individual choices, then in effect it explains nothing since it is indiscriminate.[16]

[15]Robert T. Golembiewski, "A Critique of 'Democratic Administration' and Its Supporting Ideation," *American Political Science Review* 71:4(1977):1495.

[16]Bayard L. Catron and Michael M. Harmon, "Comments in Response to Ostrom on Methodological Individualism," *Dialogue: The Public Administration Theory Network* 2:6(1979):10.

Or, as De Gregori has put it, "Self-interest, absent of any specific content, merely names, rather than predicts, action."[17]

Self-Interest and Social Action

However broadly or narrowly it is defined, self-interest—along with the concomitant assumption of utility maximizing—depicts the fundamental mode of individual action as a rational process of calculating the means by which to attain consciously known ends. This means that social interaction, including collective decision-making processes, is construed instrumentally. Its value is measured solely by its efficiency or certainty in aiding the individual in the realization of his or her interests. Since the individual's interests are assumed to be known prior to any social activity undertaken on their behalf, they are essentially separate and apart from the interests of other individuals. Buchanan and Tullock, for example, are explicit on this point when they note that it is assumed that individuals' interests differ—and for reasons other than ignorance. Thus, differences in individual interests are not only facts of political life, but are accorded by public choice an *a priori* legitimacy, as well.

The means/ends logic with which individuals relate their interests to political (decision-making) processes are, in essence, identical to the means/ends, instrumental logic that Weber describes as inherent in the bureaucratic form of organization. Rationality, assumed to be the ultimate criterion of "good" decision making, means the same for both the individual and bureaucracy. However, the *locus* of rational calculation is different, and the primary mechanism for mediating among interests is therefore significantly different. For public choice that mechanism is the market (e.g., trading), while for bureaucracy it is coercion.

What, then, are the difficulties, if any, with public choice theory's vision of human nature and the theory of organizational values that derives from it? The first difficulty is that there is reason to doubt that couching discussions of political decision making solely in terms of the satisfaction of individual interests can explain all or even most of what is important about organizing. In Chapter 11, for example, we discuss at some length the view that people often *discover* what they are (or have been) up to after the fact, through reflection. Far from this being somehow aberrant behavior, this is a more typical, in a sense a more natural, description of human action than that of the individual as a rational calculator of his utility. By ignoring the role of the unconscious, the notion of ratio-

---

[17]Thomas R. De Gregori, "Caveat Emptor: A Critique of the Emerging Paradigm of Public Choice," *Administration and Society* 6:2(1974):209.

nally self-interested action can at best only partially explain political action.

A second difficulty is that even when people self-consciously think in terms of their interests (which is not always the case even in political activity), the manner in which they define them is profoundly affected by processes of social interaction. These processes, moreover, may be intrinsically valuable, quite apart from any conscious end they may help to attain, because of the social bonds they create and sustain. Thus, in contrast to the public choice belief that social processes are regrettable costs that rational individuals seek to minimize,

> it cannot be assumed *a priori* that the time and effort people spend with one another in making decisions *is* a cost, for that is a matter of subjective definition by the decision makers themselves. Some people enjoy politics for its own sake, for example, which is to say that they more than occasionally subjectively define the "costs" of decision-making as *benefits*.[18]

By ignoring the social character of human action, public choice theory's prescriptions for improving the performance of government are thereby called into question. It is not simply that market-like structures of decision making fail to take account of the social nature of the self; rather, such mechanisms may, in turn, affect the manner in which people define their interests in the first place. No decision-making arrangement is or can be simply a neutral device for mirroring the wants of people. The process by which they define their interests (which is always a *social* act to some degree) is inevitably influenced by the institutional means that are available for expressing them.

Because people inevitably define their interests within the context created by existing institutional arrangements, there can be no normatively neutral or objectively scientific means for discovering those arrangements that best reflect those interests. Like any other decision-making arrangements, public choice mechanisms alter and help produce interests and serve to guide and constrain social action motivated by a consideration of those interests. The choice of mechanisms for decision making is ultimately governed by an implicit choice among alternative images of human nature. Moreover, through a kind of Hawthorne effect, choices about decision-making arrangements make images of human nature into self-fulfilling prophecies. The grounds for making such choices are normative and philosophical, rather than empirical or scientific.

At a more practical level, it is also questionable whether many of the public choice prescriptions are likely to produce results that are consistent

---

[18]Michael M. Harmon, *Action Theory for Public Administration* (New York: Longman, 1981), p. 159.

with its theory of values. Golembiewski, for example, notes that Ostrom's notion of a "cost calculus," if actually employed as a measure of policy effectiveness, would produce results that violate basic public choice assumptions:

> Consistent with Ostrom's emphasis on markets, "methodological individualism," and so on, it would have been seemly to argue that the scale of public organizations on the supply side is, or should be, a function of the same market forces that public choice theorists seek to energize/legitimate on the demand side. In contrast, he introduces the "cost calculus," which implies a cadre of experts, with data far beyond that available to his individual choice makers, and ostensibly with some power or authority to influence the scale of public organizations. Suddenly, Ostrom finds himself squarely facing the kind of problem that PPBS enthusiasts had promised to solve, those very centralizing, rationalist, elitist proponents from whom Ostrom otherwise seeks to distance his argument.[19]

The cost-calculus notion, in addition, does not discriminate between long- and short-term considerations, giving rise to resource allocation problems common to market structures more generally.[20]

Golembiewski also notes some "awkward probable consequences" of public choice from the standpoint of democratic theory. First, the radical decentralization of government urged by Ostrom, "is not necessarily better, more democratic, [or] more moral."[21] One cannot determine from Ostrom's account whether decentralization is effective or whether it is simply "chaotic localism." Similarly, whether smaller *size*—an apparent consequence of decentralization—will make organizations more responsive to public demands and needs is not necessarily borne out by the evidence, which is mixed and inconclusive, as well as complicated by a host of other variables.[22]

Economic criteria of effectiveness and the metaphor of the marketplace constitute both the basis of public choice theory's considerable appeal as well as its foremost limitation, at least insofar as it aspires to the status of a comprehensive theoretical paradigm for public administration. Public choice theorists, to the extent that they embrace literally the economist's vision of the political and organizational order, benefit from the powerful tools of economic analysis, especially when they employ those tools with rigor and precision. However, Western economic thinking has come under heavy criticism, from both Marxist and non-Marxist perspectives, for its dominant position as *the* implicit American social philosophy, which values moral atomism at the expense of public morality and sacri-

[19]Golembiewski, p. 1498.
[20]Ibid., p. 1497.
[21]Ibid., p. 1499.
[22]Ibid., p. 1502.

fices the human needs for community on the altar of individual self-interest. Insofar as the emerging social and political critique of economic thinking has merit, it applies by extension to public choice, which has grounded its own theory on the same assumptions.

Public choice theory goes far beyond simply recognizing the empirical fact of self-interest as a frequent motive of individual action. In advocating the creation of market-like structures for public decision making, public choice makes an implicit commitment to the self-interested individual as a normatively preferred image of human nature. The principal merits of the public choice approach lie in its often profound critique of bureaucracy and in its raising an awareness of alternative decision structures that hold promise for remedying the pathologies of bureaucracy that it identifies. Its underlying theoretical assumptions, however, tend to disguise the possible pathologies of public choice's practical proposals at least as much as they provide theoretical justification for them.

Disjointed Incrementalism: David Braybrooke and Charles E. Lindblom

Both practical and normative reasons explain the appeal of the economic marketplace as a metaphor for collective decision making. One argument is that market-like processes require relatively little in the way of conscious coordination, exercise of authority, or processing of information on the part of central decision makers. However compelling may be the internal logic of bureaucracy as the embodiment of comprehensively rational decision making, that logic is not sustained (so the argument goes) by the complexity of modern organizations and the explosion of information with which they must contend in making intelligent (i.e., rational) decisions. Beginning with Herbert Simon's *Administrative Behavior,* the psychological and cognitive limits of rationality in bureaucratic organizations have been seen as the principal elements of the critique of centralized decision making. The market, on the other hand, requires only that individuals know what is best for themselves and have enough information to make intelligent decisions. The task of the manager within such a context is procedural and fairly mundane, primarily to assure disparate individuals reasonable access to avenues of participation in the market and to insure that those individuals abide by the rules of the game.

This argument for the market as against bureaucracy sees the latter as a cumbersome and inefficient means for processing the complex information necessary to make collective decisions. Although this line of criticism underlies public choice theory, Buchanan and Tullock, and to a lesser extent Ostrom, cast their critique of bureaucracy in more explicitly normative terms, grounding it in their particular conception of democratic theory. The normative appeal of the market metaphor for them derives from the image that it conveys of autonomous individuals freely making choices in pursuit of their individual interests. Grounded as it is in the American liberal tradition of individualism, the idea of the free market stands in preferred contrast to the patterns of domination portrayed, for example, in Weber's account of the bureaucratic model of organization, the institutional prototype of centrally controlled decision making.

The normative emphasis on the market that pervades the public choice literature gives way to a practical emphasis in the so-called "incrementalist" literature. Here the argument is directed not at bureaucracy per se, but rather at the questionable efficacy of comprehensive rationality that is ostensibly the hallmark of bureaucratic decision making. The advice offered in this literature is aimed especially at those engaged in social policy analysis and evaluation. The incrementalists focus their attention primarily on the modes of analysis to be used in decision making rather than on formal decision making or organizational arrangements themselves. Nonetheless, such analysis has implications for both of the latter in view of the influence of modern policy analysis on policy (and therefore organizational) decision making.

"Disjointed incrementalism" was coined by David Braybrooke and Charles E. Lindblom in *A Strategy of Decision: Policy Evaluation as a Social Process,* published in 1963.[23] Many of the ideas associated with disjointed incrementalism have been developed in other guises by Lindblom. Rough equivalents, for example, are "muddling through" and "partisan mutual adjustment."[24] *Incrementalism* refers to the type of policy analysis and decision making that takes into account only the marginal (or incremental) differences between a proposed policy or state of social affairs and an existing one. In other words, it appraises small changes in large variables. This is in contrast, for example, to the type of policy analysis that comprehensively weighs the costs and benefits of a full range of policy alternatives against an ideal state of affairs. Incrementalism is thus concerned with only those alternative courses of action "whose known and expected consequent social states differ from each other incrementally."

---

[23]David Braybrooke and Charles E. Lindblom, *A Strategy of Decision: Policy Evaluation as a Social Process* (Glencoe, Ill.: The Free Press of Glencoe, 1963); in this section, all page references in parentheses are to this source; emphasis is in the original unless otherwise noted.

[24]See Charles E. Lindblom, "The Science of Muddling Through" Public Administration Review 19:1(1959):79–88; *The Intelligence of Democracy: Decision Making Through Partisan Mutual Adjustment* (New York: The Free Press, 1965); and "Still Muddling, Not Yet Through," *Public Administration Review* 39:6(1979):517–26.

This means the focus is only on those alternatives "whose known and expected consequences differ incrementally from the *status quo*" (p. 85).

Disjointed captures the idea that the many actors in the policy and decision process simultaneously perform incremental analyses relatively independently of one another, rather than consciously coordinating them through any kind of centralized control. The disjointed nature of policy analysis (and therefore of decision making) is roughly analogous to the public choice image of market processes and is characterized by multiple and semi-autonomous decision makers. The market metaphor is embraced only loosely in incrementalist theory, but both the metaphor and the theory reflect much of the spirit of pluralist political science. Both, therefore, emphasize the broad dispersal of political power, relatively benign competition among multiple interests, and gradual rather than revolutionary change.

Incrementalist theory is empirical insofar as it attempts to describe accurately the essence of most processes of policy analysis and decision making in organizations. It also, however, casts these processes in a normatively favorable light (mainly through Braybrooke's analysis in the latter half of *A Strategy of Decision*) by showing incrementalism to be compatible with a revised theory of utilitarianism.

Braybrooke and Lindblom offer the incremental model as a preferred alternative to comprehensive rationality or, as they call it, the "synoptic ideal." As they present it, the synoptic (or comprehensive) ideal is somewhat a straw man, used to caricature the comprehensive rational planning model. In its extreme form, the synoptic model requires that decision makers first carefully specify objectives and then develop a comprehensive list of alternative means for achieving them. These alternatives are arrayed so as to allow careful comparison of costs, benefits, and time frames. The resulting choices are presented neutrally to the decision maker, who carefully weighs them before making a reasoned decision about which alternative to select.

Braybrooke and Lindblom describe (and later argue against) two variants of the synoptic ideal, one from philosophical ethics and the other from welfare economics. Although each variant is based on quite different philosophical assumptions, each has effectively the same limitations that make it impossible to be realized in practice.[25]

The first variant is the *rational-deductive ideal,* which stresses the importance of abstract principles of moral duty as the basis for logically

---

[25]One of the "straw man" aspects of their use of the synoptic ideal is their assumption that the choice is between realizing the ideal in practice or discarding it. This is in contradiction to how one usually thinks about "using" ideals, either in the philosophical/sociological sense (e.g., Weberian bureaucracy) or the normative/ethical sense (e.g., standards of behavior). The gist of their argument is based on a crude measure of utility: Can this ideal ever be completely realized in practice?

deducing correct policies. The prototype is Kant's Categorical Imperative: "Act only on a maxim by which you can will that it, at the same time, should become a general law."[26]

> Kant thought that we can discover *a priori* a universally effective method of testing decisively every moral judgement. If it is made an axiom that one ought to do whatever the test of the Categorical Imperative requires, then this universal method furnishes a system containing every judgment that passes the test. (p. 11)

At an operational level, Braybrooke and Lindblom see the rational-deductive model as leading to the following prescription for analysis and action:

> Let ultimate values be expressed in general principles satisfactory to everybody who is ready to attend to the arguments identifying them—or, if there is no hope of that, satisfactory at least to those who are now undertaking a specific job of evaluation. Let these principles, which may embody notions of happiness, welfare, justice, or intuitive notions of goodness, be stated so exactly that they may be arranged intelligibly in an order of priority that indicates precisely which principles govern the application of others and when. Then derive within the limits of such a system intermediate principles that are suitable for application in particular cases, and that—allowing for rare cases of equality in net benefits—will indicate unambiguously which of the alternative policies is to be chosen, according to the values they would promote. (p. 9)

A quantitative variation on the rational-deductive ideal, and similar in its aspirations to comprehensiveness, is the *social welfare function*. An invention of the field of economics, the welfare function, according to Abram Bergson, is a composite of

> all the variables that might be considered as affecting welfare: The amounts of each and every kind of good consumed by and service performed by each and every household, the amount of each and every kind of capital investment undertaken, and so on. The welfare function is understood initially to be entirely general in character; its shape is determined by the specific *decisions on ends* that are introduced into the analysis. Given the decisions on ends, the welfare function is transformed into a scale of values for the evaluation of alternative uses of resources.[27]

Whereas with the rational-deductive ideal one systematically deduces

---

[26]Immanuel Kant, "Metaphysical Foundations of Morals," (1785) in Carl J. Friedrich, ed. and trans. *The Philosophy of Kant* (New York: Modern Library, 1949), p. 17. Kant also restates this slightly as "the general imperative duty": "Act as if the maxim of your action were to become by your will a general law of nature," ibid.

[27]Abram Bergson, quoted in Howard S. Ellis, ed., *A Survey of Contemporary Economics* (Homewood, Ill.: Richard D. Erwin, 1948), p. 417.

public policies from moral principles, with the welfare function one derives policies from quantitative (economic) analysis that calculates how general preferences around ends may most effectively be realized. The

> ... innovation represented by the social welfare function consists ... in substituting rules for manipulating numerical variables for the more general techniques of deduction that are envisaged in the rational-deductive ideal. (p. 13)

To Braybrooke and Lindblom, neither of these variants of the synoptic ideal represents a useful guide for policy or decision making, because neither can be put into practice for the primary reason that each presupposes initial societal agreement on values. Given the multiplicity of public values that in fact bear on any policy question, an expectation of initial agreement is unrealistic. Moreover, public values constantly shift and conflict with one another, with the result that there is no solid foundation for even beginning the complicated task of comprehensive policy analysis.[28]

The synoptic model of analysis is beset by numerous practical problems, some of which were anticipated by Herbert Simon. Braybrooke and Lindblom note, for example, the cognitive limits of people's problem-solving capacities, the limited information they typically have available to them, the costliness of comprehensive analysis in view of people's limited time and resources, and the inevitable intrusion of external political factors that necessarily alter policy analysis (pp. 49–53). Finally, the viability of the comprehensive model of analysis depends on both a logical and a "real-world" separation of facts from values and means from ends. Although Braybrooke and Lindblom do not reject the logical possibility of separating the two, they do note that "... in actual practice, continued contemplation of alternative means is often empirically inseparable from continued contemplation about values" (p. 52).

This cataloging of the liabilities of the synoptic ideal sets the stage for Braybrooke and Lindblom's description and normative defense of an approach to policy analysis better suited to the realities of political and organizational decision making. The alternative they offer, disjointed incrementalism, explicitly acknowledges the gradual nature of political and organizational change, as well as the limited time and information that analysts have available to them. In addition, this form of analysis

[28]There is, unfortunately, confusion in their work because they use the term "public values" rather loosely. At times they suggest, probably rightly, that there is no agreement at the operational level. This would indeed seem to be the case if one considers busing, antitrust actions against monopolies, or regulation of toxic waste as equivalent of "public values." On the other hand, if instead one views public values to be of a different order, then there might well not be the level of disagreement they assume. For example, equal access to education, maintenance and stabilization of the competitive arena, and protection of the public health would all seem to be fairly well-established public values, even if any particular *means* for accomplishing them may be disputed.

takes account of the fact that incremental politics is "better described as moving *away* from known social ills rather than moving *toward* a known and relatively stable social goal" (p. 71). This statement is not only descriptively accurate both of Western politics and of the manner in which policy analysis and policy making are usually carried out, but it is (they argue) normatively desirable as well. Descriptively, the incremental model suggests that policy analysts

> have an idea of present conditions, present policies, and present objectives. They seek to improve their ideas of present conditions, policies, and objectives by obtaining more information about them. . . . They often do so by comparing alternatives, all of which are similar to the status-quo. . . . A dominant characteristic, then, of their investigations is that they focus on increments by which the social states that might result from alternative policies differ from the status-quo. (p. 83)

In short, incremental analysis compares *marginal* differences, in contrast to comprehensive analysis, which assesses future ideal states of affairs against all available means for attaining them. A consequence is that the analyst and decision maker working incrementally assume that "today's and tomorrow's problems are very much like yesterday's" (p. 122).

Realizing the fundamental interdependence of ends and means, incremental analysis pursues an adaptive strategy that can be described by the following steps (p. 94):

- The analyst chooses as relevant objectives only those worth considering in view of the means actually at hand or likely to become available.

- He automatically incorporates consideration of the costliness of achieving the objective into his marginal comparison, for an examination of incremental differences in value consequences of various means tells him at what price in terms of one value he is obtaining an increment of another.

- While he contemplates means, he continues at the same time to contemplate objectives, unlike the synoptic analyst who ideally must at some point finally stabilize his objectives and then select the proper means.

The normative justification of incremental analysis derives from a sharp redefinition of the social welfare function in which no one, either singly or collectively, must formulate in advance the principles on which or the ends toward which he or she acts. The expression of preferences takes the form of *reaction against* present conditions, rather than planned action toward the attainment of some social ideal. Thus, an administrator ought to be able "to defend a policy as good without being able to specify what it is good for."[29] A further extension of this is for the administrator to eschew anticipatory proposals or analysis, because

Anticipation implies a sense of purpose or goal and the existence of a plan with a sense of direction, but for the incrementalist the notion of purpose—in the long-range sense of purposefulness—is meaningless and dangerous. It can lead to large changes in important variables, and this must be avoided at all costs.[30]

If the incremental process is managed fairly and effectively, then the consequences of incremental politics and analysis will be salutary. Or, better, the consequences are "good" if those involved deem them positive and "bad" if deemed negative. Even if Braybrooke and Lindblom's conception of the welfare function

does not eliminate controversy about values, it does shift the controversy from formulating ends to technical questions about adopting procedures, questions that seem relatively unvexed by emotive confusions and that may represent a promising new start toward working agreement on methods of introducing values into evaluation. (p. 15)

Braybrooke and Lindblom anticipate the normative objection that incrementalism, by virtue of its justification on procedural grounds, sidesteps important value questions. First, they argue that incrementalism has the effect of incorporating (albeit implicitly) a highly diverse array of values into the process of policy analysis. And secondly, incrementalism's emphasis on piecemeal movement away from social evils leads to the development of policies both grounded in experience and cognizant of the limited capacity of the human mind to process complex information.[31]

Incrementalism stipulates a preference for what Braybrooke and Lindblom call *meliorative,* in contrast to *peremptory,* values:

On the meliorative approach, judgments about accepting or rejecting any policy must wait upon a comparison of that policy with alternatives to it. On a peremptory approach, certain characteristics are looked for on the basis of which a policy would be approved or disapproved taken by itself, without any attention necessarily being given to alternatives. (p. 150)

This would appear to mean, using an extreme illustration, that the judgment "killing another human being in self-defense" is a meliorative

[29]Lindblom, "The Science of Muddling Through," p. 84.
[30]Louis C. Gawthrop, *Public Sector Management, Systems, and Ethics* (Bloomington, Ind.: Indiana University Press, 1984), p. 50.
[31]For a fuller development of this idea, see Karl R. Popper, *The Open Society and Its Enemies* (London: George Routledge and Sons, 1945).

one insofar as "in self-defense" implies a weighing against other alternative means of self-defense. "Killing is wrong," on the other hand, is a judgment coming from the peremptory approach because it explicitly disapproves an act on its face, with no comparison to other alternatives. The meliorative would seem to be situationally bounded, whereas the peremptory is not.

Meliorative values are thus associated with Braybrooke and Lindblom's revised notion of the welfare function in which values in any absolute sense need not be known or specified in advance. Peremptory values, on the other hand, are those necessary for the operation of the rational-deductive ideal as a model for policy analysis.

Included as a subclass of meliorative values are the *redistributive* ones central to contemporary theories of social justice, particularly those emphasizing the moral necessity to redistribute social and economic resources on a more equal basis.[32] To include redistribution as a meliorative value seems an odd designation, since the principle of equal justice, however defined, appears to have all the earmarks of a peremptory value. Braybrooke and Lindblom deal with this apparent contradiction by noting that equal distribution should not be regarded as an absolute value, but as a guiding "theme" whose particular application is negotiated on an *ad hoc* basis. Thus, incremental strategies may embrace values and principles that might appear peremptory in their pure state, but whose *application* is actually piecemeal and meliorative. As they note:

> Peremptory demands may be made for the observance of these principles, but, in the first place, observing them is not likely to be an "all or nothing" matter. So long as the principles of justice are only approximately satisfied, there will be meliorative and distributive questions about whether they are fulfilled more or less. One may very well adhere to peremptory principles of justice and to the associated requirement of mutual recognition and consideration, yet recognize that the only practical way of bringing fulfillment about is step by step. (p. 220)

Braybrooke and Lindblom claim that this sort of meliorative strategy for dealing with peremptory values is still well within their broad definition of utilitarianism. That definition is broad enough, in their judgment,

> that *any* theory belongs to the utilitarian family if, first, it allows meliorative and redistributive considerations a decisive role in confirming or disconfirming all moral judgments that are subject to dispute; and if, second, it supposes that, among these meliorative and distributive considerations, social welfare and

---

[32]Cf., John Rawls, "Justice as Fairness," *Philosophical Review* 67(April 1958):164–94. Interestingly, Braybrooke and Lindblom approvingly cite Rawls in support of their argument for redistributive values, even though Rawls's theory of "justice as fairness" is an explicit rebuttal of the very utilitarian political theory that they seek to rehabilitate.

group happiness justify supporting an action or policy, while their opposites do not. (p. 206)

They further acknowledge that certain moral judgments, which they call "enlightened peremptory objections," cannot be violated in the interest of general welfare. These include keeping promises, not sacrificing the lives of some people for the purpose of gratuitously making others happy, and not punishing people for crimes they have not committed (p. 212). The Bill of Rights, roughly speaking, is invoked as a hedge against the excesses of collective hedonism.

It would be misleading to suggest, as critics of incrementalism sometimes do, that Braybooke and Lindblom simply make a virtue of necessity in their defense of the incremental model. They present a plausible case not only that the synoptic ideal of policy analysis is impossible to attain in practice, but that it represents a normatively undesirable ideal, as well. The notion of incrementalism described in *A Strategy of Decision* derives its credibility not simply from its practicality, but also from the ethical considerations that accompany it. It is clearly apparent in what they write that not all (or even most) approximations of incremental analysis come close to satisfying the requirements of their ethical theory. Their own analysis is deficient by virtue of its failure to consider more fully how governmental institutions of Western democracies might be encouraged or required to take seriously, at an operational level, these ethical suggestions. This is especially important with respect to redistributive and peremptory values that the authors hold to be legitimate. In the absence of such institutional considerations, the normative requirements that accompany the incremental model amount only to good advice to policy and organizational analysis—advice that may easily be forgotten.

An Economist as Critic of the Market: Albert O. Hirschman

The belief that rational self-interest depicts the dominant motive of organizational and political actors does not unerringly lead one to an endorsement of market-like processes as a preferred mode of organizing. Albert O. Hirschman, an economist, shows how the consequences of self-interested action reveal crucial liabilities of the market as an effective basis for social organization. He stresses the complex interplay of market-like behavior with political activity in promoting organizational responsiveness. His analysis combines a normative commitment to the values of organizational responsiveness and representativeness with serious misgivings regarding the ability of market-like processes to satisfy that commitment.

In *Exit, Voice, and Loyalty,* Hirschman endeavors to explain how organizations, firms, and governments both respond and fail to respond to "repairable lapses" in their performance.[33] Although he appears to accept the systems theorists' premise regarding the desirability of organizational survival, Hirschman in effect requires that the terms of that survival also satisfy the preferences of the organization's customers and members. Thus, his theory reflects a strong democratic bias in which the survival interests of top management and political leaders are balanced against (and even integrated with) constituent and member interests. For this reason, Hirschman's theory of organization has significant implications for the full range of normative vectors in public administration.

The main elements of Hirschman's theory are revealed in his book's title. *Exit* is his abbreviated term for economic competition. It represents the decision of a dissatisfied customer to stop buying a firm's product and instead to buy those of another *or* the decision of a dissatisfied organization member to leave. *Voice,* on the other hand, "is defined as any attempt at all to change, rather than escape from, an objectionable state of affairs" (p. 30). Finally, *loyalty* represents the decision to "stick with" a firm or organization when short-term considerations of self-interest would otherwise appear to dictate an exit decision. Hirschman contends that various mixes of these three functions, rather than competition (exit) alone, are necessary to explain why it is that some organizations recover from periodic lapses in performance, but other organizations do not.

When an organization undergoes a lapse in its performance, as evidenced by declining revenues or other indicators of client dissatisfaction, three conditions are required in order for its leadership to mobilize for corrective action. First, an effective means for the expression of client (or member) dissatisfaction must be present. The availability of the exit or the voice function, however, does not alone insure that function's effectiveness as a recuperative mechanism for reasons that will be made apparent shortly.

Second, the organization's leadership must have sufficient time and resources to mend their ways before it is too late, for example, by changing their policies, management practices, or approaches to dealing with the public. Without this time, if all customers exited from Brand X to Brand Y simultaneously, the producers of X would likely go bankrupt before effective recuperative strategies could be implemented.

And third, the organization's leadership must have self-interested reasons for taking seriously the exercise of exit and voice by their clients. Such incentives for management are far from guaranteed, however, since

[33]Albert O. Hirschman, *Exit, Voice, and Loyalty* (Cambridge: Harvard University Press, 1970); in this subsection, all page references in parentheses are to this source; emphasis is in the original unless otherwise noted.

voice (in the form of protests, complaints, citizen petitions, etc.) may fall on deaf ears if it cannot be backed up by a viable threat of exit. In addition, the exit of current customers *from* an organization may often be offset by an equal number of dissatisfied customers exiting *to* it from other similarly deteriorating organizations. Thus, "No matter what the quality elasticity of demand, exit could fail to cause any revenue loss to the individual firms *if the firm acquired new customers as it loses the old ones*" (p. 26). In other words, the actual loss would not be seen as a real loss and therefore would not be seen by management as a signal that change is needed. This happens in those competitive situations where, because of the decline of quality in an entire industry, unhappy customers simply rotate from one firm to another in search of nonexistent better-quality products. In addition, and further confusing the meaning of such messages, some complacent managers will welcome exit when it unburdens them of their most troublesome customers (p. 59).[34]

For exit to be effective in signaling to managers a need for change, there must be an appropriate mix of customers, some of whom are *alert* and others *inert*.

> The alert customers provide the firm with a feedback mechanism which starts the effort at recuperation, while the inert customers provide it with the time and dollar cushion needed for this effort to come to fruition. (p. 24)

Thus, contrary to the popular mythology of private enterprise, "if all [customers] were assiduous readers of *Consumer Reports,* or determined comparison shoppers, disastrous instability might result and firms would miss out on chances to recover from their occasional lapses" (p. 25).[35]

As with exit, voice also requires a mixture of alert and inert customers in order to be effective. Alert customers are those who draw management's attention to the organization's failings, while inert customers provide the necessary slack (through their continued support) to permit recuperation. Voice works best when exit is also an option, since the threat of exit is more likely to force top management to take voice seriously. If customers see voice as effective, they will tend to postpone exit, viewing it as an option of last resort. But, other things being equal, most people will prefer exit over voice simply because the latter is more costly, especially in the

---

[34]All of this is even further muddied when there is movement of clients and customers that is unrelated to any actions of the immediate organization. For example, in the early 1970s, some school districts around San Jose, California, experienced pupil turnover in excess of 100 per cent in a year. This exit had a great deal to do with local economic conditions, which makes interpretation of these market signals, even to astute and wary managers, difficult at best.

[35]Hirschman makes an important distinction between inertia and loyalty, with the former being passive and the latter, as will be seen, active.

expenditure of time. For this reason, voice tends to be used selectively; in the private sector, for example, voice is used to express unhappiness with durable far more often than with nondurable goods and is exercised only infrequently when the sheer number of goods available is high. Meaningless product differentiation, common especially to advanced capitalist economies, thus serves as a deterrent to the activation of voice.

There is a paradoxical aspect of the relation of exit to voice that has an important bearing on the normative public administration concerns of responsiveness, representativeness, and quality of organizational processes. Voice, for Hirschman, is the means by which interests may be most directly and unambiguously expressed. It is the essence of politics, most especially democratic politics. The effectiveness of voice, both in terms of the opportunities for its expression and the seriousness with which it is heard, is the fundamental basis by which to judge the "democratic-ness" of government. The paradoxical aspect of voice in relation to exit is that while voice is likely to be taken most seriously by organizational leaders when the threat of exit is present, that very "presence of the exit alternative . . . tends to *atrophy the development of the art of voice*" (p. 43). The easier it is for consumers and clients to exit from an organization, the less likely will be their inclination to invest time and energy in "working within the system" to make it better. Moreover, consumers (or citizens) differ in the ease with which they can exit from an organization because of disparities in income, education, and social and geographical mobility. The irony is that those for whom exit is easiest and most probable are often those whom Hirschman calls "quality-conscious consumers," the same people who are able to use voice most effectively (pp. 50–51).

One consequence of quality-conscious consumers being the first to exit may be to impede the maintenance of viable public institutions. Hirschman illustrates this point by noting the competitive relationship of the public schools to private schools:

> Suppose at some point, for whatever reason, the public schools deteriorate. Thereupon, increasing numbers of quality-conscious parents will send their children to private schools. This "exit" may occasion some impulse toward an improvement of the public schools; but here again this impulse is far less significant than the loss to the public schools of those customer-members who would be most motivated and determined to put up a fight against the deterioration if they did not have the alternative of the private schools. (pp. 45–46)

Upon having exited to the private schools, however, these same parents are likely to respond to deterioration there through the exercise of voice, inasmuch as further exit alternatives will have been exhausted or at least dramatically reduced. In addition, private schools, whose continued survival directly depends on consumer satisfaction, will likely respond with greater alacrity than will their public counterparts to the voice of consumer discontent.[36]

To the extent that some sort of exit function is feasible in a particular government organization, the trick would appear to be the creation of an optimal mix of exit and voice.[37] Each function exercised without the countervailing force of the other is subject to severe limitations. Voice without the possibility of exit, for example, can render the former impotent against the power of management.[38] Exit without voice penalizes the least advantaged and deprives conscientious managers of their most effective source of feedback. Even if the two functions are combined, the exercise of voice may be discouraged if exit is made too easy.

Although he stops short of prescribing any such optimal theoretical mix of exit and voice applicable to all situations, Hirschman does provide some advice, appropriate much of the time, that specifies the conditions under which each function can be effective in relation to the other: Voice can be effective when (1) the penalties for customers exiting the organization are high enough to discourage their departing precipitously, but (2) the threat of exit is still real enough in the eyes of management that it will take voice seriously. This is where the idea of loyalty comes in.

As noted earlier, loyalty (as Hirschman employs it) is evidenced by a decision *not* to exit even though short-run considerations of self-interest would suggest that exit is a good idea. It should come as no surprise that Hirschman, as an economist, defines loyalty in self-interested rather than altruistic terms by noting that "most loyalist behavior retains an enormous dose of reasoned calculation" (p. 79). The purpose of loyalty is that it "holds exit at bay and activates voice" (p. 78). By raising the cost of exit, loyalty "pushes men into the alternative, creativity-requiring course of action from which they would normally recoil . . ." (p. 80). In view of its connection to self-interest, loyalty can seldom be induced by the organization through moral persuasion, but must instead be built into the incentive systems (either positive or negative) that govern member/client participation. Achieving an appropriate degree of severity of exit penalties entails a delicate balancing act. The penalty should not be so high that

---

[36]In addition, private schools usually have greater ability to respond quickly because of the smaller size and less complex nature of their decision-making apparatus. This is, of course, a direct function of their having considerably less public responsibility.

[37]However, exit is impossible from those agencies providing pure public goods.

[38]One of the limitations of Hirschman's notion of voice is that he implicitly restricts it to direct feedback between customers/members and an organization. In reality, in a complex world of regulatory agencies and institutionalized political influence on administrative action, change can be forced by bringing voice to bear outside of the immediate organization. Unfortunately for the managers involved, the resulting change often becomes a force outside of their control.

management needs not take voice seriously nor so low that voice atrophies or members leave too rapidly.

Hirschman's analysis of the relationship of exit and voice serves as a potent explanation of why the market, as an exclusive organizing principle, is unsatisfactory with respect to several of the normative public administration vectors. First, the market, by emphasizing the exit function, is likely to be responsive to citizen discontent only under special circumstances, in particular, when effective opportunities for voice are also present. Second, inequitable situations are likely to be exacerbated by market mechanisms, since possibilities for exit from unsatisfactory situations are far greater for the rich than the poor, the better educated than the less. Third, the quality of organizational processes as experienced especially by poorer, less educated, and less mobile citizens is likely to be low when an organization's management has little or no incentive to take voice seriously.

Taken together, these liabilities of the market serve to reinforce the notion that success, from the standpoint of market values, is conceived in almost exclusively individual, rather than communitarian terms. As Hirschman notes:

> The traditional American idea of success confirms the hold which exit has had on the national imagination. Success—or, what amounts to the same thing, upward social mobility—has long been conceived in terms of evolutionary individualism. . . . Success is in fact symbolized and consecrated by a succession of physical moves out of the poor quarters in which . . . the successful individual has been brought up into ever better neighborhoods. (pp. 108–9)

Despite the understandable appeal of this idea of success to those fortunate or skillful enough to escape their humble origins, its overall consequences are not uniformly salutary. To give but one example, "upward social mobility of just the talented few from the lower classes can make domination of the lower classes by the upper classes even more secure than would be achieved by rigid segregation. . . ." (p. 111). If, on the other hand, cooperative action by citizens is prized at least in part for the sense of community it may create, one must look to administrative mechanisms other than the market both to encourage cooperation and more generally to realize such values as equity, responsiveness, and a sense of community.

Market Theories and the Public Administration Framework

As a metaphor for public organization, the market is appealing because it encompasses such traditional American values as individual freedom, efficiency, and self-interest. From the standpoint of the public administration framework described in Part I, public choice theorists, the most literal advocates of the market-like organization, interpret these values in a way that collapses into one unified value position the framework's three normative vectors: efficiency and effectiveness, individual rights and the adequacy of organizational processes, and representativeness and the control of discretion.

Efficiency, for example, has meaning in public choice terms only insofar as it is measured by reference to the maximization of individual utility. Utility is then discernible only in terms of the adequacy of organizational and political processes through which the individual's right of free choice is exercised. In a related sense, the adequacy of organizational processes itself becomes simply a matter of efficiency, that is, maximizing utility while minimizing decision costs. Direct citizen involvement in making decisions thus obviates problems of representation and administrative discretion, since representation is seen as merely an indirect means through which citizens express their preferences. And insofar as citizens make political and organizational choices directly (via the market), the need and indeed the possibility of administrative discretion is eliminated. In short, the effectiveness of government organizations is determined by the degree to which efficiency (i.e., consumer or citizen utility) is maximized. This happens to the extent that citizens' rights to exercise individual choice are maintained, but at the same time are balanced against the requirement for keeping decision costs low.

Advocates of market-like organization appear to stand on especially solid ground when the alternatives against which they compare their own proposals appear to reinforce hierarchy, coercion, and uniformity. With such a comparison, a decentralized, market-like arrangement would appear clearly preferable to a coercive and often inefficient hierarchy. Other authors discussed in this chapter, however, are far less convinced of the virtues of market organizations. The order in which the five prominent works on market organization theory have been presented reflects a descending level of optimism regarding the market metaphor. It is viewed as increasingly problematic in two related senses: first, as the basis for explicit prescriptions for restructuring public agencies and, second, as a normatively appealing metaphor describing existing organizational arrangements and practices. Although all the works discussed here accept the premise that, at least much of the time, people's actions are motivated by considerations of rational self-interest, they differ on whether those interests can actually be realized by means of market-like organizations.

For Braybrooke and Lindblom, for example, the market metaphor is evoked only in the loosest sense in their description of the disjointed and pluralist nature of policy analysis and policy making. The existence and legitimacy of bureaucratic organization is not addressed, giving the impression that bureaucracy, Weber's dour description of it notwithstanding, is flexible enough to accommodate incremental analysis and policy making. Moreover, their endorsement of "enlightened peremptory values" and their insistence that redistributive equity be a guiding value of disjointed incrementalism require the preservation of some sort of central decisional authority (i.e., hierarchy), which is clearly incompatible with the market ideal. Even Ostrom, a leading public choice theorist, stops short of recommending the wholesale abandonment of bureaucratic organizations, emphasizing instead the notion of multiple public bureaucracies in market-like competition with one another.

Hirschman explains why the market idea is often incapable of realizing the very values that it ostensibly fosters. For him, the market is embodied in the exit function, yet the "rational" decisions of individuals to exit will fail to help them realize their interests when, as is often the case, there is no corresponding incentive for the organization to take that exit seriously. Thus, the market forces of competition are at best a partial condition for organizational responsiveness; the latter also requires effective avenues for the exercise of voice.

Conclusion

Despite the limitations of the market idea, public choice and other market theorists provide us with a unique and often valuable perspective from which to examine public organizations. It is a perspective that begins by framing institutional action, not as a process of consciously coordinated collective action, but as the interplay of interests, sometimes of groups, but more often (as in public choice theory) of individuals. The market-like interplay of interests assists in identifying important limitations to what can be accomplished through public planning efforts. These limits are not only those of the satisficing sort pointed out by Simon[39]; they are also political limits, both in terms of what can be recognized as legitimate and what can be reasonably acted on. Market theories, then, acknowledge administration as an inherent part of politics. Such a view challenges both the possibility and the desirability of the tightly structured bureaucratic organization reaching its goals of internal efficiency and control.

Consistent with the systems theorists, although they disagree on many other matters, market theorists direct our attention to the turbulent and highly politicized environments with which public agencies are, or at least ought to be, actively engaged. Also like the system theorists, the market theorists look at stabilizing turbulence in the environment by internal rule generation. The difference is that the rules of the system theorists empha-

[39]See Chapter 6.

size structural relations, whereas those of the market theorists focus on the making of decisions. The result is that the former, as we saw in Chapter 7, tends to mask (or at times, reinterpret) conflict; the latter provides a way of seeing a potential resolution of conflict.

Finally, the market theories extend the work of Herbert Simon by emphasizing the decision-making process as the most salient characteristic of organizations. The administrative process, from this perspective, is a rule-bound one that is essentially atemporal and nonhistorical. This means that the relevant question becomes "what are the rules?" rather than "where did the rules come from?" This is particularly clear in the work of Buchanan and Tullock, wherein they base their efforts on a presumed answer to a hypothetical question about "constitutional requirements," rather than on empirical evidence about how people in fact make decisions. The importance of this is that it carries Simon's emphasis on decision as the essence of administration to the extreme and, by doing so, illustrates the weakness of such a view of administration. If, in observing an organizational setting, one asks *only* the question "what are the rules?" then he or she will be unable to see how those particular rules came to be and, therefore, the factors that are likely to influence their change. The market theories focus on the immediate present in such a way as to separate it from the past and the future. This makes it difficult to understand the social (and therefore the historical) context of decision making and other administrative actions, and the way in which those actions may in some sense be socially created, modulated, or reinforced.

The limitations of the market theories derive from their often narrow adherence to a restrictive set of assumptions and beliefs. The problem with good ideas, as with moral principles, is that we may become oblivious to the pathologies they potentially generate. Virtually any idea or principle, however valid or appealing, can divert attention away from legitimate countervailing ideas and principles. Truth, or at least practical approximations of it, most often emerges from a balancing of countervailing ideas. This holds especially true as ideas are manifested in modes of social organization. Thus, "the market" as a principle of organization must be judged not only in terms of the values that it may help to realize, but also against those modes of organization that reinforce alternative values. Such values include, in no particular order of importance, those of equity, community, the maintenance of public authority, human development, and the faith that only through social processes characterized by trust and mutual respect, rather than competition, can we truly discover what our interests really are. These are the values that underlie the theories of organization considered in subsequent chapters.

10

Interpretive and Critical Theories: Organizing as Social Action

The various organizational theories presented to this point disagree so mightily on so many points that it is possible to lose sight of the issues on which they fundamentally agree. Although these agreements, at first glance, may appear to be obvious and commonsensical, they are, from other frames of reference, highly problematic for organizational theory and practice.

First, many of the theorists we have considered heatedly disagree with one another about *how* the interests of organizations and the interests of individuals may be made compatible. At issue here are what, in fact, the essential interests of organizations are, as well as how the interests of individuals should be defined. Growing out of these disputes, in turn, are conflicting proposals for structuring and administering public organizations in order to reconcile the interests of these two levels. Despite all of their differences regarding the means of this reconciliation, the theorists discussed thus far implicitly agree that:

> The basic interests of organizations and individuals may ultimately be made congruent with one another. That is, in principle there is no fundamental and irreconcilable conflict between them.

Second, disagreement persists about the practical efficacy of rational action, that is, about the limits and possibilities of organizational action for attaining goals or purposes. Opinion varies, for example, on whether rational action is more appropriately analyzed at an individual as opposed to a collective level. And often the theorists differ on whether the most important goals and purposes of organizations are known better by the theorists themselves, or by the people who actually pursue them. Disputes have also arisen concerning the cognitive capacities of organizational actors to calculate their actions so as to achieve their purposes efficiently. Nevertheless, there is common agreement that:

> Action in organizational settings is naturally directed toward and can be evaluated in terms of some known purpose. Action is and by implication ought to be conceived instrumentally as a means to an end.

Third, organizational theory is divided on significant methodological issues. Primary units of analysis, which range from the atomistic individual of public choice theory to the holistic view of systems theory, profoundly affect the methodological stances that theorists subsequently take. Despite these differences, however, virtually all the theorists we have discussed implicitly agree that:

> The basic assumptions of social science (1) are not fundamentally different from those of natural science, and (2) may be used to reveal objective, value-free accounts of organizational life.

Finally, the theorists disagree on which social and political values are most central for the normative evaluation of action in public organizations. Efficiency; personal growth and development; organizational survival, responsiveness and "health"; utility maximization; and adaptation currently compete for favor in this varied, but predominantly American, literature. Irrespective of their differing preferences regarding these values, the various schools of thought represented in that literature agree that:

> The normative evaluation of organizations is logically separate from the factual description of them. That social science and social ethics (as "facts" and "values") are logically distinct is taken for granted. A corollary to this is that social theory and social practice are similarly distinct, though possibly related, enterprises.

Introduction

This chapter considers two approaches to organization theory, the interpretive and critical theory, that challenge most (and, in the case of critical theory, *all*) of the points of agreement noted above. Their original, mainly European formulations in social and political theory differ with one another on some of those points. The contemporary synthesis of interpretive and critical theory in the American public administration literature, however, reflects a relatively unified theoretical perspective on public organizations. This is a fairly recent development, one that constitutes a radical alternative to the American mainstream of organization theory. There are six principal elements of this emerging synthesis, which summarize the thrust of this chapter:

1 Individual and organizational interests exist in fundamental tension with one another. By virtue of that tension, relationships between individuals and organizations inherently involve considerations of political power. The principal question for organization theory is not how to integrate the individual and the organization, but how the individual may transcend the organization.

2 The rational model of action is itself a problem, for it misrepresents and severely limits the understanding of action in individual, social, and organizational contexts.

3 Naturalistic social science, which is underpinned by a positivistic reliance on the notion of behavior, provides an inadequate basis for comprehending the social world. Instead, social science should be grounded in the idea of action, which directs attention toward the subjective meaning of people's everyday social experience.

4 Empirical concerns, such as accurate description and explanation, are inextricably tied to normative evaluation and social ethics. The conventional distinction between "empirical" theory and "normative" theory is misleading and unproductive.

5 The primary problem for organization theory is to understand the ways in which bureaucracy serves to reinforce social processes of domination that then produce individual alienation. Basic to such an understanding is the relationship of social structure to forms of language and discourse.

6 The purpose of theory is fundamentally practical. Theory is practical insofar as it enables self-understanding leading to responsible and autonomous action.

Social and organizational theorists are most fundamentally divided by their answers to two questions. First, what are the basic philosophical assumptions on which social science should be based? And second, what moral and practical purposes, if any, can or should theory serve? With respect to the first question, the debate turns on whether or to what degree the assumptions and methods of natural science are appropriate for the social sciences. Especially problematic are the meanings of and proper relationship between the notions of "objectivity" and "subjectivity."

Imbedded in the differing meanings of these two words are disagreements about such basic issues as the nature of social reality, human nature, and the foundations of knowledge about the social world.

The second question, which concerns the ends or interests that theoretical knowledge can or should serve, is perhaps even more divisive than the first question. The problem is not merely one of consciously deciding *which* ends and interests knowledge should serve *after* its validity has been certified, that is, after "factual" questions are settled. At first glance, this would seem to be a straight-forward "value" question. The issue is more complicated, owing to some often arcane disagreements over the issue of whether it is possible—and relatedly, whether it is desirable—to separate the generation of knowledge from the interests that it might serve.

Essentially, this debate is concerned with the extent to which social science can be, or should attempt to be, value-free as opposed to value-centered. On the one hand, it may be argued that social science knowledge is ultimately most useful when it is conceptually divorced from social purposes, the decisions about which should be decided upon in other arenas of discourse. Or, on the other hand, it may be argued that social science should be conceived as a means for enabling either the realization of shared values or the moral critique of existing social practices. The crux of the disagreement between these two opposing positions hinges on the question of whether value issues *can*, even in theory, be separated from empirical ones without trivializing—both intellectually and morally—the entire enterprise of social science.

These questions are significant not only for philosophy and social science, but also bear on practical issues of administration as well. Administration, after all, is a form of action that ostensibly uses knowledge, including theory, for practical purposes. Judging from the profound disagreements in contemporary social science, however, there is currently little consensus as to what it means to "use" theory to inform practice. As noted in Chapter 4, what it means to use theory for practical purposes is both a theoretical and a practical problem.

It is therefore necessary first to examine the assumptions underlying both interpretive and critical theories. This is followed by a discussion of each perspective, tracing its historical roots in sociological and political theory. The interpretive and critical perspectives are then synthesized in the context of the public administration framework.

Basic Assumptions of Interpretive and Critical Theory

Rather new to the American intellectual scene, both interpretive and critical theories of organization derive from long-established traditions in

European social and political thought. These traditions are marked by striking contrasts in basic assumptions from those of the writers considered in all of the previous chapters with the exception of Max Weber. Those earlier chapters have documented many of the differences, and indeed the heated disagreements, between the various perspectives. Their often obvious differences, however, mask some implicit agreements with one another about basic assumptions that interpretive and critical theorists explicitly challenge.

On the question of whether social science knowledge can or should be logically separated from matters of social practice, interpretive and critical theorists often find themselves in disagreement with one another. Interpretive theorists tend, with some prominent exceptions, to side with their counterparts in naturalistic social science in asserting both the possibility and desirability of a value-free social science. Implicit in the idea that social science should be value-free is the belief that scientific knowledge and practical human interests are conceptually distinct. As Richard Bernstein points out, critical theory, by contrast,

> has a fundamental *practical interest* that guides it—a practical interest in radically "improving human existence," of fostering the type of self-consciousness and understanding of existing social and political conditions so that "mankind will for the first time be a conscious subject and actively determine its own way of life."[1]

"Objectivist" Versus "Subjectivist" Social Science

An adequate understanding both of interpretive and critical theory, as well as the nature of their disagreements with the various perspectives discussed earlier, requires a brief lesson in the terminology of basic assumptions in social science. A helpful source here is Gibson Burrell and Gareth Morgan's *Sociological Paradigms and Organisational Analysis*, in which the authors summarize two polar philosophical perspectives in social science—the *subjectivist* and *objectivist*—along four dichotomous dimensions.[2] (See Table 10.1.)

The four dimensions are ontology, epistemology, human nature, and methodology. Each denotes a fundamental and problematic issue in the social sciences in which there are logically distinct assumptions. Collectively, the assumptions in each column constitute the basic philosophical positions of the subjectivist and objectivist approaches. Although each

---

[1]Richard Bernstein, *The Restructuring of Social and Political Theory* (Philadelphia: University of Pennsylvania Press, 1978), pp. 180–81, quoting Max Horkheimer.
[2]Gibson Burrell and Gareth Morgan, *Sociological Paradigms and Organisational Analysis* (London: Heinemann Educational Books, 1979), pp. 1–9.

TABLE 10.1

A Scheme for Analyzing Assumptions about the Nature of Social Science

The Subjective-Objective Dimension		
The Subjectivist Approach to Social Science		The Objectivist Approach to Social Science
Nominalism	ontology	Realism
Anti-positivism	epistemology	Positivism
Voluntarism	human nature	Determinism
Ideographic	methodology	Nomothetic

Source: Gibson Burrell and Gareth Morgan, *Sociological Paradigms and Organisational Analysis* (London: Heinemann Educational Books, 1979), p. 3.

assumption in its pure form logically excludes the other, they are often implicit and subject to nuances in interpretation, which leads to occasional "middle-ground" positions.

Ontology   The most fundamental assumption that scientists can make about the subject of their inquiry concerns its *ontological* status. Ontological assumptions, although they are often not made explicit, have to do with the essence of the phenomena being investigated. For organization theorists, the ontological question is: What do we mean when we say organizations exist? The objectivists in organization theory hold the view, referred to as *realism*,

> that the social world external to individual cognition is a real world made up of hard, tangible and relatively immutable structures. Whether or not we label and perceive these structures, the realists maintain, they still exist as empirical entities.[3]

By contrast, the subjectivists, who adhere to *nominalism*, reject the idea that social structures exist independent of human consciousness and action. Instead, they see the social world as a product of human consciousness, which means that the institutions and roles that constitute social reality are nothing more than labels or names.

Epistemology   The second set of conflicting basic assumptions are *epistemological*, that is, assumptions concerning what is properly to be regarded as knowledge or fact and how that knowledge is communicated and understood both in everyday life and in scientific discourse. Here the dispute revolves around the adequacy of *positivism*, the epistemological point of view of the objectivists, which seeks "to explain and predict what happens in the social world by searching for regularities and causal rela-

[3]Ibid., p. 4.

tionships between its constituent elements.[4] Serious differences of opinion can be found within the positivist camp over whether hypothesized causal relationships may be "verified" in an affirmative sense or simply "falsified" (the position popularized by Karl Popper.)[5] Positivists share, however, a common commitment to detached, objective *observation* as the surest path to the discovery of scientific knowledge. Such observations provide the data from which hypotheses may be tested in order to reveal objective and generalized explanations and predictions about social life. *Antipositivism,*[6] on the other hand, is typically less concerned with discovering underlying regularities and causal laws than with understanding the richness and nuance of their subjects' experience. In rejecting the idea of detached observation, the antipositivists seek to understand the subjective experience of those whom they study. As Burrell and Morgan note:

> For the anti-positivist, the social world is essentially relativistic and can only be understood from the point of view of the individuals who are directly involved in the activities which are to be studied. Anti-positivists reject the standpoint of the "observer," which characterizes positivist epistemology, as a valid vantage point for understanding human activities. They maintain that one can only "understand" by occupying the frame of reference of the participant in action. One has to understand from the inside rather than the outside.[7]

Along the borderline dividing these epistemological poles is the position that generalization through hypothesis testing is both possible and useful as long as the categories of generalized meaning used by social scientists accurately summarize and represent the subjective meanings of the actors under study. Here Max Weber's notion of the "ideal type," described in Chapter 5, is crucial in that it performs a pivotal role, as did Weber more generally, between two epistemological extremes. Weber, like the positivists, was very much committed to the enterprise of generalization and, more broadly, to an objective (though not "objectivist") and value-free social science. But Weber's version of an objective social science was also avowedly antipositivist, owing to his stipulation that action can only be understood in terms of the subjective meaning of acting individuals.

Human Nature The third category of basic assumptions dividing the objectivists and subjectivists is the issue of human nature, that is, the beliefs about the nature of the self that implicitly guide their respective

---

[4]Ibid., p. 5.
[5]See Karl R. Popper, *The Logic of Scientific Discovery* (New York: Harper Torchbooks, 1968).
[6]The prefix "anti" indicates the essentially reactive posture at least in the United States and Britain of the subjectivists' epistemology.
[7]Burrell and Morgan, p. 5.

inquiries. The objectivist position asserts a *determinist* view in which the doings of people may be explained by causal forces, either those in the environment or those caused by genetic endowment. Subjectivist social science takes a *voluntarist* position, which sees human nature as active or autonomous, rather than determined. Voluntarists, however, do not necessarily regard autonomous action as always consciously rational. Contemporary versions of voluntarism typically concede the important role of unconscious motivation in guiding people's actions. As Michael Harmon has noted elsewhere,

> While perhaps congenial in spirit, the active voluntarist conception shares only a superficial resemblance to earlier, heavily rationalistic, conceptions of free will characteristic, for example, of the Enlightenment period. To say that people are active is not to say that they are wholly masters of their fate. The active view of the self implies a somewhat less heroic and less autonomous view of human nature, which grants that people participate in the creation of the social world and are responsible for it by virtue of their abilities to reflect upon the meaning of their participation.[8]

As we shall see later, disagreements about the nature of the self profoundly affect the manner in which social and organization theorists variously deal with value questions. The degree of determinism or voluntarism implicit in their writings, for example, influences the degree to which people will be regarded as personally responsible, in an existential sense, for their actions. This same issue also bears upon how one should regard the appearance of predictable regularities in social conduct. Specifically, are such regularities the product of environmental or genetic forces, or are they simply evidence that people *choose* to behave predictably?

Methodology The final set of opposing assumptions captures the essence of the *methodological* debate between the objectivists and subjectivists. The alternative methodological approaches are logical extensions of the earlier-noted epistemological stances of the two general social science approaches. The objectivists, who share an epistemological commitment to generalized prediction and explanation, typically employ *nomothetic* methodologies, which base

> research upon systematic protocol and technique. It is epitomised in the approach and methods employed in the natural sciences, which focus upon the process of testing hypotheses in accordance with the canons of scientific rigour. It is preoccupied with the construction of scientific tests and the use of quan-

---

[8]Michael M. Harmon, *Action Theory for Public Administration* (New York: Longman, 1981), p. 33.

titative techniques for the analysis of data. Surveys, questionnaires, personality tests and standardized research instruments of all kinds are prominent among the tools which comprise nomothetic methodology.[9]

The alternative methodological approach, one that is congenial to the antipositivist epistemology, emphasizes a deeper understanding of social experience through the subjective frames of reference of the research subjects themselves. This so-called *ideographic* method, while it does not necessarily preclude a later interest in generalization, "stresses the importance of letting one's subject unfold its nature and characteristics during the process of investigation."[10] This approach contrasts with that of describing the subjects' behavior in terms of preestablished protocols and categories of interpretation selected by the researcher.

In describing the four sets of basic assumptions that divide the objectivist and subjectivist approaches to social science, we have not done justice to the important differences *within* each of the general orientations discussed, nor to the various points of agreement between them. Many of the subtleties of both agreement and disagreement between these two orientations will become evident as we outline the basic assumptions underlying interpretive and critical theories of organization.

Interpretive Theory

"Interpretive theory" is an umbrella term that encompasses a variety of viewpoints in social science, some of European origin and others indigenous to the United States. In the United States, interpretive theories have arisen largely in reaction against the positivist orthodoxy of American social science. As manifest in functionalist sociology, behaviorist psychology, and organizational systems theory, positivist social science has been predominant on the American scene since World War II. Although interpretive theory has reflected a minority viewpoint in the United States, it nonetheless grows out of a varied and well-established intellectual tradition in Europe.

Historical Context

The European influence on interpretive theory derives from the German idealism inspired by Immanuel Kant (1724–1804). Emerging long

---

[9]Burrell and Morgan, pp. 6–7.
[10]Ibid., p. 6.

after the time in which Kant wrote, the positivist tradition in the social sciences has consistently, if often implicitly, held to the position that sensory experience provides the primary foundation for knowledge of the social world. The methods of natural science, therefore, offer the only means by which laws governing relationships among elements of the social world can be discovered.

Kant, by contrast, held that "the ultimate reality of the universe lies in 'spirit' or 'idea' rather than in sense perception."[11] Kant's central premise illuminates the principal underlying source of disagreement between modern-day objectivist and subjectivist social science by its implications that human consciousness, rather than the seemingly self-evident world of facts and things, is the core problem of philosophical discourse. According to Burrell and Morgan, Kant

> posited that *a priori* knowledge must precede any grasp or understanding of the sense data of empirical experience. He argued that there must be inherent, in-born organising principles within man's consciousness by which any and all sense data is structured, arranged and thus understood. *A priori* knowledge was seen as independent of any external reality and the sense data which it "emits"; it was seen as the product of the "mind" and the interpretive processes which go on within it. Whilst the world in which men live may be the product of a complex interrelationship between *a priori* knowledge and empirical reality, for Kant the starting point for understanding this lay in the realm of "mind" and "intuition."[12]

The two figures of the early twentieth century perhaps most influential in the development of contemporary interpretive theory were, like Kant, both German: the philosopher Edmund Husserl (1859–1938) and the sociologist Max Weber. Husserl's highly difficult and convoluted philosophy, phenomenology, marks a systematic effort to ground philosophy in the study of consciousness itself. His purpose was to lay bare the hidden presuppositions not only of the scientific method (namely, positivism) and philosophy, but of the life world (*lebenswelt*) of everyday experience. Husserl shared with Kant the belief that consciousness is neither separate from the events of the world nor a passive receptor of sensory information. Instead, consciousness is always "intended" (that is, directed) toward the objects of its attention. Accurate description of what is "out there," therefore, necessarily entails a critical examination of the ways in which human consciousness is structured.

Husserl wrote in clear opposition to the positivistic spirit then dominating much of Western philosophy and social science. Max Weber, on the other hand, took a more intermediate role by attempting to bridge the

[11]Ibid., p. 227.
[12]Ibid.

chasm between Kantian idealism and positivistic social science. As noted earlier, Weber rejected positivism, but more for reason of its naivete concerning the "objectivity" of sense data than for its commitment to an objective, value-free social science—a commitment that Weber himself shared. Weber, however, also agreed with Husserl's view that objectivity is necessarily contingent on and derivative from the inherent subjectivity of experience. To Weber the sociologist, however, the idea of subjectivity is inherent in the descriptions of the meanings that constitute people's actions, in contrast to Husserl's philosophical concern with the innate structures of human consciousness.

Alfred Schutz and Contemporary Interpretive Theory

Just as Weber sought to bridge the gap between positivist sociology and Kantian idealism, Husserl's disciple Alfred Schutz (1899–1959) sought to merge Husserl's "transcendental" phenomenology with Weber's sociology. The cumulative product of Schutz's so-called "existential phenomenology," however, ends up being closer to Weber than to Husserl. This is due mainly to Schutz's commitment, as a sociologist, to a value-free social science concerned with an objective account of the patterns and regularities of action in the social world. Thus, Schutz did not seriously dispute the basic aims of naturalistic (objectivist) social science, nor even its methodological commitment to hypothesis testing through controlled inference.[13] His primary disagreement with naturalistic social science lay in his belief that the social world must be understood in terms of the subjective meanings or interpretations that people in the everyday world give to their experience. Schutz contrasts the role of the social scientist—the systematic interpreter of the interpretations of others—with that of the natural scientist who should, and must, determine for himself or herself the appropriate meanings of events and behaviors of the natural world:

> It is up to the natural scientist and to him alone to define, in accordance with the procedural rules of his science, his observational field, and to determine the facts, data, and events within it which are relevant for his problem or scientific purpose at hand. Neither are those facts and events pre-selected, nor is the observational field pre-interpreted. The world of nature, as explored by the natural scientist, does not "mean" anything to molecules, atoms, and electrons. . . . The thought objects constructed by the social scientist by contrast, in order to grasp this social reality, have to be founded upon the thought objects constructed by the common-sense thinking of men, living their daily life within their social world. Thus, the constructs of the social sciences are, so to speak, constructs of the second degree, that is, constructs of the constructs made by

[13]Bernstein, p. 137.

the actors on the social scene, whose behavior the social scientist has to observe and to explain in accordance with the procedural rules of his science.[14]

The second-order character of social constructs, however, does not preclude inferences of determinate relations among social units. This is a point agreed on by Schutz as well as by his adversary Ernest Nagel,[15] one of the most astute defenders of naturalistic social science. The requirement to interpret systematically the meanings that people give to their everyday experience, however, does suggest an important shift in orientation from the naturalistic approach. From the standpoint of the latter, the *social scientist's* perspective, rather than the perspective of his subjects, provides the primary basis of inquiry.

Using Wilhelm Dilthey's notion of *verstehen* (roughly translated as "interpretive understanding"),[16] Schutz criticizes naturalistic social science for naively taking for granted the external appearances of the social world. Instead, social science should systematically account "for the way in which this social reality is constituted and maintained, in what ways it is intersubjective, or how actors in their common-sense thinking interpret their own actions and the actions of others."[17] For Schutz, the idea of *verstehen* is not simply a method of the social sciences (as it was for Weber), but is also a term depicting the common-sense experience of everyday life.

Schutz's influence, along with that of some of his contemporaries (such as Martin Heidegger, Jean-Paul Sartre, and Maurice Merleau-Ponty), is evident in both interpretive sociology and interpretive organization theory, as well as to a more limited extent in social ethics. Peter Berger, often in collaboration with Thomas Luckmann, is one of the foremost exponents of Schutzian sociology,[18] while David Silverman's "action frame of reference" provides the most direct application of that sociology to the study of organization theory.[19] The works of these authors present several ideas that form the foundation of the interpretive approach, an approach

[14]Alfred Schutz, "Concept and Theory Formation in the Social Sciences," in Maurice Natanson, ed., *Philosophy of the Social Sciences* (New York: Random House, 1963), p. 232.

[15]See especially, Ernest Nagel, "Problems of Concept and Theory Formation in the Social Sciences," in Natanson, p. 209.

[16]Wilhelm Dilthey (1833–1911) attempted to extend the work of Kant to history. He separated the natural sciences from the "sciences of the spirit" (e.g., history), claiming that the latter cannot be understood except through the method of *verstehen*, that is, as meaning experienced in situations. "The natural sciences seek abstracted explanatory ultimates whereas the social sciences seek immediate understanding through insight into their raw data. . . . This is the process of subjective understanding or interpretation (*verstehen*), and we achieve such understanding through a process of 'reliving' social events." Marcello Truzzi, "Wilhelm Dilthey," in Truzzi, ed., *Verstehen: Subjective Understanding in the Social Sciences* (Reading, Mass.: Addison-Wesley Publishing Co., 1974), p. 9.

[17]Bernstein, p. 138.

[18]See especially Peter L. Berger and Thomas Luckmann, *The Social Construction of Reality* (New York: Anchor Books, 1967).

[19]David Silverman, *The Theory of Organisations* (New York: Basic Books, 1971).

that challenges the American orthodoxy of functionalism and organizational systems theory on several counts.

Action and Behavior   The notion of *verstehen*, which all interpretive theorists embrace in some form, means that people's behaviors are mainly understandable in terms of the subjective meaning that they, themselves, give to them. *Behavior*, defined as the sensorily observable and measurable movements of people, is a restrictive idea that excludes from analysis the subjective world of experience. Following Weber, who defined *action* as behavior plus the subjective meaning of the acting individual, interpretivists tend to regard the notion of behavior, alone, as far too limited and often misleading. For them, meanings and motives constitute the essence of social life. It is not just that behavior and meaning are *related*, but that action is *constitutive* of the meanings and motives of individuals. Except in rare circumstances, the study of what people do without attending to the meanings embodied in their actions omits from study precisely that which is most important.

The idea of action also bears directly on the question of human nature. In particular, are the doings of people determined, either by the environment or genetic predisposition? Or, are they the result, at least to a degree, of autonomous choice as is claimed by the voluntarists? Implicitly taking to task functionalist sociology on this matter, Anthony Giddens describes the voluntarist view of human nature this way:

> *Sociology is not concerned with the "pre-given" universe of objects, but with one which is constituted or produced by the active doings of subjects.* Human beings transform nature socially, and by "humanizing" it they transform themselves; but they do not, of course, produce the natural world, which is constituted as an object-world independently of their existence....
>
> *The production and reproduction of society thus has to be treated as skilled performance on the part of its members*, not as merely a mechanical series of processes.[20]

The Face-to-Face Encounter   All theoretical perspectives, although with varying degrees of explicitness, begin with an assumption about the primary unit of analysis that forms the foundation for their inquiries. In earlier chapters, for example, we noted that systems theory typically begins with the system, conceived holistically, as the starting point of analysis, from which explanations for the behavior and functions performed by its parts are then derived. Market theorists, on the other hand, use the ratio-

---

[20]Anthony Giddens, *New Rules of Sociological Method: A Positive Critique of Interpretive Sociologies* (New York: Basic Books, 1976), p. 143, emphasis in original.

nal, self-interested individual as their primary unit, explaining larger social units such as nation-states and organizations as aggregations of such individuals.

Interpretive theory, in particular that of Berger and Luckmann, employs the face-to-face encounter as the primary unit of analysis. Since sociology is, by definition, the study of the social, the unit of analysis must be large enough to capture the basic dynamics of interaction among people. The face-to-face encounter

> depicts a level of analysis most directly related to our concrete experience and is therefore the most elemental—and, in a sense, the most real—unit of human interaction. That is, the ... encounter is the prototypical case of social interaction from which all other cases are derived.[21]

Interpretivists exclude not only the atomistic individual as a logical starting point, but also reject the idea that the organization or indeed any larger system can serve as the primary unit. Here their nominalist, as opposed to realist, ontological stance is evident. They argue that organizations, like all other social collectivities, have no real or concrete existence, but are residual phenomena of human consciousness. Without being consciously aware of it, we think and act as if organizations were *real* entities. Organizations and institutions are constructs, products of the mind; the more encompassing they become, the more remote and abstract they are from our experience. As the primary unit of analysis, the face-to-face encounter serves as a reminder of the secondary or derivative nature of these constructs, thereby lessening the tendency to regard organizations and institutions as concrete entities.

Intentionality and Intersubjectivity   Two terms, "intentionality" and "intersubjectivity," are basic to understanding the dynamics of the production and maintenance of the social world. *Intentionality* depicts the idea that consciousness is necessarily directed toward objects of our attention; that is, we are not simply conscious, but conscious *of* something. Consciousness is an active, transactional process that involves both the objects external to us and the rules and habits of perception that affect our interpretations of those objects. The social world, which interpretive theory regards as having no concrete existence, is rather a product of consciousness. Although seemingly real and concrete in the way we experience it, the social world is really nothing more than the residue of our "sedimented" experience. Over time, this experience accumulates and is uncritically taken for granted. In this way, social phenomena are granted

---

[21]Harmon, p. 31.

the status of objects (or, to use the verb, they are "objectified"). But what we might call "objective reality" is necessarily derived from the idea of subjectivity.

Whereas intentionality describes the process by which individuals actively create social reality, *intersubjectivity* captures the *social* character of that creation. If the social world is the product of human consciousness, then one must also account for how that world is held together. Since the social world has no concrete existence, then our beliefs that lead us uncritically to take for granted its existence are necessarily the results of agreements among people. In this way, the social world is made intelligible in roughly similar ways to collectivities of individuals.

These agreements are made possible by language. Language is more than simply the instrument of communication; it is the essence of social existence. Walker Percy, for instance, argues that we are not simply conscious *of* something, but are conscious of it as *being* something, that is, as having a name or symbol that is also understood by another person:

> Besides the symbol, the conception, and the thing, there are two other terms which are quite as essential in the act of symbolization. There is the "I," the consciousness which is confronted by the thing and which generates the symbol by which the conception is articulated. But there is also the "you." *Symbolization is of its very essence an intersubjectivity.* If there were only one person in the world, symbolization could not conceivably occur (but signification could); for my discovery of water as something derives from your telling me so, that this is water for you too. The act of symbolization is an affirmation: yes, this is water! My excitement derives from the discovery that it is there for you and me and that it is the same thing for you and me. Every act of symbolization thereafter, whether it be language, art, science, or even thought, must occur either in the presence of a real you or an ideal you for whom the symbol is intended as meaningful. *Symbolization presupposes a triad of existents: I, the object, you.*[22]

Intersubjectivity not only explains the dynamics by which the social world is created and sustained in conscious awareness, but is also makes possible an awareness of the self. Schutz describes, through the vehicle of the face-to-face encounter (which he calls the "We-relation"), how individual consciousness of the social world fundamentally requires the presence of another (the "Other"):

> [E]ach of us can experience the Other's thoughts and acts in the vivid present whereas either can grasp his own only as a past by way of reflection. I know more of the Other and he knows more of me than either of us knows of his

[22] Walker Percy, *The Message in the Bottle: How Queer Man Is, How Queer Language Is, and What One Has to Do with the Other* (New York: Farrar, Straus and Giroux, 1975), p. 281, emphasis in original.

own stream of consciousness. This present, common to both of us, is the pure sphere of the "We." And if we accept this definition, we can agree . . . that the sphere of the "We" is pregiven to the sphere of the Self. . . . We participate without an act of reflection in the vivid simultaneity of the "We," whereas the "I" appears only after the reflective turning. . . .[23]

Intentionality and intersubjectivity are basic to the interpretivists' explanation of the creation and maintenance of the social world. They also reveal two crucial aspects of human nature that ground interpretive theory, however. The idea of intentionality, which is implicit in the voluntarist conception of the self, makes plausible an *active* conception of human nature. And intersubjectivity, which holds that the presence of another is a precondition for self-awareness, defines human nature as *social*. As we shall see later, this active-social conception of human nature not only guides interpretive descriptions of organization, but also profoundly influences the value stances taken by at least some interpretive theorists.

The Problem of Reification If, as the interpretivists claim, the social world is a product of consciousness, then problems arise when we lose sight of that fact. This is likely to happen because there are powerful tendencies to forget that the institutions of the social world are only products of the human mind. This kind of misapprehension is a hazard for theorists, who often unwittingly confuse their conceptual constructs with the objects of their attention. Weber offered stern warnings against this when he carefully distinguished, for example, those forms of organization that we casually refer to as bureaucracies from the ideal-typical construct of the bureaucratic model.

This tendency, however, to lose awareness of our active creation of the social world, and therefore our responsibility for it, is a problem for lay people as well. This is because it gives "the false impression that social institutions, roles, rules, and even situations possess a concrete immutability, a natural existence independent of their intersubjective creation and maintenance by social actors." [24] This confusion of the subjective for the objective, sometimes called the "fallacy of misplaced concreteness," is more typically referred to as *reification*. It is worth quoting at length here from Berger and Luckmann, who provide perhaps the most lucid discussion of reification as it pertains to the misapprehension of everyday life.

Reification is the apprehension of human phenomena as if they were things, that is, in non-human or possibly supra-human terms. Another way of saying

[23]Alfred Schutz, *Collected Papers*, vol. 1, Arvid Brodersen, ed. (The Hague: Martinus Hijhoff, 1962), p. 174.
[24]Harmon, p.131.

this is that reification is the apprehension of the products of human activity *as if* they were something else than human products—such as facts of nature, results of cosmic laws, or a manifestation of divine will. Reification implies that man is capable of forgetting his own authorship of the human world, and further, that the dialectic between man, the producer, and his products is lost to consciousness. The reified world is, by definition, a dehumanized world. It is experienced by man as a strange facticity, an *opus alienum* over which he has no control rather than as the *opus proprium* of his own productive activity.

. . . [A]s soon as an objective social world is established, the possibility of reification is never far away. The objectivity of the social world means that it confronts man as something outside of himself. The decisive question is whether he still retains the awareness that, however objectivated, the social world was made by men—and, therefore, can be remade by them. In other words, reification can be described as an extreme step in the process of objectivation, whereby the objectivated world loses its comprehensibility as a human enterprise and becomes fixated as a non-human, non-humanizable, inert facticity. Typically, the real relationship between man and his world is reversed in consciousness. Man, the producer of a world, is apprehended as its product, and human activity as an epiphenomenon of non-human processes. Human meanings are no longer understood as world-producing but as being, in their turn, products of the "nature of things." It must be emphasized that reification is a modality of consciousness, more precisely, a modality of man's objectification of the human world. Even while apprehending the world in reified terms, man continues to produce it. That is, man is capable paradoxically of producing a reality that denies him.

. . . [T]he basic "recipe" for the reification of institutions is to bestow on them an ontological status independent of human activity and signification. . . . Through reification, the world of institutions appears to merge with the world of nature. It becomes necessity and fate, and is lived through as such, happily or unhappily as the case may be.

Roles may be reified in the same manner as institutions. The sector of self-consciousness that has been objectified in the role is then also apprehended as an inevitable fate, for which the individual may disclaim responsibility. The paradigmatic formula for this kind of reification is the statement "I have no choice in the matter, I have to act this way because of my position"—as husband, father, general, archbishop, chairman of the board, gangster, and hangman, as the case may be. This means that the reification of roles narrows the subjective distance that the individual may establish between himself and his role-playing. The distance implied in all objectification remains, of course, but the distance brought about by disidentification shrinks to the vanishing point.[25]

Berger and Luckmann's discussion of reification as modality of consciousness in everyday life serves as a warning against the tendency to impute a greater objectivity to the social world than is actually warranted. As we shall see in the following section, reification is a principal issue for

---

[25]Berger and Luckmann, pp. 89–91.

interpretive organization theory, particularly in its critique of systems theory.

David Silverman's Action Frame of Reference

Interpretive theorists often hold that their perspective neither constitutes nor necessarily leads to the development of theory as we ordinarily understand the term. They differ among themselves, for example, regarding whether or to what extent generalization through hypothesis testing is necessarily the goal of theorizing. On the one hand, some insist that their intent is rather to provide an ideographic method of analysis of social, including organizational, settings and events on a case-by-case basis. On the other hand, interpretive theorists who, with Weber, do share an interest in scientific generalization require that it be based on ideal-typical constructs derived from research subjects' subjective understandings of situations, institutions, and roles.

The most influential of the interpretive theorists who have concerned themselves with the study of organizations is the British sociologist David Silverman. His approach to organization theory, which he calls the "action frame of reference," builds directly on the sociology of Weber, Schutz, and Berger and Luckmann, and is summarized in seven basic propositions. (See the accompanying box.)

In view of our discussion to this point, the meaning and import of Silverman's propositions should be reasonably clear. His nominalist, as opposed to realist, ontology is evident from Proposition 3. There he says that institutions, while they are experienced as social facts, are actually symbolic artifacts of shared meanings and orientations. Silverman's rejection of positivism is evident both in Proposition 1, which insists on a clear distinction between the natural and the social sciences, and in Proposition 7, which explicitly rejects the determinism of positivistic explanation. And his commitment to a voluntarist conception of human nature may be seen in Propositions 3 and 4, which stress the active participation of people in creating and sustaining the social world. Silverman is less committed than other interpretive theorists, however, to a strictly ideographic methodology. Drawing on the works of Weber and, more recently, Schutz, he urges the use of ideal-typical constructs for the purpose of systematic generalization.

The principal elements of his action frame of reference stand in marked contrast with mainstream social science research, which is based primarily in systems and structural-functionalist theory. Explanation of organizational action by means of the subjective meanings of actors, for example, may be seen as an implicit rebuttal of the tendency, endemic to mainstream systems theory, to explain organizational behavior in nonpersonal

---

THE ACTION FRAME OF REFERENCE

1. The social sciences and the natural sciences deal with entirely different orders of subject-matter. While the canons of rigour and scepticism apply to both, one should not expect their perspective to be the same.

2. Sociology is concerned with understanding action rather than with observing behaviour. Action arises out of meanings which define social reality.

3. Meanings are given to men by their society. Shared orientations become institutionalised and are experienced by later generations as social facts.

4. While society defines man, man in turn defines society. Particular constellations of meaning are only sustained by continual reaffirmation in everyday actions.

5. Through their interaction men also modify, change and transform social meanings.

6. It follows that explanations of human actions must take account of the meanings which those concerned assign to their acts; the manner in which the everyday world is socially constructed yet perceived as real and routine becomes a crucial concern of sociological analysis.

7. Positivistic explanations, which assert that action is determined by external and constraining social or non-social forces, are inadmissible.

—From David Silverman, *The Theory of Organisations* (New York: Basic Books, 1971), pp. 126–27.

---

and therefore deterministic terms. What systems theorists tend to regard as external forces (e.g., technology and social structure), Silverman sees as open to various interpretations by actors in the situation. Moreover, no particular interpretation should be regarded as necessarily more natural or appropriate than another.

Furthermore, such cherished ideas as the system's need to survive inevitably ignore the active choices that actors make in the course of structuring and contesting their relations with others. These active choices may have little to do with any notion of system survival and may perhaps even run counter to it. Silverman believes that action conducive to such survival is neither necessarily natural nor desirable. To assume that it is either one of these is to accept uncritically a normative stance that is inherently conservative. This stance serves the interests of present organizational leadership, whose purposes, very likely, are to maintain existing patterns of power and control. What Silverman regards as the fiction of the "universal need of system survival," moreover, can only be sustained when systems theorists and functionalists reify their theoretical constructs. As Silverman explains:

> By concentrating on the behaviour of organisations themselves, as influenced by a series of impersonal processes, functionalists run the risk of reifying the systems that they construct. One is not convinced, for instance, that the view that organisations take actions in response to their explaining history as "what had to be." One can always invent needs which made past changes inevitable. By de-emphasising the actors' definitions of the situation and the choices of action that are perceived to be available, functionalists inhibit the predictive power of their approach.[26]

Thus reification, which Berger and Luckmann earlier described as a misapprehension of the social world by people in everyday life, Silverman describes as a regrettable tendency of theorists, especially systems theorists and structural-functionalists, to confuse their theoretical constructs with the substance of their investigations. Through this form of reification, they imbue their constructs with powers of thought and action, with the result that the behavior of people is reduced to an epiphenomenon, a mechanical unfolding, of system needs or environmental imperatives. The meanings and interests of actors are thereby ignored.

Silverman's research strategy is also deliberately neutral on an additional matter about which systems and functionalist theories have questionable leanings: the issue of order versus change. Silverman, like other critics before him, chides functionalist theorists for their excessive preoccupation with explaining how the existing social order is maintained. This emphasis on order results in explanations that cast processes of change in either a needlessly negative light or, by reifying external environmental forces, view change as determined by impersonal forces.

The conventional alternative to this emphasis on order is to view the social world as inherently conflictual, with change being the natural outcome of opposing interests.[27] Silverman is also unsympathetic to this view. He argues that questions about order versus change should properly be regarded as empirical, to be settled by the weight of evidence. Answers

---

[26]Silverman, p. 67.

[27]"Conflict theories" span much of the spectrum of sociological theory, ranging from those whose intellectual roots are essentially functionalist to those that embrace either "radical Weberian" or neo-Marxist positions. See, for example, Randall Collins, *Conflict Sociology: Toward an Explanatory Science* (New York: Academic Press, 1975); Ralf Dahrendorf, *Class and Class Conflict in Industrial Society* (Stanford, Calif.: Stanford University Press, 1959); Alvin W. Gouldner, *The Coming Crisis in Western Sociology* (London: Heinemann, 1970); C. Wright Mills, *White Collar: The American Middle Classes* (New York: Oxford University Press, 1951); and J. Rex, *Key Problems in Sociological Theory* (London: Routledge and Kegan Paul, 1961).

should not be presumed in advance in the form of *a priori* theoretical assumptions that either change *or* order is a natural condition of organizational life.

Throughout Silverman's work one finds a deliberate attempt to avoid importing unwarranted theoretical assumptions into the empirical study of particular organizations. He is concerned with constructing an approach to research and theorizing, not a theory as such. To the extent that the action frame of reference is employed in developing generalized explanations of organizational action, such explanations should be carefully grounded in the meanings and motives of the people being studied. Researchers and theorists should, in other words, avoid interpretations of people's behavior in accordance with preconceived notions of what is important, interesting, natural, or desirable.

Interpretive Theory and Social and Organizational Values

In the main, interpretive theorists have sought to distance themselves from the normative and ethical implications of their theoretical orientation. In other words, they have attempted to separate their practice of social science from the realm of practical action. Their claim to neutrality is very much in keeping with both Weber's and Schutz's injunctions on the ideal of objectivity, which is to say, value-free social science. Although this commitment is also shared by exponents of positivism, interpretivists have been vigorous in their attempts to reveal the hidden value stances implicit in positivistic social science. But interpretivists have been similarly accused by critical theorists and others of disguising *their* values under a false veneer of objectivity.[28]

Despite their commitment to value neutrality, the interpretivists have been accused of being implicitly conservative in orientation, that is, of uncritically accepting what is. Nevertheless, they have served as a source of inspiration for attempts by younger scholars to "humanize" public administration theory and practice. Phenomenology, the principal variant of interpretive theory discussed in this chapter, was introduced to the American public administration literature in the late 1960s,[29] during the height of the Vietnam War and civil rights protests. This was a time when public bureaucracies were widely viewed as unresponsive to public needs, indeed as a source of rather than a means for curing social ills.

[28]See Donald L. Carvath, "The Disembodied Dialectic: A Psychoanalytic Critique of Sociological Relativism," *Theory and Society* 4:1(1977):73–102.

[29]For an early application of phenomenology to the study of public administration, see Larry Kirkhart, "Toward a Theory of Public Administration," in Frank Marini, ed., *Toward a New Public Administration: The Minnowbrook Perspective* (Scranton, Pa.: Chandler, 1971), pp. 127–64.

The appeal of interpretive theory during this period of social unrest stemmed from at least three sources. First, its acknowledgement of people's active, though often unconscious, participation in the creation of the social world appeared to be an attractive alternative to the implicit determinism of much of naturalistic social science. Because of its deterministic view of human nature, naturalistic social science seemed to offer little hope for explaining action as the activity of free and autonomous beings. Second, phenomenology, or so it seemed on first reading, appeared to be a logical counterpart, at a sociological level of analysis, to the humanistic psychology then influential in management circles. And finally, Berger and Luckmann's discussion of reification was regarded as a powerful explanation of how social institutions, especially bureaucracy, had produced pervasive alienation both within public bureaucracies and of their intended beneficiaries.

It is likely that many of the so-called "New Public Administrationists" who embraced phenomenology saw in it room for greater optimism about social and organizational change than would have been warranted by more careful reading.[30] Although the leading interpretive sociologists were, to say the least, cautious in drawing out the normative implications of their brand of social science, serious efforts to derive ethical theory from an interpretive perspective began to appear in the 1960s. One of the most significant is University of Chicago theologian Gibson Winter's *Elements for a Social Ethic*.

Gibson Winter's "Intentionalist" Social Ethics

Whether social science can or should be value-free is an issue of such contentiousness that it divides not only various theoretical perspectives from one another, but also evokes disagreement within particular schools of thought. Both sides to this dispute acknowledge, at a minimum, that values *may* affect factual description and explanation, and neither side would deny that values do and should guide the practical use of empirical knowledge. Rather, the problematic issue regarding a value-free social science turns on whether value-free description and explanation is possible in anything other than a trivial way.

Gibson Winter holds that all theoretical perspectives about the social world grapple with the problem of how to make sense of man's struggle for fulfillment within it. Theories perform this function by specifying "ordering principles," which is to say, "the unifying principles which

---

[30]For further commentary on this point, see Orion F. White, Jr., "Communication-Induced Distortion in Scholarly Research—The Case of Action Theory in American Public Administration," *International Journal of Public Administration* 5:2(1981):119–50.

make an understanding of social phenomena possible."[31] The ordering principles serve scientific purposes of description, sense-making, prediction, etc., but they also (since few if any social science perspectives are *solely* deterministic) serve as the basis for normative evaluation, as well. As Winter notes,

> When a social-scientific perspective brings to light the identity of man or society, it has to make some sense of his wrestling with values. Different models control the selective work of the sciences in defining problems and interpreting the significance of processes. The adequacy of these models varies according to the interests and problems of the sciences at any point in their development. However, the relevance of the models to an understanding of human fulfillment *in everyday terms* is of crucial significance to social ethics and the society which employs these findings. (p. 172)

The choice of an ordering principle for scientific purposes necessarily entails a judgment by the scientist about what is most fundamental about the relationship of the individual to the social world. This is inevitably a choice of values, since it implies a judgment about how the individual may attain fulfillment in a social context. The ordering principle, whatever it might be, simultaneously provides the basis for description of what *is*, but also for revealing the *possibilities* for the fulfillment of people's inherent potential. The existence of these possibilities means that value choices regarding the paths of that fulfillment are available, both to people in the everyday world and to those concerned with the subject of social ethics. Ethical postures, then, derive directly from "empirical" postures. The apparent fallacy of jumping from "is" to "ought" is obviated by the fact that empirical postures necessarily require a prior "ethical" judgment by the theorist about what is most central to an understanding of the human condition.

Although social science and social ethics are related, they are not synonymous. Winter describes both the distinction between and the appropriate nature of the relationship of these two enterprises:

> The work of social ethics is to clarify social identity more concretely than is possible or warranted in social scientific work. In this sense, social science is neither predictive nor determinative enough by its nature as a theoretical science of the social world; hence, the task of social ethical reflection is to translate the scientific formulations with reference to specific problems confronting the society. Social ethics translates the discerned regularities with which the social sciences clarify the human project into the practical context of societal

---

[31]Gibson Winter, *Elements for a Social Ethic: The Role of Social Science in Public Policy* (New York: Macmillan, 1966), p. 171; in this subsection, all page references in parentheses are to this source; emphasis is in the original unless otherwise noted.

TABLE 10.2
Ordering Principles of Scientific Perspectives

Style	Dynamic Structure	Principle of Unification	Ordering Principle
Behaviorist (Physical)	Impulses (Pleasure-Pain)	Balance of exchanges	Adjustment to external conditions
Functionalist (Vital)	Social self (Needs)	Equilibrium (Order)	Adaptation by internal and external transactions
Voluntarist (Subjectivist)	Interests	Conflict and compromise	Domination and rationalization
Intentionalist (Existential)	Intentional self	Harmony	Continuity as meaning

Source: Gibson Winter, *Elements for a Social Ethic: The Role of Social Science in Public Policy* (New York: Macmillan, 1966), p. 176.

responsibility. Social ethics converts an account of conditions into discernment of a situation; it translates an illumination of social identity on the basis of past conditions into an awareness of social possibilities in light of a human future. (p. 167)

All perspectives (Winter calls them "styles") in social science have implicit ethical postures that ultimately derive from their principal empirical interests. (See Table 10.2.) Winter claims that four basic styles currently dominate Western social science: (1) *behaviorism*, which interprets human behavior as conditioned responses to environmental stimuli; (2) *functionalism*, the organic view of society discussed in Chapter 7, which underlies much of mainstream systems theory; (3) *voluntarism*, which sees social activity as the outcome of competing interests;[32] and (4) *intentionalism*, Winter's term for the interpretive approach to social science, especially that inspired by the phenomenologist Alfred Schutz.

Underlying the rather forbidding terminology of "dynamic structure," "principle of unification," and "ordering principle" are simply some elemental assumptions about what motivates people, on what basis they manage their differences, and by what standard they may be judged successful in doing so. The empirical interests of a style are dictated by their ordering principles, which are the criteria that define the fundamental nature of human fulfillment within a social context. In addition, each style also has

[32]Winter's use of the word "voluntarism" is thus more restricted than that of Burrell and Morgan, who construe voluntarism broadly as an antonym of determinism in characterizing human nature.

what Winter calls a *principle of unification*, which defines how people's differing interests, projects, or needs are mediated among one another (e.g., through compromise, domination, integration, etc.). Finally, each style assumes, at least implicitly, a *dynamic structure*. This is Winter's term for the primary motive force from which individual action is generated. It is this prime motive force that reveals each style's basic assumptions about human nature.

Winter prefers the intentionalist style of social science and social ethics because, he believes, it captures most comprehensively people's struggle for meaning and fulfillment in their everyday lives. This is a struggle reflecting the creative tension between the needs for harmony with others and the responsible exercise of freedom within a social context. Winter regards the functionalist concern with the maintenance of order and the voluntarist preoccupation with conflict as providing necessary and important insights about social life. Their respective ordering principles, however, too narrowly confine our conception of the human project. Thus, while order and conflict are essential aspects of social life, they should be subsumed within a more encompassing, but at the same time more intimate framework of social science and social ethics.

The ethical stance of the intentionalist framework derives from Winter's particular conception of human nature, which he refers to as the "intentional self." This view of human nature, extrapolated in part from Schutz's notion of the "We-relation" (the face-to-face encounter), posits two dynamically related aspects of the self: the social and the active. The social aspect denotes the individual's natural orientation toward harmony with others. This makes possible the idea of not only a stable community, but also an intimate one, as well. The active nature of the self depicts the person's orientation toward the realization of freedom and autonomy within a human community. Thus, while functionalists and voluntarists quarrel over the relative importance of, indeed the inherent tension between, order (community) and conflict (freedom), Winter regards each of these two orientations as necessary for the meaningful expression of the other. Community in the absence of freedom produces repression and domination, whereas freedom in the absence of community results in anarchy and alienation.

The basic norms of ethical valuation derive directly from the social and active nature of the intentional self. Namely, " ... the principle of love and mutuality [is] the normative expression of man's relational being; love implies the mutuality of free initiation and free response" (p. 230). It "universalizes the relatedness of man's relational being as it is experienced in the 'We-relation.' Love in the social world expresses itself as freedom and community" (p. 250).

A significant feature of this conception of social ethics is that the beginning point for the defense of basic values, just as for empirical analysis, is at the most intimate of all social levels, the "We-relation." All other values, including those that are associated with larger social structures such as communities, societies, and organizations, are derived from love and mutuality. The idea of justice, or at least Winter's conception of it, is grounded in love and mutuality:

> [T]he *telos* of the derived [social] structures is located in human mutuality and reciprocity, so that love furnishes the criterion of adequacy for any state of justice; on this ground, the essential structure of sociality furnishes the normative elements for more complex organizations. However, the mutual openness, interpretive response, and empathic sharing which disclose love in the "We-relation" become justice in secondary structures [that is, social institutions]. (p. 233)

Interpretive Theory and Public Administration Values

In *Action Theory for Public Administration,* Michael Harmon uses Winter's intentionalist ethical theory as the basis for a normative theory of public administration. Its starting point is the criterion of mutuality that guides Winter's intentionalist perspective.

Mutuality suggests that the processes of social interaction are logically prior to and take moral precedence over the substantive ends of social action. Action is important for its own sake in that it is the means by which the impulse toward autonomy and freedom is realized. Action itself is an affirmation of the individual's active, expressive nature; it is not simply an instrumental means for the attainment of ends. The dominant Western belief is in an instrumental rationality in which means (processes) accommodate ends (substance). On the contrary, Harmon argues, processes of social interaction reveal, often only in retrospect, what those purposes or ends actually are. The purposes, therefore, cannot and should not be prespecified as the basis of an ethical theory for administration. As a "process" value, mutuality's

> preferred status is not primarily contingent upon demonstrations of its instrumental or rational utility. What are usually thought of as substantive ends are intersubjectively created symbols that provide specificity or concreteness to action, but whose value is contingent upon the process by which they are created. *The contingent character of substantive ends or goals (which are infinitely variable) on process renders as logically impossible the task of beginning the development of a theory of values by attempting to identify the ground for preferring one "substantive" end over another.*[33]

Action expresses our active nature and thus should be prized for its own sake, but it also expresses our social nature as well. Through social action, the quality of relations with others profoundly affects the projects and

[33]Harmon, p. 83, emphasis in original.

possibilities that we might discover and toward which we direct our energies. Although others may constrain our action, they also make it possible in the first place, by bounding and providing nurture for it.

Viewing mutuality as a process value also serves as a helpful warning against the temptation to regard other people simply as instruments for the attainment of our own goals. Writ large, it is also a hedge against the ubiquitous peril of totalitarianism. Along this line, Gregory Bateson says:

> We have learnt, in our cultural setting, to classify behavior into "means" and "ends" and if we go on defining ends as separate from means *and* apply the social sciences as crudely instrumental means, using the recipes of science to manipulate people, we shall arrive at a totalitarian rather than a democratic system of life.... The solution ... is that we look for the "direction," and "values" implicit in the means, rather than looking ahead to a blueprinted goal and thinking of this goal as justifying or not justifying manipulative means. We have to find the value of a planned act implicit in and simultaneous with the act itself, not separate from in the sense that the act would derive its value from reference to a future end or goal.[34]

That mutuality is inherent in action serves as a criterion for resolving the tensions between the unique needs of individuals and the general interests of collectivities. Here, interpretive theory's primary unit of analysis, the face-to-face encounter, provides not only the logical beginning point for *description* of the social world, but the initial reference point for *ethical* evaluation, as well. That is, mutuality is not only inherent in action, but it is also the normative expression of the encounter. Recognition of this dimension leads to the view that

> values such as social justice, equity, and indeed any value or normative criterion used to assess the character of, or decisions that apply uniformly to, social collectivities are by their nature *derivative*, rather than primary, and are thus "second-best" values. Put slightly differently, so-called collective values are surrogates, abstractions constructed from empathetic consideration for the well-being of people with whom we ordinarily cannot interact on a face-to-face basis.[35]

The face-to-face encounter is the normatively preferred decision unit, in contrast to more encompassing units in which decisions are made on an "aggregated" basis.[36] In aggregated decisions, all parties are treated

---

[34]Gregory Bateson, *Steps to an Ecology of Mind* (New York: Ballantine, 1972), pp. 160–61.

[35]Harmon, p. 84, emphasis in original.

[36]For a discussion of the merits of disaggregated over aggregated decisions, see Robert P. Biller, "Toward Public Administrations Rather Than an Administration of Publics: Strategies of Accountable Disaggregation to Achieve Human Scale and Efficacy, and Live within the Limits of Intelligence and Other Scarce Resources," in Ross Clayton and William B. Storm, eds., *Agenda for Public Administration* (Los Angeles: University of Southern California, 1979), pp. 151–72.

equally or differentiated only on the basis of impersonal categories. The preference for "disaggregated" decisions made at the person-to-person level affirms the idea that individuals subjectively interpret their own needs and problematic situations in unique ways that cannot be fully satisfied by standardized, which is to say, impersonal, decisions and policies. Moreover, it is only at this interpersonal level of decision making that the interpretivist commitment to processes, rather than ends, may be affirmed. As Harmon notes, rather than relying on objectivated criteria of fairness or equity,

> [d]ecisions reached as a result of intersubjective agreement [at the face-to-face level] are normatively preferable to those based upon "objective" criteria . . . because the interactive processes by which agreements are reached provide the context within which mutuality may be experienced and conflict resolved. The social as well as the active nature of the self find expression primarily through the process of acting only secondarily through outcomes. Indeed, outcomes may in a general sense be regarded favorably insofar as they enable *subsequent* action that is subjectively defined by the actors as meaningful.[37]

The preferred status of disaggregated over aggregated decisions does not imply that the latter are inappropriate or unnecessary, only that they are normatively second best. In other words, when institutional choices must be made between the two alternative decision modes, the burden of the argument rests with proponents of aggregated modes of decision making to show that practical considerations of efficiency, time, and limited resources are sufficiently compelling to warrant a departure from disaggregated, face-to-face decisions. Disaggregated decisions that take account of the unique and idiosyncratic nature of individual problems and circumstances are almost invariably expensive and time-consuming. And, when pure public goods are at issue, disaggregated decisions are even beside the point. Nevertheless, the criterion of mutuality may counteract pressures toward impersonality and uniformity that characterize public bureaucracies. The argument that links social action and mutuality to aggregated decisions and public goods is summarized in Figure 10.1.

The Interpretive Critique of Bureaucracy

A half century ago, sociologist Max Weber had recoiled from the bureaucratic future in personal horror. Like George Orwell and Aldous Huxley, he saw a strange new world in which not the brave but the dehumanized would survive. What if, instead of parroting Weber's classic characterization of bureaucracy, we started taking seriously his condemnation of its inmates?[38]

---

[37]Harmon, pp. 84–85, emphasis in original.
[38]Ralph P. Hummel, *The Bureaucratic Experience* (New York: St. Martin's Press, 1977), p. 2.

1 Mutuality, the normative expression of the encounter, is the primary value in the normative theory.

2 As a "process" value, mutuality implies a rejection ... of the assumption that means (processes) are mainly instrumentally related to ends (substantive outcomes).

3 "Disaggregated" decisions are ... preferable to "aggregated" decisions because they make possible contexts for intersubjective agreements among people, thus accounting more adequately for unique and differing preferences.

4 Disaggregated decisions are ... preferable because they allow more direct involvement in decision processes by those affected, thus facilitating the actualization of people's nature as active and social beings.

5 Equal justice, social equity, or other collective values are logically derived from, and normatively subordinate to, mutuality.

6 Aggregated decisions, that is, those which either apply uniformly to the whole population or differentiate among the population only on the basis of categories, are normatively second-best but are acceptable to the extent that

  1. pure public goods are at issue;

  2. the negative side effects that a disaggregated decision has on other actors are unmanageable through face-to-face negotiation; and

  3. the population affected is relatively homogeneous, that is, when members of the population subjectively define their needs and preferences in a relatively similar manner.

Source: Michael Harmon, *Action Theory for Public Administration* (New York: Longman, 1981), p. 92.

Figure 10.1 *Summary of the Argument for an Interpretivist Normative Theory*

Although Max Weber described bureaucracy's historical roots and the logical interrelationships of its primary elements, he was also a severe critic of bureaucracy. Recall from Chapter 5, for example, that Weber defined organizations as systems of social domination. His critique, moreover, was a natural extension of his overall perspective, an ironic fact in view of his commitment to an otherwise value-free social science. Later sociologists who followed in his footsteps (functionalists and interpretivists alike) by and large eschewed Weber's critical attitude. It is this critical attitude, however, that has recently spawned normative criticism of bureaucratic organization within an essentially interpretive framework. These criticisms of bureaucracy affect several levels of analysis. At the personal and interpersonal levels, for example, bureaucracy is charged with stifling healthy psychological development and authentic personal relations. At the political level, it has been argued, bureaucratic administration has replaced democratic government as the locus of political power and institutional authority.

Two interpretive critiques of bureaucracy will be considered here, one by Michael Harmon and the other by Ralph Hummel. Although differing in tone and practical implications, they reflect highly similar sentiments. For Harmon, the idea of hierarchy bears the brunt of criticism. The enactment of values and meanings imbued in the notion of hierarchy enables the constitution of the institutional means by which the exercise of legal-rational domination comes to be taken as given and beyond challenge. Along with other practices associated with bureaucracy, such as division of labor, specialization of tasks, and the impersonality of work, hierarchy serves to promote and support top management's claim to the rational and efficient exercise of control. An outcome of this is to mask both the relationships of power inherent in hierarchical structures, as well as the outcomes that derive from those relationships.

Defined as the division of offices into superior-subordinate relationships, hierarchy is one of five possible "decision rules" that may govern authority relationships in organizations. Defined in this way, decision rules are essential elements in the structuring (i.e., organizing) of relationships. To change a decision rule is to change in the most fundamental way an organization's structure. Decision rules not only define authority relationships within organizations, but also

between them and elements of their domains (e.g., legislatures, constituencies, the courts). Decision rules as they apply *within* organizational boundaries specify who makes decisions and the means by which those toward whom the decisions are directed (the "implementors") may be held accountable. Organizational decision rules as they apply to constituencies *external* to organizations both specify the manner in which constituents may voice their preferences effectively as well as clarify the authority of organizations over (and their obligations to) constituents.[39]

The four alternative decision rules are

- *voting* (majority rule);

- *contract*, in which both or all parties voluntarily agree to a decision, which is subsequently binding;

- *bargaining*, a market-line rule in which participants trade with one another or use an impersonal medium of exchange to reach non-coercive decisions; and

[39]Harmon, p. 95, emphasis in original.

- *consensus*, where people synthesize differing points of view in an attempt to reach a mutually acceptable (or at least tolerable) decision in which all interests are served.

In order to make consensus binding, unanimity—which is to say, conscious agreement in the absence of domination—is a formal requirement. As a social process, in contrast to the formal rule, consensus usually carries with it the idea that agreements are and should be temporary and constantly evolving, rather than seen as fixed and binding as in the case of contracts. Also underlying the idea of consensus, especially as it has evolved in the management literature, is a commitment to social processes characterized by trust and authentic communication. Described in this way, consensus also presupposes a willingness of the participants to rethink both their conceptions of the problems they must mutually confront and their personal stakes in their solutions.

If decision rules are the defining elements of formal organizational authority, then the *"selection of decision rules is the fundamental normative decision in determining the structure of public organizations."*[40] The normative problem is to establish defensible criteria for making those selections.

From his normative theory of public administration, Harmon derives four criteria for selection of decision rules:[41]

1 the extent to which the rules are likely to induce decisional processes that affirm or develop the self in its active and social aspects;

2 the extent to which the rules and associated processes acknowledge the intersubjective nature of social knowledge;

3 the extent to which rules may effectively promote, where possible, the disaggregation of decisions; [and]

4 the extent to which decision rules and associated processes affirm the reciprocal relationship between means and ends, and take due account of emotive-expressive, as well as instrumental, considerations in the pursuance of social projects.

Decision Rules and the Active-Social Self These criteria for the evaluation of decision rules all share the assumption that social processes precede in normative importance the attainment of end states. Thus, decision rules should be evaluated primarily on the quality of the social processes they help to generate. Different decision rules embody different forms of meaning and thus different value orientations. Enactments of particular

[40]Ibid., p. 104, emphasis in original.
[41]Ibid., p. 106.

decision rules have social and political implications for how relations among workers, and between workers and clients, are structured and conducted. Instrumental criteria for evaluating decision rules, such as their suitability for efficiently realizing goals, are normatively secondary considerations.

Harmon casts his critique in terms of a comparison of hierarchy with consensus, the decision rule that most nearly satisfies the four normative criteria. In terms of the first of these criteria, action that affirms the active as well as the social nature of the self expresses

> our creative potential and our need to act as autonomous beings. The social nature of the self is reflected in actions that take into account the actions and preferences of others, not merely as strategies to attain our own ends, but in ways that affirm others' creative potential and needs for social bonds. In assessing the normative adequacy of decision rules, we should be concerned with how processes logically associated with those rules are likely to reinforce or conflict with the orientations toward autonomy and community implied by the active-social nature of the self.[42]

Hierarchy constitutes an institutional means for domination by structuring organizational relationships along superior-subordinate lines. The voluntary basis of autonomous action, assumed by the active nature of the self, is thus replaced by one that is essentially coercive. Similarly, the empathic bases of community suggested by the social nature of the self is replaced, via the rule of hierarchy, by impersonal bases of decision-making. Hierarchy, in effect, serves to negate the interpretive view of human nature embodied in Schutz's notion of the "We-relation." As Hummel notes:

> In the pure we-relationship I create my social life with others who have intentions similar to mine. In the they-relationship [impersonal relationships such as those found in the bureaucratic form of organization] the social world has been preconstructed for me and my contemporaries, and the problem becomes to get to know them in terms of the significance and role assigned them by the system. It is easy to see that the we-relationship describes the situation between close friends, whereas the they-relationship describes that between bureaucrat and client, with the bureaucrat being forced to think of the client in terms predefined by the bureaucracy.[43]

By contrast, the consensus rule is normatively preferred because consensual processes most closely approximate the interpersonal dynamics of the "We-relation." Under the consensus rule, Harmon argues,

[42]Ibid., p. 106.
[43]Hummel, p. 35.

[t]he requirement of unanimity implies that agreement is based fundamentally on the presence or development of social bonds and personal commitment and only secondarily, if at all, on the basis of legal obligation, formal authority, currency, or objectivated criteria of correctness.... The rule of unanimity [consensus], more than any other rule, biases the process of decision making in directions that permit, and indeed require, modes of action that most fully express our moral nature as active and social selves.[44]

Hierarchy, Consensus, and Intersubjectivity Organizational decision rules are not only the institutional means by which decisions about social action are made and enforced, but they also constitute, in a sense, the organization's "official epistemology." That is, decision rules, as structures of authority, determine which and whose knowledge will be regarded as authoritative (i.e., correct). Decision rules, in short, not only specify what is to be regarded as correct action, but correct knowledge as well.[45]

An evaluation of decision rules may thus properly be based on the degree to which they either affirm or deny the natural processes of inter-subjective agreement posited by the interpretivists' account of knowledge creation. That is, decision rules can be evaluated in terms of the degree to which their enactment allows for the expression of the values and meanings that actors embody in their own actions and attribute to the actions of others. When seen in this light, the social and political implications of using hierarchy as an authoritative epistemological rule become apparent. As the locus of legitimate decisional authority in organizations, hierarchy appears indefensible, since it must necessarily assume the correctness of knowledge as unilaterally decided upon by those in positions of authority. If, however, the only criterion for the "correctness" of knowledge is agreement about it, hierarchy arbitrarily violates the requirement of that agreement.

Not only is hierarchically sanctioned knowledge arbitrary, but it also violates the normative injunctions implicit in Weber's idea of social action. As Hummel states,

Bureaucratic action is not social action. Social action opens me up to the entire range of meanings and needs that relevant others try to convey, because only if I open myself up to as many of the meanings, connotations, and inner feelings that others attach to their actions will I be able to understand them, cooperate with them fully, fight them sufficiently—in other words, continue to exist with them in a shared social world. Such openness is forbidden in bureaucratic action, which follows its own rules to protect itself. It is a separate world and

[44]Harmon, p. 109.
[45]For a fuller development of this argument, see Frederick Thayer, "Organization Theory as Epistemology," in Carl Bellone, ed., *Organization Theory and the New Public Administration* (Boston: Allyn and Bacon, 1980), pp. 113–39.

to break its rules is to threaten its boundaries. Against such threat, the bureaucratic world and those who have to exist within it defend themselves. It is in this sense that Weber wrote, "Bureaucracy is *the* means of transforming social action into rationally organized action."[46]

The appeal of the alternative rule of consensus is fairly obvious and needs only to be commented upon briefly. Intersubjective processes of knowledge creation are, by definition, matters of consensual argreement in which the criterion of truth is the subjective plausibility of information to the people who have an interest in its practical use. Consensus is, at the same time, both an organizational and an epistemological rule.

Projects and the Disaggregation of Decisions   Others things being equal, disaggregated decisions, which reflect the uniqueness of individual circumstances, are normatively preferred to aggregated decisions in which people are treated similarly. Hierarchy does not necessarily preclude such individualized treatment. However, the requirement of consensus—for example, between administrator and service recipient—permits a fuller exploration of problem definitions and solutions than is typical when the hierarchy rule is used. Hierarchy produces decisions conforming to preestablished problem definitions and categories of problem solution. The proper ends of action are presupposed, and administrative action is seen as an instrument for their attainment.

Following Schutz, however, interpretivists such as Winter, Harmon, and Hummel stress that the personal projects that orient action are marked by a far more fluid relationship between ends and means, between deciding and doing. Although ends and goals may orient action, action itself may also reveal new and unanticipated meaning and goals. This is an important aspect of social action that is foreign to the spirit of instrumental rationality that drives the bureaucratic machine. Rationality in the bureaucratic sense has no place for the idea that human meaning and purpose *emerge from* action, or that action itself is an end, rather than simply a means to an end. As Harmon states:

> The fluid and dialectical relation between ends and means is in part an acknowledgment that we often learn what we *want* to do by experience, rather than through rational planning, and that ends are naturally modified continually by that experience. The fluidity of means and ends is a product, as well, of the necessity to act—to undertake projects—in the absence of perfect knowledge of consequences and that useful information for subsequent action is *created*, not just made discoverable, by action motivated as much by hunches, commitment, love, and so forth, as by rational calculation.[47]

[46]Hummel, p. 5.
[47]Harmon, p. 111, emphasis in original.

However, the hierarchy rule of bureaucracy,

> which assumes that the purpose of action is the efficient attainment of ends in an instrumental sense, fails to acknowledge the dialectical relationship between ends and means that naturally exists in the pursuance of projects; and the norm of impersonality effectively denies the legitimacy of affective or expressive aspects of social action.[48]

Although their critiques of hierarchy and bureaucracy are motivated by similar sentiments, Harmon and Hummel offer differing, but perhaps in the final analysis converging, recommendations. Harmon normatively favors consensus and other alternatives to the hierarchy rule that are free of coercion and permit disaggregated decisions. He does not go as far as Frederick Thayer, who urges the outright elimination of hierarchical organizations.[49] But the justification of hierarchy on practical grounds requires a heavy burden of evidence to override the normative objections to it. Hummel, on the other hand, believes that since the essential form of bureaucracy is here to stay, the only practical strategies for surviving it are acts of resistance. Thus,

> if bureaucracy is progressive, we must, as long as we all still have an investment in tradition, balance that progress by becoming reactionary. Where bureaucracy promises more speed, we must extol the virtues of slowness and deliberation. Where bureaucracy promises efficiency, we can do with some production lags and even occasional breakdowns that give us time to breathe and rethink whether we really need to do what is being done. Where bureaucracy vows to clean politics out of administration, let us counterpose citizens groups, commissions, participatory councils and legislatures, politically appointed watchdogs and ombudsmen—for while these will bring "corruption," they are also the only way of introducing some guarantee that political goals, in the best sense, will not be totally displaced by engineering goals. In this respect, liberal democracy can be praised for one of its central faults: its fragmented myriad governments, each gouging a finger into the bureaucratic pie from above as well as from sideways and below.[50]

Critical Theory

Herbert Simon's observation that organizational decision makers are severely limited in their capacities for rational action provides an ironic

---

[48]Ibid., p. 112.

[49]See Frederick C. Thayer, *An End to Hierarchy and Competition*, 2nd ed. (New York: Franklin Watts, 1981), as well as the discussion of Thayer in Chapter 11, below.

[50]Hummel, pp. 202–3.

counterpoint to the concerns that have given rise to the "critical theory of society." Simon accepted the idea of instrumental rationality as *the* normative criterion to guide the actions of administrators, but lamented their inability to measure up to that criterion. To the critical theorists, however, it is the pervasiveness of instrumental rationality and associated practices in present-day society that pose the primary obstacles to human fulfillment. The limits of administrative rationality are a trifling problem (if, indeed, they are a problem at all) when compared with the pernicious social consequences produced by bureaucracy as the institutional embodiment of instrumental rationality.

Critical theorists seek to expose the rationalization of social relations in present-day society and, by means of critique, to liberate mankind from the structures of social domination produced by that rationalization. Their targets of criticism include not only bureaucracy, but also the modes of thought, language, and science that underlie it. In a more affirmative sense, critical theory seeks to reconstitute social science in order to serve the *practical* interest of improving human existence. As we shall see, the primary villain for critical organization theory is not bureaucracy as a discrete and objective entity, but the modes of speech, thought, and action that give rise to this mode of organizing social relationships and that permit it to dominate our existence.

Historical Background

The roots of critical theory can be traced to Georg Wilhelm Hegel's idea that

the existing "facts" of social life are . . . passing phases in the evolution of freedom and therefore more important for what they conceal than for what they reveal, since that which exists in the present is seen as limiting the evolution of freedom and therefore viewed negatively. The task of social theory becomes one of unmasking the false appearances generated in the present in order to permit expanded freedom in the future. It is through the act of critique that this is accomplished.[51]

The facts of the present, which mask the possibilities for freedom, provide the focus of critique for social theorists. This is a critique that seeks to reveal how people create forms of meaning and the attendant relationships of power that sustain social domination. Marx, who used Hegel's dialectical reasoning in his analysis of social domination, saw theory not only as a tool for interpreting the social world, but also as a means for

---

[51]Robert B. Denhardt, "Toward a Critical Theory of Public Organization," *Public Administration Review* 41:6(1981):629.

changing it. Along with Hegel, Marx provides much of the inspiration for critical theory, owing to the central importance of the idea of critique in Marx's writings. For him, critique, which performs an essentially negative (or negating) function, cannot reveal a blueprint for the future, although it can enable glimpses of it:

> [E]ven though the construction of the future and its completion for all times is not our task, what we have to accomplish at this time is all the more clear: *relentless criticism of all existing conditions,* relentless in the sense that the criticism is not afraid of its findings and just as little afraid of the conflict with the powers that be.[52]

The primary focus of Marx's criticism was the relations of domination that arose out of and were central to the maintenance of the capitalist mode of production. Modern critical theory has coupled the Marxian critique of capitalism with Weber's description of the rationalization of society by the ubiquitous instrument of bureaucracy. Although his account of the bureaucratization of modern life offers ammunition for the critical theorists, Weber's commitment to a value-free social science accords him at best marginal status among the activists of critical theory. Critical theorists reject at the outset the view that theory can, or should, be a neutral tool for description and explanation. To conceive of theory in such a manner simply leads to the perpetuation of the "facts" of social life that need to be unmasked and changed.

The term "critical theory" is associated with the founding of the Institute for Social Research at the University of Frankfurt, Germany, during the 1920s. Often linked to Marxist social thought, the so-called "Frankfurt School" has explored a wide range of subjects, including positivism, technology, the legal system, the family, bureaucracy, art, science, modes of rationality, technology, the law, music, and literature.

The unifying thread of these investigations appears in a 1937 essay written by one of the Institute's earliest and most influential leaders, Max Horkheimer. He urged, in direct opposition to Weber's commitment to value neutrality, that the social sciences be openly committed to social change, to "improving social existence."[53] The traditional social scientific commitment to interpretation and understanding should be linked explicitly to practical—which is to say, moral—interests. Understanding social and political conditions serves the human interest of emancipation, both psychologically and materially, through a revolution in human consciousness. Summarizing the thrust of Horkheimer's and other critical theorists's agenda, Richard Bernstein states:

[52]Karl Marx, *Writings of the Young Marx on Philosophy and Society,* Loyd D. Easton and Kurt H. Guddat, eds. and trans. (New York: Anchor Books, 1967), p. 212.
[53]Max Horkheimer, *Critical Theory* (New York: The Seabury Press, 1972).

Critical theory aspires to bring the subject themselves to full self-consciousness of the contradictions implicit in their material existence, to penetrate the ideological mystifications and forms of false consciousness that distort the meaning of existing social conditions. Critical theorists see the distinction between theory and action which is accepted by advocates of traditional theory, as itself an ideological reflection of a society in which "theory" only serves to foster the status quo.[54]

The Contribution of Jürgen Habermas

By far the most influential of the contemporary critical theorists is the German philosopher and social theorist, Jürgen Habermas. The scope of his interests include, among others, such diverse subjects as linguistics, cognitive-developmental theory, economics, and psychoanalytic theory. His writings are unified, however, by an overarching interest in language usage in everyday life and how the language we employ contributes to alienating us both from ourselves and others. Habermas is concerned to examine critically how the communicative practices we use distort how we see ourselves and construe and evaluate our relations with others. From this, he goes on to analyze the relation between modes of communication, the exercise of domination, and the experience of alienation that together militate against authentic human interaction. In particular, Habermas analyzes the relation of language and reason in shaping the nature and meaning of social life.

Critical theorists have a particular view of reason that can best be seen in Jay D. White's account of the interpenetration of thought and action:

Reason may be generally defined as human thought and action within the linguistic and historical context of society. It is a mental activity in the sense of thought processes such as induction and deduction, reflection and self-reflection, and dialectical negation. It is a social activity in the sense that our thoughts guide our actions, and that our actions may be judged to be reasonable or unreasonable. It is a linguistic phenomenon in the sense that language provides the symbols and rules with which to think, engage in reasoned discourse, and to judge the rationality of thought and action. Reason is historical in the sense that our past thought and action provides the framework to understand and to judge the appropriateness of our present and future thought and action.[55]

White's definition of reason aptly describes the general sense in which Habermas employs the term. To Habermas, however, reason is a crucial

[54]Bernstein, p. 182.
[55]Jay D. White, "Public Policy Analysis: Reason, Method, and Praxis," DPA degree, George Washington University, 1982, p. 63.

TABLE 10.3

The Relationship of Reason to Cognitive Interests, Social Existence, and Social Science

Cognitive Interest (mode of reason)	Dimension of Social Existence	Approach to Social Science
Technical (instrumental reason)	Work (purposive-rational action for purposes of survival)	Empirical-analytic sciences (positivism)
Practical (interpretive reason)	Interaction (communicative action based on shared meanings and consensual norms)	Historical-hermeneutic sciences (phenomenology, interpretive theory)
Emancipatory (critical reason)	Social power (emanicipation through critical insight into power relationships)	Critically oriented sciences

Source: Jay D. White, "Public Policy Analysis: Reason, Method, and Praxis," DPA degree, George Washington University, 1982, pp. 63–106.

and problematic issue for social science in view of three distinct and sometimes contradictory modes of reasoning that permeate social discourse: *instrumental* reason, *practical* (interpretive) reason, and *critical* reason. Habermas argues that an adequate theory of society must include all three, and the nature of their interrelatedness must be clearly understood. Moreover, each of the three modes of reasoning has an important bearing on three basic aspects of social life and social theory. These include, first, the *type of cognitive interest* that is served by each mode of reasoning; second, the particular *dimension of social existence* that is made comprehensible through each mode of reasoning; and third, the *approaches to social science* with which each mode is commonly associated. As a guide to the discussion below, Table 10.3 illustrates the relation of these aspects of the modes of reasoning.

Instrumental Reason   For Habermas, modern social theory and social life are infused with instrumental reason, which leads to an unreflexive use of technique in the control of social relationships. In his critique of instrumental reason, Habermas traces the connections between the rationalization of contemporary society, the relations of domination produced by it, and the experience of alienation. This rationalization is the product of, and then serves to reinforce, the idea that reason is largely limited to coordinating the means for the attainment of pregiven ends or with the following of rules.[56] Habermas does not deny the usefulness of instrumen-

[56]Ibid.

tal reason, but is critical of the modern tendency to regard it as the preeminent mode of reason. To do so, he claims, ignores or simply takes for granted the legitimacy of existing ends and rules.

The result is that instrumental reason can only serve *technical* interests such as prediction and control, rather than the larger interests of community and emancipation. From the standpoint of instrumental reason, human action is limited to "purposive-rational" action. The twin imperatives of modern capitalism and bureaucratization take on such a powerful and self-sustaining force that the legitimacy of action, without our being consciously aware of it, comes to be defined in exclusively instrumental terms. The consequence of this is that "technique" replaces a consideration of moral purpose, while bureaucratic necessity replaces the traditional values that hold society together. Thus, as Habermas points out,

> In this way traditional structures are increasingly subordinated to conditions of instrumental or strategic rationality: the organization of labor and trade, the network of transportation, information, and communication, the institutions of private law, and, starting with financial administration, the state bureaucracy.[57]

Habermas's vision of a free and responsible society is one in which as many people as possible may meaningfully participate in the "public sphere." This is the arena in which various interests may engage in free and open discourse about society's normative agenda.[58] With the rationalization of society made possible by the dominance of instrumental reason, however, the public sphere has narrowed dramatically. It is now mainly the province of those who control the institutions of purposive-rational action (i.e., business, labor, and the professions). In a sense, administration has replaced politics as the locus of legitimate social power and authority.

Habermas argues that social science inevitably serves one cognitive interest or another; it cannot be strictly neutral. What he refers to as the *empirical-analytic* sciences, which derive from a positivistic understanding of society, serve technical interests, while neglecting practical and emancipatory interests. The empirical-analytic sciences draw upon and propagate an understanding of society that underwrites positions of privilege for practitioners of science and technology. The consequences of this are, on the one hand, to mute the interests and concerns of those who, in the doing of science, are cast as objects (e.g., subordinates, clients, and citizens), while at the same time enhancing the capacity of others, such as managers and professionals, to exercise control over them.

[57]Jürgen Habermas, *Toward a Rational Society*, Jeremy J. Shapiro, trans. (Boston: Beacon Press, 1970), p. 98.
[58]Habermas, "The Public Sphere," *New German Critique* 3(1974):49–55.

To understand why this is the case, one has to remember Hegel's idea that social "facts," as well as the "laws" governing their interrelationships, *mask* rather than constitute the reality of social existence. These facts are not objectively real, but are "objectivated" (made to *appear* as real) in order to maintain existing patterns of social behavior and institutional authority. To Hegel, as well as to Habermas, the struggle for freedom entails a radical doubt and questioning of those facts; otherwise, they will imprison us. Thus, the empirical-analytic sciences, in an attempt to describe and explain the existing social reality in an objective fashion, ironically have the effect of sustaining relations of domination and the experience of alienation.

To summarize, purposive-rational action

- is enabled by instrumental reason,

- serves the technical cognitive interest of social control,

- is institutionalized in bureaucratic organization, and

- is perpetuated by the positivistic orientation of the empirical-analytic sciences.

The relations of domination produced through this confluence of factors are different from the relations of power that emerge from the exercise of physical coercion. They are embodied in the language that actors use in interpreting, describing, evaluating, and justifying their relations with each other. Thus, thought and action are not merely *related* to language, but are *constituted* by it. The significance of social institutions and social science in part derives from their impact on our language. The processes entailed in determining what sorts of language will be used in social interchange are coterminous with what people do in structuring and contesting their relations with others. Language, therefore, is a principal medium in the establishment and maintenance of social control.

Interpretive (Practical) Reason Critical theorists such as Habermas regard the interpretive theory of Husserl and Schutz as an important, but incomplete antidote against the rationalizing force of purposive-rational action. Interpretive reason, as noted earlier, "is the process of self-reflectively coming to understand and create the ends and rules of thought and action."[59] This mode of reason enables people to understand the historical and social contexts within which social decisions and policies are made and institutions created, sustained, and transformed. Consistent with the interpretivists discussed early in this chapter, Habermas holds that

[59]Jay D. White, pp. 63–64.

"[a]ccess to facts is provided by the understanding of meaning, not observation."[60] Interpretation aims at precisely that—the understanding of meaning—in order that we may then envision possibilities for consciously deciding to alter (but also to sustain, if we so choose) those ends and rules. Unlike purposive-rational action, which implies *regulation* of action to accord with present ends and rules, interpretive reason is concerned with matters of human *choice* or, as Habermas would have it, the *practical* cognitive interest of "enlightened action." To Americans, this may seem to be a peculiar meaning of practical, given our tendency to equate "practical" with "technical." To Habermas, however, practical denotes a far wider meaning that encompasses the moral choices involved in sustaining a human community.

The dimension of social existence for which practical action and interpretive reason are relevant is what Habermas calls *communicative action* (or "symbolic interaction"), in contrast to the technical interest of regulating the work environment. Communicative action involves conversation "governed by binding *consensual* norms which define reciprocal expectations about behavior and which must be understood and recognized by at least two acting subjects."[61]

Habermas's term for interpretive social science is the "historical-hermeneutical sciences." The word "hermeneutics" derives from the Greek god Hermes, who interpreted the words of the gods for humans. For many centuries, it referred specifically to the interpretation of religious texts; in the last two hundred years, its meaning has become more secular, indicating more generally the study of the relationship between reason, language, and knowledge. Hermeneutics, for Habermas, serves the knowledge interest of *maintaining* common traditions through interpretation of their historical development and contemporary meaning. Interpretive reason within the context of the historical-hermeneutical sciences reflects a conservative posture toward social change. Interpretive reason and hermeneutical analysis are *necessary* for the realization of freedom in the Hegelian sense. But they are ultimately insufficient for that purpose, since they neither provide a vision of what freedom means nor explain the conditions required to attain it. This brings us to the subject of *critical* reason and the role of speech in enabling human emancipation.

Critical Reason   To serve the interest of emancipation, Habermas's idea of communicative action requires some additional features. Because of its binding nature, a consensus may be, and often is, a product of asymmetries (inequalities) of power among those who are a party to it. These power

---

[60]Habermas, *Knowledge and Human Interests*, Jeremy J. Shapiro, trans. (Boston: Beacon Press, 1971), p. 309.
[61]Habermas, *Toward a Rational Society*, p. 92, emphasis in the original.

asymmetries can produce communicative distortions, since conversations will be mediated in terms of domination interests by the more powerful and self-protection interests by the less powerful. The result is that the search for truth will be sacrificed in the struggle of winners and losers. Even in the absence of power asymmetries, the search for truth in the interest of emancipation will not be successful so long as the existing consensus is uncritically taken for granted.

This leads to a crucial distinction that Habermas draws between communicative action and *discourse*. Whereas communicative action assumes an existing consensus about mutual expectations, discourse calls that consensus into question:

> Discourses help test the truth claims of opinions (and norms) which the speakers no longer take for granted. In discourse, the "force" of the argument is the only permissible compulsion, whereas co-operative search for truth is the only permissible motive.[62]

Discourse is necessary in order to distinguish an *accepted* consensus, which is taken for granted within the interpretive mode of reason, from a *rational* one. But how are we to determine whether a consensus is rational? Judging its rationality on the basis of its substantive content is ruled out, since proof of substantive "correctness," assuming it were possible, could then be used as a ground for limiting discourse. Such limitation would entail the use of authoritative means, which brings us back to domination.

Instead, the rationality of a consensus can only be determined with reference to the processes that give rise to it. The process of discourse is itself the end. In a somewhat different sense, however, this "end" has no end, no final stopping point. This is, of course, consistent with Hegel's dictum that the evolution of freedom is a continuous process, one whose termination can signal only renewed domination.

If the rationality of a consensus through discourse may only be determined through reference to processes, then what are the characteristics of rational processes? The answer is found in Habermas's notion of undistorted communication enabled by what he terms the "ideal speech" situation. Ideal speech is a form of discourse in which only the force of argument, rather than domination, can carry the day. This requires a symmetry (equality) of power among participants to prevent the occurrence of communicative distortions that flow from domination. Such symmetry is required not only at a face-to-face level, but must be reinforced by social institutions and social practices that encourage free and unconstrained

---

[62]Habermas, "A Postscript to Knowledge and Human Interests," *Philosophy of the Social Sciences* 3(1973):168.

communication. To summarize Habermas's overall argument in the words of Thomas McCarthy:

> The analysis of "truth" leads to the notion of a discursively achieved consensus. The analysis of "consensus" shows this concept to involve a normative dimension. The analysis of the notion of a grounded consensus ties it to a speech situation which is free from all external and internal constraints, that is, in which the resulting consensus is due simply to the force of the better argument. Finally, the analysis of the ideal speech situation shows it to involve assumptions about the context of interaction in which speech is located. The end result of this chain of argument is that the very structure of speech involves the anticipation of a form of life in which autonomy and responsibility are possible. "The critical theory of society takes this as its point of departure." Its normative foundation is therefore not arbitrary, but inherent in the very structure of social action which it analyzes.[63]

The ideal speech situation describes the kind of discourse that makes emancipation—the goal of critical reason—possible. But what *is* emancipation and how do we achieve it? Richard Bernstein answers the first part of the question by defining emancipation as "the ideal state of affairs in which nonalienating work and free interaction can be manifested."[64] Regarding the second part, the social context of the ideal speech situation enables emancipation through acts of critical self-reflection. Drawing from Kantian, Marxian, and Freudian analyses, Habermas describes self-reflection as the process of critical self-understanding whereby one is able to release oneself from an unconscious dependence on hypostatized powers.[65] By "hypostatized powers," he means construction of meaning and modes of practice that we unconsciously reify. Through reified thinking we are unable to perceive the possibilities for responsible and autonomous action. Self-reflection, accordingly, is the means by which we negate the powerful forces toward reification that abound not only in the social world that is extrinsic to us, but also within us. More generally,

> [s]elf-reflection is the ability to see one's self in relationship to one's object of attention be it a material object, another person, a concept, an ideological constraint on thought or action, or an unconscious constraint on thought or action. This self-reflective turn allows us to judge the truth and desirability of our relationship to things in our environment.[66]

It is important to remember that self-reflection is a critical process by

---

[63]Thomas A. McCarthy, "A Theory of Communicative Competence," *Philosophy of the Social Sciences* 3(1973):153–54; quoted in Bernstein, p. 213.

[64]Bernstein, p. 189.

[65]Habermas, *Knowledge and Human Interests*, p. 310.

[66]Jay D. White, p. 98.

which we *deny* the certainty, and thus the binding nature, of the "facts" of social existence. Only through critique can we truly comprehend and thus transform existing configurations of power that otherwise dominate thought and action. Critical reason and self-reflection are both the means and the ends of human emancipation. Or, as Jay White has put it, "the end of critical reason is itself."[67]

Critical Theory and Public Administration

The influence of critical theory on the study of public administration did not become evident until the late 1970s.[68] Since that time, a small but impressive body of literature has appeared that extends the Frankfurt School's perspective to a critical analysis of public bureaucracy, public management, and public policy. These analyses range from such everyday practical concerns as open communication in organizations to broader subjects such as the human struggle for meaning and fulfillment in the bureaucratic age.

A principal contributor to the critical theory of public organizations, Robert Denhardt, uses Habermas's notion of communicative action to diagnose an apparent crisis of legitimacy in the public service. At issue is the pervasive distrust of, and even hostility toward bureaucrats by citizens. This distrust, according to Denhardt, may be construed as

> a perceived lack of congruence between the interests of bureaucrats and those of the public. Under these circumstances, it may well be that the contradictions of interests which appear to exist are, in fact, based in systematically distorted communications between the various parties. Thus, the analysis of structural limitations in communicative practices called for by critical theory would seem a useful place to begin.[69]

In terms of the distinction made earlier between technical and practical interests, bureaucracy serves to reinforce the former. Citizens, on the other hand, especially those who desire more humane treatment or an active role in public discourse, are concerned with the latter. Because of bureaucracy's hegemony over the machinery of public authority, technical interests in efficiency and control leave little if any room for citizens' practical interests in public discourse. In addition to restricting citizen participation in the public sphere, this dominance of technical rationality, Denhardt argues,

[67]Ibid., p. 99.
[68]See, for example, Robert B. Denhardt and Kathryn G. Denhardt, "Public Administration and the Critique of Domination," *Administration and Society* 11:2(1979):107–20; William N. Dunn and Bahman Fozouni, *Toward a Critical Administrative Theory* (Beverly Hills, Ca.: Sage, 1976); and Hummel, *The Bureaucratic Experience.*
[69]Denhardt, "Toward a Critical Theory," p. 632.

manifests itself in an objectification of members and clients and serves the interests of efficiency, but in its preoccupation with the external "objective" world,
acts to depersonalize and rigidify administrative processes. The idea seems to
be that control may be achieved by treating people as data to be manipulated
or as functionaries to be directed from above. The first result of this situation
is that persons are separated from one another and, as a consequence, treat one
another as impersonal objects. A second result is that managers and others are
distracted from *self* reflection. It is this combination of increasing "objectivity"
and decreasing reflexivity which is at the base of both alienation within the
bureaucracy and alienation from the bureaucracy.[70]

As Denhardt sees it, the crucial problems for public administrators are
not primarily problems of effectiveness or efficiency. By definition, these
are *technical,* rather than practical, standards by which to judge administrative performance. Rather, a critical approach to the theory and practice of public organizations would be concerned with exposing patterns
of power and domination both within bureaucracy and in its relations
with the citizens who are served by it. These patterns are mainly evident
in the distortions of communication that are embedded in social institutions, such as bureaucracy, in which power asymmetries are present.

Drawing on Habermas's work, John Forester proposes a framework for
analyzing communicative distortions in organizations. His normative
objective is to enable organizational conditions conducive to discourse
and open communication. Forester begins by identifying how, in ordinary
language, people judge the validity of what they hear and say on the basis
of four claims:[71]

1 a *truth claim* referring to the existence of some state of affairs (e.g.,
   the time of day, another's action, someone's presence, and so on);

2 a *legitimacy claim* to be "appropriately in context," because the
   same words mean different things in different situations;

3 a *sincerity claim* that the speaker really means and intends to say
   what is being said; and

4 a *comprehensibility* or *clarity claim* that what is said has an ordinarily clear and coherent meaning (when this claim is in doubt we
   ask, "What do you mean? Would you say that again?")

When, on any of these four grounds, the listener doubts the validity of
what he or she has heard, a communicative distortion has occurred. This
distortion is experienced by the listener as an affront, because he or she,
unless thoroughly jaded, anticipates that an uncoerced consensus is both

[70]Ibid.; emphasis in original.
[71]John Forester, "Critical Theory and Organizational Analysis," in Gareth Morgan, ed.,
Beyond Method: Strategies for Social Research (Beverly Hills, Ca.: Sage, 1983), pp. 236–37.

possible and natural. Doubt, often sensed only at a subconscious level of awareness, leaves the person feeling misled, deceived, manipulated, or coerced. These feelings may be the result of idiosyncrasies of the particular speaker (for example, from tone of voice), *or* they may result from communicative distortions that are systematically structured into the formal roles mediating the relationship of speaker and listener.[72] This is especially so when institutional roles reflect asymmetries of power. Thus, those in subordinate positions (such as clients and citizens) are likely to feel powerless to confront the validity claims of those who are more powerful (such as government officials). As Forester notes:

> When organizations or polities are structured so that their members have no protected recourse to checking the truth, legitimacy, sincerity, or clarity claims made on them by established structures of authority and production, we may find conditions of dogmatism rather than of social learning, tyranny rather than authority, manipulation rather than cooperation, and distraction rather than sensitivity. In this way critical theory points to the importance of understanding practically and normatively *how* access to, and participation in, discourses, both theoretical and practical, is systematically structured.[73]

Forester's critical approach differs in two related senses from the more conventional human relations strategies described above in Chapter 8. First, he regards *power,* rather than effectiveness, as the principal subject in the analysis of communication. And secondly, the *structural conditions,* in addition to the interpersonal behaviors, that produce distorted communication assume a prominent place in his scheme of analysis. As Forester concludes·

> Because critical theory provides a means of examining how such systematic *institutional* distortions of communication may undermine and threaten our most ordinary sense of what seems to be the case, it provides a provocative, politically and morally illuminating structural phenomenology for examining the nature and consequences of various modes of human organization.[74]

From this discussion, it should be evident that critical theory's perspective on management provides a clear alternative to the efficiency-effectiveness emphasis of mainstream management theory and practice. Although much of its literature has dealt with communication analysis, critical theory's principal message should not be lost amid its often esoteric terminology. Namely, the democratization of social relationships should take precedence over the technical concerns of effectiveness and efficiency. This means that the political significance of discourse about effectiveness and efficiency ought to be exposed and subjected to critical review.

---

[72]Role, in this sense, refers to the forms of meaning that are to be embodied in the actions of persons occupying positions with a given structuring of relationships.

[73]Forester, pp. 239–40; emphasis in original.

[74]Ibid., p. 244; emphasis in original.

This is perhaps the most problematic issue for a theory of public organization, for it raises a fundamental question about the relationship of the individual to the organization. The early management literature was, by and large, sanguine—indeed, took for granted—that organizational and individual needs were basically compatible. From Frederick Taylor to Chester Barnard, organization and management theorists in the United States were unstinting apologists for American capitalism, which was predicated on the assumption of the compatibility of those needs.

With the writings of the managerial humanists such as Argyris and McGregor, doubt began to surface about the ostensibly happy coincidence of management's and workers' needs. Management theory's most pressing question during the 1950s and 1960s became one of how to "integrate" the individual and the organization. In the absence of an explicit social and political theory to guide it, managerial humanism pinned its hopes on a variety of "enlightened" management philosophies and practices in order to bring about that integration. There is, however, an ambivalence evident in its literature about whether, if forced to choose, its loyalties ultimately lie with the individual or with the organization. To defend participation or organization development mainly on the grounds that they are "cost effective" or produce "organizational health" suggests, by implication, that the imputed needs of a reified entity—the organization—are more important than the concerns, interests, and wants of individuals.

The critical theorists offer no utopian alternatives to the bureaucratic approach to organizing. Only through relentless criticism of practices and constructions of meaning associated with bureaucracy can the pathologies that these produce be brought to light, questioned, and contested. To the extent there is a real basis for even that modest hope, the question of two and three decades ago must be recast. As Denhardt has posed it: *"The central question is no longer how the individual may contribute to the efficient operation of the system, but how the individual may transcend that system."*[75] Clearly, this is a time for heroes, not for functionaries.

Interpretive/Critical Theory and the Public Administration Framework

In the sociological literature, interpretive theory and critical theory represent two fairly distinct theoretical perspectives.[76] Although they share

---

[75]Denhardt, *In the Shadow of Organization* (Lawrence, Kan.: The Regents Press of Kansas, 1981), p. 131; emphasis in original.

[76]Some significant attempts to integrate, but also to appreciate the crucial differences between these two perspectives include Bernstein's *The Restructuring of Social and Political Theory* and Anthony Giddens, *The Constitution of Society* (Berkeley: University of California Press, 1984).

somewhat similar epistemological stances, as reflected in their common commitment to the subjective understanding of social action and the similarity of their critiques of positivist social science, they are nevertheless clearly divided on other issues. Principal among these is whether it is either possible or desirable to separate meaningfully the social-scientific interest in description and explanation from the practical and moral interest in improving social existence. With some prominent exceptions, interpretive sociologists in effect answer "yes" by virtue of their endorsement of Weber's commitment to objective, value-free (but still antipositivist) social science. On the other hand, the critical theorists dispute the possibility of value-free social science by claiming that intendedly value-free description and explanation inevitably reinforce and legitimate the "facts" of the current world, with the result that human emancipation from those facts is made difficult, if not impossible.

Although this difference of opinion is a serious one, it appears to have been transcended (or perhaps glossed over) in the American public administration literature. There, interpretive and critical theorists have drawn rather freely from one another and in so doing have forged the foundation, at least, of a synthesis of their positions that overshadows their occasional squabbles with one another. For example, Ralph Hummel, even while declaring himself a phenomenologist, borrows heavily from the critical theory of Jürgen Habermas in his normative critique of public bureaucracy, in addition to the more conventional sources of phenomenological thinking such as Weber and Schutz. Similarly, Michael Harmon, whose "action theory" is mainly influenced by the interpretive theorists, reads in their writings the implicit basis for a normative theory of public administration not greatly dissimilar in intent from Habermas's theory of communicative competence. Finally, Robert Denhardt, usually considered to be a critical theorist, also draws upon phenomenology in support of his critique of public bureaucracy.

It is in its critique of bureaucracy that the synthesis of interpretive and critical theory in the American public administration literature is most clearly evident. In essence, that critique holds that the rationalizing imperative to bureaucracy produces pervasive alienation among both the members of public organizations as well as the citizens who are served by them. Thus, bureaucracy stifles politics and public discourse as traditionally conceived, with the result that bureaucracy becomes the primary arbiter of public values. The practical value of *theory* for that critique is that it provides an important means for systematically exposing the alienation and other social pathologies generated by bureaucracy.

At first glance, bureaucracy's apparently low esteem in the public eye, coupled with mainstream organization theory's frequent insensitivity to the practical uses of theory, would appear to make highly attractive the emerging synthesis of interpretive and critical theory in the American public administration literature. With regard to its critique of bureaucracy, for example, the interpretive/critical position seems to be congenial in overall sentiment with the ambivalent feelings that Americans typically hold about bureaucracy. Much of this ambivalence derives from a traditional American distrust of government generally, for which bureaucracy has served as a convenient, if somewhat abstract, whipping boy. The skepticism with which Americans view bureaucracy, however, is not simply the residue of conservative, antigovernment sentiments. Skepticism also runs deep at the political center, as well as the left, which, beginning in the 1960s, roundly condemned public bureaucracies for being unresponsive to the plaints of the poor and the politically disenfranchised.

Similarly, the avowedly practical role of theory urged by the interpretive and critical synthesis would seem to offer encouragement for practicing administrators who, for quite understandable reasons, have heretofore doubted the value of theory for informing administrative practice. It would be uncharitable, as well as inaccurate, to dismiss these doubts as evidence merely of an implicit anti-intellectualism among practitioners. But it is also true that Americans, including their public servants, usually demand evidence of the "cash value of ideas," to borrow a term from William James, that grows out of their pragmatic political and social heritage.

A comparison of earlier chapters reveals divided opinions about the values and modes of practice that can and ought to be embodied in administrative processes. The conflicts among these proposals typically stem from differing beliefs about the operational definitions of those criteria, the levels of analysis for which they are most appropriate, and their normative priority relative to one another. Despite their many important differences, however, the theorists considered in those earlier chapters are unified by their implicit commitment to a purposive-rational view of organizational action. Not only do they assume that action is naturally directed toward the attainment of some known end, but they also hold that action should be evaluated by how well it succeeds in attaining that end.

By challenging the descriptive and normative bases of rational action, interpretive and critical theorists also suggest radically expanded boundaries of the normative vectors. Efficiency and effectiveness, individual rights and the adequacy of organizational processes, and representation and the control of discretion assume new meanings for these writers, who propose bases for judging the efficacy of action in public organizations that are very different from those offered by theorists representing more established perspectives.

Efficiency and Effectiveness

It is with respect to these most traditional of public administration values that interpretive and critical theory most dramatically part company with the mainstream of organizational theory. Their objections are not primarily to the wisdom of efficiency and effectiveness as such. For example, no one, including the theorists reviewed in this chapter, would prefer (other things being equal) inefficiency to efficiency or ineffectiveness to effectiveness. What is questioned is the belief that bureaucratic efficiency is necessarily, or even very often, compatible with more fundamental values, both of the people who are served by bureaucracy, as well as those who work within it. The mind set of purposive rationality is objectionable because it force fits the unique needs of individuals into uniform and impersonal categories, thus serving the bureaucratic interest of efficient and authoritative disposition. Whatever may be the virtues of efficiency in some larger sense (such as keeping taxes down), its "benefits," in a more immediate sense, are often ones that we would wish neither on ourselves nor our close friends.

In addition to criticizing the impersonality generated by a preoccupation with efficiency, interpretive and critical theory also question a more basic assumption on which the idea of efficiency rests. Specifically, efficiency only has meaning when the ends of action are known in advance. Efficiency is thus an instrumental criterion for judging how quickly and cheaply a particular end is achieved, but it cannot tell us what that end should be. In principle, this would not appear to pose a serious problem. One could simply declare that efficiency is a legitimate criterion for evaluating action when ends *are* known, whereas other criteria, such as equity, fairness, or personal development, should be invoked when the task is to discover what those ends ought to be.

Appealing as this neat division may first appear, however, interpretive and critical theorists argue that the problem is not as simple as consciously deciding among alternative values. Values are not simply matters of conscious, rational choice made by public officials, however well-meaning and conscientious they might be. Instead, values are made manifest in actions defined by the interests and imperatives that accompany formal organizational roles. They have less to do with conscious choice than with the modes of consciousness that have historically emerged through the rationalization of society. As Weber was so keenly aware, the bureaucratic functionary is more an unwitting captive of legal-rational authority than a self-aware and venal oppressor. Against the bureaucratic imperatives of impersonality, control, and technique, even good and humane intentions are unlikely to make much of a difference.

Rights and the Adequacy of Process

As Gibson Winter argued, all social science styles inevitably evaluate social processes within the context of some conception of human fulfillment. With the exception of the present chapter, the theories considered to this point variously depict that fulfillment in terms of the satisfaction of prespecified ends. Sometimes these ends are consciously known by the actors involved, either individually or as they are shared with others. At other times, the basic ends of human action are presupposed by the theorist. In these latter cases, the ends may pertain either to individuals (such as their psychological "needs" or economic self-interest) or to collectivities (including organizational survival, the maintenance of order, adaptation, goal attainment, or the maximization of utility). Underlying each instance, however, is the belief that social processes are merely the instrumental means for attaining those ends.

Accompanying this instrumental view of social process is the way in which mainstream theories conceive individual rights. Consistent with the American liberal tradition, they regard individual rights in an essentially negative manner. That is, rights are seen only as protections against external, usually authoritative, intrusions into one's private affairs. The desire to protect one's rights, furthermore, is assumed to be motivated by acquisitiveness. The individual's *interest*, whatever the particular content, is to receive as much as possible (or at least a fair share) of the scarce supply of society's blessings.

The theorists discussed in this chapter regard this negative conception of individual rights as symptomatic of modern society's moral disintegration. To the extent that it glorifies an atomistic, hedonistic individualism, liberalism is oblivious to the resulting alienation of the individual from society. Alienation results not only from the domination fostered by hierarchical authority, but also from the misguided belief that any single individual's fundamental interests are separate and apart from those of others. Interpretive and critical theory do not deny the necessity to protect the individual from unwarranted intrusions in his or her private life. They object, however, to an emphasis on individual rights that ends up by obscuring the inherently social character of human existence. In other words, protection of the individual from domination by rational, impersonal, and hierarchical authority is necessary for individual fulfillment *within* a social context, not apart from it.

Consistent with their critique of this negative conception of individual rights, interpretive theory and critical theory hold that individual fulfillment is realized through the social processes of a human community. Processes are intrinsically important, inasmuch as they provide the context within which individual projects are developed and human relationships nurtured. The adequacy of social processes, apart from considerations of personal intimacy, must be judged by the degree to which they enable noncoerced discourse and the exercise of self-reflective, critical reason.

Each constituted by language, discourse is overtly social, while self-reflection is a form of internal conversation that is nevertheless profoundly influenced by prior communicative interaction with others. Two principal tasks for organization theory may be inferred from the relationship of language to discourse and self-reflection. The first is to determine how the authority structures in organizations may be altered so as to enable discourse and self-reflection. The second, and related, task is to examine how the formal and informal roles in organizations may inhibit discourse by distorting communication. More broadly, the task of social and organizational theorists is to reveal the means for fostering practical action through undistorted communication both within public organizations, as well as in the larger public sphere.

Representation and the Control of Discretion

The issue of administrative discretion concerns the extent to which administrators do or should make independent judgments in the day-to-day implementation of public policies. Most of the literature on this subject is explicitly normative and is best represented by the classic debate between Carl Friedrich and Herman Finer. Friedrich holds that administrative discretion is indispensable given the complexities of modern government and the inherent ambiguity of public policies. In noting the absence of clear prescriptions for action to cover all possible cases, he argues for the necessity of discretion based on professional expertise and discernment of the prevailing "popular sentiment."[77] Arguing against this position, Herman Finer holds that only the public, through its elected representatives, is capable of defining the popular sentiment (or, as Finer called it, the "public interest"). Administrative discretion, or administrative responsiveness based on felt needs and wants, constitutes a threat to democratic government by undermining the legitimate basis of public authority.[78]

From the standpoint of interpretive theory, much of this traditional debate about administrative discretion misses the mark. Discretion, or any other form of administrative action, necessarily involves not only interpretation of the policy but also interpretation of the particular context to which it applies. Social action, including both the creation and implementation of public policy, is fundamentally an interpretive process. Although one might well propose criteria for wise and judicious interpretation, some form of interpretation—which is to say, discretion—is an inescapable feature of administration. Unless administrators are reduced to mind-

---

[77]Carl J. Friedrich, "Public Policy and the Nature of Administrative Responsibility," in Friedrich and Edward S. Mason, eds., *Public Policy 1* (Cambridge: Harvard University Press, 1940), p. 12.

[78]Herman Finer, "Administrative Responsibility in Democratic Government," *Public Administration Review* 1:2(1941):355–50.

less technocratic functionaries, as Weber feared they would be in bureaucracy, discretion is a fact of life.

Another unsettling aspect of most discussions about administrative discretion is their implicit presumption of its unilateral nature. To the interpretivists, however, the choice is not between strict obedience to rules as opposed to wise and enlightened judgments made singly by the administrator. Rather, the more relevant issue is who and how many are to engage in the interpretation of general policies when they are applied to particular contexts. Moreover, if and when discretionary decisions should be made collectively, rather than unilaterally, then what kinds of authority relationships should govern the making of those decisions? These questions, in turn, affect the meaning of representation.

From the standpoint of interpretive and critical theory, the meaning of representation differs in two significant respects from much of the mainstream public administration literature. First, critical theorists such as Denhardt argue that the imperatives for rational-instrumental action render bureaucracy incapable of representing the citizen's most fundamental interest, which is to participate actively in the public sphere. "Representation" is an uncommon word in the critical theorists' lexicon because it typically implies a passive role for those whose interests are to be satisfied by public agencies. To have any meaning for critical theorists, representation would need to be redefined to promote active engagement by citizens in public decision making, not merely the passive receipt of material things or government services.

Secondly, there is the question of how adequately the interests of the individual citizen can truly be represented by general policies that apply uniformly to all. Often, when practical necessity dictates or when pure public goods are at issue, the question is moot. But, when individuals vary greatly in their subjective understanding of their interests, general or aggregated policies will likely be incapable of accounting for those variations. In such cases, decisions will be "representative" only when those who are served by public organizations actively participate in making the decisions, according to their frameworks of meaning and in terms of what is significant to them.

Conclusion

Chapter 4 suggested several ways in which theory can be of practical use to administrators: as an aid to critical self-reflection, as the basis for normative evaluation, and as a device for understanding the past and the present in novel and counterintuitive ways. It is probably fair to say that, of the perspectives presented thus far in Part III, interpretive and critical theorists explicitly construe the purposes of theory in a manner most fully in keeping with these practical suggestions. Ironically, however, interpretive/critical organization theory may often appear to be the very antithesis of practicality to practicing administrators, at least in part because of its often-arcane vocabulary.

More important, however, is its rejection of the instrumental meaning of practicality that is typically assumed by practicing administrators and mainstream organization theorists alike. The interpretive/critical perspective's critique of instrumentalism and, by extension, of the rationalization of contemporary life induced by bureaucracy have led to both unfamiliar and highly arguable meanings of practicality for public administrators. The result has been to challenge, and even reject outright, some long-accepted beliefs in public administration theory and practice. In their place, interpretive and critical theory have argued that the *practical* use of theory is synonymous with its *moral* purpose.

Where the interpretive and critical theorists of public administration differ from mainstream organization theorists is in their effort to identify the nature of the individual's struggle for freedom and meaning in a bureaucratic age. They see this struggle not only as a moral issue, but as an epistemological one as well. That is, one cannot know or comprehend the existence of that struggle solely through reference to the facts of the social world as they are presently manifested in our conscious awareness. The truth of the struggle's existence lies at least partially hidden in the unconscious. This suggests that the definitive characteristic of the interpretive/critical perspective as revealed in the contemporary public administration literature is the vital distinction that it implicitly draws between "truth" and "fact." To insist that truth is in principle distinguishable from fact does not require a knowledge of the former's particular content, only the acknowledgment of its logical separation from the facts of the current world.

From the interpretive/critical perspective, the positivists of mainstream organization theory, by naively equating fact with truth, fail to recognize the struggle for freedom and meaning. In a similar vein, the interpretivists in sociology, by virtue of their exclusive concern with the subjective character of "social facts," are often inattentive to the wellspring of those facts' creation. Thus, both positivism and interpretive sociology remain essentially conservative and conformist because neither offers a moral perspective within which to comprehend the individual's search for truth, and therefore freedom, amidst the otherwise oppressive and reified facts of the social world. The project of the interpretive/critical theorists in public administration is to offer such a moral perspective.

11

Theories of Emergence: Organizing as Discovered Rationality

The preceding chapter on interpretive and critical theory documented a radical turn away from the mainstream American literature on organizations in several significant respects. First, positivist social science, which regards organizations as unproblematic "facts," was rejected in favor of an epistemology that views organizations as projections of human consciousness—as figments, as it were, of our collective imaginations. Second, the idea that the doings of people are explainable mainly in terms of observable behavior was discarded in favor of Weber's notion that social action is constituted by the subjective meanings that actors give to their behavior. Third, instrumental rationality, traditionally seen as the normative imperative for organizational action, was depicted as a tool for psychic and social domination. Finally, integration of individual and organizational purposes gave way to the notion of individual transcendence of organization.

The present chapter offers four theoretical perspectives on organizations that incorporate broadly similar sentiments. Labeled here as "theories of emergence," their stances with regard to society and politics derive from an essentially psychological orientation.[1] At the same time, the loose

[1]One of the authors dealt with here, Frederick Thayer, would qualify this description, arguing that all social science, including psychology, is derivative of organization theory.

designation of "theories of emergence" only temporarily disguises many differences between them that will become readily apparent as the chapter progresses.

First to be considered is the "integrative" perspective of Mary Parker Follett (1868–1933), whose writings spanned the first third of this century. Heavily influenced by the American pragmatist movement, Follett saw enlightened management as the key to reshaping liberal democratic society so as to promote individual psychological development within a cooperative social context. The extent of Follett's influence, fairly restricted even during her lifetime, waned in the decades following her death. In recent years, however, her thinking has enjoyed a mild resurgence of appreciation, which we intend to encourage further here through a summary of her principal contributions to the organizational literature.[2]

Of the three contemporary approaches discussed in this chapter, only one directly acknowledges Follett's ideas. All do, however, emphasize the emergent rather than the rationally planned quality of organizational action. The first is Karl Weick's "natural selection" theory of organizing, which is based on the belief that organizational purposes and goals are typically discovered retrospectively. Organizing, according to Weick, is largely a sense-making activity performed subsequent to action, which is more or less spontaneous and unplanned. Orion White and Cynthia McSwain's "transformational" approach deals with many of the same themes as Follett and Weick, but chiefly from the psychoanalytic framework of Carl Jung. For White and McSwain, the emergent character of action requires explanation in terms of a theory of the self that accounts for the relationship of unconscious energy to conscious awareness.

Finally, Frederick Thayer's controversial proposal to eliminate hierarchical organization (as well as economic competition and voting) is presented as a radical counterpoint to the more conservative stance toward organizational change proposed by White and McSwain. Thayer, working directly from Follett's ideas, regards the formal requirement of consensual as opposed to hierarchical decision making as essential for the preservation of social, and indeed physical, life on the planet.

Introduction

The idea of rational, instrumental action is so firmly embedded in our thinking about organizations that their very existence seems to be defined by its presence. That *deciding* what to do precedes the *doing* of it is so commonsensical that we may be hard pressed to imagine that action

[2]A recent example of this resurgence is the prominent role her work plays in Louis Gawthrop, *Public Sector Management, Systems, and Ethics* (Bloomington, Ind.: Indiana University Press, 1984).

occurs any other way. Embedded in our common experience, rational action appears intuitively plausible as a description of our everyday activity both within and outside of organizational contexts. This is especially true in the former, so much so that organizations are ordinarily assumed to be the institutional embodiments of rational action.

The belief that rationality may largely explain organizational activity has been the foundational assumption on which, until quite recently, virtually all organization theory rested. At least since Herbert Simon warned of the limits to rational action, few have seriously held to the heroic presumptions of rationality that marked early public administration and management thought. Despite alerting us to the human limitations of intelligence, time, information, and other scarce resources, Simon (like most mainstream theorists) nonetheless regards the *intention toward* rationality as the primary motivation underlying organizational action.[3] Much like the idea of original sin, the belief that we do not always act rationally because we *cannot* do so casts that inability in a distinctly negative light.

The perspectives in this chapter assert that this conventional belief in rational action is unwarranted as both a descriptive and a normative assumption in organizational analysis. The approaches here all argue, from a variety of premises, that such a conception of rational action is a misleading, artificial reconstruction of human action. Each claims that our awareness of the meaning of action (why we act as we do) emerges from social experience. That is, people act more or less spontaneously—either in response to the nature of social situations, changes in their environments, or through the unfolding of unconscious energy—and then seek after the fact, through reflection, to discover what they have done. The implications of this interpretation of action, to the extent it is accurate, are so profound that they force a sweeping revision of both organizational theorizing and the commonsense assumptions that guide our understanding of organizational life.

Although the differences among the theorists here are both numerous and important, their writings share a half-dozen unifying themes that provide coherence to this perspective:

1 Contrary to the instrumentally rational view in which thought precedes, gives rise to, and orients action, it is action that precedes conscious thought. Thus, organizational action, like all other forms of

---

[3]Although we believe that this still reflects his general attitude toward rationality, as described in Chapter 6 above, in a recent work Simon devotes some attention to the idea of "planning without goals" with an eye toward improving the learning-adaptive capacities or organizations. See Chapter 6, "Social Planning: Designing the Social Artifact," in Herbert A. Simon, *The Sciences of the Artificial*, 2nd ed. (Cambridge, Mass.: The MIT Press, 1981), pp. 161–91.

human action, is most appropriately conceived as a process of retrospective sense making, that is, of understanding what we have done after we have done it.

2 Social purposes emerge from social processes. Processes, therefore, are not mainly instrumental means for the attainment of pregiven purposes; rather, social processes are chiefly important insofar as they *generate* rather than achieve social purposes.

3 Change is more natural than stability in organizations. The chief problem for people in organizations is to identify and remove the blockages to change, not to try to create change.

4 Organizations and organizing are logically, as well as historically, prior to politics. A truly democratic theory of politics can only be derived from a humane theory of organizing.

5 Responsible administrative action is fundamentally a matter of self-awareness, rather than one of assuring institutionally or "objectively" correct action. By implication, the task of the administrator is to facilitate self-awareness and, therefore, responsible action—both in others and in himself or herself.

6 Theorizing is a valuable means for facilitating self-aware action, both individually and organizationally. Organizing and theorizing entail essentially similar processes in that both are sense-making activities enabling self-aware action.

Integrative Public Administration: Mary Parker Follett

America's historical belief in progress has been buttressed by an implicit faith in the beneficence of its institutions. For this century's early liberal reformers, who drew their main intellectual inspiration from home-grown philosophical pragmatism, their faith was placed in the *possibility* that institutions could effectively guide social progress. But in their often-sweeping proposals to transform democratic institutions, American reformers nonetheless clung to the belief that individual development and orderly social progress could, and must, go hand in hand. That social and political institutions, in practice, often fell short of societal expectations was evidence more of unenlightened leadership than of the need for revolution.

Just as the intensity of the reform spirit in the United States during this century has ebbed and flowed, so also has the image of public administration as a key instrumentality of that spirit. More often than not, the legitimate societal role of American public administration has been viewed as that of neutral handmaiden to existing political institutions. Woodrow Wilson's vision of an efficient and dutiful bureaucracy has continued to be, all things considered, the preferred normative image, compared with, for example, that of the "New Public Administration" activists of the late 1960s and early 1970s. Although the reality of public administration's inevitably political character has long been recognized, that recognition has also been clouded by an ambivalence stemming from the absence of any widely accepted normative theory to legitimate it.

Fully fifty years before the emergence of the New Public Administration, Mary Parker Follett sought to transform public administration into a vital participant in the democratic order.[4] An "unrestrained pragmatist," Follett envisioned a dynamic industrial age. The new order that she saw constituted a radical yet benign alternative to Marxist revolution, to the prevailing pluralist conception of politics in which static and entrenched interests were pitted against one another, and to the technocratic conception of administration proffered by Woodrow Wilson and many of the writers of the *Papers on the Science of Administration* described earlier in Chapter 6.

Follett's interests as a writer, reformer, and consultant reached far beyond public administration to include vocational education, industrial and labor relations, business management, and the administration of the League of Nations. All of her activities, however, were unified by two deeply held beliefs: (1) her commitment to the pragmatists' idea that experience rather than detached intellectual reflection was the surest guide to the discovery of truth, and (2) a psychology that held that the self does not exist prior to social interaction. Taken together, these two beliefs suggest that human meaning and purpose emerge from social experience. She argued that the task of management is to promote the harmonious integration of individual development within a democratic conception of social progress.

Follett roundly criticized any and all ideas at variance with her central beliefs. A brief summary of some of these ideas provides a clue to the direction of her thinking. First, Follett rejected the view that the *raison d'etre* of industrial organization was the maximization of profits and that workers were mere instruments of economic production. The legitimate

---

[4]For an account of Follett's influence on public administration thought, see James A. Stever, "Mary Parker Follett and Integrative Public Administration," paper presented at the annual meeting of the American Society for Public Administration, Denver, April 1984. Follett's principal works include *The New State: Group Organization the Solution of Popular Government* (New York: Longmans, Green, 1918); *Creative Experience* (New York: Longmans, Green, 1924); and *Dynamic Administration,* Henry C. Metcalf and L. Urwick, eds. (New York: Harper & Brothers, 1940). All page references in parentheses in this section are to the latter two sources; emphasis is in the original unless otherwise noted. The following abbreviations refer to Follett's works: *Creative Experience,* "CE," and *Dynamic Administration,* "DA."

social role of business, she argued, was in effect no different than that of public organizations, namely, to contribute to the broader purposes of human fulfillment and social progress.

Second, Follett criticized the pluralists' notion that politics inherently involved the clash of and, ultimately, the compromise between fundamentally opposing interests. In this vein, she disputed the strategies of organized labor, which saw the interests of workers as inevitably at odds with those of management. Follett was thus a champion of Frederick Taylor, who provided an ostensibly scientific means for integrating organizational goals of productivity with the workers' goals of higher wages and better working conditions.[5]

Finally, Follett was a steadfast opponent of behaviorist psychology, which depicts the individual as passive, pliable, and therefore subject to facile manipulation by external forces and higher authority. Rather, she said, in addition to being inherently social, the individual is (or at least has the potential to be) an active participant in the creation of his or her own experience.

Purpose, Experience, and Rationality

Mary Parker Follett's theory of management and organizaton challenged the assumption of rationalism implicit in the leading management thought of her day. Traditional as well as much now-contemporary management literature sees organizational action as naturally oriented toward the achievement of preconceived ends or purposes. Follett, who regarded this teleological conception of purpose as at best incomplete, insisted that "[a]ctivity always does more than embody purpose, it evolves it" (*CE*, p. 83). Although she shared the liberal's faith in progress, it was a faith that stemmed from an openness to experience produced in creative social process, rather than from a belief in the force of intellectual thought and consciously willed action. For example:

> When we see end [purpose] as involved in the process, we cannot "choose" our ends as we would choose a cause to be loyal to. Life is richer than this: we have a far greater responsibility, a nobler ethics, not less but a larger freedom. Choice is not given up but is put further back in the process. (*CE*, p. 84)

Further:

> Empty will can no longer masquerade as a spiritual force. We can rely neither on facts nor ... on our "strong will," but only on full acceptance of all the

---

[5]She was, in fact, so implacably committed to the possibility of uniting seemingly opposing interests that she gently but firmly rebuked Mahatma Gandhi for failing to seek a "common ground" with the British, who had ruled India for more than a century (*CE*, pp. 103–4).

responsibility involved in our part in that unfolding life which is making both "facts" and ourselves. (*CE,* p. 150)

Follett is perhaps the first "process" theorist of stature in American management thought. She stands clearly apart from the rationalist tradition in boldly asserting that purposes *emerge from social experience,* as do the "facts"[6] of social activity that bear on those purposes. Moreover, there is a distinctly moral tenor evident in Follett's notion of emergent purpose, since the same social processes that give rise to it are also the formative stuff of the individual's development. "Responsibility," mentioned in each of the two preceding quotations, is possible only by active and reflective participation in the social processes through which collective purposes unfold. Responsibility, here, does not mean adherence to an objective standard of truth arrived at through abstract intellectual thought nor obligation to a superordinate source of authority. Rather, in the personal sense that Follett intends, it refers to the self-understanding and self-realization that individuals experience when they invest their emotional energies in collaborative endeavors.

Integration and the Law of the Situation

Follett's idea that responsible action is linked to the emergence of collective purpose gives rise to what she calls "the law of the situation":

> [I]f taking a *responsible* attitude toward experience involves recognizing the evolving situation, a *conscious* attitude toward experience means that we note the change which the developing situation makes in ourselves; the situation does not change without changing us. (*DA,* p. 65)

Whereas the responsible attitude entails commitment, the conscious attitude enables reflection about oneself and the situation so that a kind of objectivity about the latter may be attained. Through this reflective objectivity (our term, not Follett's), both superiors and subordinates would "take their orders" from the situation. One result of the mixture of the responsible and conscious attitudes is to depersonalize orders by *repersonalizing* social relationships. By contrast, the giving and taking of orders that are inappropriate to the situation at hand thwarts both the development of the individual and the emergence of shared purposes. As Follett notes:

> We, persons, have relations with each other, but we should find them in and through the whole situation. We cannot have any sound relations with each other as long as we take them out of that setting which gives them meaning

---

[6]Follett often places quotation marks around the word "facts" to denote their contingent status.

and value. This divorcing of persons and the situation does a great deal of harm. I have just said that scientific management depersonalizes; the deeper philosophy of scientific management shows us personal relations within the whole setting of that thing of which they are a part. (*DA,* p. 60)

For any of this to make sense requires, at a minimum, agreement on one of Follett's basic assumptions, namely, that organizational purposes and individual needs are in the final analysis compatible. Follett obviously parts company here with the critical theorists, although both they and she, starting from radically different premises, end up in much the same place: committed to the democratization of organizational relationships. But while Follett is optimistic about the possibilities for reconciling the individual and the organization, their integration is far from automatic. Integration, in fact, is the defining and most problematic element of effective leadership. The leader, she said, is *not* the one

who is able to assert his individual will and get others to follow him, but . . . the one who knows how to relate these different wills so that they will have a driving force. He must know how to create a group power rather than express a personal power. He must make a team. (*DA,* p. 248)

One should not mistakenly read into Follett's words a disguised organizational boosterism intent on swallowing up the individual in the interests of attaining organizational goals. Although individualists, whether rugged or philosophical, might wince at the collectivist tone of her preachments, Follett is sincerely convinced that the individual's freedom is attained *through* organized relation, not apart from it. Freedom is not freedom *from* others, but freedom expressed through and, especially, *with* others. In this sense, Follett is truly communitarian in her primary sentiments, in contrast with many of her contemporaries whose faith in progress derived from the atomistic individualism of social contract theory.[7]

Follett takes pains to distinguish integration from compromise, which divides individual from individual, group from group, and nation from nation:

[C]ompromise is suppression, and as we have been shown that a suppressed impulse in the individual will be his undoing later, so we see again and again that what has been suppressed in the compromises of politics or labor disputes crops up anew to bring more disastrous results. If according to the Freudians the sane man is one in whom there are no thwarted wishes, the sane industrial group would be one in which neither employer nor workman had compromised, the sane nation would be one not based on log-rolling, the sane league

---

[7]Follett forcefully criticizes contract theory as the philosophical basis of liberal society in Chapter 15, "From Contract to Community," in *The New State,* pp. 122–36.

of nations one in which no nation had made "sacrifices," but where each sought enrichment. Suppression, the *bête noire* of modern psychology, is, in the form of compromise, the evil of our present constitution of society, politically, industrially and internationally. (*CE,* p. 164)

Apparent in this excerpt, and indeed in her writings as a whole, is Follett's attempt to comprehend her own experience in terms of a synthesis of psychology, moral philosophy, and political theory. Follett's theory of management is in effect a theory of politics; this profoundly affects the manner in which she speaks about such perennial concerns in political thought as power, consent, and participation.

On power:

There is an idea prevalent, which I think very harmful, that we give up individual power in order to get joint activity. But first, by pooling power we are not giving it up; and secondly, the power produced by relationship is qualitative, not a quantitative thing. If we follow our rule throughout of translating everything into activity, if we look at power as the power to *do* something, we shall understand this. (*CE,* p. 191)

On consent:

The theory of consent rests on the wholly intellectualistic fallacy that thought and action can be separated. The theory of consent rests on the assumption that we think with our "minds" and we don't. Political leaders are supposed to put something before our minds to which we respond with our minds. Yet how often we see cases where we have not been able to persuade people, by our most careful reasoning, to think differently, but later, by giving them an opportunity to enter on a certain course of action, their "minds" are thereby changed. . . . Mill long ago told us of "torpid assent"—it is not a vital process. (*CE,* p. 198)

On participation:

Thinkers about democracy have passed the stage of merely perfecting mechanisms of voting and representation; their aim is to train minds to act together constructively. The democratic problem is now recognized as the problem of how to get collective action that is socially valid, that is satisfying by the criteria of enlightened living; the problem of how to maintain vigor and creativeness in the thinking of everybody, not merely of chosen spirits. (*CE,* p. 211)

Coordination

Four years after her death, one of Follett's last papers, retitled "The Process of Control," was included in Gulick and Urwick's *Papers on the*

Science of Administration.[8] Predictably, Follett rejected the idea that control should mean domination, either by force of personality or the exercise of hierarchical authority. Control, she said, "is coming more and more to mean fact-control. . . . [Moreover,] Central control is coming more and more to mean the correlation of many controls rather than a superimposed control" (*PC,* p. 161). Control, in sum, is collective self-control and is made possible through coordination. Coordination, in turn, is not an activity performed only by the occupants of particular roles, but is an ongoing process involving everyone in the situation. Therefore, Follett is less concerned with offering instrumental advice about **how to** coordinate than with describing what coordination is. She consistently avoids instrumental prescription in favor of description (albeit heavily laden with evaluative terminology) of what the process of coordination involves. This tone is reflected in what she regards as the four fundamental principles of organization (*PC,* p. 161):

1 Co-ordination as the reciprocal relating of all the factors in a situation.

2 Co-ordination by direct contact of the responsible people concerned.

3 Co-ordination in the early stages.

4 Co-ordination as a continuing process.

By "reciprocal relating" Follett intends to convey the idea that the facts of a situation are constantly altered through a process of mutual adjustment among actors. Facts attain significance by virtue of this process of adjustment, which reveals to the participants the "law of the situation." Individuals derive meaning from their participation, which is necessary in order that they might discover what their interests really are. The individual's real interests cannot be preconceived intellectually prior to cooperative action, but are realized through it. Follett says that

> this reciprocal relating, co-ordinating, unifying is a process which does not require sacrifice on the part of the individual. The fallacy that the individual must give up his individuality for the sake of the whole is one of the most pervasive, the most insidious, fallacies I know. (*PC,* p. 163)

[8]Follett, "The Process of Control," in Luther Gulick and Lyndall Urwick, eds., *Papers on the Science of Administration* (New York: Institute for Public Administration, 1937), pp. 161–69. Originally titled "Basic Principles of Organization," the paper was first presented in a series of lectures that Follett delivered at a conference sponsored by the Department of Business Administration of the London School of Economics in January 1933. It parallels an earlier (1932) American paper, "Individualism in a Planned Society," subsequently published in Metcalf and Urwick's collection of Follett's papers, *Dynamic Administration,* pp. 295–314. Page references to this paper, in parentheses and preceded by the abbreviation "PC," are to the Gulick and Urwick volume.

Follett's second principle, "co-ordination by direct contact of the people concerned," highlights her conviction that coordination cannot be achieved by the vertical giving and receiving of orders. If control is necessarily *self*-control, order giving violates the internal processes by which the individual comes to terms with himself in relation to the situation. This is less a moral dictum than a psychological principle:

> We know that every individual has many warring tendencies inside himself. We know that the effectiveness of an individual, his success in life, depend largely on these various tendencies, impulses, desires, being adjusted to one another, being made into a harmonious whole. Yet no one can issue a fiat by which I am adjusted, I can only be helped to adjust myself. (*PC*, p. 164)

Thus, "direct contact" seems to suggest that horizontal relationships, which by definition preclude order giving, will reveal to actors the relevant facts of the situation. Free from coercion, they make their own adjustments, both intrapersonally and to other actors in the situation.

The third and fourth principles, "co-ordination in the early stages" and "co-ordination as a continuous process," are warnings against the dangerous tendencies for individual actors to fix upon positions prematurely and to assume that, once decided upon, those positions should remain in place. In view of Follett's belief that sensible action emerges from collaborative experience, preconceived and individually held positions tend to thwart the creative processes required for the emergence of such action. Moreover, situations and facts continually change, creating new problems as old ones are solved.

Follett Concluded

Mary Parker Follett's contributions can only be fully appreciated when we consider both the multiple levels to which her writings apply, as well as what might superficially appear to be the paradoxical sentiments that guided her thought. She was a psychologist, but also a political and organizational theorist. She was a moralist; at the same time she was eminently practical. Finally, although Follett rejected socialism, she was not an apologist for business-as-usual, laissez-faire capitalism. She saw the twin evils of coercion and divisiveness underlying both forms of social and economic organization. Alternatives to them were to be found in a profound trust in both the lessons of experience and social unification made possible through cooperative effort:

> We aim then at co-ordination in business because we know that through unity an enterprise generates its own driving force. And this self-generated control does not coerce. But I do not think that this kind of control is sufficiently

understood. Everyone knows that our period of laissez-faire is over, but social-
ists wish to give us in its place state control, and they mean by that state coercion—we find again and again in their pamphlets the words force, coerce.
Those using these words are making the fatal mistake, I believe, of thinking
that the opposite of laissez-faire is coercion. And it is not. The opposite of laissez-faire is co-ordination. (PC, p. 168)

Natural Selection Theory: Karl Weick

We emphasized in Chapter 4 that the most useful theories are often those
that aid us in rethinking our taken-for-granted assumptions about the
world, by leading us to doubt both our senses and our intuition. Karl
Weick's *The Social Psychology of Organizing* provides a provocative
source of such doubt.[9] Because the tone of his book is often whimsical, it
is possible to miss the radical counterintuitive nature of its substance. Virtually every chapter reverses the cause-and-effect assumptions that underlie the conventional wisdom about organizations. Take, for example,
Weick's use of "organizing" in the title of his book:

> The qualifier "organizational" has a kind of stiffness and frozenness that the
> word "organizing" does not. "Organizational" as a qualifier also suggests that
> the topic of interest is substance rather than pattern and form. We believe
> instead that the crucial issues in organizational inquiry turn on issues of pattern
> and form, not on issues of substance. (p. 34)

This, then, prompts a warning and some advice:

> Whenever people talk about organizations they are tempted to use lots of
> nouns, but these seem to impose a spurious stability on the settings being
> described. In the interest of better organizational understanding we should urge
> people to stamp out nouns. If students of organization become stingy in their
> use of nouns, generous in their use of verbs, and extravagant in their use of
> gerunds, then more attention would be paid to process and we'd learn about
> how to see it and manage it. (p. 44)

Weick then proceeds to define organizing in a manner that initially
appears offbeat or even perverse. Organizing, he argues, is a *"consensually
validated grammar for reducing equivocality by means of sensible interlocked behaviors"* (p. 3). The idea of "consensual validation" suggests that
through tacit agreement people make real to themselves and one another
the objects and, especially, the processes of their collective attention. By

[9]Karl E. Weick, *The Social Psychology of Organizing*, 2nd ed. (Reading, Mass.: Addison-
Wesley, 1979); in this section, all page references in parentheses are to this source; emphasis
is in the original unless otherwise noted.

contrast, if the subject of discussion were the noun "organization," the tendency would likely be to regard "it" as existing somehow apart from the active doings of people. Just as in the use of language, *grammar* provides the means by which the activities among people become stable and mutually understandable:

> Organizing is like a grammar in the sense that it is a systematic account of some rules and conventions by which sets of interlocked behaviors are assembled to form social processes that are intelligible to actors. It is also a grammar in the sense that it consists of rules for forming variables and causal linkages into meaningful structures . . . that summarize the recent experience of the people who are organized. The grammar consists of recipes for getting things done when one person alone can't do them and recipes for interpreting what has been done. (pp. 3–4)

Events and conversations mean different things to different people, which is to say that they are *equivocal.* Happenings that represent a change from what has gone before are also equivocal and are precisely the experiences around which people exert their organizing efforts. Things that do not change simply do not require this effort. Further, such acts are meant to be *sensible,* that is, appropriate to the situation, although not necessarily rational in any narrow sense of being consciously directed toward the achievement of a previously determined end. Finally, organizing is necessarily a social activity characterized by the interdependence of social actors, evidenced by what Weick calls *interlocked behaviors.*

What Weick omits from his definition of organizing is as significant as what he includes. He makes no mention, for example, of goals, either of organizations as collectivities or of the individuals who populate them. Thus, the systems theorists' preoccupation with the goal of organizational survival, as well as the public choice theorists' postulate that individual action is motivated by the goal of utility maximization, are implicitly regarded as perhaps interesting fictions but hardly the real motive forces behind organizing activity. At most, the idea of rationality is an explanation used by organization members and theorists to reconstruct meaning from organizational action after the fact.

Indicative of Weick's attitude toward goals, for example, is his commentary on planning, ordinarily assumed to be vital to goal attainment. Citing Michael Cohen and James March, he notes that plans are *symbols* that signal messages to the environment about what the organization is doing or might do; they are *advertisements* used to attract investors and clients; plans are *games* "used to test how serious people are about the programs they advocate" (p. 10).[10] Finally, plans are *excuses for interaction* in that

[10]See Michael D. Cohen and James G. March, *Leadership and Ambiguity* (New York: McGraw-Hill, 1974).

... they induce conversations among diverse populations about projects that may have been low-priority items. The interactions may yield immediate positive results, but such outcomes are usually incidental. (p. 11)

However, for Weick, planning in the sense of a rational, goal-oriented activity is relatively unimportant as an organizational activity. Implicitly echoing the incrementalist critique of comprehensive rational planning described above in Chapter 9, Weick invokes Herbert Simon's idea of "bounded rationality" to argue that decision makers often operate in relative isolation and with limited knowledge about the long-term, overall consequences of their actions. This means that they act in the "here-and-now," engaging mainly in short-term problem solving. To impute rationality to these activities, Weick argues, typically requires a *post hoc* explanation that bears little if any relationship to the conscious, shared motives of the actors.

Although he cites Simon in support of his argument, Weick's theory of organizing has more far-reaching implications in at least three important respects. First, Weick's view of organizing is one that reverses traditional ideas both of cause and effect between activities and events in organizations and of the temporal relationship between them. He approvingly quotes, for example, Cohen, March, and Johan Olsen's description of organizations as "garbage cans":

> An organization is a collection of choices looking for problems, issues and feelings looking for decision situations in which they might be aired, solutions looking for issues to which they might be the answer, and decision makers looking for work.[11]

Taken literally, this definition no doubt overstates the point its authors intend, which is simply that causal relationships in organizations tend to be multidirectional, rather than unilateral. Weick notes that managers' failure to recognize this often creates serious problems for them:

> Most managers get into trouble because they forget to think in circles. I mean this literally. Managerial problems persist because managers continue to believe that there are such things as unilateral causation, independent and dependent variables, origins, and terminations. Examples are everywhere: leadership style affects productivity, parents socialize children, stimuli affect responses, ends affect means, desires affect actions. Those assertions are wrong because each of them demonstrably also operates in the opposite direction: productivity affects leadership style ... , children socialize parents ... , responses affect stimuli ... , means affect ends ... , actions affect desires.... In every one of these examples causation is circular, not linear. And the same thing holds true for most organizational events. (p. 86)

[11]Cohen, March, and Johan P. Olsen, "A Garbage Can Model of Organizational Choice," *Administrative Science Quarterly* 17:1(1972):2, quoted in Weick, p. 21.

Consistent with his preference for verbs over nouns, Weick contends that processes are logically prior to, and are therefore more important than, substantive ends. To quote Weick, "The basic property of interdependence [in organizations] is that patterns and *relations* among variables are the realities that you have to deal with; substances are trivial" (p. 79). Part of the reason for this is his belief, which he shares with Floyd Allport,[12]

> that people converge first on issues of means rather than on issues of ends. Individuals come together because each wants to perform *some* act and needs the other person to do certain things in order to make performance possible. People don't have to agree on goals to act collectively. They can pursue quite different ends for quite different reasons. All they ask of one another at these initial stages is the contribution of their action. (p. 91)

The logical priority of process over substance suggests that what we refer to as structure, as depicted by the noun "organization," is merely a derivative of the patterns of relationships. An organization's structure consists of, to use Weick's term, "repetitive interstructured behaviors" (p. 97). Thus, what is most real are the patterns of relationships among people. There is no underlying reality to organizations that awaits our discovery, since "organizations" are the inventions of people (pp. 11–12).

A further consequence of Weick's emphasis on verbs and processes is to highlight the idea that change, rather than stability, is the rule in organizations. Because verbs have the capacity to depict activity in a way that nouns typically do not, they direct attention to those events that people make happen. Stability, on the other hand, is a necessary but nonetheless artificial condition that humans impose on that change. If change comes about too quickly, we are unable to make sense of it; hence, we need to be able to freeze it, break it up, impose some temporary order on the flow of activity (p. 117).

Another implication of Weick's emphasis on the priority of process over substance is that it suggests our experiencing of organizational events is necessarily indirect. Metaphors are the most common devices employed in making sense of such experiencing and the subsequent explanations of it to others. Metaphors are not merely nice, they are also necessary. Problems arise when people in organizations (and theorists) lack conscious awareness of the metaphors they inevitably must use and thus become wedded to inappropriate or destructive ones. Weick advises managers, therefore, to expand their repertoires of metaphors in order to enhance their awareness of possibilities for understanding and acting creatively. This is advice that Weick, himself, took to heart in writing *The Social Psychology of Organizing,* which is filled with scores of evocative and

---

[12]See Floyd H. Allport, "A Structuronomic Conception of Behavior: Individual and Collective," *Journal of Abnormal and Social Psychology* 64:1(1962):3–30.

sometimes bizarre metaphors, poetry, and cartoons from *Mad Magazine* and *The New Yorker*.

Double Interacts and Organizing

The primary unit for the analysis of organizing, according to Weick, is the *double interact,* which is similar to the face-to-face encounter used by interpretive sociologists. As a primary unit of analysis, it denotes the behavior of at least two people, in obvious contrast to the atomistic individual postulated by most market theorists. Weick, in other words, sees organizing as an inherently social activity in which the

> behaviors of one person are contingent on the behaviors of another person(s), and these contingencies are called *interacts.* The unit of analysis in organizing is contingent response patterns, patterns in which an action by actor A evokes a specific response in actor B (so far this is an interact), which is then responded to by actor A (this complete sequence is a *double interact*). (p. 89)

Double interacts serve to reduce equivocality in a sensible manner.

Natural Selection and Retrospection

What are the dynamics of the organizing process and in what interesting and important ways does that process differ from our usual understanding of it? In broad brush, Weick casts his answer in the metaphor of Darwin's theory of natural selection. Just as Darwin saw evolutionary processes in nature, Weick views analogous processes in social organization as neither good nor bad, which is to say that no assumption of "progress" is implied. Nor is there any assumption that evolution is directed toward a particular end or goal; it is, in other words, nonteleological.

At the same time that Weick takes the natural selection metaphor seriously, he does not take it literally, recognizing that the social and natural worlds differ in ways significant for organizational analysis. For Weick, metaphors may illuminate understanding, but they are neither valid bases of nor substitutes for social philosophy.

His evolutionary model of organizing is based on four interrelated assumptions:

- *Processes* of organizing are primary, while ends or goals are secondary.

- *Change* is a natural condition of organizing, while stability is either an artificially imposed condition or simply does not generate organizing activity.

- Organizing should mainly be thought of as a *sense-making* activity.

- This activity of sense-making is ordinarily performed *retrospectively* (i.e., after the fact), rather than prospectively.

Together, these assumptions help to make comprehensible the most significant, though seemingly cryptic and whimsical, sentence in *The Social Psychology of Organizing*: "How can I know what I think until I see what I say?" (p. 133).

Weick's model of organizing contains four basic steps: ecological change, enactment, selection, and retention. The steps are listed and explained below in their logical sequence, but they are highly interactive, a fact that is crucial to deciphering the implications of his question.

Ecological Change   People engage in organizing activities in response to changes in their environment. This is not to say that *ecological changes* in any way compel people to act in particular ways; only that such changes provide the "raw materials for sense-making" (p. 130). Environments in Weick's model play a far less deterministic role than in, say, mainstream systems theory. Moreover, the reference to change simply captures the commonsense notion that organizing is not likely to occur when things in the environment stay the same. The most significant aspect of ecological change is its relation to the second step of the model, enactment.

Enactment   Weick frequently refers to "enacted environments," a term intended to convey that people, through organizing, actively create the environments that subsequently impinge on them. Seen in this light, the environment is as much an output as a source of inputs (p. 228). *Enactment* depicts the idea that perception (a word Weick prefers to avoid because of its often passive connotation) of the environment is a highly active process, and, unlike the latter two steps in the model, enactment is the only step in the organizing process in which people actively engage with the raw materials of ecological change. This is where a person "wades into the swarm of 'events' that surrounds him and actively tries to unrandomize them and impose some order" (p. 148).

Enactment is an attempt to freeze our experience of events so that we may hold them up for inspection. We should remember, however, that these events are not just "out there" awaiting our discovery, for we play important roles either in creating those events or in attributing importance to them. Weick describes this process as *efferent sense-making.*:

> The modifier *efferent* means centrifugal or conducted outward. The person's idea is extended outward, implanted, and then rediscovered as knowledge. The discovery, however, originated in a prior invention by the discoverer. In a crude

but literal sense, one could talk about efferent sense-making as thinking in circles. Action, perception, and sense-making exist in a circular, tightly coupled relationship that resembles a self-fulfilling prophecy. (p. 159)

Enactment provides the key for understanding the nature of environments and thus of ecological change. Environments, quite literally, are not external to us. To assume a logical separation of the individual and the environment "excludes the possibility that people *invent* rather than discover part of what they think they see" (p. 166).

Selection   Organizational enactments are virtually always equivocal in their meaning. Those events in the environment that we selectively perceive and toward which we tentatively direct our attention are, like puns, subject to a variety of interpretations as to their meaning and importance. *Selection,* the next step, is the process by which we make sense of organizational enactments. In Weick's formula "How can I know what I think until I see what I say?" enactment is "saying," that is, engaging directly with the events (raw materials) of one's environment. Selection depicts the process of imposing interpretations on enactments, that is, "seeing," retrospectively, what has been said. Selection, by placing interpretations on what we have directed our attention to, reduces the equivocality of enactments and thus enables us to construct a context within which we may act sensibly:

> Selection is the organizational process that generates answers to the question "What's going on here?" The selection process selects meanings and interpretations directly and it selects individuals, departments, groups, or goals indirectly. The selection process houses decision-making, but it is crucial to remember that decision-making in the organizing model means selecting some interpretation of the world and some set of extrapolations from that interpretation and then using these summaries as constraints on subsequent acting. (p. 175)

The direction of causality in the model (enactment followed by selection) may often be reversed. That is, our predispositions to see events in the environment in a particular way may lead us to reduce the equivocality of our enactments to a greater degree than may be otherwise warranted by the situation. As a practical matter, then, Weick advises managers to be wary of cognitive processes of selection that may impose an unwarranted degree of order upon the environment. Enactments, in other words, should be "loosely structured" in order to allow for adaptive actions that are flexible and improvised (p. 187). Sensible action, it appears, requires (1) an ability to discern a degree of equivocality roughly proportional to the degree of "variety" in the environment, while (2) reducing equivocality to a degree sufficient to permit an orderly context for action. In our efforts to strike a reasonable balance between these two requirements, however, Weick sees the first as the more difficult to sustain:

> At least perceptually, the problem for organizations is *not* one of entropy and the loss of order, it's just the opposite. Orderliness is overestimated and erroneously given credit for adaptive success. Having been credited, orderly actions are implemented again in the future, perhaps tightened even more, and suddenly . . . the organization finds itself saddled with an antiquated, tight structure. (p. 186)

Only in exceptional circumstances, Weick suggests, is the degree of equivocality so great that it paralyzes action. Order, in a word, is a bigger problem than chaos.

The retrospective nature of action, including organizing, is also explained by Weick's view that enactment (saying) precedes selection (seeing). Put more briefly, and in obvious contrast to the rational model of action, "Action precedes thought" (p. 194). Doing something requires such an active and immediate engagement with the objects of our attention that only *afterwards* are we able to stop and reflect on, to "see," what we have done.

To leave the matter at that, however, may give the false impression that action is merely accidental, random, or purposeless. To correct this, Weick draws from Alfred Schutz's idea of "future perfect" thinking and its relations to acting. Cast in Weick's terminology, future-perfect thinking is a way of imagining (enacting/"saying"/doing) an action by viewing (selecting/"seeing") it as already having been done. He quotes Schutz on this subject, who said that:

> The actor projects his action as if it were already over and done with and lying in the past. It is a full blown, actualized event, which the actor pictures and assigns to its place in the order of experience given him at the moment of projection. Strangely enough, therefore, because it is pictured as completed, the planned act bears the temporal character of pastness. . . . The fact that it is thus pictured as if it were simultaneously past and future can be taken care of by saying that it is thought of in the future perfect tense.[13]

The idea of future-perfect thinking, then, retains the core idea that action precedes thought, but permits a prospective view of action in a temporal sense in which we imagine the meaning of it as if it were already accomplished, thus enabling us actually to perform that action.

[13]Alfred Schutz, *The Phenomenology of the Social World* (Evanston, Ill.: Northwestern University Press, 1967), p. 61, quoted in Weick, p. 198. See Chapter 10 for a discussion of Schutz's phenomenology of thinking.

Retention   The final step of the organizing model depicts "meaning" or "believing" ("knowing what I think"). Retention is the process of holding onto, for periods of time, those interpretations of experience that appear to have longer-term validity. Retention involves, among other things, the storage of "cause maps" that tell us how some events, procedures, and actions relate to others over time. This term conveys the idea that some of the enactments that people select are retained in memory, whereas others are forgotten.

The importance of retention lies in the fact that remembered beliefs about the significance of particular events and of patterns of cause and effect help us establish routine ways of doing things. This helps us maintain a degree of order amid the constant flow of organizational events. Retention, however, works directly at odds with enactment, the process by which changes in the environment are first identified and held up for scrutiny. The degree to which a belief is retained varies inversely with our ability to identify changes when they occur, that is, to create new enactments. Established procedures, including taken-for-granted ways of seeing the world, dampen our capacity to identify environmental change when it occurs and therefore inhibit the development of alternative modes of action to respond to that change.

The tension between retention and enactment brings to mind novelist E. McGlashan's comment that "Man must remember if he is not to become meaningless, and must forget if he is not to go mad."[14] Creating the proper balance between remembering and forgetting constitutes, for Weick, a most crucial and enduring practical problem for people in organizations. But they ordinarily err on the side of memory, which, he says, should be treated as a pest (p. 221). Thus, it is important for managers to retain less than they ordinarily do, and this requires a term to describe the opposite of retention, namely *discrediting*.

Discrediting involves doubting what we know or assume to be true by imposing equivocality on previous enactments, selections, and retentions. Sometimes, the equivalent of discrediting occurs when accidents, external events, or superordinate decisions serve to eliminate the sources of institutional memory. For example, records are lost, the enemy bombs the files of the bureaucratic apparatus (as Albert Speer approvingly reported in *Inside the Third Reich*), or manuals of standard operating procedures are deliberately destroyed. (U.S. National Park Service Director George Hartzog reportedly did this in the late 1960s so that subordinates would have to decide for themselves how to act sensibly.)

Although large-scale discrediting may sometimes be accomplished institutionally, discrediting in a more personal sense simply involves a dif-

---

[14]E. McGlashan, *The Savage and Beautiful Country* (Boston: Houghton Mifflin, 1967), p. 5; quoted in Weick, p. 205.

ferent way of thinking about the relationship between acting and doubting. While, in part, discrediting means to doubt what one knows for certain, it also may mean to act *decisively* in the face of doubt, to impose a certainty that denies one's doubts:

> To doubt is to discredit unequivocal information, to act decisively is to discredit equivocal information. When things are clear, doubt; when there is doubt, treat things as if they are clear. That's the full and symmetrical meaning of discrediting. (p. 221)

Organizing and Theorizing

The Social Psychology of Organizing is less a book about theory than about theorizing. In view of Weick's preference for verb forms, we should not be surprised at this. But the fact that "organizing" and "theorizing" are both verb forms is more than simply an interesting parallel or a reassuring sign that Weick thinks and writes consistently. Rather, although Weick himself does not quite make the point explicit, organizing and theorizing amount to virtually the same thing. After all, Weick's entire discussion of organizing, including his definition of it, describes that process as fundamentally a *sense-making* activity.

Similarly, theorizing, although it *may* be much more than that, is at the very least a sense-making activity as well, one of the few aspects of theorizing on which there is general agreement. If we accept as useful or plausible Weick's definition of organizing, then what theorists mainly do is organize, and what organizers (such as managers) do is theorize. In a quite literal sense, then, practicing managers theorize all the time, a fact that should force us to reconsider what we ordinarily mean by the so-called "theory/practice gap." Since managers do theorize continually, the overall thrust of Weick's advice is that they should do so much more self-consciously, with greater variety and imagination than they often now employ and with an expanded awareness of how existing organizational routines and habits of thought inhibit effective theorizing.

As an intendedly practical book about theorizing, *The Social Psychology of Organizing* is far less concerned with empirical findings than with images and metaphors. Although Weick scatters his own metaphors in great profusion, his book offers an invitation, a framework, and a series of methodologies to assist managers in creating their own metaphors and images for sense-making. The four-step model of organizing, seen in this light, should not be regarded mainly as a theory to be proved or disproved, but as a "metatheory" on the basis of which managers may construct theories appropriate for their particular circumstances.

Weick Concluded

Weick concludes his discussion with the admonition to "complicate yourself" (p. 261). "To be complicated is to take pleasure in the process rather than pleasure in the outcome. That holds true for the process of theorizing as well as for the process of managing" (p. 263). In fact, the idea that process is intrinsically important, rather than simply a means to an end, is perhaps the most persistent theme in *The Social Psychology of Organizing*. Weick's organizing model depends not upon a grudging recognition of the cognitive and psychological "limits" to rationality noted by Simon and various systems, human relations, and market theorists reviewed in earlier chapters. Instead, the retrospective view of organizing, in which "rationality" is discovered after the fact, depicts for Weick the natural processes involved both in organizing and in acting more generally. Only with an appreciation of his belief in the primacy of process over substance can one understand why he intends the last sentence of his book to be taken with utmost seriousness:

> Organizations keep people busy, occasionally entertain them, give them a variety of experiences, keep them off the streets, provide pretexts for story-telling, and allow socializing. They haven't anything else to give. (p. 264)

Transformational Theory: Orion White and Cynthia McSwain

Although Weick presents a novel, and in many respects an appealing, discussion of *how* organizing processes occur, it is outside the scope of his inquiry to explain *why* they occur. He gives us few clues regarding the wellspring, the prime motive force that leads people to engage in organizing activity or, more generically, to act. He is clearly unsympathetic to the determinism of the more positivistic variants of systems theory (not to mention behaviorist psychology) that explain acts of organizing almost exclusively in terms of system or environmental "imperatives." And he would no doubt regard as sterile and simplistic those psychological theories that attempt to explain action in terms of a limited number of psychological needs or drives. Finally, his "retrospective" stance regarding rationality would presumably lead Weick to look askance at the self-interest/utility-maximizing motive postulated by the market theorists.

For Weick, motives at a conscious level of awareness follow rather than precede action (at least in terms of articulation and self-understanding). He thus sees people as active, rather than passive, but guided by motives that they usually understand more fully only after acting. His rejection of the view that action derives from consciously rational motives, however, makes all the more glaring the absence of a theory of the self (or the psyche) to explain even in general terms the psychological dynamics of his organizing model. This absence of a theory is crucial, because we are left without guidance in considering some basic value questions regarding public organizations or for determining, in the context of Weick's own model, why some processes of organizing are preferable to others. To be consistent with the major themes of the natural selection model, such a theory of the psyche should see people as active agents, but not as especially consciously rational in their actions. That is, the psychological theory should account for the retrospective (or emergent) nature of rationality through reference to unconscious forces that govern action and personal development. Any such theory of the psyche would reflect Weick's bias toward the primacy of processes, rather than "substance" or end states.

Of the contemporary literature in public administration, these requirements appear to be most nearly satisfied by transformational organization theory, presented in the works of Orion White and Cynthia McSwain. Inspired principally by the analytical psychology of Carl Jung, transformational theory not only grapples with some important issues that are not dealt with by Weick, but offers a provocative basis for understanding the nature of organizational change and development. In doing so, it addresses some of the most significant value questions in public administration.

Like most other developments in organization theory, the transformational approach grows out of an acute disillusionment with, in part, existing theoretical approaches, but more particularly with organizations and governments whose failed efforts reflect the failed theories on which those efforts are implicitly based. The failure of mainstream organization theory, as White and McSwain see it, may be traced to its neglect of the vital role of unconscious energy in shaping both individual development and social life.

Levels of Organizational Reality

The vantage point of this perspective is the individual self, or psyche, which confronts the world simultaneously on four levels of reality: structural, social relations, nomological, and human-encounter. Movement from the structural to the human-encounter level brings us ever closer to what White and McSwain regard as the prime motive force behind organizing activity, as well as human action more generally.

The first of the four (see Figure 11.1) is the *structural level,* which depicts what we usually mean when we think about organizations as large

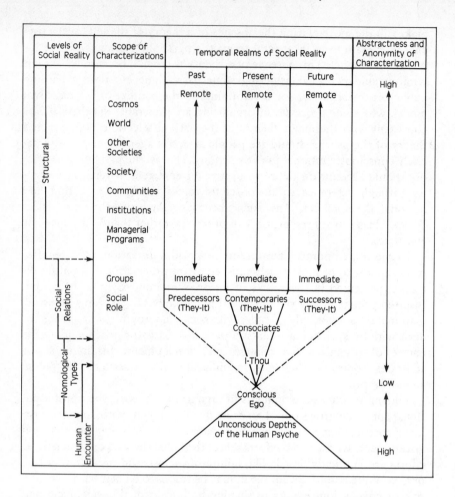

Figure 11.1 *A Transformational Approach to the Analysis of Social Reality*

Source: Orion F. White, Jr. and Cynthia McSwain, "Transformational Theory and Organizational Analysis," in Gareth Morgan, ed., *Beyond Method; Strategies for Social Research*, Beverly Hills, Calif.: Sage Publications, 1983, p. 239.

and discrete entities. It is, however, the least real of the four levels in the sense of individual consciousness, because it is the most remote from our immediate lived experience. Consistent with the interpretive theorists of the preceding chapter, White and McSwain note that "These patterns can be construed as a residual phenomenon" of human consciousness, rather than having an existence independent of consciousness.[15] The second level, *social relations,*

> refers to the realm of social consciousness or life world, in which individuals negotiate and renegotiate with others. It is the world of directly lived experience in which individuals engage and interact with others through conversation and other modes of discourse. This level provides the focal point of action in organizational life.[16]

These first two levels of reality correspond closely to the usual focuses of analysis used by sociologists and social psychologists. The final two levels, by contrast, delve into two psychological areas rarely addressed by either of these, that of conscious awareness and, finally, the unconscious. The *nomological,* as the third level,

> ... refers to the realm of individual consciousness. This realm contains many types of consciousness through which individuals experience and construe reality in different ways, ... These different modes of consciousness reflect preferences or styles of coping with the outside world. In these different kinds of conscious attitudes, psychic energy assimilates and integrates information from experience in different ways. . . .[17]

The fourth level, and for White and McSwain the primary beginning point of analysis, is the *human-encounter level,* which

> involves a dialogue with the deepest levels of the human psyche. This process is activated by energy from the depths of the psyche, flowing through the medium of symbols into the conscious ego and the external world. This unconscious energy exerts a major impact on thought and action in the world, whether this is directly recognized or not.[18]

Individual consciousness (the nomological level) is unconscious energy that has been transformed. Personal maturation is the process by which this energy increasingly comes under the control of the person and therefore becomes more available to conscious awareness, thus enabling autonomous action. "The project of human life is seen as the development of an appropriate relationship to the unconscious such that unconscious energy is transformed or made available to consciousness."[19]

---

[15]Orion F. White, Jr. and Cynthia J. McSwain, "Transformational Theory and Organizational Analysis," in Gareth Morgan, ed., *Beyond Method: Strategies for Social Research* (Beverly Hills, Calif.: Sage, 1983), p. 294.

[16]Ibid.

[17]Ibid.

[18]Ibid.

[19]Ibid., p. 295.

The unconscious plays the preeminent role in the individual's maturation; this also profoundly influences, via the notion of *projection,* the individual's relation to others and to the social world. That is, unconscious energy supplies the force that links the four levels of social reality. In view of the highly technical nature of explaining why this is so, we take the liberty of quoting at length a portion of White's summary of Jung's analytical psychology:

> Roughly speaking, analytical psychology sees the human being as existing simultaneously in two co-equal worlds: the everyday world of physical reality which operates by causal laws; and synchronous to this world, the world of "non-ordinary reality," to borrow a term, which consists of the psychic forces within the individual and which are acausal in nature. This world of psychic forces is the unconscious, consisting of a personal and a "collective" or transpersonal element. Jung apparently saw the psyche of the individual in evolutionary terms, as highly structured and conservative as the human body itself. The unconscious psyche, that is, its collective element, can operate autonomously and govern the individual's life as a set of instinctual reactions. In a totally unconscious state, as one imagines the primitive mind to be, the unconscious psyche in the form of instincts totally determines the individual's life. In this state, without consciousness, the individual cannot see reality at all, in that the instincts operate by causing powerful "projections" to occur within the individual and to which he reacts instead of to real situations. Hence, the primitive feels his dreams to be as real as his waking experiences. The task of personal psychological development, then, is seen as being able to bring these powerful instinctual forces under control, such that one becomes free of the projections they cause and is better able to encounter reality. . . .
>
> [T]he transformation of psychic energy involves what is essentially a scientific process, a process whereby the individual seeks to see reality instead of his own projections about it. But the key to the process is not mechanically to follow a method, but to maintain a scientific, that is to say, an *open* attitude toward information coming from the other. It is this attitude which is the essence of all science.[20]

Social Relationships

Individual psychological development entails two seemingly paradoxical aspects of the individual's relationship with others. First, such development requires that a healthy distance be maintained between the individual and society. This distance is necessary in order that the individual may make choices based on his or her personal wants. When such distance is maintained, social relations are characterized by *interaction* among

---

[20]White, "Psychic Energy and Organizational Change," Sage Professional Paper in Administrative and Policy Studies, 1,03–001 (Beverly Hills, Calif.: Sage, 1973), pp. 24–25.

people. The opposite and pathological tendency is toward *crowding,* wherein distance in social relations is obliterated, with the result that genuine individual choice is precluded. Crowding most obviously occurs in anarchic mobs, but, ironically, arises also from formal social arrangements designed to prevent crowding. One such example is the overuse of authority through the device of the *command.* As White describes it:

> The command, as a form of symbolic action, is a "reaching out" of one individual into the space of another so as to "shove" or "push" the person. A direct connection (no space in between) is thereby established and both the commander (or the master) and the commanded (the slave) become participants in a crowd dynamic which ensures a negative fate for both—the loss of their humanity or their human possibility. They begin to suffer the oppression of each other, which is of course the prototype phenomenon of the crowd.[21]

For White disorder in the social system results from problems in the *relations between* people, rather than from pathologies inherent in the people themselves. "[A]s long as the wants occur to the individual under conditions where the conscious and the unconscious attitudes are in dialectical balance," we have nothing to fear from the authentic expression of those wants.[22] Thus, the Jungian view of the individual's natural developmental orientation is an optimistic one as judged by the salutary social consequences that accrue from that development.

Social distance, then, is required between the individual and the social order so that interaction rather than domination may mediate their relations. Paradoxically, such distance is developed and maintained by social relationships characterized by trust and mutual acceptance. Only when such relationships exist is it possible for the individual to perceive clearly (i.e., nondefensively) himself or herself in situations and in relation to others, rather than see those situations and relations in terms of unconscious projections. Relationships governed by mutual acceptance, in other words, are needed to help the individual mediate the dialectic between unconscious energy and conscious awareness.

Language and Social Relationships

If domination is the means by which healthy social distance is collapsed and individual choice denied, then the question arises as to how such dom-

---

[21] White, "Psychological Aspects of Action Theory: An Apologia (Qualified) for Bureaucratic Jargon and Other Ugly Language—Including Awkward Titles," paper presented at the annual meeting of the American Society for Public Administration, April 1978, p. 18. For a provocative examination of the pathologies associated with crowding, see Jerry B. Harvey, "The Abilene Paradox: The Management of Agreement," *Organizational Dynamics* 3:1(1974):63–80.

[22] White, "Psychic Energy," p. 18.

ination, or indeed any form of social control, is achieved in the first place. The transformational perspective, consistent in some respects with the position taken by Weick, argues that domination is mainly a function of the forms of language that people employ in their conversations with one another. Like Weick, the transformational theorists view all situations as (1) inherently equivocal (that is, subject to numerous interpretations of what is going on) and (2) essentially unique in that each situation is sufficiently different from other situations that generalized standards of assessment and judgment have only limited applicability. The equivocality and uniqueness of situations, however, require modes of conversation that differ greatly from the *judgmental* mode implicit in the model of rational action associated with bureaucratic behavior and large-scale programmatic action:

> The process of action in the traditional model proceeds from analysis, to decision, to implementation. The centerpoint is *conclusive decision* or *judgment* about what is the most satisfactory course of action. The language of policy analysis and administration is a language of evaluation and judgment. These are its central concerns. What is represented in the alternative being raised to replace judgmental action is a mode of action that includes a much greater emphasis on perception, or finding out what the situation is before one acts because little credence is any longer given past judgments about what are effective lines of action. What is valued is not *knowledge* (information evaluated, categorized and stored), but *information* itself—currently perceived data.[23]

Judgmental language, then, imposes an artificial and often unwarranted uniformity across situations that denies their inherently equivocal and unique character. Such appearances of uniformity are represented by language and are maintained authoritatively through acts of domination. These acts of domination not only produce a false sense of certainty about situations, but, by limiting open communication, also inhibit healthy individual development by eliminating the necessary distance between the individual and the social (or organizational) order. Drawing upon the critical theory of Jürgen Habermas, White describes the oppressive effect that judgmental language produces in individual development and social relations:

> [J]udgment creates a form of false consciousness of meaning in interpersonal communication, whereby the individual comes to believe that conversation that is evaluative of others is of greater interest than conversation that is descriptive of one's own life experience and of the experience that one is having in relation

---

[23]White, "Some Notes on Language and the Politics of Paradigmatic Change," paper presented at the annual meeting of the American Society for Public Administration, April 1976, p. 15, emphasis in original.

to the other party in the conversation.... [This is] a form of language that typically speaks only *about* but not *of* experience and as such is alienating and oppressive in the most insidious of ways. In this form of language judgment is the sole content.[24]

To counteract the insidious tendencies of judgmental language, White proposes two normative criteria of language that may assist in maintaining a healthy social distance between people so as to promote a dialectical balance between the unconscious and the conscious attitude. The first criterion of language is that of *reflexivity,* that is, language that vividly reflects back to the individual what he or she has been doing. Such language is descriptive, rather than judgmental; specific, rather than general; and intends to capture the idiosyncrasies of the particular situation in which the individual finds himself or herself. "A reflexive language is one that describes behavior in such a manner that the actor is 'faced' with his or her actions," so as to hold the person's attention and mobilize reflection.[25] This idea is implicit, for example, in the widely taught techniques associated with interpersonal "feedback" or "leveling." Here learners are urged to avoid prescribing what another person *should* do in favor of accurate and vivid description of what he or she *is* (or seems to be) doing. Nonreflexive language, on the other hand, tends to be not only judgmental and general in nature, but also tends to "gloss" over what the person has been doing by, for example, being overly nice or euphemistic.

The second normative criterion of language is its *relationality,* that is, language that acknowledges the distance between one individual and another. Instead of implicitly claiming to be "objectively true" statements about the other person (thereby intruding into that person's life space), relational statements are those that "own up" to the speaker's subjective and therefore possibly fallible interpretation of what the other person *seems* to be doing. The typical form that relational statements take is to begin with the pronoun "I," rather than to attribute a meaning or motive to the other person through the use of "you." In the parlance of organizational development practitioners, "I-statements" show a willingness to acknowledge the personal and subjective character of one's statements, thereby respecting the other person's right to make independent choices. Even the act of questioning, though often regarded as evidence of an innocently inquiring mind, is subtly dominative and violates social distance by "demanding that the other enter your own taken-for-granted world."[26] That is, questions are almost invariably "leading" and thus manipulative to some degree. Like statements that pretend to be objective, questions

---

[24]Ibid., p. 16, emphasis in original.
[25]White, "Psychological Aspects of Action Theory," p. 24.
[26]Ibid., p. 26. For further explication of this argument, see Schutz, *The Phenomenology of the Social World.*

dissolve the social distance between people that is required for autonomous choice.

Transformational Processes Versus Achievement of End States

For reasons similar to Follett's and Weick's, transformational theorists
place much greater emphasis, both descriptively and normatively, on processes than on substance or end states. This emphasis on process flows
almost automatically from the belief that we cannot consciously know, at
least in any fundamental sense, what are the goals or end states toward
which individual (much less, organizational) action and development
should be directed. Given the central role played by the unconscious, the
specification in advance of a preferred end state of either individual or
organizational development is necessarily arbitrary, thus requiring legitimation by means of domination. Further, the presumption that one particular end state of development is appropriate for everyone denies the
unique pattern by which unconscious energy unfolds in each individual.

The transformational perspective also shares Weick's belief that "rationality"—the meanings and intentions of one's actions—is gradually discovered retrospectively. This calls into question the wisdom of using the
instrumental model of rational action to judge the "correctness" of action.
If action cannot legitimately be judged as correct or incorrect in terms of
the instrumental criterion of a prespecified end, then we are left with no
alternative but to concern ourselves with the quality of the *processes* by
which individuals mature and develop. In particular, our concern more
properly should rest with facilitating processes that encourage *responsible*
action that is self-aware and critically reflexive, rather than with trying to
ensure "correct" action as determined instrumentally by standards, judgments, moral principles, or the exercise of authority.

Action as Conversation: What to Say Next

From the preceding analysis, we can discern two interrelated aspects
that ground our understanding of what organizational action is: (1) *processes* by which unconscious energy unfolds and is made accessible to conscious awareness via (2) *language,* which mediates social interaction and
enables us to understand what we have been doing (retrospection) and to
visualize what we *might* do in the future. As with Weick, then, *doing* is
saying. From White's perspective, action is seen

> as essentially a flow of information and affect (emotion or personal energy) that
> is carried in conversation and other forms of speech and out of which, if one
> wishes to insist on the distinction, physical action flows. In our view, though,

all action can be seen as speech and can be considered, to the extent that it is problematic, as a speech problem. What it comes down to, then, is that the issue of action amounts to the question of *what to say next.* This question, in turn, involves a centrally important personal moral issue that is equivalent to the issue of public morality, viz., "who am I if I 'say' (this)?" or "What does 'saying' (this) mean about who I am or me as a person?" . . .

We can extend our analysis of action to one final point: Effective action becomes, in light of our alternative conceptualization, *being able to think of something to say next,* and as a corollary, *maintaining the personal disposition* (i.e., *feeling good enough) to continue talking.*[27]

The idea that action should be understood as processes of speech gives us some insight, then, about how to regard *problems* in acting. Note that in the instrumental/rational model of action, problems are defined as the inability to achieve a prespecified end or goal. Viewed from the transformational perspective, however, "'problems' occur only when the action process becomes stalled. Problems are *stopped process.*"[28] Generally speaking, these stalled processes result from "glossed perception," which means that the actor is out of touch with what is going on in the situation. Unblocking action is achieved, at least in part, through conversation with others (and also in internal dialogue) that employs highly reflexive and relational language. Conversation that employs such language is intended to be *confrontational,* that is, "designed to face the actor with the task of constructing the situation—of focusing concretely on it and finding new meanings in it."[29] In general, then, language forms are crucial by virtue of their power to clarify, or alternatively to distort, the individual's understanding of his or her relationship to a particular situation.

Managing as Facilitating Personal Action

The role of the manager, to the transformational theorists, is to *facilitate personal action.* This entails assisting employees in identifying the reasons for blocked actions by helping them to see disparities between their feelings and attitudes toward their organizational roles, on the one hand, and the apparent requirements of the particular situations in which they find themselves. Accordingly, the manager "must work from the presumption that only the people directly involved in the problematic situation do and can have a direct apprehension of it."[30]

---

[27]White, "A Structuralist Approach to Organizational Action," paper presented at the annual meeting of the American Society for Public Administration, April 1983, pp. 21–22, emphasis in original.

[28]White, "Public Management as the Facilitation of Personal Action," *Praxis* 2:2(1977):14.

[29]Ibid., p. 14.

[30]Ibid., p. 15.

It follows, then, that the exercise of managerial authority entails confronting employees with the personal nature of their responsibility, rather than unilaterally imposing, through meting out rewards and punishments, courses of correct action. As White notes,

> [T]he manager must be willing to *confront*, . . . to *face* the actors to the situation when it appears their perceptions of it are glossed or stereotyped. This means in more conventional terms that the manager must be willing to stand on the authority of his or her office and represent the necessity of "owning" one's own part in problematic situations. The role of authority is in helping block projections of responsibility onto others.[31]

The meaning of responsibility, as described here, is primarily a psychological one. It describes the process by which the employee, with the assistance of the manager, is encouraged to view himself or herself in situations realistically—which is to say, in a critically self-reflexive manner—rather than to construct those situations on the basis of unconscious projections of psychological energy. There is also an implicit premise, deriving from their optimistic assumptions about people, that when employees "know what they are doing" in this critical, self-reflexive sense, their actions by and large will satisfy the usual social or organizational tests of responsible action. Such a view of responsible action for employees also carries with it the presumption that the manager, in order to be credible to his or her subordinates, should be capable, and be perceived as being capable, of responsible action, as well. That is, if the manager is perceived as unreflexively acting out his or her own unconscious projections, subordinates will inevitably see the manager's actions as inauthentic, manipulative, and therefore irresponsible.

The Role of Ethics and Values

The public administration literature offers up numerous guides for administrative action. Although their contents may differ, they agree that some overriding ethical value or premise ought to be employed in evaluating a particular administrative action. Two assumptions underlie this approach to administrative ethics, both of which are eyed with doubt by the transformational theorists. The first assumption is that the primary orientation of administrative action in particular, as well as personal action more generally, comes out of a *conscious attitude*. The second, and closely related, assumption is that a particular end state or condition can be identified to provide a relatively stable reference point in order to deter-

---

[31] Ibid.; emphasis in original.

mine "good" or "proper" behavior. To the extent this second assumption is warranted, then stable rules and guidelines may be developed (and enforced) to orient action. Ethical action, in this view, is correct action. This produces a legalistic emphasis on "blame, proof or innocence, and subsequent punishment."[32]

Several features of the transformational viewpoint both challenge this stance and suggest an alternative conceptualization of the whole issue of administrative ethics. The principal feature, which by now should come as no surprise, is the role of the unconscious in orienting action. Earlier, in the discussion of language forms, we noted the transformationalists' admonitions against the use of judgmental language, as well as their preference for language that is self-reflexive and relational. Ethics, like action, is a form of language as well.

From the transformational viewpoint, particular ethical principles can have no "objective" and transcendental validity, as least insofar as they presume to define the essence of an ideal state of affairs. In view of the transformationalists' emphasis, instead, on processes of *individual* development, ethical discourse should be regarded in terms of its contribution to that development. As McSwain and White argue,

> All moral value positions or ethical values are ultimately arbitrary and are to be valued only for the role they play in establishing a dialectical, reflexive relationship to the unconscious, wherein the original value commitments will be revised and transcended. Our only point of moral reference, then, becomes the process by which aspects of the unconscious are transformed and brought to the apprehension of the conscious side of the psyche.[33]

Ethical language, like language generally, may be considered "good" insofar as it helps the individual reflexively understand situations so as to enable responsible action. Traditional ethics necessarily involves arbitrary, and therefore situationally inappropriate, judgments regarding the correctness of an individual's actions. When the individual fails to live up to the standards or principles underlying those arbitrary judgments, he or she will either reject, usually with good reason, the standards as appropriate to him or her in that situation or experience feelings of guilt. Guilt, say McSwain and White, is a feeling that does nothing to promote responsible action or personal development, because it fails to help the individual understand his or her role in the situation. Moreover, by generating feelings of rejection rather than personal acceptance of responsibility, the feeling of guilt is divisive of the sense of community (i.e., of caring and

---

[32]McSwain and White, "The Case for Lying, Cheating, and Stealing—Personal Development As Ethical Guidance for Managers," *Administration and Society,* forthcoming, p. 22 (in manuscript).

[33]Ibid., p. 18.

authentic social relations) that is otherwise necessary for personal development to occur. It is not just the "errant" individual, however, whose
development suffers from this blame-and-punishment approach to ethics;
the organization suffers as well. The reason for this is that in parceling
out individual blame and punishment, organizational leaders are likely to
be less reflective about how either their own actions or the institutionalized mores of the organization may have contributed to a "wrong" action
by an individual.

The alternative to this blame-and-punishment orientation is *confrontation*—not only of the individual by the organization, but also of the
organization by itself (including the individual whose behavior is in immediate question). From a personal development perspective, confrontation
initially involves establishing

> the conditions within organizations that will lead people to see that their great-
> est interest is in determining if lying, cheating, and stealing are occurring, *from
> the point of view of the unconscious.* From this perspective, i.e., that of the
> unconscious, these behaviors are all simply avoidances, in one form or another,
> of facing the task of coming to terms with and integrating unconscious mate-
> rial. Whether or not facts are misstated is an ambiguous and relatively unim-
> portant matter to the unconscious. The central question in such instances con-
> cerns whether or not the ambiguity around the facts represents an ambivalence
> in facing some aspect of one's self and one's life. Willingness to proceed with
> such facing is what the Jungians call "the moral attitude," and this label indi-
> cates the only firm point of reference for morality: the register of individual
> development. . . .[34]

Among other things, then, the role of ethics in the transformational
approach is less one of establishing and enforcing definitive standards of
judgment than of generating confrontive conversations in order to foster
responsible, rather than correct, action and personal maturation.

Theory and Practice

For transformational theorists, the proper purpose of theory is much
the same as it is for Karl Weick, namely, to assist in the *practical* project
of increasing organizational actors' understanding of situations in order
that they may act sensibly. It should be recalled that for White the generic
problem of action is "what to say next." As with Weick, "doing" (acting)
is equivalent to "saying," which is a way of conveying the idea that action
is carried out primarily through language. Moreover, the meanings we
attach to our uses of language comprise the stuff, the raw materials, from

---

[34]Ibid., p. 425; emphasis in original.

which we "construct" situations and the social and organizational worlds generally. "Theory," by extension, is simply a way of talking about and attributing meaning to situations that is self-consciously intended to generate *reflexive conversation* about those situations. The purpose of the reflexive conversations is temporarily to freeze the flow of events in a situation in order to see relationships among them. In describing how practical theorizing works, White uses the metaphor of a frame on a painting, which sets

> proportional relationships such that the elements of the painting stand in proper and sensible relation to each other and are distinguishable from their surroundings. As such theories can provide a certain amount of security of understanding when one faces a complex and changing reality. They can, furthermore, yield suggestions for how to talk about a situation. Theoretical predictions and definitions are usually of sufficient interest to inspire conversation and thereby can be a direct aid to what we consider to be effective action.[35]

By temporarily freezing the situation, theory, very often in the form of metaphors, allows us to see what *might* be going on (note that these assessments are always tentative, given the inherent equivocality of situations) in order to decide what might be sensible to say next. Theorizing, then, serves "as a method for developing a *reflexive codification* of organizational situations, which is to say, a continuing and grounded dialogue" about them.[36]

The standards of good theorizing that apply to practitioners of management also hold for organizational scholars and analysts. When all is said and done, good theory, which is to say *practical* theory, is that which we find interesting. As White and McSwain put it:

> *Something is true to the extent that it is interesting.* So also it is good. As Arendt pointed out that evil is banal, we point out that banality is evil. Valid knowledge is knowledge that is interesting—in that it acts as an effective analogue in drawing out the energy of the person viewing it.[37]

An End to Hierarchy and Competition: Frederick Thayer

Try to imagine how organizations, construed broadly to include all forms of social, political, and economic organization, might be structured and administered if we took Mary Parker Follett seriously. Recall that she

---

[35] White, "A Structuralist Approach to Organizational Action," pp. 22–23.
[36] Ibid., p. 24.
[37] White and McSwain, "Transformational Theory," p. 298, emphasis in original.

abhorred competition, broadly hinted at the need to eliminate the nation-state, saw the idea of representative government as divisive and outdated, rejected the individualism of Western liberalism in favor of a communitarian ideal, viewed leadership as facilitation rather than unilateral decision making, and opposed coercion in any form, including state socialism and laissez-faire capitalism.

The implicit assumption that unified Follett's beliefs was that politics derived from the more encompassing idea of organization. This may seem to be a startling notion, since historically our self-conscious awareness of the phenomenon of formal organization emerged long after our awareness of politics. Further, the Western democratic tradition of representative government sees organization (more precisely, administration) as derived from and subordinate to politics. But the idea that organization is logically prior to politics seems plausible when we consider that collectivities for cooperative endeavor, which we call organizations, *must* have predated the authoritative distribution of power, resources, rights, and duties, which we ordinarily think of as politics. Of the two, organization is therefore the more generic idea. That we have long forgotten this fact may well have created problems so grave that the quality of social life and the survival of the planet are thereby imperiled.

This, in brief, is the argument that Frederick Thayer presents in his controversial book, *An End to Hierarchy and Competition*.[38] Like Follett, Thayer proposes a radical vision of a new world based on a noncoercive theory of organization to replace contemporary theories of politics, economics, and organization. In one rather brief book, Thayer urges the elimination of the three principal institutions of the Western world of the last two centuries (and in the third instance, of the last six thousand years), namely:

- political democracy, as predicated on the ideas of representation and voting;

- economic competition; and

- hierarchy.

In their place, Thayer proposes a form of social, political, and economic organization that he terms "structured nonhierarchy," in which no decision may be made without the agreement of all those affected by it. The implications of this apparently simple change in the official rules of organizational conduct are so far-reaching, however, that we may both

---

[38]Frederick C. Thayer, *An End to Hierarchy and Competition: Administration in the Post-Affluent World,* 2nd ed. (New York: Franklin Watts, 1981); in this section, all page references in parentheses are to this source; emphasis is in the original unless otherwise noted.

wonder about the possibility of its being accepted and ask why, for Thayer, such drastic measures are needed in the first place. In this regard, he concedes with doleful irony that "a world without hierarchy *may be* impossible to sustain, whether it be the first such attempt or the partial re-emergence of something tried before. The social world in which we now live *is* the truly impossible world to sustain" (p. A-36).

The plausibility of Thayer's proposal to restructure social institutions along consensual lines hinges on his argument that existing modes of social organization are impossible to sustain or are not worth sustaining. The chief offender in Thayer's analysis is hierarchy, with political democracy and economic competition playing supporting roles. Since Thayer's arguments concerning economic competition are not central to the purposes of this book, we shall deal with them here only in passing. Briefly, his condemnation of competition is equally as severe as his condemnation of hierarchy and "democracy." His proposed alternative to competition, just as for hierarchy and "democracy," is structured nonhierarchy, that is, economic planning and decision making through continual and overlapping consensual processes.

Competition, which Thayer depicts as the economic equivalent of political anarchy, achieves for us "absolutely no benefits at all" (p. 183). Quite independent of the social and political critiques of capitalism from the political left (e.g., that competition produces alienation), economic competition fails on its own terms of efficient allocation of economic resources. In oligopolistic competition, for example, prices are

> two to three times higher than they should be—something traceable to the *competitive waste* of companies which do not compete on the basis of price reductions but instead use massive advertising, limitless schemes of promotion, and irrationally excessive capacity and distribution systems, all designed to lure a few customers away from each other. Where we commonly believe that these problems can be overcome by "more perfect" competition, this leads only to huge *overproduction,* dangerously declining prices, widespread failures, and a social chaos overcome only by government intervention. (p. 83)

Hierarchy, "Democracy," and Alienation

Thayer argues that "Conventionally, alienation is thought to exist when the world, society, or organization does not respond to the individual member, and subjects him to forces he can neither comprehend nor influence in a meaningful way" (p. 47). Alienation, while much talked about, is elusive because we have probably never experienced a state of *un*alienation and therefore can only guess what it might be like. Moreover, the most influential explanations of how and why alienation persists,

Thayer argues, are probably all misguided. He criticizes, for example, Marx's view that alienation stems from contradictions inherent in the capitalist mode of economic organization. Thayer notes both that alienation most likely existed long before the advent of capitalism and continues when ownership, even in "enlightened" socialist countries such as Yugoslavia, is shifted from the private to the public sphere. Equally dubious is Jacques Ellul's contention that alienation results from the depersonalizing effects of technology in the industrial age, in contrast to the "personalized" relationships characteristic of feudal societies.[39]

Social relationships, whether personal or impersonal (and regardless of their particular historical epoch), are alienating insofar as there exist disparities of institutional power and authority (i.e., hierarchy).[40] "The formal, or officially acknowledged, interactions within any hierarchical structure are those of *ruling* and *being ruled, issuing commands* and *obeying them, repressing* and *being repressed*" (p. 52). The fault of Marx's and Ellul's explanations lies in their failure to recognize that pre-capitalist and feudal societies, like capitalist and post-feudal societies, were also hierarchical and no less alienating.

"Democracy,"[41] as we now practice it, provides no satisfactory alternative, inasmuch as it is predicated on an assumption of hierarchy:

> Even at its best, "democracy" has tended only to *limit* the power of rulers, without changing the fundamental *relationship* between those who rule and those who are ruled. This is because all theories of "democracy" contain within them the pervasive assumption that hierarchy is inevitable, desirable, and necessary, the assumption that *no organization (family, church, corporation, public agency, nation-state) can achieve its social purposes other than through the interaction of those designated "superiors" and those labeled "subordinates."* (p. 44)

Thayer condemns political democracy as undemocratic for several reasons. First, the idea of majority rule inevitably results in hierarchical domination. Voting is simply a means for determining who are the winners (the majority) that may then dominate the losers (the minority). In the case of democratic elections,

> this fundamental act of citizenship, as we now define citizenship—a lonely act performed infrequently and out of sight and sound of all other human beings— is intended to discard or defeat a candidate we have learned to hate or at least

[39]See Jacques Ellul, *The Technological Society* (New York: Vintage Books, 1964).

[40]It is important to see that Thayer uses "hierarchy" to describe *any* superior/subordinate social situation, not merely those formalized in bureaucratic settings.

[41]Thayer says that "'Democracy' refers throughout to our conventional approach to government. It implies that we must transform ourselves if the quotation marks are to be removed" (p. 44).

thoroughly dislike. Although we often think of voting as a positive step preliminary to our version of the good life, this attractive camouflage cannot conceal its negative meaning. Indeed, the act is kept secret so that those we seek to repress cannot retaliate by repressing us. (p. 54)[42]

Second, by institutionally separating (at least in theory) policy making from policy implementation, political democracy sets the stage for hierarchical domination through bureaucratic organizations. Alienation is produced not only by virtue of the bureaucratic arrangement of offices into superior and subordinate roles, but is made even worse by the formalistic impersonality (first documented by Weber) that accompanies those roles. As the primary instrumentality of social and political organization, bureaucracy subverts the democratic values of personal freedom and participation that it is intended to promote and protect. As Thayer explains:

> The fiction of freedom and independence, and the corollary objective of political equality, encourage us to believe that as *persons* we interact with each other in free and equal fashion. In organizations, we are *not* free and equal, so we describe ourselves not as persons, but as roles; we "act out" the norms prescribed by other roles. We interact, in other words, as *nonpersons*—a framework in which we are automatically alienated from one another and from ourselves. (p. 50)

Although in many respects Thayer's analysis of hierarchy and alienation bears a strong resemblance to the critical theorists' critique of bureaucracy, his proposed alternative of structured nonhierarchy more closely parallels the thinking of Mary Parker Follett. Any summary of the essential features of structured nonhierarchy, however, requires an examination of the theoretical assumptions on which it is based, as well as the developments in contemporary management practice that lend it plausibility.

Consensus Through Structured Nonhierarchy   The theory of structured nonhierarchy is predicated on a set of beliefs about human nature that challenge the implicit individualism both of liberal democratic theory and Protestant Christianity. Reversing the assumption that the moral individual is corrupted by an immoral society, Thayer invokes H. Richard Niebuhr's position that the individual can have no moral existence independent of society. Society logically precedes and makes possible the individual's awareness of himself. Contrary to the contractarian view of a society populated by atomistic individuals, the fundamental social unit is

---

[42]Management theorists, including Mary Parker Follett, have long argued, however, that voting is one of the least effective forms of group decision making, since it stifles free and open discussion in the interest of winning and creates social divisiveness and distrust that later emerge in lowered commitment to collective purposes and even sabotage.

the "face-to-face community in which unlimited commitments are the rule and in which every aspect of every self's existence is conditioned by membership in the interpersonal group."[43]

If human association is fundamental to being, it follows that what people value can emerge only through that association. Echoing Follett, Thayer says that "*value* can be defined only as an attribute of being-in-relation-to-being" (p. 124). The implications of this moral view of the self are far-reaching and suggest the basis for a theory of society, politics, and organization that is radically distinct from hierarchy:

> This moral theory can, almost of itself, be translated into an operating social and political theory. No individual, even an officially designated decision-maker, can have values of his own which direct or command him to impose those values upon others. Values (objectives, goals, ends) can emerge only from social interaction in which the parties are unable to coerce each other. The individual brings to the interaction not values, but opinions; values (objectives, goals, ends) can be created only through *collective* processes. Values can be carried over from one social process to another only as they are adopted by the members of that second process. The effect of this approach is to de-objectify both individuals and values, transforming both into the consensus outcomes of interpersonal and intersubjective interaction. The unit of social action can *never* be the individual, *only* the group. (pp. 124–25)

Support for Thayer's vision of a new political and social order is indeed scarce in contemporary American political thought, whose mainstream, chiefly political pluralism, still embraces the atomistic individualism of contract theory and market economics. From the standpoint of modern management theory, however, Thayer's analysis appears far less radical. Requiring that organizational and political decisions be made consensually merely formalizes and makes politically legitimate what enlightened managers, as a matter of personal style, already do for very practical reasons. The reason why participative management and consensus do not work better than they do is because they contradict the formal theory of hierarchy implicit in democratic political theory and institutionalized in formal organizations. But despite the official theory of hierarchy, several well-documented organizational trends show promise of undermining it. For example,

> *Transorganizational processes* cut across permanent organizational boundaries, compelling us to think of "open systems" of action. Within organizations, especially in middle management, activities grouped under the title "Organization Development" (OD) seek the democratization of decision processes.

---

[43]H. Richard Neibuhr, *The Responsible Self* (New York: Harper and Row, 1963), pp. 71–73; quoted in Thayer, p. 124.

From the outside come *demands from clients, customers, or citizens,* those affected by organizational decisions, for involvement in the making of decisions. Finally, an increasing *malaise among low-level employees,* especially assembly-line workers, is forcing *the redesign of industrial technology.* (pp. 10–11)

Although these trends signal reasons for optimism regarding the eventual elimination of hierarchy, Thayer cautions that their influence in reshaping organizations and society may not withstand the still-ubiquitous imperatives of hierarchy. Worse still, he sees the organizational development movement, as currently practiced, as subject to manipulation by hierarchical superiors in service on their own ends.

Consensus and Political Rights   Thayer is simultaneously concerned with such traditional organizational values as effectiveness (albeit broadly interpreted) and political rights. In terms of the latter, he agrees with Henry Kariel that we should accept as democratic "nothing less than a society all of whose members are active participants in an interminable process [of cooperative activity]—*and who would not mind such activity.*"[44] If this is what democracy is truly about, then the role of organizational leaders (who, in Thayer's scheme, would include most of us at one time or another) is not to *make* decisions, but to *facilitate* their emergence through consensus-building. This, in fact, is "the *primary act of citizenship*" (p. 38) and "that *to deprive the individual of such involvement is to remove his or her political franchise*" (p. 40).

Consensus as Creative Bargaining   The consensual processes that Thayer proposes, terming them "creative bargaining," are far from revolutionary, except that in structured nonhierarchy there is no legal and politically legitimate alternative to using them. Drawing from contemporary management theory and practice, Thayer describes five steps involved in consensus building (p. 137):

- Getting a sharply defined perception of the essential aspects of the conflict.

- Developing a disturbing concern for the satisfaction of opposing interests.

- Discovering new possible aims or interests, in which conflicting ones can be absorbed to the larger advantage of all.

- Embodying the new aims in a practical program.

[44]Henry S. Kariel, *Open Systems: Arenas for Political Action* (Itasca, Ill.: F. E. Peacock, 1969), pp. 96–98; quoted in Thayer, p. 129.

- Expressing all ideas used throughout the process in ways which enable everyone to identify deficiencies in those ideas as they are now used.

Consensus and Organizational Interdependence   Although Thayer gives no quarter in his opposition to hierarchy, the alternative of structured nonhierarchy, by outward appearances, might not differ greatly from existing organizational structures, both internally and as they relate with one another. Their *processes* would differ, however, owing to the requirement of consensus. Consensus at the small-group level is a familiar idea, but the more difficult question is how (and whether) it can work across multiple groups, organizations, and even nation-states. In order for consensus to succeed, "we must abandon the notion of organizational autonomy" (p. 173) by recognizing that a consensus of one group or organization will usually have to be altered when it is synthesized with that of other groups and organizations. Representatives of organizations will necessarily have to regard the consensuses they initially represent as tentative positions, subject to alteration and integration with those of other units:

> Because no policy process can produce a decision of its own, and because of the multiple overlapping, all the consensus plans so produced can, over time, become the *collective will* of *all* those involved in *all* the processes. The model explicitly requires us, of course, to abandon the notion that any single unit of government (and any organization) can produce a suitable plan for its own future that is not interlocked with those of other units of government (and other organizations). (p. 173)

The requirement of consensus, which is continually evolving across and within organizations, is the only way to manage interdependencies without either resorting to domination or degenerating into anarchy. In the latter regard, Thayer is adamant that the alternative to hierarchy is *not* anarchy. The consensual future will likely be *more* structured than is the present, hence the awkward but deliberately chosen term "structured nonhierarchy." Since, for more than 6,000 years,[45] the social world has been structured hierarchically, it is impossible to provide anything more than a tentative sketch of some of the essential features of organizations (not to mention the world as a whole) without hierarchy. Although Thayer offers neither proof nor a definitive blueprint of the future, he does speculate about some likely consequences of eliminating hierarchy, including

---

[45]In the second edition of his book (pp. A1–A36), Thayer includes a new chapter, "Hierarchy and the Human Brain," in which he argues that hierarchy is a rather "recent" invention, dating back about 6,000 years. Extrapolating from some provocative anthropological theory, Thayer concludes that the emergence of hierarchy led to the invention of written language and the consequent genetic shift from right- to left-brain dominance.

the decline of the nation-state and war; the eventual equalization of salaries, with a concomitant end to the idea of promotion; and the elimination of the taboo against sex in organizations, a taboo that currently exists because sex in organizations so often involves exploitation and domination by hierarchical superiors (usually men) of subordinates (typically women). The consensual future is, among other things, a sensual one.

Thayer Concluded

In his attempt to present a convincing case for transforming the world of hierarchy and competition into a consensual one, Thayer faces at least two formidable obstacles. First, he must convince his readers that in fact they *are* alienated and that a barely imaginable state of *un*alienation is preferable. Inasmuch as knowledge of one's alienation is, for most people, only marginally available to conscious awareness, Thayer's message may strike a responsive chord only in those few already predisposed to hear it.

Once convinced of their alienation, readers must then be prepared to imagine, and to want to live in, a consensual world. It is a world about which even Thayer, much less those whose imaginations are more limited, can merely speculate. Whatever the drawbacks of hierarchy, most of us seem to accept it as a necessary evil. The known evil of hierarchy, even if we accept Thayer's critique of it, may seem safer than the promise of a brave, but largely unknowable, new world, however sensual.

Even for those who are able to comprehend their own alienation and who feel personally unafraid of a consensual future, hard questions still remain about the possibilities of our actually creating it. First, a world without hierarchy is a world without authority, at least as we ordinarily understand the word. If White and McSwain are correct in their view that confrontation with authority is an indispensable requirement for personal maturation, we might well wonder what authority's surrogate would be in a world of structured nonhierarchy.

Further, even if Thayer's diagnosis of the relationship of hierarchy to alienation is correct, can the requirements of our material subsistence be met in the absence of that organizational instrument of efficiency called bureaucracy? Thayer's answer, of course, is "yes," although, as Weber and many others have argued, hierarchy may be alienating while at the same time highly efficient. Even writers who agree with Thayer's linking of hierarchy (and by extension, bureaucracy) to alienation stop short of urging hierarchy's complete elimination. To mention only one example here, Alberto Guerreiro Ramos has carefully argued that bureaucratic organizations are indispensable requirements for our material survival; the best that we can do is attempt to limit their influence by separating them from other domains (or "enclaves") of social life.[46]

Those who might facilely dismiss Thayer's proposals as grossly impractical should consider them in light of the alternative of maintaining the status quo. If there is merit to Thayer's arguments regarding the impossibility of sustaining for very long the institution of hierarchy and an economy based on competition, then the only alternative may well be a consensual world, however implausible it may first appear. How radical structured nonhierarchy really is, however, depends on how one looks at it. From the perspective of modern management theory and practice, it may even be interpreted as a rather minimalist proposal. The change in a single rule—i.e., that no one be allowed to make unilateral decisions that are binding on others—simply formalizes what effective, and truly democratic, managers have been doing all along.

The "Emergence" Critique of Rationality and Liberalism

The sequence of the chapters in Part III reflects a progressive departure from the spirit of rationalism and instrumentalism that marked much of the classical organizational literature, as well as portions of its current mainstream. It is probably safe to say that people's everyday beliefs about organizations by and large are products of that same spirit. In one sense, this is a spirit of optimism about the human condition that is especially prominent in Western societies. Rationalism and instrumentalism bespeak a desire, at least, to believe that at a conscious level of awareness, we know who we are, what we want, and, through individual and collective effort, how to get it. To the extent that we encounter obstacles along the way, they may be attributed either to technical difficulties that may be overcome through hard work or to deficiencies in particular individuals who are needful of improvement or, if that fails, control.

This is not to say, however, that people are uniformly confident that modern organizations will invariably serve as effective instrumentalities for promoting the collective good and satisfying individual wants. It has long been commonplace for observers to note, and citizens to experience, profound tensions between the requirements for a stable social order and the satisfaction of their personal wants. This tension may be thought of as a competition between two levels of rationality: the rationality of individual utility and the rationality of institutional survival. In political

---

[46]See especially Chapter 7, "Theory of Social Systems Delimitation: A Paradigmatic Statement," in Alberto Guerreiro Ramos, *The New Science of Organizations: A Reconceptualization of the Wealth of Nations* (Toronto: University of Toronto Press, 1981), pp. 121–34.

terms, it is simply a restatement of the classical dilemma of Western liberalism—the tension between the demands for individual rights and the requirements of the collective order.

Follett, Weick, White, McSwain, and Thayer each challenges the assumptions underlying the optimistic spirit of our rationalist intellectual tradition. By extension, they also cast doubt on the wisdom of how we typically frame questions about managing the tensions between rationality as it is expressed at these two levels. As emergence theorists, they assert that rationality is at best "discovered" after the fact. In effect, they ask us to suspend our commonsense belief that action may be adequately understood in consciously rational terms, as well as the concomitant belief that action is correctly judged by whether it satisfies goals or corresponds to consciously held principles of conduct. Stated more broadly, these authors ask us to shift the level of our discourse about organizations from the *political* level—the struggle among consciously known and usually opposing interests—to the *psychological* level—where the struggle plays out mysteriously within ourselves, that is, within our psyches. It is this shift from the political to the psychological, from a conscious to an unconscious attitude, that informs the emergence perspective's critique of contemporary liberalism and the assumptions about human nature on which it is based.

Beliefs about the nature of the self invariably influence beliefs about the nature of the social order. For example, the assumption that rational individuals will act in order to maximize their interests evokes a view of a social order that is held together on a contractual basis. In a liberal, contractual order, differences in people's preferences are granted legitimacy through guarantees of individual rights. The attitude of one person toward another is one of toleration, and rights are the institutional means by which we protect ourselves from occasional lapses in that tolerant attitude. The contractual order is bound not only by toleration, but also by obligation or duty, the particular meanings of which are taught or learned through experience. That is, feelings of obligation to both tolerate and protect others derive from sources that are external to the natural proclivities of the human psyche, rather than intrinsic to it. Thus, whereas liberalism may be optimistic about the capability of individuals for rational action deriving from the conscious attitude, it is far less sanguine about the social consequences of action resulting from the natural unfolding of unconscious energy.

From a psychological perspective, the liberal view seems to share with both Thomas Hobbes and Sigmund Freud the same bleak image of man as naturally at war both with others and himself. Insofar as this image of human nature is correct, good taste and good manners require that its expression be regarded as a private matter, unfettered by the presumption of a public morality. As Jean Bethke Elshtain describes it:

Liberalism, as such, is indifferent to the ways of life any individual chooses to pursue—unless his actions harm anyone else. Holding as self-evident a view of the person as a bearer of inalienable rights who must be free to determine his own ends, liberal society promulgates and protects "negative freedom." The citizen is free *from* a public morality he may not share, and free as well from the intrusions of his neighbors into his "private" affairs. Our political morality, in other words, is agnostic about alternative conceptions of the "good life."[47]

The liberal ideal seems plausible so long as one accepts the idea that individuals are in essence independent selves consciously pursuing their private ends. Such a view dictates that opportunities for their attainment be protected both from infringement by other individuals, as well as from, except in extreme circumstances, a more encompassing version of the public good. At least in theory, it is relatively easy to separate private wants from public goods, with the former carrying with them the presumption of a prior moral legitimacy. From what has been said, then, the appropriate role of the public official is to maintain the conditions under which individual rights are protected and, when collective action is necessary, to enforce the terms of the social contract that make such action possible.

To the emergence theorists, liberalism misunderstands both human nature and the nature of the social order. Transformational theory, for example, holds that, since action is the unfolding of unconscious energy whose meaning is revealed retrospectively, it is therefore false to regard human action, in a fundamental sense, as consciously directed toward the achievement of known ends. The liberal commitment to individual rights as the primary value in political life, however, makes sense only if the ends in whose service action is taken *are* known in advance. Secondly, although it is certainly true that people do often define interests that they later act upon, liberalism seems unaware not only of the role of the unconscious but also of the *social* nature of the process by which interests are created. Interests are neither pregiven nor autistic creations of the mind, but are created and discovered within a web of human relationships whose influence is only partially open to conscious awareness.

The dialectical process by which conscious awareness and unconscious energy interact is profoundly influenced by the quality—which is to say, the authenticity—of social relationships. The atomistic individual of liberalism, with its preeminent emphasis on individual rights, exaggerates and creates an unhealthy distance between the private life of the individual and the large community of which he or she is a part. Rights invoked to *protect* people from one another, if carried to the extreme, serve to destroy the bonds of community that provide the conditions wherein indi-

---

[47]Jean Bethke Elshtain, "The New Porn Wars," *The New Republic,* June 25, 1984, p. 18.

viduals may discover, create, and act upon "interests" that serve their own development. By placing a heavier burden on the idea of individual rights than it can possibly bear, liberalism may ironically create the conditions under which mass society finds itself unable to tolerate the differences of interest that liberalism intends to protect.

All of the emergence theorists share in the view that healthy psychological development requires a much more communitarian stance toward the social order, one that acknowledges the uniqueness of people's individual developmental needs, but also of their common project. Acknowledging the importance of the community thus replaces, or at least supplements, liberalism's private individual with a more positive role of a public-regarding citizen.

Theories of Emergence and the Public Administration Framework

The emergence theorists optimistically envision the possibilities inherent in political and organizational life. But the communitarian ideal, which they propose in a decidedly hopeful mood, is, in the minds of others, also borne of the fear of the totalitarianism spawned by social disintegration. As Michael J. Sandel comments:

> [I]ntolerance flourishes most where forms of life are dislocated, roots unsettled, traditions undone. In our day, the totalitarian impulse has sprung less from the convictions of confidently situated selves than from the confusions of atomized, dislocated, frustrated selves, at sea in a world where common meanings have lost their force. As Hannah Arendt has written, "What makes mass society so difficult to bear is not the number of people involved, or at least not primarily, but the fact that the world between them has lost its power to gather them together, to relate and to separate them." Insofar as our public life has withered, our sense of common involvement diminished, we lie vulnerable to the mass politics of totalitarian solutions. So responds the party of the common good to the party of rights. If the party of the common good is right, our most pressing moral and political project is to revitalize those civic republican possibilities implicit in our tradition but fading in our time.[48]

The issue of community bears not only on politics, but also on social organization. Since this is an age in which formal organization may have transcended politics as the dominant institution of public authority, it is especially important to see how this critique of liberalism affects basic public administration values.

[48]Michael J. Sandel, "Morality and the Liberal Ideal," *The New Republic,* May 7, 1984, p. 17.

Efficiency and Effectiveness

From the standpoint of the emergence perspectives, efficiency and effectiveness assume the status of, at best, second-order criteria for judging the adequacy of organizational action. Since these two criteria derive from the means-ends logic of the rational model of organization, their appropriateness necessarily depends on the degree to which that model both accurately depicts organizational life and provides a preferred normative image of it.

Weick's dual emphasis on the retrospective nature of rationality and the importance of organizational adaptation leads not so much to a rejection of efficiency and effectiveness as legitimate values as to a recognition of their inevitable tension with the value of adaptation. Efficiency and effectiveness are values predicated on the assumption of certainty in the face of equivocality. This prompts Weick to advise managers to be wary of institutional pressures toward valuing these two criteria when the more important issue may be *what* to do, not how best to do it. As *instrumental* criteria, efficiency and effectiveness serve as measures of accountability for organizational action. This probably explains much of their appeal in that they seem, at least, to provide standards of *correct* action. Too great a concern with correctness (and therefore with accountability), however, may assume greater stability in situations than is really warranted, with the consequence that efficiency and effectiveness become valued at the expense of adaptation.

Individual Rights and the Adequacy of Process

Liberalism's preoccupation with individual rights as the cornerstone of its normative theory leads to the judgment that organizational processes may be evaluated on procedural grounds. This is a rule-oriented, legalistic view of organizational processes, one that is intended either to protect people from one another or to insure fair distribution of material things among citizens. Organizational processes are thus judged instrumentally, that is, by the extent to which they guarantee such protection and fair distribution.

The transformationalists' critique of liberalism, much like Follett's, challenges the wisdom of this position by arguing that organizational processes may be regarded as desirable insofar as they promote healthy development of people. This is less a matter of a procedural rules and formal organizational design (at least not initially) than a concern with the authenticity of personal relationships. Such relationships are necessary in order that people might discover what their interests really are, both as individuals and in terms of collective projects shared with others. These relationships, then, are characterized by commitment to, rather than freedom from, others.

Both the liberal and emergence viewpoints share a common commitment to "autonomous" action by individuals. The psychological perspective of the latter, however, interprets autonomous action as a much less consciously rational, and a far more social, activity than does the former. The core of Follett's, Weick's, and the transformationalists' critique of the liberal attitude toward organizational processes is their belief that processes of human action are *intrinsically* important. The fact that action cannot properly be seen solely in rational/instrumental terms does not signify a regrettable human limitation. Rather, it is simply a feature of the human condition in which the search for meaning supersedes in importance the attainment of goals. Formal organizational procedures may often be necessary in order to protect individual "rights." But, such procedures should properly be seen as codifications of naturally evolving social processes, rather than ensconced as inviolable principles of conduct.

Representativeness and the Control of Discretion

The proper extent of administrative discretion in the interpretation and implementation of public policies has been a perennial subject of dispute in the public administration literature. The question, at least in the mainstream literature, largely revolves around the extent to which discretionary judgments may accurately represent either the intent of particular policies or the public interest more generally. To Follett and the transformationalists, this formulation of the discretion issue is rather badly misconceived. Follett argues that discretion is unavoidable at all levels of organization. She says that workers "must exercise discretion in their work because, unless they do, the work does not get done, and no amount of supervision can compensate for the absence of discretion" (*DA*, p. 85).

Moreover, the problem to Follett is not primarily one of "representing" interests that already exist, but of creating the conditions under which interests, if one insists on the term, may be created and discovered. To "represent" interests is to integrate evolving interests, rather than to seek compromise among static, preconceived interests. Rather than regard the representative process as compromise or as a struggle between winners and losers, "We should send men to 'conference' to confer, not to fight for something already decided upon before meeting" (*CE*, p. 253). The implied role of the administrator, therefore, is mainly that of a facilitator of social processes who enables people to discover and integrate their interests through cooperative effort.

Transformational theorists harbor doubts about whether "macro" social policies that mandate large-scale programmatic action can, by themselves, adequately represent the unique needs of citizens. Even though such policies may be necessary, their effectiveness requires the availability of avenues for collaborative decisions in their implementation. Discretion, insofar as the word is still useful, must be reinterpreted to mean consultation and participation as the basis for action.

The quarrel of the transformationalists with the traditional view of discretion is mainly a cognitive one. The traditional debate tends to cast the problem as one of deciding, on the basis of competing consciously held values, what kind and how much, if any, discretion is warranted in a given situation. For the transformationalists, however, discretion defined as consciously deciding among competing values is at best derivative of the more important question of how *reality* judgments—"what is actually going on here?"—are influenced by unconscious projections of psychic energy, as well as how conflicting definitions of reality are mediated. What we are tempted to call problems of "discretion" may often disguise an absence of critical self-awareness and a consequent inability to fathom how and why others define the same situation differently.

Conclusion

Readers who are generally sympathetic to the emergence perspectives may reasonably be troubled by at least two lingering concerns about them. The first pertains principally to White and McSwain's transformational approach, which relies so heavily on the analytical psychology of Carl Jung. Specifically, Jung and the public administration scholars who have drawn from his work hold to what many would regard as an excessively optimistic vision of social action stemming from the natural unfolding of unconscious energy. A similar optimism is also found in the writings of Follett and Thayer, who regard healthy individual development as deriving from a social context characterized by cooperation, rather than external control.

Not all psychologists, however, share their optimistic vision. Freud, to mention only the most prominent alternative, presents us with a much less encouraging picture. It is one in which unconscious forces must, both in the interests of self and society, be restrained and brought under control, rather than allowed to find their natural and authentic expression. The optimism of Jung and the pessimism of Freud parallel a less sophisticated, but a more socially consequential, division within the public consciousness about the relation of the individual to the collective order. The appeal of the emergence perspectives rests on the highly problematic assumption that the more optimistic vision is correct. Yet, the plausibility of that vision depends, as does its alternative, far less on a conscious choice than on a far deeper, much less conscious, comprehension of our experience— both of the social world and of ourselves. In view of the profound difficulty of that comprehension, a definitive resolution of these two conflicting attitudes, at best, appears distant.

The second concern is one that divides some of the authors reviewed within this chapter from one another. It involves the question of whether formal change of organizational structure is a precondition for the kind of personal development that writers such as Follett, White, and McSwain describe. Although all of the authors discussed here share similar sentiments on the normative priority of personal development, two seemingly polar positions are evident regarding the relationship of structural change to that development. White and McSwain hold to the more conservative view that structural change follows from personal development. Thayer, on the other hand, says that structural change is a precondition for it. More specifically, individual development, he would argue, is inevitably impeded by hierarchical structures of authority in which social relations are mediated by systems of reward and punishment. Whether a middle ground between, or a synthesis of, these two positions is possible is very much an open question, as well as an important one.

IV
CONCLUSION

12

Wicked Problems, Theoretical Diversity, and Responsible Practice

The great diversity of theoretical perspectives on organizations presented in this book might, quite understandably, seem overwhelming not only to practicing administrators, but also to scholars of organization theory. For administrators, this diversity particularly poses a problem insofar as they construe the practical value of theory as solely to provide the basis for correct definitions and solutions to problems. The proliferation of various theoretical perspectives simply accentuates the already formidable difficulties they experience in finding and using theoretical insights for the practical purpose of getting things done. To scholars, on the other hand, diversity often signals an unwelcome challenge to the presumed correctness of their own particular perspectives.

We believe both quests for certainty are misguided—and for what amounts to much the same reason.

In Chapter 1, we emphasized the growing recognition of the "wicked" character of the problems that typically confront public administrators. Wickedness, it may be recalled, is an attribute of those problems with multiple, conflicting definitions and no clear solutions, and whose necessarily imperfect solutions beget further problems. For administrators, accepting the notion that problems are wicked is analogous to accepting the diversity of theory. Both require an attitude that rejects the possibility of definitive solutions to problems, recognizing that no particular theory can provide an unassailable, correct framework for problem analysis. The wickedness of problems is proportional to (as well as the product of) the variety of theoretical perspectives available for comprehending those problems.

Similarly, theorists seeking definitive justifications for their theories run the risk of denying the wickedness of those problems to which their researching and theorizing is addressed. Research problems, just like other problems, do not objectively exist independent of the researcher's frame of reference. Rather, problems are inevitably defined *in terms of* that frame of reference. The interactive nature of theory and problem definition reveals the wickedness of both.

For those theorists intent on demonstrating the truth of their assumptions, Gareth Morgan warns that "it is fallacious to conclude that the propositions of a system of thought can be proved, disproved, or evaluated on the basis of axioms within that system, since the process becomes self-justifying."[1] The self-justifying nature of that process results from the wicked quality of theory's interaction with problems, whether "research" or "practical." The belief that a theory's basic assumptions can be either logically proved or conclusively established through research, Morgan argues, rests on the highly arguable assumption that the objects of the researchers' attention exist in an external world independent of their frames of reference:

> [T]he "independence" of this external world, and hence its validity as a fixed point of reference against which the claims of scientific theories can be evaluated, begins to break down once we introduce the idea that the independence of subjective mind and objective reality is no more than an assumption. As soon as we entertain the idea that what the "Eye of the Mind" sees in the external world may be as much a consequence of the nature of the eye as it is of the object seen, we create severe problems for the view that the "truth claims" of scientific theories can be judged in terms of a criterion of objective knowledge based on an ability to mirror or reflect the nature of the external world.[2]

At a variety of points throughout this book we have stressed that theory and practice, and more generically, thought and action, are not merely related, but are actually constitutive of one another. It is because of this connection, Morgan argues, that theory is not to be valued for the definitive answers that it offers, but for the basis it provides for self-reflexive conversations about potentially sensible ways to understand and act in the world. The apparent wickedness of practical problems and the diversity of theory do not together constitute a problem in a larger sense, but

---

[1]Gareth Morgan, "Toward a More Reflective Social Science," in Morgan, ed., *Beyond Method: Strategies for Social Research* (Beverly Hills, Calif.: Sage, 1983), p. 370.
[2]Ibid., p. 371.

instead provide opportunities for self-understanding and for appreciating why we are divided from one another.[3] Differences in theories not only reveal alternative aspects of the world that we perceive as existing external to us, but also reveal variations in the ways in which we can understand ourselves in relation to that world. In the absence of definitive standards either of truth or of correct action, administrators and theorists alike are confronted with the same basic problem of making moral choices in the face of practical uncertainties and theoretical diversity.

All of this, however, runs counter to the ways in which theory and practice have generally been conceived of by those who engage in public administration study and activity. Instead, the last several decades have seen an increasing reliance on a single perspective, the rational science model, as the basis for both action and study in public administration. This emphasis has given a very narrow meaning to both theory and practice, as well as to the relationship of the two. One consequence of reliance on this model has been to bring into question the efficacy of governmental process in the service of society. The model and its relationship with public administration theorizing and practice are discussed in the next section.

In order to move away from this model as a primary mode of action and theorizing requires a two–fold effort on the part of public administrators. First, they must reconceptualize the notion of administrative responsibility; this is briefly outlined in the third section. Next, they must recognize the intrinsic diversity of theory as a means of illuminating organizational action. To this end, the final section provides a cross-cutting summary of the various perspectives examined here, offering six dimensions across which theorizing can be usefully assessed.

Theory and Administrative Practice: A Change in Direction

In the twenty years of American history between the inaugurations of Presidents Kennedy and Reagan, the role of government shifted dramatically. Concomitant with this shift was the development of what can best be called an "operant social theory," a dominant way of thinking about appropriate governmental action. This operant theory took two forms, the programmatic and the regulatory, and was paralleled by developments in the literature of public administration around the question of the relationship between theory and practice.

Many practitioners and writers in public administration have commented on (and bemoaned) the current relationship of theory to practice. Most have assumed the issue is merely one of making theory more rele-

[3]Ibid., pp. 381–82.

vant to practice in order to improve the latter. The solution, this argument runs, lies on the side of more and better theory. Yet when one reads the literature of public administration, there is a strikingly discordant note: Theories never seem to do what we want them to do, namely, to tell us how to act tomorrow. At the same time, the practice of public administration is rife with theory; there is no substantive area of public administration (health, education, welfare, science) that is not replete with its own theoretical literature, not to mention the grander theories of public policy embodied in Keynesian and supply-side economics.

All of this is usually characterized as the "theory/practice gap." But what is the "problem" embodied in this gap? In answer, we argue three things:

- The increasing public disenchantment with government evidenced over the last twenty years is in large part the result of disillusionment with the operant theory of social control, which assumes that programmatic and regulatory action are *the* appropriate means for addressing social problems.

- Paralleling the operant theory is academic public administration's historical belief in theory as a means for explanation and prediction for purposes of social control. This makes it nearly impossible for the literature to address the concerns of practitioners, namely, by providing them practical knowledge in a form useful for understanding their day-to-day public work settings.

- It is therefore essential to revise our thinking about both government action and public administration theory by reassessing our commitment to the idea of social control. Such a reassessment requires a quite different mind set for both acting as a public administrator and theorizing about public administration.

The Operant Theory: From John Kennedy to Ronald Reagan

Americans like to measure their history in decades and to use their presidents as touchstones for their alternating periods of national consciousness. The two decades between the elections of John Kennedy, the youngest president in this century, and Ronald Reagan, the oldest in the history of the republic, provide a time expressive of both the hopes and the frustrations of administrative technology. If there was any sense of direction to things during the entire twenty years, it was decidedly down. Sociologists, for example, charted this through public opinion surveys by asking people about the alienation they felt in relation to the society around them: In 1966, 29 percent of those surveyed said they felt alienated;

by 1982, this had increased steadily to 56 percent. The same pattern shows up as well in surveys of Americans' attitudes toward their social institutions, which indicate an increasing disenchantment with large-scale organizational activity.[4]

One thing that did go up during this time (besides interest rates, inflation, and unemployment) was government—the money we spent on it, the extent to which we asked it to regulate our lives, the quantity of services we demanded of it, but most of all, our perception of it as something sitting apart from (and on top of) us. The early 1960s belief in the positive role of government had changed, by the end of the next decade, to a belief in the oppressiveness of government.

If one word characterizes those twenty years, it would be *rules.* Considerable energy was devoted to making, breaking, and reshaping the rules by which American society lives. Civil rights and sex discrimination, energy conservation and ecology, regulation and deregulation were all about rules. And in these twenty years, the public administrator came to play the central role of both rule-maker and rule-enforcer.

Behind all this promulgation of rules was an operant theory about social control: The behavior of individuals and groups can be determined by ordering and structuring, in predetermined ways, their interactions with each other and with their immediate environment. This had a corollary: Negative reinforcement (usually in the form of threats of lawsuit or fiscal sanction) is the most effective form for ensuring compliance with the rules formulated on the basis of the operant social theory. Both the theory and its corollary were expressed in one of two basic forms, the programmatic and the regulatory.

Programmatic activity seeks to solve a perceived problem by structuring the social environment around the problematic area. It does this, for example, by establishing agencies to oversee programs whose stated objectives are to manipulate and control the elements assumed by that agency (and its enabling legislation) to be the causal factors of the defined problem. Hence, there was the Office of Economic Opportunity of the Johnson years, the Law Enforcement Assistance Administration of the Nixon years, and the Energy Department of the Carter years. In each of these and other similar cases, the purpose was the same: To specify objectives in terms of outputs or outcomes as a function of altered behavioral characteristics and then to fund agents who were invested with the authority to intervene in the problematic situation. With the initiation of a program came an inevitable expectation, for both program recipients and the public at large, that the desired results would come to pass. However, what

---

[4]The data in this paragraph is from an address by Amitai Etzioni, George Washington University, February 1983. These same findings are borne out in numerous studies and has been especially popularized in works such as John Naisbitt, *Megatrends: Ten New Directions Transforming Our Lives* (New York: Warner Books, 1982).

often followed was a disappointment, because this expectation was seldom met as quickly as hoped (if at all); this in turn often resulted in a cynicism about such programmatic action.

Such disenchantment has been explained in several ways, including reference to the propensity of legislative bodies to enact broad (and basically unrealizable) objectives. However, what has seldom been questioned, but must be, is the operant social theory upon which such programmatic activity is based. Its operating assumption is that there exists a necessary, direct, linear relationship of cause and effect between institutionally specified objectives (such as legislative mandates) and individual or small group behavior. One way to view the increasing malaise with government and institutional action is to see it as reflective of a growing cynicism toward this theoretical stance.

The other form of governmental structuring of the social environment, the *regulatory,* can also be seen in the same light. In addition, however, the primary thrust of regulatory activity has always been that of rationalizing (and therefore stabilizing and regularizing) the actions of individuals and groups within a particular social configuration.

The rationalizing logic that underlies the regulatory insists on ordering and standardizing the boundaries of a particular milieu and the individual actions within it. It does this through a process of hierarchical rule generation. This is structured in terms of the power of the state to use legitimated force to ensure compliance with its mandates. There is also a hierarchy of knowledge; expertise is used to produce generalized solutions (rules) to day-to-day-specific problems. In both instances, the specification of both problem and solution are placed in the hands of those with the coercive power. The effect of this, for purposes here, is to anesthetize the operant social theory from serious examination.

Theory for Control: The Rational Science Model

By virtue of public administration's ambiguous status as either (or perhaps both) an academic discipline or an area of professional activity, students of the field have long been obliged to grapple with complex questions about theory's relation to practice. The word "theory" is itself sufficiently ambiguous that it embodies several meanings and, as a consequence, may serve a variety of purposes. In order to deal with this ambiguity, public administration scholars often distinguish among the meanings and purposes of theory by means of formal categories. One representative and influential categorization is provided by Stephen K. Bailey, who identifies four general categories of theory found in the public administration literature:

1 *Descriptive-explanatory theory,* which encompasses those propositions and models whose intent is systematically to explain and predict action in or related to public administration.

2 *Normative theory,* whose objective is "to establish future states prescriptively,"[5] by elucidating the *value* premises on which administrative action should be taken and judged.

3 *Assumptive theory,* which includes those "propositions which articulate the root assumptions about the nature of man and the tractability of institutions."[6]

4 *Instrumental theory,* which refers to those theories whose purpose is the application of knowledge to practical tasks of accomplishing administrative objectives.

For Bailey, instrumental theories

are the "pay-off" theories. All else is pedantry. A man may be knowledgable about reality, inspired in his sense of what is needed, and profound in his understanding of human nature. . . . But if he lacks instrumental wisdom . . . he might just as well have stood in bed.[7]

Bailey's four-part categorization, and in particular his emphasis on instrumental theory as the culmination and payoff of theorizing, reflects some common presumptions of both scholars and practitioners about what theory is and what it should do. The primary purpose of academic theory, just as for the operant social theory, is to enable control. Implicit in this notion of control is an assumption that the relation between theory and practice is unidirectional, specifically, that theory informs and drives practice—*not* the other way around. Thus, while practice provides the data on which theory is based, once theory is formulated, it is then the rationale for altering practice. This conception of theory in public administration mirrors the operant social theory by supporting both a programmatic and a regulatory thrust.

One characteristic of this orientation is epistemological: Theory (ideas about the world) rather than practice (action in the world) is assumed as the basis of valid knowledge. Another characteristic is political: The relationship between theory and practice is a hierarchical specification of power. Just as in the operant social theory, it is policy that drives admin-

---

[5]Stephen K. Bailey, "Objectives of the Theory of Public Administration," in James C. Charlesworth, ed., *Theory and Practice in Public Administration: Scope, Objectives and Methods* (Philadelphia: American Academy of Political and Social Science, October 1968), p. 129.

[6]Ibid., p. 133.

[7]Ibid., p. 136.

istration, so theory here drives practice. In both cases, the relation is one of subordination in which the interests of the second are seen as deriving from and being guided by those of the first. Finally, a third characteristic is normative: The way in which the relationship between theory and practice is structured reveals a particular value stance toward human consciousness and responsibility. Theory, because it deals with behavior (observed action mediated through the value system of the observer), becomes normatively superior to and therefore more meaningful than practice, which merely deals with action (human intentionality tied to concrete events).

Especially in recent years, however, these traditional beliefs about theory's relation to practice have been hotly contested throughout the social sciences. Disagreement about them also pervades the public administration literature and is a major source of friction among contending factions. It is also the primary basis of difference between the various perspectives outlined in Part III. But this is not a debate limited to academics; it is part and parcel of the larger debate (and malaise) about the role of government in American society. This debate turns not only on the question of what government should (or should not) do, but also on what government can and cannot do. The issue can be formulated relatively clearly: Can the actions of people be explained, and therefore predicted and controlled, through the use of those deterministic notions, such as cause/effect and stimulus/response, that are concomitant with this view of theory and made operational by programs and regulations?

The Operant Social Theory—Again

Much of both the writing about and work of public administration between 1960 and 1980 was predicated on the operant social theory. This has been the source of frustration, both within and without government, about the latter's ability to solve the various social problems that have afflicted the nation with such regularity. When our theories break down and fail to provide adequate explanation, the tendency has been to blame our government rather than our science or our theories.

The rational science model has two characteristics that bear scrutiny, because together they connect closely with the operant social theory. The *direct causal assumption* in such theory building is imbedded in the programmatic aspects of the operant social theory. Likewise, its intellectual cousin, the *rationalizing presumption,* is part and parcel of the regulatory aspect. This presumption suggests that careful analysis of a problem or policy will *necessarily* enable rational determination of the needed inputs and decisions that may appropriately guide action.

The causal assumption and the rationalizing presumption, like the operant social theory itself, have guided much of the administrative activity in the decades between the inaugurations of Kennedy and Reagan.

They have also come to be at the heart of our thinking about what government should or should not do. Both support a particular kind of social control, one that emphasizes external forces as against individual motivation, coercion and compliance as against persuasion and agreement, and hierarchical planning toward prestated objectives as against mediation of interests toward discovery of mutual objectives.

Theory and Practice

All of which brings us once again to the notion of "theory versus practice" that has pervaded the last several decades of thinking about and doing public administration. This has evolved, in effect, into a principle of "theory as administration." As the influence of government has grown over the last twenty years, the role of the public administrator as a key player in governing society has substantially increased. As such, the public administrator has become the central actor in administering a particular theory: By manipulating the environment (and the people in it) and by rationalizing the processes of this manipulation, it is necessarily possible to create a bigger and better world for all. In the 1930s and 1940s, we manipulated plants and animals to increase geometrically our food production. We did the same with our machinery and production processes in the 1950s in order to increase our economic productivity. During the 1960s and 1970s, we tried to do the same with our social institutions themselves. All through this, but especially in the last two decades, the primary mover (though by no means the only one, as some would assert) has been government—government in the person of the administrator, the caseworker, the policy analyst, the policymaker.

In his discussion of public administration theory, Stephen Bailey makes an offhand remark: "The utility of theory as an exercise in understanding for purposes of control need not be belabored."[8] Yet, perhaps it is after all the very thing that we must belabor, if we are to understand the limits of that control and thereby the limits of theory as a means for facilitating it. And this we must do if we are to use the administrative technology of public administration as a vehicle for governing society, rather than merely controlling it, and for making choices about our collective future.

Administrative Responsibility

Our argument above is simply that the rational science model has so fully infused our conceptions of theory and practice that it now stands as the dominant paradigm for both government action and public administra-

---

[8]Ibid., p. 128.

tion theorizing.[9] Although the benefits reaped from its use are undeniable, it is also evident that we have learned the rational model too well, without learning its limitations. These are not only limitations in our *abilities* to control, but also limitations in the *desirability* of control as the premier mode of government action. This paradigm effectively denies both the wickedness of problems and the necessary diversity of theory.

On the other hand, effective and humane action in and by government, we assert, would not only control when appropriate to do so, but would also reflect an ability to learn from and trust the processes of social experience. To learn from our experience requires a far different role for theory than that of control as implied by the rational model. Instead, theory must increasingly be regarded as a means for interpreting, criticizing, reflecting on, and generally making sense of what we do as administrators, as citizens, and collectively as nations and governments.

At the same time, theory, in all of its diversity, can variously serve all of these interests only so long as we recognize that personal judgment, reflective understanding of ourselves and our collective experience, and deciding what we should value must all precede our efforts to control. As public administrators, we must therefore deal first with the issue of administrative responsibility; only then can we profit fully from a look across the perspectives presented here.

The role of the administrator is to mediate, not merely to judge or to solve problems, but to interpose between two parties as the equal friend of each. The administrator mediates not just between the policy of the government and the governed, but also between the interests that make up both sides of that traditional equation. Performing this essential role thus requires that the administrator be responsible in each of three senses: professionally, politically, and personally.

Professional Responsibility

Acting in a manner that is professionally responsible requires both a state of mind and a morality. It means having sufficient knowledge of the task at hand to appreciate its consequences, yet not allowing that knowledge to dominate the appreciation of the situation. This suggests that being objective is necessary in the sense of having the ability to weigh the available evidence both impersonally (without concern for personal gain) and impartially (without concern for where the benefits accrue). In other words, being professional simply means making no decision on subjective factors alone and being conscious that this is one's professional responsibility.

[9]Much of this section is based on Richard T. Mayer and Michael M. Harmon, "Teaching Moral Education in Public Administration," *Southern Review of Public Administration* 6:2(1982):217–26.

This sense of being a professional—or better, of acting professionally—seems to be what Laurin Wollan attempts to describe. He argues that, despite all the different definitions of profession, there are three things that most would acknowledge professionals as being: ethical, vocational, and learned.[10] The ethical element that is conjured up when one speaks of acting professionally has to do with precepts and codes perhaps, but even more important, it has to do with the sense that any such elements are both internalized and not unique to the particular individual. The professional is semiautonomous, self-governing, and self-disciplined. Professional action is thus based on a self-directed understanding of proper action.

"Vocational," as Wollan uses it, speaks to the sense of a calling that one brings to one's work, a summons to service. It is not coincidental that we use such phrases as "the public service," "military service," "civil service," and "social service." They present us with images of being oriented beyond one's individual self.

Finally, there is the element of being learned. By this Wollan seems to mean not just training, yet more than being knowledgeable or formally educated. There is a body of knowledge that one is able to call upon as a professional, a body of knowledge that is learned by study *and* by doing.

Political Responsibility

Acting in a manner that is politically responsible means being cognizant of the dominant societal values as expressed not only through the pronouncements of the regime currently in power, but also through the law and the Constitution, and through society's historical development. It means comprehending that any decision made by a public administrator that affects people's lives (both corporate and individual), no matter how seemingly technical and value-free, is always in part a political decision because it allocates public resources through the mediation of interests. Finally, it means recognizing that administrative decisions are made in the name of the public—not merely in the name of the organization, agency, or bureau—and therefore necessarily speak politically to the public interest, no matter how poorly this may be defined.

To be politically responsible is also to be responsibly political. Although the Wilsonian dichotomy of politics and administration has long been intellectually undermined as an analytical tool, both a conceptual and a real-world difference between the two remains. Knowing that there is and must be a difference that matters prods us to define in explicit,

---

[10]Laurin A. Wollan, Jr., "Lawyers in Government—'The Most Serviceable Instruments of Authority,'" *Public Administration Review* 38:2(1978):105–12.

though still general, terms the proper relationship of politics in and to administration. Part of that definition, not surprisingly, was articulated by Woodrow Wilson when he clearly emphasized that the then-emerging science of administration be adapted to the unique features of the American political system. Within the value consensus of the system, he urged, administrators should be granted broad decision-making discretion in execution of the law.[11]

Subsequent writers have taken a more generous view of what it means for administrators to be responsibly political. In view of the complexity of modern administration, however, it is doubtful that Wilson would vigorously disagree with some of their conclusions. Carl Friedrich's advice, for instance, that administrative discretion should be informed by popular sentiment as well as by standards of professional conduct hardly violates Wilson's prescription.[12] Nor does Gibson Winter's more contemporary description of the administrator's role as the executor of public policy:

> Policy has to do with man's problems in coping with the future—man's problem as a maker of history as well as being made by history. Policy brings to statement what is judged to be possible, desirable, and meaningful for the human enterprise. In this sense, policy is the nexus of fact, value, and ultimate meaning in which scientific, ethical, and theological-philosophical reflections meet.[13]

Certainly there is room for debate about the proper limits of administrative discretion—as should be evident by the discussion in all the previous chapters—especially in determining what is "possible, desirable, and meaningful for the human enterprise." It is also clear that such debate can no longer be couched in absolute terms. The limits are likely to be found—and re-found, just as wicked problems are regularly re-solved—by examining the tension between political and professional responsibilities.

Personal Responsibility

Acting in a manner that is personally responsible is to acknowledge that it is one's actions that affect people's lives. Social forces, institutions, parties, and even government itself are chimera: They are ways we have

---

[11]Woodrow Wilson, "The Study of Administration," *Political Science Quarterly* 2:2(1887):197–220.

[12]Carl J. Friedrich, "Public Policy and the Nature of Administrative Responsibility," in Friedrich and Edward S. Mason, eds. *Public Policy 1* (Cambridge: Harvard University Press, 1940), pp. 3–24.

[13]Gibson Winter, "Toward a Comprehensive Science of Policy," *Journal of Religion 50* (October 1970):352.

of speaking about, generalizing about, the combined actions of others, and they are ways of recording our history. They are real to the extent that we stand outside of them and to the extent we allow them to alter and define our lives. At root, however, they consist of those actions taken by innumerable individuals, each of whom is responsible—that is, can be held accountable by other members of society—for the consequences of the collective action. The utility of framing responsibility in this sense lies not in arousing paroxysms of guilt, but rather in reminding each of us who works, thinks, teaches, and learns in an administrative environment that we cannot escape from the consequences of our actions. We cannot shift the burden of those actions to others, to institutions, or to rules. And we cannot hide our actions under a blanket of rhetoric about orders, requirements, or the like.

Professional, political, and personal responsibility are neither additive nor exclusive notions. Each is meaningful only in relation to the other two. Each provides a check against those pathologies of the others that would develop were they alone to guide the actions of administrators. Political responsibility, for example, rescues both professionalism from being a narrow instrumentalism and personal responsibility from being either ethical narcissism or moral dogmatism. Professional responsibility, in turn, checks both the tendency of the political to degenerate into opportunism and the personal to lapse into naive impracticality. Finally, personal responsibility helps clarify the difference between political responsibility and unquestioning obedience, as well as between professionalism and mindless technicism.

What is required is an accommodation with and call for the constant negotiation of the tensions between the three aspects of responsible administrative action. One aspect of this comes in dealing with, thinking about, and working in organizations. Given the theoretical landscape that we have crossed in this volume, it should be clear that we believe there is no such thing as *the* perspective that explains organizational action. Each perspective that has been investigated here—and, we would submit, all those we have not touched upon—offers useful insights while blinding us to important aspects of people organizing themselves.

Summarizing the Diversity of Organization Theory

All of this argues for structuring a summary view of organization theory's diverse perspectives around how they relate to the general questions that administrators should consider when drawing upon theory for practical insights. Therefore, rather than summarizing each theoretical perspective separately, we have instead provided comparisons of the perspectives from the standpoint of the six general dimensions outlined earlier in Chapter 2. Each dimension suggests corresponding questions of practical interest to administrators:

1 *The cognitive interests of the theoretical perspectives.* Why, in the first place, do or should you want to know about theory? What practical purposes do you hope that it will serve?

2 *The dominant metaphors implicit in the various perspectives.* What general images are, or might be, helpful in ordering your understanding of organizations and organizing?

3 *The primary units and levels of analysis of the perspectives.* Whose point of view should you take: that of an external, disinterested observer; a concerned citizen; top management; an ordinary worker? How broadly or narrowly, given your present interests or circumstances, should you focus your attention?

4 *The basic assumptions that the perspectives make about the relation of the individual to the organization and society.* Should people, yourself included, be integrated more fully with organizations, protected *from* them, enabled to transcend them? Are organizations primarily instruments of social domination, or are they benign associations of cooperative activity?

5 *The meaning and locus of rationality assumed by each perspective.* Individually or collectively, to what extent can we know (a) why we do what we do, and (b) what the consequences of that action will be? Does thought precede action—or is it the other way around? In other words, does our experience mainly follow from our conscious decisions about goals and objectives, or do goals and objectives emerge out of our experience?

6 *The primary values explicitly or implicitly embodied in the theoretical perspectives.* Which is most important: achieving goals, being efficient, acting according to principle, understanding what you and others are doing, promoting humane social processes, being left alone? Whose side are you on? Do "sides" have to be chosen?

Cognitive Interests

In Chapter 10, we discussed Jürgen Habermas's argument that the social sciences can be distinguished from one another according to the three generic types of cognitive human interests they serve: technical control (the empirical-analytic sciences), interpretive understanding (the historical-hermeneutic sciences) and human emancipation (the critically oriented sciences). Like all such categorizations, Habermas's typology of "cognitive interests" is of course disputable, including his beginning assumption that social science necessarily serves, in a direct way, *any* "interest"—save that of knowledge for its own sake.

If, however, we accept the idea that organization theory serves practical interests, then how can the various perspectives discussed in Part III be usefully distinguished from one another? Table 12.1 provides a framework for answering this question by (1) using Habermas's categorization to indicate the cognitive interests that each theoretical perspective promotes and by (2) describing the kinds of practical interests of administrators that each perspective addresses. In reading Table 12.1, some cautionary notes should be borne in mind. First, *any* perspective might serve a broad interest in interpretive understanding (Habermas's second type of cognitive interest) by virtue of its providing a novel framework for viewing organizations and organizing. Second, several types of cognitive interests might be served by a theoretical perspective; however, one type is ordinarily primary. Third, we have deliberately construed emancipation (Habermas's third type of cognitive interest) more broadly than he intends, by including within that designation those theoretical perspectives whose humanistic sentiments reflect a strong concern with the project of personal development. Finally, in light of the diversity of views found *within* the perspectives, we have noted where appropriate the major practical concerns suggested by each of the principal contributors we have discussed.

Dominant Metaphors

The use of metaphors is unavoidable in perceiving, making sense of, and producing the social world. In view of our inability to apprehend aspects of social life solely through sensory observation, we use metaphors, though we are often unaware of doing so, as the lenses through which we absorb and filter out sense data, order and arrange them into meaningful patterns, and then act as if those metaphors had objective validity as representations of the "real world." When our own metaphors match those of people with whom we associate, they will tend to regard us as sensible and realistic. When our metaphors are vivid and evocative, and resonate with the unconscious, repressed, or merely forgotten experience of others, they might regard us as leaders, as influential, or even as visionaries. When there is no match or resonance at all between our own metaphors and those of others, they may well regard us as deranged.

Theorists also employ metaphors, though typically with a greater degree of self-consciousness and explicitness than that of people in everyday life. For organizational and other social theorists, metaphors may guide and even determine the directions and methods of their analyses, whereas in other instances seemingly apt metaphors may be discovered or invented after analysis in order to summarize or make sense of what they have observed. In either case, however, theorists may be so forceful in arguing for their preferred metaphors that they, like the rest of us, end up by ascribing to their metaphors an objective validity, sometimes asserting them as foundations for a "scientific" account of the social world.

Table 12.2 offers a brief comparison of the dominant metaphors implicit in the perspectives presented in Part III. Highlighting the differing metaphors in this way, we hope, will discourage the tendency to regard any particular metaphor as synonymous with a "truthful" representation of organizations or organizing. In suggesting these metaphors as concise images of the various theoretical perspectives, we make no claim that they necessarily match those used by any particular theorist in contributing to those perspectives.

TABLE 12.1

Cognitive Interests and Practical Uses of Theory

Theoretical Perspective	Cognitive Interest	Practical Interests Served for Administrators
Neo-Classical Theories	Technical	Explanation and prediction to enable rational choice, given high uncertainty and imperfect information
Systems Theories (Katz & Kahn, Thompson)	Technical	Understanding factors related to organizational survival and stability; reducing uncertainty so as to achieve control over or adapt to the environment
(Buckley)	Technical, but also interpretive	Same as above; but also to understand how the organizational order is negotiated among its members
(Ackoff & Gawthrop)	Unclear: technical or emancipatory	Developing collective strategies for democratic organizational change
Later Human Relations Theories	Unclear: technical or emancipatory	Integrating individual and organizational needs through participative processes and democratic leadership styles
Market Theories Public Choice (Buchanan & Tullock, Ostrom)	Technical	Maximizing aggregate utility; responding to the diversity of client needs; enabling noncoerced choices by private individuals

continued next page

continued

Theoretical Perspective	Cognitive Interest	Practical Interests Served for Administrators
Incrementalism (Braybrooke & Lindblom)	Technical	Ameliorating rather than definitively solving problems; adjusting for inability to utilize comprehensive analysis
Interpretive & Critical Theories (Schutz, Silverman)	Interpretive	Understanding differences in situational and problem definitions, and how those differences lessen the effectiveness of working relationships
(Winter, Harmon, Hummel, Denhardt, Forester)	Emancipatory, but also interpretive	Same as both above; but also understanding how organizational structures and associated modes of language and reason create power inequalities, domination, and alienation
Theories of Emergence (Follett)	Interpretive and emancipatory	Understanding how noncoerced decisions produce shared experiences that enable the discovery of sensible goals
(Weick)	Interpretive	Understanding how differing metaphors may retrospectively illuminate the meaning and consequences of organizing
(White & McSwain)	Interpretive and emancipatory	Understanding how unconscious energy affects possibilities for self-aware, responsible action
(Thayer)	Interpretive and emancipatory	Understanding how decision structures affect the quality of social process, the levels of individual alienation, and sensible allocation of resources

Primary Units and Levels of Analysis

Although the primary units of analysis used by organizational theorists may appear to be merely convenient starting points for investigation, they typically reflect the theorists' beliefs as to what is most real about and most basic to an understanding of the subjects of their inquiry. The choice of a primary unit of analysis constitutes an assertion as to what the understanding and explanation of organizations ultimately rely on. Thus, the primary unit embodies a philosophical commitment as much as a methodological vantage point for the theorist.

Primary units of analysis are distinguishable in part by the levels (or encompassing-ness) of the phenomena to which they refer. In the termi-

TABLE 12.2

Dominant Metaphors and Theoretical Perspectives

Theoretical Perspective	Dominant Metaphor	Aspects of Organizing Highlighted by the Metaphor
Neo-Classical Theories	Decision set	Means by which and premises on which actors attempt to make rational choices
Systems Theories	Biological organism	Interdependencies with the environment; input, processing, and output of energy
Later Human Relations Theories	Integration	Social processes by which individual and organizational needs and goals may be satisfied simultaneously
Market Theories	Marketplace	Processes of economic and social exchange, resource allocation, and mutual adjustment among individuals and groups
Interpretive and Critical Theories	Language	Rules and processes for negotiating, maintaining, and changing patterns of social relations
Theories of Emergence	Emergence	Social and psychic dynamics that affect the unfolding of individual energy and the discovery of shared purposes

nology of Part I's public administration framework, particular units of analysis are likely to bias inquiry toward one of the three organizational arenas: the inter-organizational, the intra-organizational, and the organization-to-individual. The appeal of a particular unit of analysis for administrators may well depend on which arena they regard as most salient to an understanding of their everyday activities. Where you stand, as they say, depends on where you sit. An awareness of those units of analysis that appear *less* salient to one's own activities, however, may lead to an appreciation of why *others* stand, and sit, where *they* do. The vantage point of top management is different indeed from that of the mid-level supervisor, the computer programmer, the client, the concerned citizen, and one's political masters.

One must be cautious, however, because primary units of analysis differ not only with respect to the levels to which they direct attention, but also in terms of the particular motives or purposes that they embody. Both the market theorists and the later human relationists, for example, employ the individual as their primary unit, yet attribute very different fundamental motives to that individual. The self-actualizer of Abraham Maslow is a far cry from the self-interested utility-maximizer of Buchanan and Tullock.

Moreover, these differences in the basic motives of individuals are also significant insofar as they embody commitments to certain values. To Maslow, people *should* self-actualize; to the public choice theorists, *good* government promotes and protects the individual's right to pursue his or her self-interested ends; and to the systems theorists, the satisfaction of organizational needs for survival, homeostasis, control, or adaptation are positive benefits, at least implicitly.

Table 12.3 summarizes the six theoretical perspectives according to (1) their primary units of analysis, (2) the organizational arenas to which they direct most immediate attention, (3) the kinds of organizational issues for which they mainly offer illumination, and (4) the question of from *whose* point of view within the organization the primary unit has greatest relevance.

TABLE 12.3
Primary Units and Arenas of Analysis

Theoretical Perspective	Primary Unit (& Arena) of Analysis	Issues Illuminated by the Primary Unit (From Whose Point of View)
Neo-Classical Theories	Decision (intra-org)	Premises underlying and limits to rational decision making (from the decision maker's point of view)
Systems Theories	System viewed holistically (inter-org, intra-org)	Maintenance and direction of organization as a whole in the face of environmental uncertainty (from top management's viewpoint)
Later Human Relations Theories	Self-actualizing individual (org-to-ind)	Promotion of individual growth and development, while meeting goals of the organization (as negotiated by the worker and the manager)
Market Theories	Self-interested individual (org-to-ind, inter-org)	Design of efficient structures for allocating resources; maximizing aggregate utility, while adjusting for negative side effects (from the viewpoint of designers of decision structures)
Interpretive/ Critical Theories	Face-to-face encounter; the alienated individual (org-to-ind, intra-org)	Development of noncoercive processes for achieving consensus around shared purposes and social relationships (subjective meanings of all actors, including organization members and citizens)
Theories of Emergence	Human/intrapsychic encounter; shared social experience (org-to-ind, inter-org)	Promoting individual growth through reflexive understanding of psychic experience; discovery of shared purposes emerging from social experience, rather than rational thought (from the viewpoint of the reflexive individual)

Relation of the Individual to the Organization

Assumptions that social theorists make about the relation of the individual to society necessarily reflect a combination of beliefs about human nature and the nature of the social order. An assumption about one is the mirror image of the other. As microcosms of the larger social order, organizations are similarly viewed by theorists as special types of social collectivities that exist in particular kinds of relation to the individuals who comprise or inhabit them. The ways in which theorists variously conceive the fundamental nature of that relationship are not the result of empirical investigation, but are instead prespecified on the basis of philosophical reflection, experience unique to the theorist's personal biography, or simply unreflected intuition. Theorists' beliefs about the relation of the organization to the individual are also intimately linked to their particular cognitive interests and the metaphors and primary units of analysis that guide their inquiries.

Two polar positions illustrate the range of opinion about this dimension. One is Chester Barnard's conviction that individuals derive their moral nature by virtue of their willing participation in organizations. Although, most assuredly, organizations may be mismanaged, Barnard sees *effective* management as virtually synonymous with the realization of the organization's naturally benign, indeed benevolent, nature. The image of the individual thus implied is that of a highly social self whose own interests, if only he or she has the wit to realize it, are identical to those of the organization.

At the other extreme are the critical theorists, who regard the putative "facts" of the social world, including organizations, as shackles that impede the individual's natural struggle for emancipation. Where Barnard sees cooperation, the critical theorists find deeper and unconscious patterns of domination. What Barnard might regard as individual deviancy, the critical theorists would likely take to be evidence of healthy, autonomous action. For Barnard, observed mismatches between organizational purposes and the actions of recalcitrant individuals constitute aberrations, and are thus *management problems* that need to be solved. For critical theorists, those same mismatches are inherent in the human condition and, as such, are evidence of a *political* struggle that requires uncovering and explication.

There are, of course, middle-ground positions between these two polar extremes. Deeply conflicted as to their own sentiments, the later human relationists, for example, seek either to balance or integrate the competing interests of individuals and organizations. Still others, including public choice theorists and some interpretive and emergence theorists, regard only *particular forms* of social organization—chiefly hierarchy—as divisive of the two levels. To the former, the principal remedy may be found

TABLE 12.4

Organization-to-Individual Relations and Criteria for Human Fulfillment

Theoretical Perspective	Normatively Prior Level	Criterion of Individual Fulfillment
Neo-Classical Theories	Organization (implicit)	Individual rewards derived from the efficient attainment of organizational goals
Systems Theories	Organization (but in later writings moving to synthesis with individual needs)	Successful accommodation to and integration with the organization as a social system; achieving shared purposes (sometimes determined democratically)
Later Human Relations Theories	Individual (ambivalent by accepting legitimacy of organizational goals)	Self-actualization—within legitimate constraints imposed by the organization's leadership
Market Theories	Individual (organization is merely an aggregation of private individuals)	Exercise of free choice in pursuit of private interests; reduction of the costs of social interaction in decision making
Interpretive/Critical Theories (Public Administration synthesis)	Individual (organization is derived of face-to-face relations)	Self-realization enabled by noncoercive social relations and discourse; emancipation through self-reflexivity
Theories of Emergence	Individual (organization is the product of shared experience)	Retrospective discovery of the meaning of social and psychic experience

in the idea of the *marketplace,* whereas for the latter two perspectives, the answer lies in *consensual* organizations.

Table 12.4 summarizes the six perspectives of Part III in terms of their differing stances regarding the relation of the individual to the organization. Each perspective is briefly described, first, in terms of whether the organization or the individual is considered as normatively prior, and, second, in terms of its criterion for successful individual fulfillment in relation to the organization.

The Meaning and Locus of Rationality

Although virtually all organization theorists grapple with the problem of rational action, the meanings and normative importance of rationality vary widely in their writings. This is an issue of immense practical significance, since the meanings of rationality largely determine the particular manner in which organizational effectiveness and efficiency are construed and ranked in relation to other normative criteria of organizational performance. Differences of opinion about the meaning of rationality reflect differing priorities regarding the relation of ends (and associated terms such as goals or purposes) and means (i.e., social processes). Additionally, theorists disagree as to the level of analysis in which rationality (or the possibilities for it) is located. Is the primary locus of rationality, for example, the consciously aware individual or is it the organization as a unified whole?

At the root of these controversies is the question of whether thought logically precedes action (experience) or action precedes thought. As with our previous discussion of primary units of analysis, two polar positions can be identified with respect to this question. The first is that of Herbert Simon, whose strict separation of ends from means, values from facts, necessarily implies that thought precedes, or at least *should* precede, action. To Simon, rationality has little, if anything, to do with the way in which ends are initially specified; rather, it is the criterion by which action is linked to, and evaluated in terms of, its correspondence with previously chosen conscious ends. Action is an instrument for their efficient attainment. Thus, whereas ends, themselves, have no necessarily rational basis, their conscious specification precedes and provides the standard against which action is subsequently judged. Despite the *limits* to rational action of which Simon was acutely aware, the intention toward rationality is nevertheless the defining characteristic of human action.

The other polar extreme is reflected in the writings of Mary Parker Follett (and also other emergence theorists) who flatly declared that action precedes thought. Ends, which to Follett were necessarily social or collective in nature, are *products of* social experience, rather than preconceived through conscious, intellectual thought. The "law of the situation," which is properly understood as a gradual unfolding of collective experience, enables us to grasp only retrospectively the "rationality" of our collective purposes. The value of ends is discoverable through recognition of the inherent value of authentic and creative social processes.

As with the other dimensions that we have summarized, many of the theorists discussed in Part III take positions somewhere in between those two polar extremes. Often, their treatment of rationality is less explicit than Simon's and Follett's, requiring perhaps imperfect inferences as to their actual stances on this issue. Nevertheless, Table 12.5 summarizes the range of views in the six theoretical perspectives as they bear on the meaning and locus of rationality and the relationships of thought and action thereby implied.

Primary Values

The social values affirmed by organization theories are seldom the products of intellectual choices made prior to and independently of other analytical considerations. Nor are they arbitrarily added on to frameworks for organizational analysis after the fact. Rather, values are *embodied in* frameworks of analysis and are inseparable from the five dimensions

TABLE 12.5
The Meaning and Locus of Rationality

Theoretical Perspective	Locus of Rationality	Meaning of Rationality (Relationship of Thought and Action)
Neo-Classical Theories	Decision maker	Instrumental attainment of preconceived ends under conditions of uncertainty (thought precedes action)
Systems Theories	Organization as a whole	Adapting to imperatives for organizational survival; attaining collective purposes (thought precedes action at individual level)
Later Human Relations Theories	Self-actualizing individual	Meeting needs for self-actualization in the face of organizational imperatives for instrumental rationality (thought and action are interactive)
Market Theories	Self-interested individual	Maximizing individual and aggregate utility at least cost (thought, i.e., decisions about ends, precedes action)
Interpretive/Critical Theories	Individual (informed by interpretive and critical reason)	Rationality involves the use of interpretive and critical reason in order to understand oneself and social processes (action mainly precedes thought)
Theories of Emergence	Social and intrapsychic processes	Rational action is discovered retrospectively through cooperative social experience and self-confrontation (action precedes thought)

just discussed. Values are, at the same time, the products of and the driving forces behind those five dimensions. To the extent that there are differences among or within the theoretical perspectives with respect to the five dimensions, such variation is reflected in the differing values that the perspectives embody. Being clear about these values assists us in understanding why the theorists have written what they have written. More importantly, they provide summary clues as to the probable consequences of taking organization theories seriously and of discovering where their "cash value" truly lies. Table 12.6, then, may be viewed as a summary of summaries, with each perspective identified by the primary values that it represents or seeks to promote.

Conclusion

Throughout this book we have stressed those descriptive and normative aspects of public administration practice that together form a unique con-

TABLE 12.6

Primary Values Embodied in Organization Theories

Theoretical Perspective	Primary Values
Neo-Classical Theories	Efficiency, rational goal attainment
Systems Theories	Organizational survival and adaptation to environment; achieving collective purposes through democratic means
Later Human Relations Theories	Achieving organizational goals by promoting individual self-actualization
Market Theories	Free individual choice and maximizing aggregate utility; ameliorating known social ills; responding to diverse organizational and environmental interests
Interpretive/Critical Theories	Promoting noncoercive discourse and processes of organizational decision making; reducing individual alienation through emancipation from reified social and organizational structures
Theories of Emergence	Discovering shared purposes through humane, noncoercive social processes; facilitating reflexive self-awareness to enable responsible personal action

text for examining organization theory. Both in Part I and in this concluding chapter, we have attempted to show how that context illuminates the distinctively wicked character of the problems that public administrators are obliged to define, solve, or tame, if only temporarily and imperfectly. For these efforts, or so we have argued, the practical value of theory is not mainly instrumental; rather, its value lies chiefly in informing the moral task of clarifying what we both do value and should value. It is probably not coincidental that the organization theorists who have most clearly recognized the moral character of theory are those few who have also been great administrators themselves. Certainly, Chester Barnard was one; another was Sir Geoffrey Vickers, who, shortly before his death, pondered the question of why, to begin with, we should want theory. He argued forcefully against the prevailing belief among social scientists that organizational decision makers needed or could even benefit from having a theory for the instrumental purposes of explanation, prediction, and control. Rather than dismiss theorizing as impractical, however, Vickers concluded on an encouraging note with which we would join:

> But wait—there is one sense in which I warmly agree that one needs a theory of decision making. Somewhere, I think in the *Art of Judgment*,[14] I say that the process of decision is directed to learning what to want rather than learning how to get. If that is a theory then surely we need it. The criterion of method is that it should present . . . the alternative mixes of value that are in fact avail-

[14]See Sir Geoffrey Vickers, *The Art of Judgment: A Study of Policy Making* (New York: Basic Books, 1965).

able. And the result is that we finish up not merely decided on what to do but changed in our norms of what is worth doing. So we start from a different place next time.... I hoped everyone knew by now that merely instrumental decisions (how "best" to get what you want) are an unimportant class of decision making unless the criteria of "best" are themselves open to evaluation.[15]

Seeking right action, as Vickers knew, does not imply a moral "one best way." Informed by the passions embodied in moral precepts, right action also appreciates the moral ambiguity inevitably attending administrative decision making. The diversity of theory serves as a continuous reminder of that moral ambiguity, while theorizing provides the necessary means for acting responsibly.

[15]Vickers, "Notes," *Dialogue, The Public Administration Theory Network* 1:3(1979):4.

Bibliography

Ackoff, Russell. *Redesigning the Future: A Systems Approach to Societal Problems.* New York: John Wiley and Sons, 1974.

Allison, Graham T., Jr. *Essence of Decision: Explaining the Cuban Missile Crisis.* Boston: Little, Brown, 1971.

Allison, Graham T., Jr. "Public and Private Management: Are They Fundamentally Alike in All Unimportant Respects?" In *Setting Public Management Research Agendas: Integrating the Sponsor, Producer and User.* OPM Document 127–53–1, pp. 27–38. Washington, DC: Office of Personnel Management, February 1980. Reprinted in Richard J. Stillman II, pp. 453–67. *Public Administration: Concepts and Cases,* 3rd ed. Boston: Houghton Mifflin, 1984.

Appleby, Paul. *Big Democracy.* New York: Alfred A. Knopf, 1945.

Appleby, Paul. *Policy and Administration.* University, Ala.: University of Alabama Press, 1949.

Appleby, Paul. *Morality and Administration.* Baton Rouge, La.: University of Louisiana Press, 1952.

Argyle, Michael. "The Relay Assembly Test Room in Retrospect." *Occupational Psychology* 27(1953):98–103.

Argyris, Chris. *Personality and Organization.* New York: Harper & Row, 1957.

Argyris, Chris. *Integrating the Individual and the Organization.* New York: John Wiley and Sons, 1964.

Argyris, Chris. *Intervention Theory and Method: A Behavioral Science View.* Reading, Mass.: Addison-Wesley, 1970.

Argyris, Chris. "Being Human and Being Organized." In Warren G. Bennis, ed., pp. 17–26. *American Bureaucracy.* Hawthorne, N.Y.: Aldine, 1970.

Argyris, Chris. "Some Limits of Rational Man Organizational Theory." *Public Administration Review* 33:3(1973):253–67.

Argyris, Chris. "Organization Man: Rational *and* Self-Actualizing." *Public Administration Review* 33:4(1973):354–57.

Argyris, Chris. *Reasoning, Learning, and Action: Individual and Organizational.* San Francisco: Jossey-Bass, 1983.

Argyris, Chris, and Schön, Donald. *Theory in Practice: Increasing Professional Effectiveness.* San Francisco: Jossey-Bass, 1974.

Argyris, Chris, and Schön, Donald. *Organizational Learning: A Theory of Action Perspective.* Reading, Mass.: Addison-Wesley, 1978.

Bachrach, Peter. *The Theory of Democratic Elitism: A Critique.* Boston: Little, Brown, 1970.

Bailey, Stephen K. "Objectives of the Theory of Public Administration." In James Charlesworth, ed., pp. 128–39. *Theory and Practice in Public Administration: Scope, Objectives and Methods.* Philadelphia: American Academy of Political and Social Science, October 1968.

Baretz, Loren. *The Servants of Power.* Westport, Conn.: Greenwood Press, 1974.

Barnard, Chester. *The Functions of the Executive.* Cambridge: Harvard University Press, 1968; first published in 1938.

Barnard, Chester. *Organization and Management.* Cambridge: Harvard University Press, 1948.

Barrett, William. *The Illusion of Technique.* Garden City, N.Y.: Anchor Books, 1979.

Bateson, Gregory. *Steps to an Ecology of Mind.* New York: Ballantine, 1972.

Bellone, Carl, ed. *Organization Theory and the New Public Administration.* Boston: Allyn and Bacon, 1980.

Bendix, Reinhard. *Max Weber: An Intellectual Portrait.* Berkeley, Calif.: University of California Press, 1960.

Bennis, Warren G. *Changing Organizations.* New York: McGraw-Hill, 1966.

Bennis, Warren G., ed. *American Bureaucracy.* Hawthorne, N.Y.: Aldine, 1970.

Berger, Peter L., and Luckmann, Thomas. *The Social Construction of Reality.* New York: Doubleday, 1967.

Bernstein, Richard. *The Restructuring of Social and Political Theory.* Philadelphia: University of Pennsylvania Press, 1978.

Biller, Robert P. "Toward Public Administration, Rather Than an Administration of Publics: Strategies of Accountable Disaggregation to Achieve Human Scale and Efficacy, and Live within the Limits of Intelligence and Other Scarce Resources." In Ross Clayton and William B. Storm, eds., pp. 151–72. *Agenda for Public Administration.* Los Angeles: University of Southern California, 1979.

Bion, Wilfred R. *Experiences in Groups.* New York: Basic Books, 1961.

Blake, Robert R., and Mouton, Jane S. *The Managerial Grid: Key Orientations for Achieving Production Through People.* Houston, Tex.: Gulf, 1964.

Blankenship, L. Vaughan. "Public Administration and the Challenge to Reason." In Dwight Waldo, ed., pp. 188–213. *Public Administration in a Time of Turbulence.* Scranton, Pa.: Chandler, 1971.

Blau, Peter M., and Scott, W. Richard. *Formal Organizations: A Comparative Approach.* San Francisco: Chandler, 1962.

Braybrooke, David, and Lindblom, Charles E. *A Strategy of Decision: Policy Evaluation as a Social Process.* Glencoe, Ill.: The Free Press of Glencoe, 1963.

Buchanan, James M., and Tullock, Gordon. *The Calculus of Consent.* Ann Arbor, Mich.: University of Michigan Press, 1962.

Buckley, Walter. *Sociology and Modern Systems Theory.* Englewood Cliffs, N.J.: Prentice-Hall, 1967.

Buckley, Walter, ed. *Modern Systems Research for the Behavioral Scientist.* Chicago: Aldine, 1968.

Buckley, Walter. "Society as a Complex, Adaptive System." In Jong S. Jun and William B. Storm, eds., pp. 198–213. *Tomorrow's Organizations: Challenges and Strategies.* Glenview, Ill.: Scott, Foresman, 1973.

Burrell, Gibson, and Morgan, Gareth. *Sociological Paradigms and Organisational Analysis.* London and Portsmouth, N.H.: Heinemann, 1979.

Carey, Alex. "The Hawthorne Studies: A Radical Criticism." *American Sociological Review* 32:2(1967):403–16.

Carvath, Donald L. "The Disembodied Dialectic: A Psychoanalytic Critique of Sociological Relativism." *Theory and Society* 4:1(1977):73–102.

Catron, Bayard L., and Harmon, Michael M. "Comments in Response to Ostrom on Methodological Individualism." *Dialogue: The Public Administration Theory Network* 2:6(1979):8–11.

Charlesworth, James, ed. *Theory and Practice in Public Administration: Scope, Objectives and Methods.* Philadelphia: American Academy of Political and Social Science, October 1968.

Churchman, C. West. *The Design of Inquiring Systems.* New York: Basic Books, 1971.

Cohen, Michael D.; March, James G.; and Olsen, Johan P. "A Garbage Can Model of Organizational Choice." *Administrative Science Quarterly* 17:1(1972):1–25.

Cohen, Michael D., and March, James G. *Leadership and Ambiguity.* New York: McGraw-Hill, 1974.

Collins, Randall. *Conflict Sociology: Toward an Explanatory Science.* New York: Academic Press, 1975.

Cyert, Richard M., and March, James G. *A Behavioral Theory of the Firm.* Englewood Cliffs, N.J.: Prentice-Hall, 1963.

Dahl, Robert A. "The Science of Public Administration: Three Problems." *Public Administration Review* 7:1(1947):1–11.

Dahrendorf, Ralf. *Class and Class Conflict in Industrial Society.* Stanford, Calif.: Stanford University Press, 1959.

De Gregori, Thomas R. "Caveat Emptor: A Critique of the Emerging Paradigm of Public Choice." *Administration and Society* 6:2(1974):205–28.

Denhardt, Robert B. *In the Shadow of Organization.* Lawrence, Kan.: The Regents Press of Kansas, 1981.

Denhardt, Robert B. "Toward a Critical Theory of Public Organization." *Public Administration Review* 41:6(1981):628–35.

Denhardt, Robert B. *Theories of Public Organization.* Monterey, Calif.: Brooks/Cole, 1984.

Denhardt, Robert B., and Denhardt, Kathryn G. "Public Administration and the Critique of Domination." *Administration and Society* 11:2(1979):107–20.

Downs, Anthony. *Inside Bureaucracy.* Boston: Little, Brown, 1966.

Dunn, William N., and Fozouni, Bahman. *Toward a Critical Administrative Theory.* Beverly Hills, Ca.: Sage, 1976.

Ellul, Jacques. *The Technological Society.* New York: Vintage, 1964.

Etzioni, Amitai. *The Active Society: A Theory of Societal and Political Processes.* New York: The Free Press, 1968.

Etzioni, Amitai, ed. *A Sociological Reader on Complex Organizations.* New York: Holt, Rinehart and Winston, 1969.

Fayol, Henri. *General and Industrial Management.* Constance Storrs, trans. London: Sir Isaac Pitman and Sons, 1949.

Finer, Herman. "Administrative Responsibility in Democratic Government." *Public Administration Review* 1:2(1941):335–50.

Follett, Mary Parker. *The New State: Group Organization the Solution of Popular Government.* New York: Longmans, Green, 1918.

Follett, Mary Parker. *Creative Experience.* New York: Longmans, Green, 1924.

Follett, Mary Parker. *Dynamic Administration,* Henry C. Metcalf and L. Urwick, eds. New York: Harper & Brothers, 1940.

Forester, John. "Critical Theory and Organizational Analysis." In Gareth Morgan, ed., pp. 234–46. *Beyond Method: Strategies for Social Research.* Beverly Hills, Ca.: Sage, 1983.

Frankfurt Institute for Social Research. John Viertel, trans. *Aspects of Sociology.* Boston: Beacon Press, 1972.

Frederickson, H. George. "Toward a New Public Administration." In Frank Marini, pp. 309–31. *Toward a New Public Administration: The Minnowbrook Perspective.* Scranton, Pa.: Chandler, 1971.

Frederickson, H. George, ed. "A Symposium: Social Equity and Public Administration." *Public Administration Review* 34:1(1974):1–51.

Frederickson, H. George. *New Public Administration.* University, Ala.: University of Alabama Press, 1980.

Friedrich, Carl J. "Public Policy and the Nature of Administrative Responsibility." In Friedrich and Edward S. Mason, eds., pp. 3–24. *Public Policy 1.* Cambridge: Harvard University Press, 1940.

Garfinkel, Harold. *Studies in Ethnomethodology.* Englewood Cliffs, N.J.: Prentice-Hall, 1967.

Gawthrop, Louis C. *Public Sector Management, Systems, and Ethics.* Bloomington, Ind.: Indiana University Press, 1984.

Gerth, H. H., and Mills, C. Wright, trans. and eds. *From Max Weber: Essays in Sociology.* New York: Oxford University Press, 1946.

Giddens, Anthony. *New Rules of Sociological Method: A Positive Critique of Interpretive Sociologies.* New York: Basic Books, 1976.

Giddens, Anthony. *The Constitution of Society.* Berkeley: University of California Press, 1984.

Goffman, Erving. *The Presentation of Self in Everyday Life.* Garden City, N.Y.: Doubleday, 1959.

Golembiewski, Robert T. *Men, Management, and Morality.* New York: McGraw-Hill, 1976.

Golembiewski, Robert T. *Public Administration as a Developing Discipline, Part II.* New York: Marcel Dekker, 1977.

Golembiewski, Robert T. "A Critique of 'Democratic Administration' and Its Supporting Ideation." *American Political Science Review* 71:4(1977):1488–1507.

Golembiewski, Robert T. "Observations on Doing Political Theory: A Rejoinder." *American Political Science Review* 71:4(1977):1526–31.

Golembiewski, Robert T., and Eddy, William, eds. *Organization Development in Public Administration, Part I.* New York: Marcel Dekker, 1978.

Goodsell, Charles T. *The Case for Bureaucracy: A Public Administration Polemic.* Chatham, N.J.: Chatham House, 1983.

Gouldner, Alvin W. *The Coming Crisis in Western Sociology.* London: Heinemann, 1970.

Green, Phillip, and Levinson, Sanford, eds. *Power and Community: Dissenting Essays in Political Science.* New York: Pantheon Books, 1969.

Gulick, Luther, and Urwick, L. *Papers on the Science of Adminstration.* New York: Institute of Public Administration, 1937.

Gulick, Luther. "The Twenty-Fifth Anniversary of the American Society for Public Administration." *Public Administration Review* 25:1(1965):1–4.

Habermas, Jürgen. *Toward a Rational Society.* Jeremy J. Shapiro, trans. Boston: Beacon Press, 1970.

Habermas, Jürgen. *Knowledge and Human Interests.* Jeremy J. Shapiro, trans. Boston: Beacon Press, 1971.

Habermas, Jürgen. "A Postscript to Knowledge and Human Interests." *Philosophy of the Social Sciences,* 3(1973): 157–85.

Habermas, Jürgen. "The Public Sphere." *New German Critique* 3(1974):49–55.

Habermas, Jürgen. *Legitimation Crisis.* Boston: Beacon Press, 1975.

Hampden-Turner, Charles. *Radical Man.* Garden City, N.Y.: Doubleday, 1971.

Harmon, M. Judd. *Political Thought: From Plato to the Present.* New York: McGraw-Hill, 1964.

Harmon, Michael M. "Organization Development in the State Department: A Case Study of the ACORD Program." *Report of the Commission on the Organization of the Government for the Conduct of Foreign Policy,* Volume 6. Washington, DC: U.S. Government Printing Office, June 1975, pp. 65–78.

Harmon, Michael M. *Action Theory for Public Administration.* New York: Longman, 1981.

Hart, David K. "Social Justice, Equity, and the Public Administrator." *Public Administration Review* 34:1(1974):3–11.

Harvey, Jerry B. "The Abilene Paradox: The Management of Agreement." *Organizational Dynamics* 3:1(1974):63–80.

Held, Paul. *Introduction to Critical Theory: Horkheimer to Habermas.* Berkeley, Calif.: University of California Press, 1980.

Herzberg, Frederick. *Work and the Nature of Man.* Cleveland: World Publishing Co., 1966.

Herzberg, Frederick. "One More Time: How Do You Motivate Employees?" *Harvard Business Review* 46:1(1968):53–62.

Hirschman, Albert O. *Exit, Voice, and Loyalty.* Cambridge: Harvard University Press, 1970.

Horkheimer, Max. *Critical Theory.* New York: The Seabury Press, 1972.

Hummel, Ralph P. *The Bureaucratic Experience,* 2nd ed. New York: St. Martin's Press, 1982.

Jay, Martin. *The Dialectical Imagination: A History of the Frankfurt School and the Institute of Social Research, 1923–1950.* Boston: Little, Brown, 1973.

Kariel, Henry S. *Open Systems: Arenas for Political Action.* Itasca, Ill.: F. E. Peacock, 1969.

Katz, Daniel, and Kahn, Robert L. *The Social Psychology of Organizations,* 2nd ed. New York: John Wiley and Sons, 1978.

Kaufman, Herbert. "Administrative Decentralization and Political Power." *Public Administration Review* 29:1(1969):3–15.

Kaufman, Herbert. *The Limits of Organizational Change.* University, Ala.: University of Alabama Press, 1971.

Kirkhart, Larry. "Toward a Theory of Public Administration." In Frank Marini, ed., pp. 127–64. *Toward a New Public Administration: The Minnowbrook Perspective.* Scranton, Pa.: Chandler, 1971.

Kuhn, Thomas S. *The Structure of Scientific Revolutions,* 2nd ed., Chicago: University of Chicago Press, 1970.

Landsberger, H. A. *Hawthorne Revisited.* Ithaca, N.Y.: Cornell University Press, 1958.

LaPorte, Todd R. "The Recovery of Relevance in the Study of Public Organization." In Frank Marini, ed., pp. 17–48. *Toward a New Public Administration: The Minnowbrook Perspective.* Scranton, Pa.: Chandler, 1971.

Likert, Rensis. *New Patterns of Management.* New York: McGraw-Hill, 1961.

Likert, Rensis. *The Human Organization.* New York: McGraw-Hill, 1967.

Likert, Rensis, and Likert, J. G. *New Ways of Managing Conflict.* New York: McGraw-Hill, 1976.

Lilla, Mark T. "Ethos, 'Ethics,' and Public Service." *The Public Interest* 63:1(1981):3–17.

Lindblom, Charles E. "The Science of Muddling Through." *Public Administration Review* 19:1(1959):79–88.

Lindblom, Charles E. *The Intelligence of Democracy: Decision Making Through Partisan Mutual Adjustment.* New York: The Free Press, 1965.

Lindblom, Charles E. *Politics and Markets: The World's Political-Economic Systems.* New York: Basic Books, 1977.

Lindblom, Charles E. "Still Muddling, Not Yet Through." *Public Administration Review* 39:6(1979):517–26.

Long, Norton E. "Power and Administration." *Public Administration Review* 9:3(1949):257–64.

Lowi, Theodore. *The End of Liberalism.* New York: Norton, 1969.

Luthans, Fred. *Introduction to Management: A Contingency Approach.* New York: McGraw-Hill, 1976.

March, James G., ed. *Handbook of Organizations.* Chicago: Rand McNally, 1965.

March, James G., and Simon, Herbert A. *Organizations.* New York: John Wiley and Sons, 1958.

Marini, Frank, ed. *Toward a New Public Administration: The Minnowbrook Perspective.* Scranton, Pa.: Chandler, 1971.

Marx, Karl. *Writings of the Young Marx on Philosophy and Society,* Loyd D. Easton and Kurt H. Guddat, eds. and trans. New York: Doubleday, 1967.

Maslow, Abraham. *Toward a Psychology of Being.* Princeton, N.J.: D. Van Nostrand, 1962.

Maslow, Abraham. *Eupsychian Management.* Homewood, Ill.: Richard D. Irwin, 1965.

Maslow, Abraham. "The Superior Person." In Warren G. Bennis, ed., pp. 27–38. *American Bureaucracy.* Hawthorne, N.Y.: Aldine, 1970.

Mayer, Richard T., and Harmon, Michael M. "Teaching Moral Education in Public Administration." *Southern Review of Public Administration* 6:2(1982):217–26.

Mayo, Elton. *The Human Problems of an Industrial Civilization.* New York: Macmillan Co., 1933.

McCarthy, Thomas A. "A Theory of Communicative Competence." *Philosophy of the Social Sciences* 3(1973):135–56.

McCarthy, Thomas. *The Critical Theory of Jürgen Habermas.* Cambridge, Mass.: The MIT Press, 1978.

McGregor, Douglas. "The Human Side of Enterprise." *Management Review* 46:11(1957):22–28.

McGregor, Douglas. *The Human Side of Enterprise.* New York: McGraw-Hill, 1960.

McGregor, Douglas. *Leadership and Motivation: Essays of Douglas McGregor.* Warren G. Bennis and Edgar Schein. eds. Cambridge, Mass.: MIT Press, 1966.

McGregor, Douglas. *The Professional Manager.* Warren G. Bennis and Caroline McGregor, eds. New York: McGraw-Hill, 1967.

McSwain, Cynthia J. "Administrators and Citizenship: The Liberalist Legacy of the Constitution." *Administration and Society* 17:2(1985):131–148.

McSwain, Cynthia J., and White, Orion F. "The Case for Lying, Cheating, and Stealing—Personal Development as Ethical Guidance for Managers." *Administration and Society,* forthcoming.

Mead, George Herbert. *Mind, Self, and Society* 18:4(1987):411–432.

Meier, Kenneth J. *Politics and the Bureaucracy.* North Scituate, Mass.: Duxbury Press, 1979.

Merton, Robert K. "Bureaucratic Structure and Personality." *Social Forces* 18(1940):560–68.

Merton, Robert K. *On Theoretical Sociology.* New York: The Free Press, 1967.

Michael, Donald N. *On Learning to Plan—and Planning to Learn.* San Francisco: Jossey-Bass, 1973.

Mills, C. Wright. *White Collar: The American Middle Classes.* New York: Oxford University Press, 1951.

Mills, C. Wright. *The Sociological Imagination.* New York: Oxford University Press, 1959.

Morgan, Gareth, ed. *Beyond Method: Strategies for Social Research.* Beverly Hills, Calif.: Sage, 1983.

Mosher, Frederick C. *Democracy and the Public Service.* New York: Oxford University Press, 1968.

Mosher, Frederick C., ed. *American Public Administration: Past, Present, Future.* University, Ala.: University of Alabama Press, 1975.

Mouzelis, Nicos P. *Organisation and Bureaucracy: An Analysis of Modern Theories.* Chicago: Aldine Publishing Co., 1967.

Mueller, Dennis L. "Public Choice: A Survey." *Journal of Economic Literature* 14:2(1976):395–433.

Nagel, Ernest. "Problems of Concept and Theory Formation in the Social Sciences." In Maurice Natanson, ed., pp. 189–209. *Philosophy of the Social Sciences.* New York: Random House, 1963.

Natanson, Maurice, ed. *Philosophy of the Social Sciences.* New York: Random House, 1963.

Neibuhr, H. Richard. *The Responsible Self.* New York: Harper and Row, 1963.

Nozick, Robert. *Anarchy, State and Utopia.* New York: Basic Books, 1974.

Olson, Mancur. *The Logic of Collective Action.* Cambridge: Harvard University Press, 1965.

Ostrom, Elinor. "The Design of Institutional Agreements and the Responsiveness of Police." In L. Rieselbach, ed., pp. 274–299. *People vs. Government.* Bloomington, Ind.: Indiana University Press, 1975.

Ostrom, Vincent. *The Intellectual Crisis in American Public Administration,* rev. ed. University, Ala.: University of Alabama Press, 1974.

Ostrom, Vincent. "Some Problems in Doing Political Theory: A Response to Golembiewski's Critique." *American Political Science Review* 71:4(1977):1508–25.

Parsons, Talcott. *The Social System.* New York: Free Press, 1951.

Percy, Walker. *The Message in the Bottle: How Queer Man Is, How Queer Language Is, and What One Has to Do with the Other.* New York: Farrar, Straus and Giroux, 1975.

Perrow, Charles. *Complex Organizations: A Critical Essay,* 2nd ed. Glenview, Ill.: Scott, Foresman, 1979.

Pfeffer, Jeffrey, and Salancik, Gerald R. *The External Control of Organizations.* New York: Harper and Row, 1978.

Popper, Karl R. *The Open Society and Its Enemies.* London: George Routledge and Sons, 1945.

Popper, Karl R. *The Logic of Scientific Discovery.* New York: Harper Torchbooks, 1968.

Ramos, Alberto Guerreiro. *The New Science of Organizations: A Reconceptualization of the Wealth of Nations.* Toronto: University of Toronto Press, 1981.

Rawls, John. "Justice as Fairness." *Philosophical Review* 67(April 1958):164–94.

Rawls, John. *A Theory of Justice.* Cambridge: Harvard University Press, 1971.

Redford, Emmette S. *Democracy in the Administrative State.* New York: Oxford University Press, 1969.

Rex, J. *Key Problems in Sociological Theory.* London: Routledge and Kegan Paul, 1961.

Rittel, Horst W. J., and Webber, Melvin. "Dilemmas in a General Theory of Planning." *Policy Sciences* 4:2(1973):155–69.

Roethlisberger, F. J., and Dickson, William J. *Management and the Worker.* Cambridge: Harvard University Press, 1939.

Rourke, Francis E. *Bureaucracy, Politics, and Public Policy.* Boston: Little, Brown, 1976.

Rourke, Francis E., ed. *Bureaucratic Power and National Politics.* Boston: Little, Brown, 1978.

Runciman, W. G., ed. *Max Weber: Selections in Translation.* Cambridge: Cambridge University Press, 1978.

Schutz, Alfred. *Collected Papers,* vol. 1. Arvid Brodersen, ed. The Hague: Martinus Hijhoff, 1962.

Schutz, Alfred. "Concept and Theory Formation in the Social Sciences." *The Journal of Philosophy* 51:9(1954):257–73.

Schutz, Alfred. *The Phenomenology of the Social World.* Evanston, Ill.: Northwestern University Press, 1967.

Scott, William G. "Organicism: The Moral Anesthetic of Management." *Academy of Management Review* 4:1(1979):21–28.

Scott, William G., and Hart, David K. *Organizational America.* Boston: Houghton Mifflin, 1979.

Scott, William G.; Mitchell, Terrence R.; and Birnbaum, Philip H. *Organization Theory: A Structural and Behavioral Analysis,* 4th ed. Homewood, Ill.: Richard D. Irwin, 1981.

Seidman, Harold. *Politics, Position and Power: The Dynamics of Federal Organization,* 2nd ed. New York: Oxford University Press, 1975.

Selznick, Philip. "Foundation of the Theory of Organizations." *American Sociological Review* 13:1(1948):25–35.

Selznick, Philip. *Leadership in Administration: A Sociological Interpretation.* New York: Harper & Row, 1957.

Silverman, David. *The Theory of Organisations.* New York: Basic Books, 1971.

Simon, Herbert A. "The Proverbs of Public Administration." *Public Administration Review* 6:4(1946):53–67.

Simon, Herbert A. "'Development of Theory of Democratic Administration:' Replies and Comments." *American Political Science Review* 46:2(1952):494–96.

Simon, Herbert A. "Organization Man: Rational or Self-Actualizing?" *Public Administration Review* 33:4(1973):346–53.

Simon, Herbert A. *Administrative Behavior: A Study of Decision-Making Processes in Administrative Organization,* 3rd rev. ed. New York: Free Press, 1976.

Simon, Herbert A. *The Sciences of the Artificial,* 2nd ed. Cambridge, Mass.: MIT Press, 1981.

Simon, Herbert A.; Smithburg, Donald W.; and Thompson, Victor A. *Public Administration.* New York: Alfred A. Knopf, 1950.

Sykes, A. J. "Economic Interest and the Hawthorne Studies: A Comment." *Human Relations* 18(1965):253–63.

Taylor, Frederick Winslow. *Scientific Management.* New York: Harper & Brothers, 1947.

Thayer, Frederick C. "General System(s) Theory: The Promise That Could Not Be Kept." *Academy of Management Journal* 15:4(1972):481–94.

Thayer, Frederick C. "Organization Theory as Epistemology." In Carl Bellone, ed., pp. 113–39. *Organization Theory and the New Public Administration.* Boston: Allyn and Bacon, 1980.

Thayer, Frederick C. *An End to Hierarchy and Competition: Administration in the Post-Affluent World,* 2nd ed. New York: Franklin Watts, 1981.

Thompson, James D. *Organizations in Action.* New York: McGraw-Hill, 1967.

Vaill, Peter B. "Management as a Performing Art." *Personnel* 53:4(1976):12–21.

Vaill, Peter B. "Integrating the Diverse Directions of the Behavioral Sciences." In Robert Tannenbaum, Newton Margulies, and Fred Massarik, eds., pp. 547–77. *Human Systems Development: New Perspectives on People and Organizations.* San Francisco: Jossey-Bass, 1985.

Vickers, Sir Geoffrey. *The Art of Judgment: A Study of Policy Making.* New York: Basic Books, 1965.

Vickers, Sir Geoffrey. *Freedom in a Rocking Boat: Changing Values in an Unstable Society.* Baltimore: Penguin, 1970.

Von Bertalanffy, Ludwig. *General Systems Theory.* New York: George Braziller, 1968.

Wahba, Mahmoud A., and Bridwell, Lawrence G. "Maslow Reconsidered: A Review of Research on the Need Hierarchy Theory." *Proceedings of the Academy of Management* 1973:514–20.

Waldo, Dwight. *The Administrative State: A Study of the Political Theory of American Public Administration.* New York: The Ronald Press, 1948; 2nd ed. New York: Holmes and Meier, 1984.

Waldo, Dwight. "Development of Theory of Democratic Administration." *American Political Science Review* 46:1(1952):81–103.

Waldo, Dwight, ed. *Public Administration in a Time of Turbulence.* Scranton, Pa.: Chandler, 1971.

Waldo, Dwight. *The Enterprise of Public Administration: A Summary View.* Novato, Calif.: Chandler and Sharp, 1980.

Weber, Max. *The Protestant Ethic and the Spirit of Capitalism.* Talcott Parsons, trans. London: G. Allen & Unwin, 1930.

Weber, Max. *Economy and Society.* Guenther Roth and Claus Wittich, eds. Berkeley, Calif.: University of California Press, 1968.

Weick, Karl. *The Social Psychology of Organizing,* 2nd ed. Reading, Mass.: Addison-Wesley, 1979.

White, Jay D. "Public Policy Analysis: Reason, Method, and Praxis." DPA dissertation, George Washington University, 1982.

White, Leonard. *The Study of Public Administration.* New York: MacMillan, 1939.

White, Orion F., Jr. "Psychic Energy and Organizational Change." Sage Professional Paper in Administrative and Policy Studies, 1, 03–001. Beverly Hills, Calif.: Sage, 1973.

White, Orion F., Jr. "The Concept of Administrative Praxis." *Journal of Comparative Administration* 5:1(1973):55–86.

White, Orion F., Jr. "Public Management as the Facilitation of Personal Action." *Praxis* 2:2(1977):12–15.

White, Orion F., Jr. "Communication-Induced Distortion in Scholarly Research— The Case of Action Theory in American Public Administration." *International Journal of Public Administration* 5:2(1981):119–50.

White, Orion F., Jr., and McSwain, Cynthia J. "Transformational Theory and Organizational Analysis.'" In Gareth Morgan, ed., pp. 292–305. *Beyond Method: Strategies for Social Research.* Beverly Hills, Calif.: Sage, 1983.

Wildavsky, Aaron. *The Politics of the Budgetary Process,* 4th ed. Boston: Little, Brown, 1984.

Wilson, Woodrow. "The Study of Administration." *Political Science Quarterly* 2:2(1887):197–220.

Winter, Gibson. *Elements for a Social Ethic: The Role of Social Science in Public Policy.* New York: Macmillan, 1966.

Wren, Daniel A. *The Evolution of Management Thought.* New York: Ronald Press, 1972.

Index

Accountability, 6, 23, 34, 47–53, 116–117, 130–131, 225, 236, 381. *See also* Responsibility, administrative
  Friedrich, Carl J., on, 49
  and POSDCORB, 131
Ackoff, Russell, 185–187, 196
  on expansionism, 186
  on interactive planning, 185
  on teleology, 186
Action
  and behavior, interpretive theorists on, 294–295
  as a means to an end, 15. *See also* Rationality, instrumental
  personal versus organizational, 13–15
  social
    Max Weber on, 73, 74–78
    as an interpretive process, 334
    public choice theory on, 262–264
  and thought. *See* Thought and action, relation of
Administration. *See also* Democratic administration
  as politics, 23, 26
  principles of, 22, 132–134, 135, 151. *See also* Gulick, Luther
  as "proverbs," 133, 136–139, 255–256

science of, 22, 24, 126, 131
Administrative responsibility. *See* Responsibility, administrative
Alienation, 330, 394–395
  Habermas, Jürgen, on, 319, 321
  Thayer, Frederick C., on, 373–374, 379
Antipositivism, 288
Appleby, Paul B., 22–25, 35, 48
  and political nature of administration, 23–24
Argyris, Chris, 33, 97, 199–200, 204n, 213–219, 225–226, 228, 232, 237, 329
  on characteristics of healthy individuals, 213–214, 218
  on "double-loop" learning, 217
  exchange with Herbert Simon, 199, 201–202
  on organization development, 215–217, 237
  and Schön, Donald
    on espoused theory and theory-in-use, 216–217
    on organizational learning, 216–217

Bachrach, Peter, 226, 237–238
Bailey, Stephen K., categories of theory, 396–397